W9-BWC-875

RAVE REVIEWS FOR THE <u>NEW</u> DIVORCING BIBLE:

"An up book, long on optimism and hope."
—*Los Angeles Times*

"Required reading for anyone contemplating a divorce...Readers needing sound, well written and practical advice will find it here." —*Library Journal*

"Krantzler's eloquent chapters have the kind of thoughtful advice everyone—married or separated—should read." —*Milwaukee Journal*

"Belli provides clear and detailed information."
—*Single Parent*

"The most comprehensive, practical and clearly written book I've ever seen on the subject."
—*The Women's Newspaper*

DIVORCING

MEL KRANTZLER, Ph.D.
AND
MELVIN M. BELLI, Sr.

WITH CHRISTOPHER S. TAYLOR

ST. MARTIN'S PAPERBACKS

The poem "Eskimos Have No Word for Divorce" is from *The Double Bed* by Eve Merriam. Copyright © 1972 by Eve Merriam. All rights reserved. Reprinted by permission of Marian Reiner for the author.

Grateful acknowledgment is made to William M. Lamers, Jr., M.D., for his permission to reproduce the "Grief Cycle" chart that appears on page 109.

"Address to a Penis Owner" by Sabina Sedgewick is from *Ladies' Own Erotica.* Copyright © 1984 by the Kensington Ladies' Erotica Society. Published by Ten Speed Press, Berkeley, California. Reprinted by permission.

DIVORCING

Library of Congress Catalog Card Number: 87-38264

ISBN: 0-312-92744-4

Printed in the United States of America

St. Martin's Press hardcover edition published 1988
St. Martin's Press trade paperback edition published 1989
St. Martin's Paperbacks edition/February 1992

10   9   8   7   6   5   4   3   2   1

Contents

Acknowledgments

This book would never have materialized in its present form without the major professional contribution of my wife, Patricia Biondi Krantzler, who is an outstanding marriage and divorce counselor in her own right, as well as the co-director of our Creative Divorce, Love and Marriage Counseling Center in San Rafael, California. Her conceptual ideas and extensive research regarding all of the issues dealt with in *Divorcing* have profoundly influenced the form and content of this book. My appreciation of the dedicated effort and expertise she has given this book is greater than words can express.

In addition, I am deeply indebted to Dr. Seymour Boorstein for the spiritual guidance and encouragement he gave me, which enabled my writing to turn into chapters in this book.

—MEL KRANTZLER, PH.D.

Introduction

If you are considering divorce or are living through a divorce or its aftermath, you need one book that will provide you with *all* of the expert advice that will enable you successfully to ride the giant shock waves in your life that the divorce experience typically creates. The objective of this book is to fill your need, to give you the best possible assistance at the time you need it most.

Divorcing is the result of a unique collaboration of the two of us, Melvin Belli and Mel Krantzler. In our separate professions as a lawyer (Melvin Belli) and as a psychological counselor (Mel Krantzler), we have specialized in assisting thousands of men and women to cope skillfully with the myriad problems in their divorces, and in doing so we have helped them improve the quality of their lives as newly single persons. We will be sharing with you in the pages of this book all of the knowledge we have derived from our work on the divorce firing line over many decades, so that you too can triumph over the psychological, emotional, social, economic, and legal complexities and adversities that can arise when a breakup occurs.

We ourselves are no strangers to divorce in our personal lives. Melvin Belli has been divorced four times and Mel Krantzler once. We both have journeyed through the divorce labyrinth that you may be entering now. And if you feel at times that the light at the end of the divorce tunnel may only be the headlight of an oncoming train, rather than the light of greater happiness, self-renewal, and the excitement of a new beginning, we too once felt that way when our own marriages were ending: the shock, the denial of the reality, the uncertainty, the frustration, the sadness, the resentment, the anger, the fear, the guilt, the hatred, the anxiety, the self-pity, the sense of failure and rejection, the loneliness, the legal hassles, the everything-seems-out-of-control and will-this-divorce-ever-end feelings.

But since both of us had a passionate interest in learning why our marriages broke up and why we were experiencing such emotional disarray in going it alone, we were able to take more effective charge of our own lives and use our divorces as a stepping-stone to greater personal fulfillment. We know that you can do the same, once you have the necessary information at your disposal, which you will find in this book. We are human beings first; our professional expertise flows from that basic fact, for we are no different from you at basic emotional levels. Our claim that we can help you arises from our empathy and human experience, which we have communicated to our clients along with the specific knowledge of what to do and what not to do in a divorce. What we have learned the hard way may help you to avoid the pitfalls and to take advantage of the possibilities that exist in your divorce.

At the time you are reading this book, you may feel there is no such thing as a bright side to your breakup. Or you may have thought everything would be delightful once you left your spouse, but now find life as a newly single person unexpectedly difficult. Or, if you were the person left by your spouse, it may seem like the end of the world. It is our purpose to alert you to the possibilities for a better life that exist in the very pain you may be experiencing. As your friendly guides throughout the chapters of this book, we will be pointing out the roads you can follow that will lead you to a brighter future rather than to a dead end.

Our objective is to bring to you the most comprehensive, helpful book on divorce you can obtain, one that you can use as your "bible" of divorce. We have written it because, until now, no such book has satisfied this urgent need. Our book is as up-to-date as the newspaper you read this morning. It incorporates all of the tremendous discoveries made in the past decade about the nature of divorce: its effect on the individuals experiencing it; its impact on children and other family members; the changed attitudes of society toward divorce; the new support systems that society and the churches have created for the divorced; the new dating patterns and social etiquette for singles; the physical as well as the psychological impact of divorce; the economic crises and credit-, job-, and housing-related situations you might experience; the trend toward remarriage; and the emergence of new forms of intimacy, such as the living-together arrangement. All of these aspects of the divorce experience will be explored by Mel Krantzler.

Like it or not, divorce as a personal experience and divorce as a legal arrangement are inseparable. Consequently, a book that aspires to be the "bible" of divorce must also offer you the best legal advice possible, which attorney Melvin Belli will do in the legal chapters in this book. He will translate intimidating legal jargon into everyday language that you can understand and use to your benefit. He will inform you about the qualities that make for a good divorce lawyer and tell you how you can contact one, how you can get the most effective service from him or her, what legal costs you can expect to incur and how to minimize them; he will explain the advantages and disadvantages of a do-it-yourself divorce, or of utilizing a mediator rather than a lawyer.

And since the legalities of divorce have changed so dramatically during the past decade, he will focus on those changes that may directly affect your welfare, such as the new concept of no-fault divorce; changes in division of property and tax laws; new principles of alimony or spousal support; new child visitation and custody rights; the rights of lesbian mothers and gay fathers; antidiscrimination laws for the divorced; and the legal rights and obligations of couples in palimony disputes.

This is a how-to-see-it as well as a how-to do-it book of divorce. For it is our firm conviction, validated by the positive results in the clients we have counseled, that a change in the way you view your divorce can profoundly influence the way you live through it.

If you regard your divorce as an unmitigated disaster, the world you live in today and tomorrow will confirm that belief; you will blind yourself to your opportunities for leading a better life, since you will only focus on the disasters. You will ignore the possibility that occurrences you think are disastrous could prove to be positive in the long run. Divorce is a crisis, the greatest crisis you may experience in your lifetime, apart from the death of a loved one. The Chinese word for *crisis* is composed of the characters meaning *danger* and *opportunity*. What you emphasize in your divorce crisis is what you will receive.

In the process of coming to terms with our own divorces, we did some harmful things that we later regretted. However, saints are for heaven, and we are only human beings, as fallible as anyone else. But it is precisely because we ourselves have fallen into some of the same pitfalls you might encounter that we can be of help to you. For we can alert you to the danger signals we overlooked, thereby enabling you to avoid harming yourself and others. We know that wallowing in regrets over the past is about as useful as trying to buy a cup of coffee for a nickel in a restaurant. Consequently, the focus of our book is to assist you in utilizing your divorce as an opportunity to take more effective charge of your life, to improve your love relationships in the future, and to become a more human, compassionate, caring, and empathetic individual in the process of doing so.

You are indeed entitled to know more about the two of us regarding our own personal divorce experiences and what we have learned from them. Your confidence in our advice to you necessarily will reside in our own capacity to fully understand the confusion, trauma, and pain you may be experiencing as a human being in your own divorce. Our professional abilities as a lawyer and as a divorce psychologist will count for little in your eyes without that confidence. We'll begin with Melvin Belli's story.

1

Divorce and Self-Renewal

Melvin Belli: Divorce in My Life

I was born in 1907 and grew up in a time when divorce was an unmentionable subject. At best it was considered a dirty little secret if it happened to some poor unfortunate, and at worst it meant that such a person was a dreadful sinner. "Fallen woman" was the term then used to label any divorced woman, a diseased person to be feared, scorned, and avoided.

I was an only child who lived with my parents in a large home on Main Street in the little Bret Harte/Mark Twain country town of Sonora, in northern California. I wasn't lonely, since I lived in the midst of a crowd of relatives—a grandmother, three uncles and aunts, and a host of cousins. Divorce was never thought of by any of my relatives as something that could ever happen to themselves. On the very rare occasions when a divorced person's name would come up (I remember, in my childhood, listening to their comments as I hid under the table after a big family dinner), one of my parents or relatives would inevitably label the divorced man a "villain." The divorced man, however, always got the better of the bargain, since most of the condemnation was heaped on the woman.

My upbringing inculcated in me a belief that an intact

family life was one of the most valuable experiences a
human being can have—a belief that has never left me.
Although I am now in my seventy-eighth year, I can still
remember, as if it were yesterday, sitting in front of the big
fireplace at my aunt and uncle's house at the other end of
town from where my parents lived. I see the logs sparkling
and the fire reflected in the highly polished black high-
buttoned shoes of my dad (the town banker) and my uncle
(the county health officer for forty years).

I can still hear the family talk about the war (World War
I was then happening) and the chitchat about the latest
doings of my relatives. That was the time in my life when
I used to visit my grandmother, Anna Mouron, at her drugstore. She came from Germany and was the first woman
druggist in California, and ran the town drugstore after her
husband's death. Grandpa Mouron had been the town doctor, and Grandma used to regale me with stories about how
he would saddle up the team of horses in the middle of the
night to visit a sick person.

On what turned out to be his last ride, he was caught
in the middle of a cloudburst; he survived the storm, only
to die of pneumonia. The remembrance of my grandfather's
dedicated public service to people in real need is one of the
reasons why I'm a lawyer who fights for the rights of the
average person.

I was fortunate to spend my first ten years in a delightful small town. Every holiday was a big, festive, family occasion, like Thanksgiving with all of my aunts, uncles, cousins,
and grandparents present, and the huge turkey cooked in
the woodstove. Grace would be said, then a tremendous
meal would be eaten. When the dishes had been cleared
away, stories about the family doings would be told. I tried
to stay awake, listening to them long past my bedtime, because they were so interesting. At the close of the evening,
there would be excited conversation about which relative
would act as host for the next holiday dinner.

Experiences such as these made me feel that family life
was forever, and how wonderful that was. My first shock in
realizing some families are not forever came when I was
about fifteen, when the first divorced woman I ever met
appeared at a tea party my mother had given. I remember

how I went into the party room a number of times to get a look at this strange creature. But, oddly enough, I felt very disappointed, because she didn't look like someone from outer space at all. I had to admit reluctantly that she looked like all the other women present, but perhaps a bit more beautiful and intelligent than most of them. I then discounted that fact by telling myself there must be something terrible about her that she was clever in disguising, even fooling my mother!

It wasn't just my religious background that made me so intolerant of divorce as a child; it was the security and sanctity of the family. I resented either spouse destroying that, let alone an outsider like a judge or a lawyer. My religious upbringing certainly reinforced my early bias against divorce. My dad, with his Italian background, probably should have been a Catholic, but for some reason he became an Episcopalian at an early age, and later a Mason and a member of the Knights Templar. The Catholic priest would come to our home and, in amazement, hear my father say that he was an Episcopalian. I liked the Catholic priest. I wished we were Catholic, but I've always remained an Episcopalian and am a Mason, as were all the male members of my family (the female members belonged to the Eastern Star). I do visit the Catholic church when I'm abroad, and if I can't find a Catholic church, I have no objection to going into, say, a Buddhist temple and praying as I did in Lhasa, Tibet.

I don't want to give the impression that there weren't any storms in my parents' lives when I was a child. Mom and Dad had their quarrels, some of them very bitter indeed, particularly when Dad wanted to move to San Francisco at the urging of A. P. Giannini, the founder of the Bank of America, who wanted my father to be a young partner in his business. In those days a wife's role was to follow her husband wherever he decided to move, but Mom never saw it that way.

I'm certain that, at times like this, my mother and father felt estranged from one another, but divorce never entered their minds. The saying, "I've often thought of murdering my spouse, but never of divorce," must occasionally have occurred to them, as it has to many other couples.

Given my background, it may seem strange to you that I've been divorced four times, but there is no contradiction here. Like the family I grew up in, I never intended to get divorced. In fact, my first divorce was one of the greatest traumas in my life. My first wife, Betty Ballantine, had been a student at the University of California when we were married in 1933. She wanted the divorce, and I was bitterly opposed to it. We had been married eighteen years, and I felt that the divorce would be a personal failure.

I was agonizingly concerned about the fate of our four children; Richard was fourteen years old, Johnny was twelve, Jean was nine, and Suzie was six. The divorce was a very bitter one, played out in public with reams of three-ring-circus publicity. That was back in 1951, when there was no such thing as no-fault divorce; you had to prove at that time that your spouse was a wicked woman or a son of a bitch to "win" a divorce. Well, nobody won in my case. Our harshness estranged Betty and me. I can remember saying I could never forgive her for getting custody of our children and changing their last names from Belli to Ballantine, with our children siding with their mother.

That divorce modified my belief in staying married at all costs. Since there was no hope of improving the marriage, we would have been doomed to a life that would have been utterly destructive to ourselves and our children. Painful as it was, my divorce did allow for the possibility of my living a better life as a single person. However, I believed then and I believe now that a good marriage is a wonderful thing, one of life's greatest joys, and I've pursued that quest again and again. I can smile now when I remember saying, after my divorce from Betty, that I'd never marry again, but later I had to acknowledge to myself that I didn't like living alone and that I loved women. I was determined that my next marriage would be a better one.

Well, it didn't quite work out that way. I married again only six months after my divorce from Betty. This time it was to Toni Nichols, a reporter-photographer. It was one of those cases of "marry in haste, repent at leisure," and we were divorced two years after our marriage. Again, I was accurately quoted in the press when I announced, "You can say I am through with women from here on out." And again

I revised my attitude, once the pain of my divorce dimin-ished, when I married Joy Turney, a sweet stewardess, two years after my divorce from Toni. We had a son, Caesar, named after my father and grandfather, which made me feel young at fifty. Caesar is now twenty-seven and practices law with me. However, that marriage ended after nine years on the grounds that I seemed to be married more to my law practice than to my wife.

I was still optimistic in my quest for a good, permanent marriage at the age of sixty-five, and my optimism was re-warded: I married Lia Triff, who was twenty-three, back in 1972. (My marriage in 1966 to Pat Montandon, a beautiful and talented San Francisco writer, model, and television personality, was little more than a footnote, since it ended in an annulment a few months after the ceremony.)

Lia, an outstanding student, had majored in art history and anthropology at the University of Maryland, and is now actively engaged in politics and in the struggle for women's rights. Thirteen years ago, Lia gave birth to Melia, our daughter. Having a thirteen-year-old daughter at seventy-eight keeps me from ever feeling old; she's a delight.

That my marriage to Lia has lasted as long as it has, and continued to become better with each passing year, rein-forces my conviction that divorce, painful as it is, can be a stepping-stone to a better life. I've been a slow learner, no doubt, but I have learned how to handle the divorces of others in a more constructive way than I have often handled some of mine.

And I think that being a romantic optimist who, down deep, truly likes and loves women helped me enormously in eventually establishing a marriage that really works well. I'm an example of the old adage that "it's never too late to learn," and have experienced the reality that divorce is not the end of the world. I recall the story of the farmhand who is shoveling away happily at a mountain of manure in the barn, whistling while he works. "With a terrible job like that, why are you so happy?" he is asked. "Well," the farm-hand replies, "I figure that underneath all of this manure there has to be a pony!"

There is indeed a "pony" after divorce, but first you have to clear away the debris. If I had it to do all over again, here is how I would handle my own divorce: I would recognize that it takes two to make a marriage turn sour. That means I have shared in the responsibility for my marriage ending in divorce. Not intentionally, but because I let things that were going wrong drift, and believed everything that created arguments and tension was always the other person's fault. I think I finally got the message from a law partner of mine, who told me, when one of my marriages was falling apart, "Goddammit, Mel, you work all the time. You never go home at night, but sleep in the office in your clothes instead. If I were you and had a family, I'd go home nights and spend time with my wife and kids. You'll be in trouble if you don't."

How right he was! I had neglected my wife's needs, expecting her to adjust to my schedule.

If I had it to do over again, here is how I would handle my divorces: I would not voice my bitterness, anger, and feelings of rejection to the world. I remember how clever I thought I was when I made smart-aleck, sarcastic cracks to the press about my soon-to-be ex-wife. And I thought I was being clever when I paid $3,500 to my ex-wife's attorney by sending him the money in two sacks of small change. It made me feel self-righteous at the time, but left a legacy of bitterness and hostility that enveloped me and my ex-wife like a black cloud for years long after the divorce. In fact, I haven't seen or heard from my first wife to this day, and am not proud of that situation.

I would be kinder. Being kind, not vengeful or permanently bitter, toward your ex-spouse will enable you to feel better about yourself and to lead a happier life as a single person, rather than with a permanent scowl and a grudge against the world.

I learned that lesson well from my first divorce. I am on friendly terms with all of my other ex-wives, and feel all the better for it. That lesson of acting kinder in a divorce was brought home to me when I was present while Errol Flynn was going through one of his divorces. His wife was claiming what objectively appeared (but apparently not to her) to be an exorbitant amount of the property. This had stalled all proceedings and could have led to a very bitter battle, until one day, at a meeting suggested in the lawyer's office, Flynn

walked in in his most debonair manner, presented a big
bouquet of beautiful red roses to his wife, gave the startled
young lady a fond kiss, and said, "Honey, my lawyer's going
to lay it all out on the table, and you take what you think
you're entitled to!" Errol gave one of his gallant bows and
swept out of the room. The wife burst into tears, and when
she finally composed herself, she was receptive to a more
reasonable compromise agreement that was fairer to both
parties.

I don't for a moment suggest that this approach is uni-
versally applicable. But as a general principle, the way you
act toward your ex spouse will determine whether or not
you will be scarred with hate and vengefulness or feel
renewed as a better person, and this is something you
should be seriously concerned about. Divorce is one situation in which what you willingly give away, even though
you know you're being taken, you get back in your own
self-respect and what others think of you. And a person who
"takes" his or her ex-spouse will regret it later on.

Today I would be more attentive to how divorce would
affect my children, and try to minimize the pain, anxiety,
confusion, uncertainty, and estrangement. Every missile
you hurl has a homing device, and it will hurt not only you
but your children to be the author of the vituperation you
heap on your spouse and your divorce. The mutual bitterness between my first wife and me resulted in the very thing
I feared the most, my loss of a father connection with my
first four children for many years, although my relationship
is good with them now. But how much needless pain I endured by allowing my bitter feelings about the divorce to
keep me from being more attentive to my children in those
early years of their lives. I made certain with Joy, who is
Caesar's mother, that this would not happen. Joy and I
agreed upon my visitation rights with Caesar, and we always
cooperated in paying attention to Caesar's needs when he
was a child. The result has been a happy relationship with
my son, although I must admit I'm a somewhat indulgent
parent. (And, he's a very independent person and lawyer
now!)

Out of my own experience, I advise my clients (no matter how much the parents may dislike each other at the time

they are divorcing) to cool their anger toward each other when they are with their children, and to say to them, "Daddy and Mommy love both of you. You're our children forever, so if we do get a divorce it only means that Daddy won't be living here but somewhere nearby, and will see you regularly, will go to school with you, will take you to dances and to church, will read with you, and you will go over to his new home and play with him and the animals."

Don't ever vilify or criticize your spouse in front of the children. Though they may seem to side with you, they will be so bewildered and traumatized that they won't know what to do or where to go. Even though they may seem to side with you, they will resent someone talking negatively about their father or their mother. Tell them what to say at school, to their teachers, to their ministers, and to others.

If I had it to do over again, I would lead a more balanced family life that might prevent a divorce. I think that in all my four divorces, the prime factor was not enough time at home and too much time at the office. I love my work, and because I was so intensely involved in it, I failed to see the problems that were developing at home, so I never dealt with them. Well, those problems don't go away just because you don't attend to them; instead, they continue to accumulate until they are insurmountable.

I come to my office every holiday, Saturday, and Sunday, and have done so these last fifty years. I try to get in now by 8:00 A.M., and I seldom leave before 7:00 P.M. I work all day Saturday and Sunday; any time I have to devote to my family is taken from my law, whether I am working on a case, writing, or reading generally. I do a tremendous amount of writing; I've done sixty-two law books, as well as lectures and TV appearances, and have tried cases outside of California and indeed outside of the United States.

Not spending enough time at home obviously has a tremendous effect upon one's children. They unconsciously resent their dad "going to the office." Before long "the office" becomes almost an inanimate suitor for their father's affections, and the children can actually become jealous.

After a period of time, even worse than the children missing the absent father is that they take these absences for granted, and this causes them to look less frequently to the father for advice, comfort, recreation, and simply *being* a father. When it gets to that point, immediate drastic action is necessary—a vacation, a change in life-style, perhaps a sit-down with the children and the wife and detailed promises to change problem-creating habits, like not reading to the children at night. And these promises can't be broken.

With my Melia, now thirteen, I tried a different tack: I made her a part of the office. I gave her a mailbox at the office, in which I put advertisements in her name, pieces of gum, candy, and toys. She is the one now who wants to come to the office. Frequently she will say, "I have to go to the office." She has had her own chair and desk and drawing pad here in the old Belli Building since she was five. Indeed, the other day, of her own accord, she announced she was going to be a trial lawyer like her father, that she was going to Yale, and that the Belli Building now belongs to her and to my twenty-seven-year-old son Melvin Caesar Belli, Jr. Indeed, on the building is the legend "Belli, Belli and Belli." Melia and Caesar are both very proud of that; they speak of the building as "their" building, and their advice is asked about what flowers are to be planted, what painting is to be done, what furniture and computers and such are to be gotten. They understand these things are being put into "their" building. Caesar is beginning to put as much time in at the office as I do, and Melia, though she's still going to school, proudly brings her friends to the office and shows them around. It is a ritual that she has Saturday luncheon with me and some of my lawyers. She often brings a friend, who will frequently comment, "I wish my dad took me to his office."

Just a little thoughtful, meaningful attention *each day* under a motivated plan to take one's children and wife into one's profession in life goes a long, long way. Staffers in the office, whether secretaries, paralegals, nurses, or trial lawyers, are asked to say something to Melia when she comes in, and she's very happy and very proud to be taken into consultation.

Melia's mother, Lia, is about as busy as I am. She was President Jimmy Carter's special affairs assistant in the White House, and indeed the Reagan administration asked her to stay over, but she declined since she wanted to go into politics on her own. For the second time, she is chairman of the California Democratic Caucus, and goes all over the state, making speeches regularly.

A professional man's wife, who is herself a professional, Lia understands the lure of the law, since she herself is turned on by her own independent calling. She and I know that compromises have to be made. We make them knowingly, and in doing so, we are amazed at how much time we can allocate to both our professions and our family life.

As a bonus, I'll include something here that I wouldn't change if I had it to do all over again. I wouldn't change my belief that adversity, as Disraeli remarked, is the greatest teacher, provided one learns from one's past, rather than repeating it. And it's all right if you're a four-time repeater like me, because eventually you'll get the right message about how to improve your life if you are motivated to do so. No matter how old I become, I'll still "rage against the dying of the light."

When you read my technical legal advice in the subsequent chapters, I hope you will first remember me as a person who has experienced many a dark night of the soul, as you may now be doing. But also remember me as a person who knows that you can, with proper guidance, turn that dark night into a sunny morning.

Mel Krantzler has his own story to tell, so I'll let you hear from him now.

Mel Krantzler: My Personal Encounter with Divorce

My local supermarket illustrates how much society's attitude toward divorced persons has changed since the time of my own divorce, in 1970. As I push my shopping cart around the aisles on this bright Saturday morning eighteen years after my breakup, I see many divorced men, some with their children, doing the same thing. I wave to some of my male friends, and give an acknowledging smile to others who are acquaintances. None of them seem uncomfortable or ashamed at being "caught in the act" of doing

what only their wives used to do, shopping for their daily
meals. It's a taken-for-granted part of their lives these days.

How different this all was, back in 1970. At that time I
felt anxious and demeaned, the only man amid a sea of
women, shopping like a woman. I would glance furtively
around, praying that I would not be recognized. I would
slump down as I pushed my cart, hoping my six-foot frame
would shrink into invisibility. In record time I would beat
a hasty retreat from the store, after almost randomly choosing the canned and frozen foods that would be my meals the
next week. Sighing with relief, I would drive my car (if I was
lucky, my ten-year-old Ford would still start) back to my
strange new home. "Home" was an incredibly uncomfortable, one-and-a-half-room basement apartment that I
rented during the first year of my divorce, after leaving the
large and comfortable two-story home in which my twenty-
four-year marriage had ended. The listing in the paper had
said the apartment was "furnished." The joke was on me,
since the three fragile chairs, scratched table, and lumpy
bed were more like throwaways from a Salvation Army
store. There was a constant cacophony of police sirens,
shouts, the screeching of brakes, and arguments from the
nearby business street and the neighborhood tavern. I felt
like the loneliest human being in the supermarket, and like
a man in purgatory in my apartment: a failure in life at fifty,
an over-the-hill outcast, were my definitions of myself in
that bleak time.

It's very different today. The divorced men in the supermarket neither slink nor hurry. They are comfortable in
doing what seems to come naturally; it's no big deal doing
what once was considered "women's work." And when they
look for their favorite packaged or canned foods, they can
choose from a host of products in single-portion sizes, in
acknowledgment that divorced persons are human beings
also, who have their own special needs. But I can still remember the time when I was forced to buy family-size cans
and packages, since companies weren't making single-portion units of their products. The food I wasted by buying
items designed for consumption by two or more persons
often exceeded the amounts I used. How often I hoped that
someone would invent one-person amounts as the mounds

of half-used containers accumulated in my garbage can! The
family-size portions made me feel I was a nonperson because I was now single.

My supermarket today has a generous display of greet-
ing cards that were inconceivable back in 1970. The divorced person who shops there can choose a card that
announces a divorce rather than a marriage, a card for a
stepmother, or a Mother's Day card for fathers who have
sole custody of their children. New cards for new relationships.

If my supermarket now validates the fact that divorced
persons are people too, so does the daily newspaper. When
I pick up my morning paper to scan the ads for the weekend
specials at the supermarket, I also find listings of the special
events available for divorced persons during the week: a
divorce self-help group, a dance for singles, a lecture on
loneliness, listings of Catholic, Unitarian, Episcopalian, and
Jewish programs for divorced members of their congrega-
tions, and a single-parent conference at the local community college. Next to this listing may be a prominent boxed
ad by a law firm announcing reasonable rates for individuals
who want a divorce.

Where could I find such support systems when I was
wandering around in a daze of uncertainty and bewilderment in the early months of my divorce? Nowhere, since
they were nonexistent then.

Another page in the paper lists the TV shows, and it is
a rare day that doesn't include a talk show on divorce, a
movie-of-the-week about problems that divorced people experience, a sitcom like "Kate and Allie" dealing with divorced parents, or a documentary on children of divorce.

Only yesterday the subject of divorce was considered a
shameful and unnatural dirty little secret, while today we
have even elected a divorced man as President of the
United States! It seems like another century, but it's only a
few decades ago that a divorced person, like Nelson Rocke-
feller, was considered political poison because of that fact.

Certainly I felt ashamed and guilty when I was divorced in 1970, almost as if I had a scarlet *D* branded onto
my forehead. The unspeakable had happened to me after a
twenty-four-year marriage, and at a time when my two

daughters were teenagers. The first divorce in my family. What would my relatives, friends, work associates, and boss think of me?

Weighed down with guilt, anxiety, and fear, I sought out support systems for myself in my time of distress, and found none available. I had vaguely heard of a relatively new organization called Parents Without Partners, which was then only fifteen years old. Apart from that organization, a dark void existed in which a divorced person seemed to be considered a nonperson until he or she married again. Since I was soured on marriage at the time of my breakup, and had no intention then of remarrying, I seemed doomed to be another of those nonpersons. However, life is full of surprises, for my own anguish and disarray proved to be the motivating force for me to improve on my past life rather than wallow bitterly in regret and hopelessness. Two wise sayings by the philosopher Nietzsche gave me sustenance at that time:

"He who has a *why* to live can bear with almost any *how.*"

"Whatever does not kill me makes me stronger."

I applied this vision of life to my divorce, refusing to accept the conventional opinion in 1970 that divorce was a form of penal servitude and that escape from its stigma could only be achieved through an immediate remarriage. Indeed, wasn't an agonizing marriage the ultimate jail penalty? I was to learn from my divorce how to relate to myself and others in a more loving, compassionate, and skillful way. To stumble into an immediate remarriage out of fear of living alone would have been utter folly. To believe that a divorce was all the other person's fault didn't make sense to me, since both the husband and wife bear equal responsibility for a breakup. I knew at bottom that my ex-wife and I were not villains and evildoers, even though I experienced surges of those feelings about myself frequently during the early months of my divorce. Instead, we were two well-intentioned people who had fallen in love twenty-four years ago and now had fallen out of love.

I was determined to make my divorce a creative experience, creative in the sense of making a fresh start, a new and better life for myself as a separate person rather than as part of a couple. Since there were no divorce self-help groups available for the general public back in 1970, I created such a group in order to help myself as well as other men and women who were in the same position I was in: single and confused in a Noah's Ark world. I reasoned that divorce could be taught like history or any other subject. "Learn from your past rather than repeat it" was my motto. To that end, I made up a twelve-session seminar series that I titled "Creative Divorce: A New Opportunity for Personal Growth," which I began teaching in the continuing education department of my local community college. I later learned that this was the first such program established for the general public in the entire country. Much to my surprise and delight, the initial seminar was filled to overflowing.

I can truthfully say I learned as much about myself as my students learned from me in the course of that first seminar. I discovered I was not alone, for here were sixty students, ranging in age from twenty-five to sixty, who were experiencing the same kind of emotional "craziness" in their divorce as I was. And, most encouraging of all, they were as eager as I was to use their divorce experience as a stepping-stone to a better life.

That first seminar was the beginning of an entirely new career for me. I left my job as a psychological rehabilitation counselor in a state agency, became one of the first full-time divorce counselors in the nation, and wrote a book bearing the same title as my seminars, which was published in 1974. I still give these seminars and counsel divorced people every day at my Creative Divorce, Love and Marriage Counseling Center, located in San Rafael, California, as well as training people in other parts of the country to do similar work.

However, the more things change, the more they remain the same. Even though society now accepts divorce as a normal aspect of American life (each year more than two million men and women and one million children are involved in a divorce) and while you now can have a no-fault divorce based on "irreconcilable differences" (instead of legal battles designed to prove your spouse was a "bad person"), the *emotional realities* of divorce remain the same as they always were. For there are universal psychological reactions to divorce that transcend time and national boundaries, despite cultural and social differences. Men and women experiencing divorce in Japan or Israel or France or Russia feel the same emotional uproar inside themselves as you may be feeling when the marriage bond is severed.

I see emotional reflections of my own divorce experience in every man and woman I counsel in my office who is currently living through a breakup, even though my divorce occurred eighteen years ago.

Ann, an attractive forty-two-year-old woman, sits before me with tears in her eyes and fear and anger in her voice. "Why me?" she wails. "Harry moved out two weeks ago. I gave him the best years of my life, twenty-two years, and now it's all for nothing. I've never lived alone before. The kids are grown up and on their own, and I'm scared. It's not fair, I'll never be able to make it on my own."

In that moment her fear becomes my fear once again, as my mind travels back to the first month of my own divorce. For, just like Ann, living with someone else was my taken-for-granted way of life, and I felt I could not survive as a single person, yet I could not return to a marriage that was over.

I thought I couldn't ever find a place to live; I didn't even know how to operate a washing machine or cook a meal or clean and dust, believing these tasks were woman's work. My married friends didn't call me, and my associates at work gave me odd looks as they saw my productivity plummet to near zero. I was isolated and alone and feeling oh-so-sorry for myself . . . and then I discovered that no one was going to take care of me except myself.

Yes, life is unfair—who guaranteed it to be otherwise?—but I could either drown in self-pity or make my life fairer. In choosing the latter, I was able, bit by bit, to take charge of my own life! I *did* find an apartment, and, uncomfortable though it was, it turned out to be a stepping-stone to a better one later on. I *did* learn to operate a washing machine and make my own meals—it wasn't so difficult after all!—I *did* improve my work, and I had a better relationship with my co-workers, but only after I reached out to them by telling them of my temporary shock and disarray, which they responded to by giving me sympathy and support.

As for my married friends, I discovered that I had to reach out to them and make them feel it was all right to talk about my divorce, and that I wanted to remain friends with them. My true friends remained true when that happened.

David's wife has left him after a thirteen-year marriage, taking their two boys, ages nine and eleven, to live with her. His tortured face makes him look ten years older than his thirty-seven years. "I love my children, but now they'll never want to see me again, since my wife has been brainwashing them by telling them what a bastard I am." Tears and panic over the possible loss of his children flood his face.

As he shares his agony, the poignant feelings I had about my own two teenage daughters during the first few months of my own divorce return. They would never want to see me again, I believed. But they responded when I wrote to them, called them, and had them visit me in my little apartment. My youngest daughter made up a book of simple recipes for me to use, a book I still cherish. That book became my cooking teacher. I learned from personal experience what I had always known in theory: children love *both* their parents, since they are products of two parents. That love will never die, except in the rarest of instances.

I knew that David and his children would reconnect once he and his wife would begin to understand that while they could divorce each other, they could never divorce their children. Since both parents loved their children in their own ways, they would eventually put aside their present hostility toward each other when it came to deciding what was in the best interest of their children's welfare: agreement on flexible visitation rights and custody, and no bad-mouthing of each other in the children's presence.

"Don't tell me about the millions of people who get divorced, I know all about that," says Mary, twenty-nine. "I feel like a personal failure, because I didn't marry in order to get divorced. I was going to be married for life, and now it's over after five years. I wanted a family, at least two kids, because my time is running out, but Jerry would have none of that. Oh, why did I make such a terrible mistake in marrying him?"

Her words, *mistake* and *personal failure*, were old acquaintances of mine. How I flagellated myself with these same words in the early stages of my own divorce! Today, just as in 1970, the first emotional reaction of most people encountering divorce is a sense of failure—in God's eyes, in friends' and relatives' eyes—even though one may be fully aware *intellectually* that divorce is now an acceptable alternative to an impossible marriage. It's one thing to read about *other* people's divorces, but quite another to experience one's own divorce. Marriage is one of the most important and valuable relationships in life, so it's really quite natural to believe you are a personal failure if that relationship ends. And since a good marriage is in reach for all of us, it's also natural to believe you have made a mistake in choosing a partner you no longer love.

No matter how acceptable divorce becomes in society's eyes, it will always be a devastating *personal* experience in which feeling that one is a personal failure and has made a mistake will be the initial reaction to one's own divorce. So it is in the more enlightened present, as it was in the benighted seventies. However, accepting the normalcy of these feelings in the initial stages of your divorce is only one side of the coin. For I soon learned in my own case that I had the choice of making a lifetime career out of labeling myself as a personal failure who had made a horrendous marital mistake *or* of thrusting my life into a more positive direction.

To accomplish the latter, I had first to forgive myself and my ex-spouse for the unintentional harm we did to each other. We were neither saints nor sinners, but fallible human beings who, with the best of intentions, had unskillfully dealt with our marital problems, and this had resulted in our breaking up. In other words, we were the same as millions of other married couples in our country who arrived at the same dead end.

Second, I had to substitute the words *learning experience* for *personal failure* and *unawareness* for *mistake*. Otherwise, I would be drowning in self-pity, remorse, and timidity for the rest of my life. To continue to see myself as a failure would guarantee my acting like a failure in my new single life. To label my marriage a mistake would mean I would go through life afraid of making other major mistakes. I would paralyze myself: to venture nothing would ensure that I would make no new mistakes, but would also guarantee me a totally empty, fear-obsessed existence.

How liberating my shift of focus turned out to be! When I saw my previous marriage as a learning experience, I was able to center on the positive as well as the negative qualities of my marriage: what went wrong and why, and how I could improve my life in the future by utilizing what had been best in my marriage and eliminating the worst.

For example, at the time of my breakup, I believed my twenty-four years of marriage were all for nothing, a waste of my life. However, in viewing marriage as a learning experience, I realized it had been tremendously valuable. It had proved I had the capacity to love (for my wife and I had married because we loved each other to the extent that we knew what love was about in our early twenties); it had proved I was a caring person, since I was always alert to my family's welfare; it had proved I had the capacity for empathy, kindness, tenderness, patience, playfulness, and concern for others in nurturing my own daughters through their childhood years; it had proved that sharing common goals, such as having children, taking vacation trips, improving our living standard, and participating in family events with the one special person in my life made that life interesting and adventurous; it had proved that companionship with the one person in life who cared more about me than anyone else was an infinitely desirable way to live; it had proved I was a survivor who could overcome unemployment, illness, and the deaths of my parents, and could weather the storms of job changes and family crises.

Even though my marriage eroded, as the differences between my wife and me resulted in alienation from each other in place of the earlier closeness we had, those positive elements in my marriage remained within me. They only *seemed* lost at the time of my divorce, but subsequently I found those resources available for my use in living alone.

As for my marriage being a mistake because it ended

in divorce, it wasn't a mistake at all. Sad and painful and necessary as my divorce was, it didn't mean I was prone to making gigantic errors. But it did mean that my marriage had ended out of my own unawareness of the drift toward divorce that was occurring in our relationship long before the final breakup, a drift of over half a dozen years. The danger signals had been right before my eyes, but I never had seen them: my dissatisfaction with my job, which had translated into marital dissatisfaction; my inability to share my deepest hurts and fears with my wife; my refusal to share in household chores; the arguments that festered since they were never resolved; the contradictory sleeping schedules (my wife going to bed early every night, while I would overdose on television until two in the morning); our neglecting to seek counseling help in the early stages of our estrangement, rather than waiting until it was too late; and above all else, my unawareness that a good marriage doesn't happen by accident. When marriage is taken for granted it becomes a desert, and I had taken it for granted.

In taking this inventory of my past marriage, I learned that I had not been the victim of a chain of events that had resulted in my divorce. Instead, I had been a contributor to that end. Blaming myself for that fact was irrelevant, since I had been unaware of that fact at the time. What was most significant was my dawning recognition that I had had the personal power to influence my marriage negatively in the later years and positively in the earlier years. My image of myself had changed from that of the victim to that of the person who made things happen for better or for worse. And if I possessed that personal power in my marriage, I also possessed it in my life as a divorced person. With that newfound understanding, I was able to *make the effort* to make positive things happen to me. I could now permit myself to make "mistakes" in full awareness that I would be the gainer in venturing into unexplored territory, rather than a person always fated to lose. There were no guarantees that I would succeed, but it would be the only way to have some successes in life again. For if I didn't make such an effort, I would guarantee my achieving nothing after my divorce.

Claire, thirty-eight, is bewildered as she asks me, "Will my divorce *ever* end? I thought it would be all over when I got my decree. That was over five months ago, but I'm still being hassled by that creep I married. Phone calls in the middle of the night telling me what a bad wife I was, and complaints about how I'm not bringing up my children right. It's like I've never been divorced."

Claire is as bewildered as I was after I received my divorce decree. "At last, it's ended!" I had thought. How disappointed I was to discover that the divorce decree was only a piece of paper, not a resolution of all of my problems. My divorce was a relatively friendly one in the sense that there was agreement on the way we would handle our two children, and there was no interference in each other's lives after our separation. But there certainly was self-created interference in my own mind and heart that remained unresolved for many months after my divorce became "final" on paper. For I *still* thought of myself as a married man, and as a person of little value or worth now that I was on my own.

The freedom I had longed for was a very mixed blessing. Now I was accountable to no one except myself. But who, indeed, was "myself"? For twenty-four years I knew "myself" as a married man, accustomed to a daily routine I thought boring and anguishing: nine to five at a dead-end job; dinner at 6:30 P.M.; resentment over last night's marital spat that had reached no conclusion; dead silence after dinner, or else a new argument; two persons becoming lonelier than one as I worked over my stereo equipment hobbies in the basement, while my wife upstairs busied herself with reading or calling friends; then she would go to bed and I would follow after my dose of late-night boob-tube movies. And each day and night was a repetition of the previous day and night.

Who needed that? There must be more to life, I used to think at that time. Ah, to be free. Yes, there was to be more to life after divorce, but it didn't come automatically with our separation or after the divorce papers. That fact was the surprise in the divorce package I lived with during my first year as a single person.

I was shocked to find that I initially *missed* that deadening routine in my marriage. At least it had provided me with a structure to my life. At desolating times during the first months of my living alone, a disconcerting yearning inside myself to return to that structure would overwhelm me. I didn't know then that "freedom" could be scary as well as exciting. The territory of singleness was like a menacing jungle, since I had no experience as a single person in my middle years I didn't know what to expect.

Instead of feeling relieved at living alone, I found myself fleeing every night from my chosen apartment as if it were jail, going into neighborhood bars, wandering into movie houses just to exhaust myself enough to return to sleep in the solitary emptiness of my bed. Sometimes a woman would be in that bed with me, but orgasm was a release of biological tension rather than emotional fulfillment. And so I discovered that two could be lonelier than one, even after divorce. Even my relationship with my job turned into something unexpected. In those early months of living alone, I actually found myself veering toward becoming more attached to the very job I had claimed made me so unhappy. But I now found myself working longer hours than I had before I separated. At 5:00 P.M. I had been out of the office like a rabbit on the run.

Now I would frequently linger at my desk until eight or nine in the evening, shuffling papers, half-absorbed in writing bureaucratic reports that meant nothing. I would wonder why I was staying in an office I had been so eager to leave, yet feel compelled to remain rooted at my desk. And most of all, I would puzzle over why, why, why the divorce didn't end with my final decree. Why was I still feeling more like a married person than a single person now that my marriage had ended?

This maelstrom of contradictions all began to make sense to me when I started to focus on the *real* meaning of freedom. Freedom meant more than freedom from something, the leaving of a situation I had felt jailed in. That was only half of the freedom equation. The other half was the freedom to make a new reality for oneself that would improve upon the past. This was far more easily said than done, for it meant I would now have to take personal responsibility in order to make my own freedom a positive adventure in life rather than a continuation of my past despair in my marriage.

At the time of my own confusion and fear, Dave, a divorced friend of mine, was sitting with me in my tiny apartment and said, "You know, Mel, I went through what you're going through, although you wouldn't know it, since now I feel good about myself and the way I'm living. I got to where I am now when I learned that at rock bottom the only arm I could reliably count on to get me out of the mess I was in was my own right arm."

I'll never forget Dave's words. I was ready to understand their meaning only when I had lived out my illusions about what I thought divorce meant, which had been "off with the old, on with the new, each in its own separate compartment." When the past kept interfering with my present life as a single person, that was telling me that I had to give up my illusion that divorce was just a simple legal matter. Divorce had turned out to be a complicated mixture of remorse, regret, sadness, and pain about the past; anger and hostility at discovering that living as a single person in those early months of separation seemed to be no better than living with my former partner; fear over the loss of my identity as a married man, since no single-person identity was yet emerging inside me.

And I had also felt a towering resentment over the fact that *now* I had no one else to blame for my misery. How easy it had been for me to believe it was all my wife's fault for our mutual unhappiness while I was married. That prop of self-righteousness was knocked out from under me when I was divorced. I was accountable now only to myself for my continued unhappiness. "How dare she do this to me," I would think, and then stop and realize the absurdity of what I had been telling myself.

I could no longer pass the buck to anyone else (but, oh, how that yearning to do so persisted!), and yet I refused to confront the bitter but necessary realization that the buck stopped with me and no one else. I suppose I was on the verge of confronting the unpalatable fact that I would remain a victim as long as I continued to see myself as victimized by others, such as my former wife, my job, my old friends who seemed to avoid me, the unfamiliar world of divorced society, which was why Dave's blunt words became a beacon of light shed on my dark life in that gloomy apartment.

"To rely on my own right arm" meant taking personal responsibility to shape the direction of my life, and to be accountable to myself, rather than anyone else for my actions. Freedom means exactly that, taking personal responsibility for one's own behavior, which is the awesome but necessary demand that divorce imposes on every man or woman who separates from a spouse. A very wise man, George Bernard Shaw, once defined freedom as accepting such personal responsibility, and then he added, "that's why so many persons fear freedom."

Yet it was only when I accepted my own personal responsibility for my behavior, *in spite of my continuing fear of doing so,* that positive things began to happen in my life as a divorced person. The less I saw myself as the person to whom bad things were happening, the more my life assumed a brighter hue: instead of waiting for old friends to call me, I would call them. Some were relieved and welcomed my call, while others gave me the feeling I should get lost.

I learned who my good friends were, and separated out those who were friends by habit only and those who were truly empathic and accepting of me. Instead of blaming my ex-wife for all my troubles, I began to see that I was at least equally responsible for our breakup.

I was appalled at my own blindness in my marriage, once I faced the facts of what I had done to make our marriage sour. My own self-righteousness; my assumption of male superiority; my failure to hear my wife's pain with the marriage; my hiding behind a newspaper or in front of the television set as a way of not dealing with the basic hurts in our marriage; my foolish belief that if I didn't talk about our problems, they would go away.

Assuming my share of the responsibility for my divorce had a liberating effect on me. It became a learning experience that made me relate in a healthier manner to the new women in my life that I dated. It helped me to see these women as separate individuals apart from my own needs. It put me on the road to a more empathic understanding of women, their needs, their hopes and dreams, and how they were programmed to relate to men. If a relationship of mine broke up (and many of them did, during the first two years of my divorce), I would focus on myself. "How did I contribute to the breakup?" I would ask myself, rather than saying, "Good riddance, I didn't like the bitch anyway." In this way I could acknowledge my own personal power to influence a relationship. It followed that if I had the personal power to influence a relationship negatively, I also had the personal power to influence it positively. Every relationship then became an exciting new experience in which I learned more about myself and how I could correct my self-defeating behavior.

Instead of complaining about my job (at the same time using it as a crutch to avoid people), I took steps to leave it for something better. In my off-hours I would assemble groups of divorced men and women in what I called Creative Divorce Seminars. I did not precipitately quit my old job, but when I saw I could make a living at what I had originated, I gave notice to my employer. That was one of the happiest days in my life.

Instead of feeling ripped off in the financial settlement of my divorce, I no longer complained about "getting the shaft." Living in the present was all I had in life, and I had the resources to survive: I was intelligent; I had professional skills; I had survived near-starvation in months of unemployment in my earlier years; I had been fired from earlier jobs and attained better ones thereafter; when my job as a sales manager for a plywood firm was eliminated through a merger, I had returned to college to get an advanced degree in psychology in my mid-forties.

At fifty, I had a rich inheritance as a survivor. What I lost in money in my divorce, I could always make up again. Although marriage had defined my sense of who I was, I now had the opportunity to discover for the first time who I was as a separate individual, rather than as part of a couple. That could be an adventure instead of a disaster.

Instead of believing I had no identity, now that I was single I began to total up the survival skills that I had learned through fifty years of living. These were the building blocks of my new identity through divorce, for I was still a wage-earner, a father, a friend, a relative, a risk-taker, a person who had coped with extreme adversity in the deaths of my parents. These were resources I carried with me in my single state and could use to advantage if only I would permit myself to tap them.

Then why did I think of myself as a man with no identity, which really meant a man with no resources at his disposal to lead a decent life? Only the breakup of my marriage could have given me the answer; in a world in which marriage is accepted as the norm, the loss of that status has a devastating personal impact. No one can really know how profound that impact can be unless one has experienced divorce. In addition, you have shared the deepest parts of yourself with another person, you have marched together through the basic joys and adversities of life; you have made and nourished your children together; you have loved each other before that love died, with the full intensity of your being. Small wonder, then, that such a precious set of experiences, now ended, should temporarily destabilize you. Like me, most divorced men only discover the enormous extent to which marriage has defined their personal identity when they are confronted with a future of living alone.

Nothing that is valuable in a marriage is ever lost, once a divorce has occurred. In my own case, the rich experiences in my own marriage enabled me to become a more mature human being, fallible like any other, but a person who had the capacity to live my life in a less hurtful way to myself and others. It took the jolt of my divorce to experience that reality, but it took the lived experiences of my marriage to give me the capability of attaining that goal. No, my marriage had not been all for nothing.

However, it seemed that way during the first month of my divorce. But slowly a self-healing process emerged. My feeling that I was starting from scratch began to disappear when I found I could survive one day at a time: each day I went to work on time, even though I thought I could never get out of bed again; I learned to cook for myself, since I could not afford to eat out all the time and it was a choice of either cooking or starving; despite the fact that I had been known as a fumble-fingers, I achieved the ultimate for me, sewing buttons on my shirts; I had visits from my daughters and friends after I reached out to them; when I felt like running away from my apartment to become unhappy in a bar, I would surprise myself by occasionally preferring to stay home and read a book, listen to music, or write letters; instead of remaining in my office, I began to disengage myself from that unfulfilling womb and turned it into a nine-to-five job again; I started my first evening Creative Divorce Seminar and began to make new friends out of that group. Each new day became a challenge and an opportunity rather than another essay in hopelessness.

I only became aware that this was happening to me after it began. Jan, a friend, brought this to my attention when she said to me over lunch, four months into my divorce, "You look so much better now, Mel. There's less sadness in your face. You have a nice smile and you're using it more." That remark made me realize I was experiencing the *process* of divorce, rather than the *label* of divorce. From that time on I would notice that process at work in myself, share my observations with my divorce groups, and find confirmation that all the men and women in those groups were also undergoing a similar process.

By the end of the first year of my divorce, I evaluated my findings about myself and all the other divorced men and women who had shared their experiences with me. Yes, there was the legal aspect of divorce, but that piece of paper did not end the *emotional* connection that still remained within me to my past marriage and the way that marriage shaped my personal identity.

To let go of the past, and the seductive trap of wallowing in self-pity, I had to make the effort to prove to myself, first, that I was a person who could survive physically and emotionally as a single person instead of as part of a couple. In doing so, I would validate the fact that I was a person of value and worth in my own right. Nobody could give me that sense of my own value and worth except myself. When I would feel that way about myself, then other people would confirm what I myself radiated. To achieve that goal, I had to recognize that divorce, apart from the legal piece of paper, was predominantly *a psychological process of self-renewal.* Understanding that process, and moving myself ahead in accordance with it, was the key factor that would make my life happier after my breakup. That process involved the following four steps:

1. *Terror time.* Initial separation and the feeling that everything in life is now out of control.
2. *Mourning time.* Laying the past marriage to rest in your feelings, in the same way you would mourn the loss of a loved one who died, since divorce is indeed a death, the death of a relationship.
3. *Living-in-the-present time.* Responding skillfully to each new day as a challenge to ensure that the best in your life is yet to come, rather than as a remembrance of past pleasures.
4. *Self-renewal time.* The product of experiencing the three previous processes so that you arrive at a stage of being where you wonder why you ever thought it was impossible to survive happily both physically and emotionally on your own.

It is this process that I personally experienced and that I encourage the divorced men and women attending my seminars to incorporate in their own lives. It is a process that can also enable you to take positive charge of your life, as the subsequent chapters of this book will demonstrate.

"Marriage is for the birds! I'll never marry again." It is a rare day when I don't hear a divorced man or woman defiantly shout those words to the world at some time during a counseling session with me.

I know the fear behind that defiance, the fear of men and women that no one will ever love them again. For it was that same fear I felt in the first year of my own divorce. It was a form of self-protection, an I'll-reject-you-before-you-reject-me attitude toward the opposite sex. I married for life, yet here I was, divorced and in pain.

So marriage became the culprit, a con game played on kids who thought they were adults just because they took out a marriage license. Just like Melvin Belli, I loudly proclaimed to anyone who would listen to me, including the

press, that I would never, never, marry again. In fact, I
continued to wave my anti-marriage banner for almost four
years after my divorce.

And in that fourth year I married again!

No, I hadn't lied to myself, nor had I betrayed my
deeply held conviction that another marriage was to be
avoided at all costs. As I look back at that time, I believe I
was right and honest with myself when I said I would never
marry again, but I was also right and honest with myself
when I decided to remarry.

The change in my attitude was the result of my allowing enough time after my divorce to enable me to establish
a single-person identity that proved to me I was a person of
value and worth in my own right. To do that, I had to
experience the initial separation terror of the early months
of living alone, then mourn the death of my marriage, and
subsequently make positive things happen (leave my job
and establish a new career; take personal responsibility to
make new friends; pursue new interests, such as teaching
and writing; make a closer connection with my children;
date new women).

Tuning into this divorce process enabled me to learn to
trust myself to become more insightful, understanding, and
empathic with women I dated, and made me understand
that I was *not* the same callow youth today that I had been
when I was first married. I now knew why marriages turned
sour, and the steps needed to prevent that from happening.
Within that four-year period, I discovered that I was running away from intimacy, which meant running away from
the best part of myself. For without intimacy—the capacity
to give and receive love—life becomes a desert. A good
marriage is an ultimate expression of intimacy, and is to be
welcomed rather than feared.

But it had been right for me to fear that kind of intimacy as long as I felt like a victimized loser, as I did in the
early stages of my divorce. How afraid of myself I was at that
time, for how could I ever trust the sad-sack image I saw in
my mirror not to make the same "mistake" again? Wouldn't
I wind up in another marriage that would be a repetition of
the past, divorce included?

I was able to protect myself from hastily remarrying

only by acknowledging to myself how needy I was for someone to take care of me and make me happy. In fact, my own
lawyer told me at the time I received my final decree, "Mel,
I'm going to give you the advice I give to all my divorced
clients: stay away from getting married again too soon, not
for another two years at least. Otherwise, you'll wind up in
my office again in another divorce."

This was very valuable advice, although I didn't realize
it then. I absolutely had no intention of marrying again;
there was no woman waiting in the wings for me, because
my divorce was based on mutual incompatibility. I followed
his advice, however, in my own way by distancing myself
from a close commitment to any one woman through the
disdain I heaped on the institution of marriage. At that time
it was hard enough to get through one day successfully, let
alone engage in a committed relationship.

My attitude toward marriage began to change when I
myself had changed, when I began to feel happy about the
way I was personally taking charge of my life. I then began
to *want*, not *need*, a new relationship with one special person that perhaps might lead to marriage. Although I was
happy with myself, I felt I would be *happier* with a person
I loved who could share my hopes and dreams, who would
be my best friend and companion and equal partner. I could
give that person my new-found strength rather than my old
weaknesses. She, in turn, would have the same vision of such
a commitment as I did.

I met that person at a party I didn't want to go to,
believing it would be a boring affair. It was, except for her.
She was Patricia Biondi, a divorced lady of thirty-eight with
two teenaged children, who had been married for eighteen
years.

It wasn't love at first sight. We were initially attracted
to each other, but were committed to making our own personal lives better by ourselves, and so we almost scared each
other to death because we didn't want to become closely
involved. Both of us had then been divorced for one year.
We very cautiously started out as acquaintances, then as
friends, and didn't make love during the early months of our
relationship. The friendship blossomed into love as we be-

came stronger within ourselves in resolving our separate problems arising from our divorces.

In the third year of our relationship, we took the step of living together, still fearful of marriage. When this arrangement proved we could relate in ways that fulfilled each other's needs, in contrast to our past marriages, we exorcised the horror-movie idea of marriage that had haunted our minds for four years. We wrote our own marriage ceremony in which the word *obey* was eliminated and the words *care for each other as equal partners* were substituted in its place.

We will be celebrating our fifteenth anniversary this year, and we like and love each other more rather than less as the years accumulate. We don't have a happily-ever-after story to tell. What we do have is a marriage of mutual respect and a commitment to communicate openly and resolve problems that inevitably arise when two persons live together permanently. Of abrasions, tensions, and crises there are plenty. But we face them when they arise, knowing we are each other's best friends. And by talking out our hurts, fears, resentments, and vulnerabilities, we arrive at resolutions of our difficulties rather than allow them to fester into alienation. We have learned from our past, not repeated it.

The quest for new intimacy that resulted in my remarrying is a quest most divorced men and women eventually undertake. In fact, four out of every five divorced persons eventually remarry. Most of them are as soured on marriage immediately after their divorce as I was, but they too discover that when they say they will never marry again, that "never" is not forever, for the quest for intimacy is built into the human condition.

If you are not involved in that quest at the present time, don't be surprised if it becomes a new priority in your life as a single person. There is a readiness time for it to occur, which will be dealt with in a subsequent chapter. Of course, there are some men and women who learn from their divorces that they are not the kind of people for whom marriage will ever again be an appropriate arrangement. They will be perfectly happy living out the rest of their lives as single persons. Their choice is right for them; they have discovered this most important fact about themselves as a result of their divorces.

However, the number of people opting for a permanent single life-style after divorce is relatively small. Whether you are one of those persons will not be determined by what you say, but by how you will feel most comfortable in the many years that follow your divorce.

Melvin Belli and I have shared with you our commitment to divorce as a stepping-stone to our own personal self-renewal, which made our futures brighter than our past. We are not exceptions, which is why we are charting the way for your own self-renewal in the subsequent chapters of this book. We invite you to experience the realities of divorce as an adventure in learning, so that you can experience each new day in your single life as a time for positive achievement rather than as an exercise in regret.

2

Toward the World Beyond Marriage: The Basic Realities

≡

"What about all those thousands of people out there who are thinking right now about whether or not to get a divorce, or those who have already begun legal action but are having second thoughts about ending their marriages? You know, Mel, you never addressed yourself to these issues in any of your previous writings, yet they are terribly important."

This criticism was raised by Mary, a dear friend of mine who was first divorced in the mid-1970s, when I told her some months ago that I was going to write this book with Melvin Belli. I had to agree that she was right, which is why this chapter will deal with some of those issues.

Throughout my many years as a divorce counselor, I have observed how important it is to be very certain that your decision to divorce is based on the reality that there is no hope left for your marriage. Even the person who tells me on a first visit, "I want out. It's impossible to live with that horror I'm married to any longer," may still have many mixed feelings, misconceptions, and apprehensions about throwing in the towel. To jump out of the frying pan impulsively might land you in the fire, which is what happened to my friend Mary.

She told me, "If I had not rushed for a divorce and had thought more about its pros and cons, I would be better off today. It's even conceivable I might still be married to my first husband if we had both tried harder to make our marriage work. Or it might not, but I would feel better today if I had really been more aware of the consequences of a divorce."

Since her first divorce, Mary has divorced a second husband and recently ended a year-long living-together arrangement. "I must be a slow learner," she said, "but I'm finally getting the message that I need to think long and hard before I will ever again allow my emotions to overwhelm me into making a snap decision whenever I experience problems in a relationship. Maybe my example can be of help to your readers."

The result of my talk with Mary is to be found in this chapter. Do you have mixed feelings about whether or not you should divorce? Is your marriage truly dead? If your marriage is dead, do you have illusions about divorce that might prevent you from dealing effectively with the problems you will face as a single person? Do you know how to find a good divorce lawyer and determine whether or not he or she is right for you? Are you aware of how you can minimize the legal hassles and expenses of a divorce?

Let's begin to answer these questions by starting where all divorces begin, with marriage itself:

To married men and women, the world of the divorced is a blank sheet of paper on which they will draw their own fantasies. The happily married may paint single life in dark and frightening colors, while those who consider their present marriages to be jail sentences may envision divorce as a rainbow-colored future of freedom. Neither of these views is accurate, since both are reflections of states of mind rather than photographic representations of the complex reality the millions of adult single men and women in our country actually experience in their daily lives.

The way in which you live inevitably colors your perception of your personal world. For example, if you are in a fairly long first marriage and are over thirty and have children, you see your daily reality through a married person's eyes, from the time you wake up until you go to sleep. You wake up with your spouse in a bed warmed by the both of you, in a house or apartment alive with the chatter of children. There is the routine pandemonium of dressing, preparing breakfast, and then the flight to work or school. You know what to expect when you come home from work: the family dinner at the usual time, during which a recounting of what happened to the kids that day and news about the job, friends, or relatives may be covered.

The rest of the evening may involve both of you with the good and bad deeds of the children, their discipline, homework, and bedtime; then maybe a drink and some TV, or talk, arguments, or alienated silence between you and your spouse. Suddenly it's time to go to bed. You know what to expect when you wake up the next morning, since it will be more of the same, day after day, year after year; the married-life habit defines your sense of who you are without your even being consciously aware of that fact.

Your shopping, washing, housecleaning and upkeep, gardening, clothing repairs, and meal preparations are married-life chores, since they nurture your spouse and family, not just you yourself. You are you, but plus one in almost everything! The house or condominium or apartment in which you live has been marriage-chosen, since it was selected because there was space enough for you and your spouse and your children. Even your social life is marriage-defined: most of the friends you see regularly are married couples like yourself, with similar interests and children; the relatives you visit are connected through your marriage; your holidays, religious observances, and vacations are spent with your spouse and usually with your children.

Married-life habits generate married-life emotions. You always have to take into consideration how your decisions and feelings will affect others in your family. Even if you don't do so, the effects will show anyway, since your children and spouse are quick to pick up and interpret (or misinterpret) any silence, sadness, anxiety, despair, or self-isolation on your part as noncooperative, nonloving disenchantment with them. In turn, their constant physical presence, their emotional impact on your personality, pervades the everyday reality of your own life. Consciously or unconsciously, you've learned to depend on others for your almost every act!

The enveloping impact of your marriage on your behavior, emotions, and sense of self cannot be underestimated. Whether or not you have children, or have been married a short two years or a long twenty years, its effect is potent. The marriage stamp on your personality intensifies as the years accumulate. Since most marriages in North America are of relatively long duration (divorce typically occurs after seven years of marriage, with almost one-third of all divorces taking place after fifteen years of marriage), a breakup will shatter or reassemble your elaborate network of family, social, and economic relationships to an unprecedented extent. Most people who are considering a first divorce are not aware of this basic fact prior to their separation from their spouse; family, social, and economic problems will end, so they believe, if they divorce.

Divorce is seen at that time through the tunnel vision of their unhappy marriage as the solution to all of their problems. This resembles the plight of the parched wanderer in a desert who is convinced life would be happy if only he could find an oasis. However, once the water is discovered and drunk, the wanderer is still unhappy. Finding the water may be the precondition to remaining physically alive, which would enable the wanderer to solve his problems, but this is not the cure-all for unhappiness. Similarly, divorce may very well be the absolutely necessary precondition to your remaining emotionally alive; it could be an opportunity to free yourself to create your own happiness, but it is no guarantee in and of itself that the act of divorcing will create that happiness for you.

Should Your Marriage Be Saved?

If, as you read these words, you feel your marriage is at a dead end, look hard before you leap into a divorce, since divorce, even when it is the only possible solution to a soured marriage, can be one of the most traumatic experiences in your life, second only to the death of a loved one in its shattering intensity. The quality of your future years may well depend upon your accurate assessment of whether or not divorce is the *only* road toward greater happiness for yourself. Divorce, indeed, can offer you such a chance for personal improvement, but the divorce road is the hardest of all possible routes to that end. It is a fact of life that nobody, but nobody, works harder to put the pieces of his or her life back together again than a divorced person. It will take far less of your energy to work at improving your marriage, given goodwill and motivation to do so on the part of you and your spouse.

Quite frequently, people who yell at their spouses and say they want a divorce really want positive changes in their marriages instead. In a survey I recently made, lawyers invariably told me that half of the men and women who barge into the office yelling, "I want a divorce!" are not really interested in filing for one, but wish instead to alert their spouses that major improvements in their marriage are needed.

You didn't marry in order to get divorced. You have worked very hard to make your marriage a success, nevertheless, you find yourself in an insufferable marriage and consider divorce as the only possible next step. If this is the way you are now feeling, you join the ranks of millions of other married persons in our society. Must you take the next step of separating? Only if there is no possibility of improving your marriage.

Most married people work very hard to have a good marriage, but they work at the wrong things in the wrong ways, and wind up in a dead-end situation. However, if your marriage seems to be at a dead end, there is always the possibility that the dead end is a new beginning in disguise. The dead-end feeling may be telling you that your old ways of relating to each other don't work and that new ways that will work can be substituted instead. You may be misreading the dead-end sign to mean divorce, when it really means "take a detour to better your marriage."

There is a popular magazine column called "Can This Marriage Be Saved?" The intent of the column is admirable, but the question it poses is the wrong one. In today's times, the question to be asked is "*Should* this marriage be saved?" For a marriage that is not based on love, mutual respect, equality, accommodation to each other's needs, friendship, caring, empathy, forgiveness, and relevant communication not only cannot be saved, but *should not* be saved. A loveless marriage that makes you feel less than human is not worth saving. If you are feeling this way, however, make certain, for your own subsequent piece of mind, that you are not misinterpreting your situation. Your marriage may not be terminally ill if:

1. You and your spouse still believe there is a residue of love left in your relationship beneath all the pain, hurt and resentment you are experiencing with each other. (You may be complaining, "We love each other, but can't stand living with each other.")

2. Both of you realize it takes *two* to make a bad marriage, and that the two of you are equally responsible for the unhappiness you are experiencing.

3. Rather than blaming each other, you both recognize that you are doing harmful things to each other out of *unawareness*, not because you are wicked persons who like to hurt each other.

4. Since you can't resolve your problems by yourselves, both of you are willing to seek outside help. Both of you recognize that it is the strong person, rather than the weak one, who seeks outside help. Consequently, the two of you, understanding that you are too close to your situation to see it clearly, are willing to seek help from a good marriage counselor who can view your marriage objectively.

5. Both of you are open to changing the destructive, habitual ways in which you communicate with each other and are willing to change those ways once you are given the tools to do so by a good marriage counselor.

6. Both of you decide you would rather be happy than right. This means the letting go of your

righteous anger toward each other, and allowing forgiveness rather than "getting even" to
take place between the two of you.

7. Both of you are motivated to work through
   your problems with the aid of a good marriage
   counselor, rather than run away from them.
   This will be difficult to do, since old habits die
   hard, but can be done if the willingness is present.

8. The goal the two of you set for yourselves is to
   create a new marriage *within* your marriage,
   since the old one doesn't work, characterized
   by love instead of alienation.

Many couples who have sought my counseling help
have been able to improve their marriages, even though
they initially had thought only of divorce, because they
were willing to look for solutions within the framework of
the eight conditions listed above. If, at this time, you are
considering divorce, making the effort to engage your
spouse in this prior attempt to improve your marriage before that ultimate step is taken would be well worth the
try. Even if that effort doesn't work, or your spouse refuses
to undergo counseling with you, it will enable you to minimize your feelings of guilt and regret once you opt for
divorce.

As I write these words, I hear the plaint of a client of
mine, Harry, forty-five, divorced for six years, who told me
sadly, "I only wish I had taken my wife's advice and gone
to a marriage counselor with her when she suggested it. We
may have remained together, knowing what I know now,
rather than break up. Now I'll never know if that was possible."

Of course, the search for a good marriage counselor
should be made in good faith. That effort should not be used
on your part as a halfhearted attempt to prove that only a
divorce is possible; nor should your spouse agree to counseling if he or she is convinced in advance that it is all to no
avail, but simply a delaying action prior to divorce. Indeed,
these kinds of game-playing only confirm that your marriage is over.

When Does Your Divorce Begin?

Practically every married person has thought at one time or another, "Wouldn't it be great to be divorced from this turkey I'm married to?" It's a normal and natural reaction to the difficulties experienced in living together in one of the most complex arrangements ever invented by human beings. For couples whose marriages are intrinsically in excellent shape, the desire to divorce is only a fleeting fantasy twinge. However, if the idea of divorcing becomes a daily visitor in your soul because the pain of remaining together keeps escalating in intensity over time, then legal divorce action may very well be the realistic next step.

A divorce, however, doesn't begin when you visit a lawyer for the very first time. The legalities of divorce are only the end product of a divorce that has occurred *in your feelings* for a long time before that visit to the lawyer occurs. You married in the first place because you believed your spouse was the number-one person in your life: the person who cared more about you and loved you more than any other nonrelated adult in this world (and vice versa). When those beliefs die inside of you, marriage turns into a world of pain. Consequently, your *emotional divorce* will take place at the time when your belief that you are the number-one person in your spouse's life has irrevocably died. It is possible that your spouse may be experiencing these very same feelings about you. In my counseling practice, I have discovered that an emotional divorce of this kind can take place many years before a legal divorce is initiated. These are the most frequently encountered types of emotional divorce:

The Honeymoon Divorce You may discover in the first month of marriage that the two of you are grossly mismatched. Sexual incompatibility, value differences, and power struggles emerge that may pervade the marriage for years before a legal divorce takes place. Your number-one position in the marriage may have ended at your marriage ceremony.

The My-Relatives-Come-First Divorce Fairly soon after your marriage, you or your spouse may discover you are more attached to your family than to your marriage partner. Priority is always given to your parents' needs and demands and their ordering of your lives, so that you nourish your family instead of each other. When the number-one "person" in your or your spouse's life is the parental family, and that childhood bond is not replaced by a mature adult relative relationship, your emotional divorce has occurred.

The My-Career-Is-More-Important-than-Your-Career Divorce Most married couples today are dedicated to two-career marriages. In the process of choosing a career, getting and holding a job, and advancing up the career ladder, both of you may become more passionately involved in your separate careers than in each other. You may feel that every night you're coming home to a board of directors meeting, rather than a marriage partner. The career becomes an obsession, the number-one "person" in your life. Working differing hours and evenings and weekends leads to the conclusion that the career has taken precedence over one's spouse. Your emotional divorce begins when that takes place.

The Baby-Makes-a-Triangle Divorce With the onset of pregnancy and the birth of a child, attention in your marriage is focused on the new member of your family. You may have been a husband who felt you were no longer the number-one person in your wife's life, since all of the love you once received seems now to be directed toward the newborn infant. This can also happen if you are a wife and your husband seems to be concerned with caring for the child to the exclusion of your needs.

You and your spouse will have laid the groundwork for your divorce if you have never given up the belief that your children are number one, rather than each other, throughout the duration of your marriage. It is one thing to be number one with your children as a parent, but quite another to consider your children as substitutes for a number-one adult relationship with your spouse.

The Great-Expectations-Turned-Sour Divorce You may have been a husband or wife who married in the belief that your spouse would make "good marriage material." He or she would "make you happy" by having a successful career and a high income. When this bubble burst in the years you lived together, resentment and hostility may have replaced the feeling that you were number one to each other. The failure of the dream of material success may have become the number-one focus of your marital life, and the longer that focus was primary in your marriage, the more inevitable your legal divorce became.

The Hobby-Widowed Divorce It is one thing to have a hobby as an element that adds salt to a marriage, but quite another if a hobby becomes an obsession that substitutes for a shared marital relationship. "You're not married to me, you're married to that damned hobby of yours," is a frequent complaint of couples I counsel who are on the verge of a divorce.

Today, you hear a lot about "computer widows," wives who feel abandoned because their husbands are more enamored of hardware and software of their computers than of their wives. In former times, the term "golf widow" was used for the wife who felt her husband's golf game was more important to him than she was. As long as a spouse seethes with resentment over not being number one in the marriage, because excessive personal involvement with a computer or any other hobby excludes the chance to nourish the marriage, feelings of loneliness and estrangement are generated.

The Bloom-Is-Off Divorce Some people fall in love with love instead of a person. Passionate romance, Technicolor orgasms, and a permanent high of self-centered excitement may have been their definition of what marriage was all about. They are the men and women who say, "The romance has gone out of my marriage," as they become confronted with the prosaic activities that make up a significant portion of married life. When the romantic bloom fades, as it must to some extent, since the "high" of romance is primarily based on the newness of a relationship, disillusionment with marriage quickly occurs in such people. When married life is equated solely with romantic excitement, an emotional divorce can quickly occur, with a legal divorce shortly thereafter, which may account for the fact that over a quarter of all legal divorces occur within the first two years of marriage.

The Drugs-Are-My-True-Love Divorce The major drug in our society is the homely drug of alcohol. There are some 20 million problem drinkers in our country, a fact that contributes enormously to the deterioration of millions of marriages. Add to this the increase in consumption of more exotic drugs, such as cocaine, and you have a situation in which drugs become the number-one "person" in many marriages. When a spouse becomes less of a turn-on than a substance, an emotional divorce occurs.

The Trust-Is-Broken Divorce When the practice of monogamy in a marriage becomes the exception rather than the rule, basic trust between a husband and wife is broken. Even if an affair is only a one-time fling in a marriage that is otherwise monogamous, mutual trust is extraordinarily difficult to restore. An affair-addicted spouse may be perfectly content to remain in the marriage; however, the spouse who has been victimized no longer believes he or she is number one in the marriage and experiences an emotional divorce when the affairs become known. Such a marriage may drag on for years after the erosion of trust occurs.

The I'm-in-Love-with-Someone-Else Divorce It seems to come out of nowhere when a husband or wife says, "I'm in love with another person and want a divorce!" The recipient of that shocking news usually replies, "But I thought we had a good marriage. I never felt anything was going wrong." However, when the reasons for the breakup in such a marriage are explored in depth, the "other" woman or man is never the basic cause. The illusion of a "good" marriage hid the reality of profound discontent with the relationship that both the husband and wife may have experienced for years. Frequently the person who is shocked by this revelation has massively denied the reality that *both* husband and wife were emotionally divorced from each other long before the "other" person entered the scene. No one can "win" or "take away" a spouse from his or her partner unless that spouse was ready to be won or taken away. What seems like a quick subsequent legal divorce is really the end result of a long-standing estrangement from each other within the marriage.

The Is-This-All-There-Is-to-Life? Divorce In this emotional divorce, the number-one "person" in the marriage has become the dream of absolute freedom from the responsibilities of married life. This oh-to-be-single-and-wild-and-free dream frequently erupts as a towering flame in a husband's or wife's middle years, but it usually has been present as a banked fire in one's feelings for many years prior to the eruption. Obsessed with the belief that time is running out (look at all the deaths of friends and relatives and the onset of chronic illnesses and terminal diseases in others!), one last exciting chance for personal freedom becomes the reason for ending a marriage that is experienced as chained servitude to a boring partner. When such a person decides to divorce, it may seem to his or her spouse that this is a "sudden" occurrence. But it is not sudden at all. For the number-one relationship between husband and wife may have died of undernourishment long before the sudden outburst.

The You're-Not-the-Person-I-Married Divorce A husband and wife may have seen only the tip-of-the-iceberg of each other at the time they married; he may have seen her previously as a compliant homemaker and vivacious sex object; she may have seen him as a take-charge, strong and silent provider. The longer the marriage lasts, the greater will be their disillusionment with each other, should she become manipulative, complaining, and usually "too tired" for sex, and should he become an uncertain provider whose silence masks resentment and fear rather than strength. They are no longer number one to each other if they remain attached to the original distorted image of the person they *thought* they married, rather than resolving constructively the ongoing difficulties between them. The number-one "person" then becomes the betrayal of the illusion they had harbored about what their spouse was like, in contrast to what that person is really like.

The Changing-Years Divorce The only unchanging certainties in life are birth and death; in between, every person changes, along with his or her priorities for living. A married couple's failure to adjust to these changes and accommodate themselves to new circumstances in their marriage will destroy their number-one feeling toward each other. This is particularly evident in the middle or later years. When the children leave home, a husband and wife may discover they have neglected their couple relationship over decades of marriage; the children had been their only binding element, and with the children's leaving, home has now become a desert. Or when the specter of retirement nears, the prospect of experiencing living with an abrasive ever-present spouse may be too anguishing to accept. In these instances, fear of a future together becomes the number-one "person" in the marriage, and the emotional divorce may subsequently turn into a legal reality.

The Power-Struggle Divorce The impact of the women's movement has had a profound affect on what couples expect in a marriage. For women, marriage is seen as a relationship based on mutual respect and full equality in decision-making. A man may agree to this in principle, but find it hard to practice, since his societal programming from birth has made him believe that women are second-class citizens and that major decisions are his province, since he earns more money than his wife.

When a husband continues to act this way in the marriage, while the wife resents and balks at the attitude that she must do all the housework and child care and defer to the "king of the castle" in all key decisions, a power struggle occurs. A husband, in turn, may resent the fact that his wife is trying to be "ruler of the roost" in instances where she earns more money at her job than he does. The struggle for power then becomes the number-one "person" in the marriage and can result in an emotional divorce when a husband or wife is more in love with being the dominant power in their relationship instead of being in love with each other.

Departure Time and the Seven Deadly Emotions

The fact that your emotional divorce may have occurred long before the physical act of your leaving each other takes place can reinforce the irrevocability of your decision to live permanently apart from each other and divorce legally. You will need this reinforcement, since actually separating is no simple matter. For this action, even when contemplated, may open up the floodgates to wildly mixed feelings within yourself that may completely surprise you. Your head will have told you that living apart from each other is the only logical answer to your marital problems, but your heart may pound you with enormous reservations about taking that action. Your decision to act may be assaulted by the following Seven Deadly Emotions that can turn that decision into a nightmare:

Fear. Thoughts such as, "I may not be able to survive on my own. . . . It's impossible to find a place to live. . . . My savings and income will disappear and I might live in poverty. . . . Maybe I'm unlovable and doomed to live a lonely life. . . . My family will reject me, and my friends won't want to see me anymore. . . . I may lose my job. . . ."

Guilt. Thoughts such as, "My children will think I'm a rotten parent. . . . My spouse is a nice person whom I don't want to hurt; he [or she] will believe I'm a bitch [or a bastard]. . . . Friends will no longer think I'm a nice person, and my parents will have heart attacks when they find out we're divorcing. . . . My spouse can't make it on his or her own, so I'll be the cause of a possible suicide. . . ."

Self-pity. Thoughts such as, "I've been too trusting, but I'll never trust anyone again. . . . I'm never going to let anyone hurt me again. . . . I'm such a warm, decent, reasonable person, but my spouse was too blind to see me that way. . . . Nobody else is suffering like I'm suffering. . . ."

Failure. Thoughts such as, "My marriage was supposed to be for life, but I've failed to make that happen.... All of my relatives and married friends will now look at me as a personal failure.... My children will be pointing their fingers at me because I failed them by making them live in a broken home...."

Anger. Thoughts such as, "I'm in this horrible situation because of that rotten spouse of mine. ... He [or she] is forcing me into breaking up, and disrupting my life.... Our marriage was all a mistake from the start.... Cold, mean, unfeeling, selfish—that's the person I married...."

Self-Flagellation. Thoughts such as, "How stupid of me to have married the person I did. ... What an idiot I was to remain in my unhappy marriage for so many years.... I'm just a bumbler who always makes mistakes.... What's the use of doing anything, I'm bound to screw it up...."

Hatred. Thoughts such as, "I'll get even with that bitch [or bastard] who has rejected me and ruined my life.... I'll take my case to the Supreme Court, even if I lose every dime I've got.... He [or she] is never going to see the children again.... I'll raise a stink he [or she] will never forget.... Murder, that's what I'll do, murder him [or her] for what's been done to me...."

The above are the basic emotions that may overwhelm you *after* the decision to separate has taken place. That is what is so surprising, since you may have thought all you needed to do was to make an intellectual decision that would make actual separation a cut-and-dried affair. You are much more complex than you may have thought, since human beings are neither computers nor programmed software. In the arena of interpersonal relationships, intellectual logic takes second place to *emotional* logic.

The nonintellectual needs for acceptance, validation, love, affection, tenderness, trust, mutual respect, friendship, sharing, feedback, and commitment are paramount in their demand for fulfillment in a marriage. When they are not fulfilled, the Seven Deadly Emotions outlined above take their places. This is the emotional logic of separation, in contrast to intellectual logic: emotional logic allows you to experience mutually opposed emotions *at the same time.* For example, you may feel hatred toward your spouse, and simultaneous guilt for feeling hatred. Or self-pity and the feeling of personal failure may be mixed with guilt, anger, hatred, and fear.

In addition, each of the Seven Deadly Emotions has its own complexity: fear, for example, may exhibit itself in an unwillingness to take new chances in life; anger may mask fear; guilt may cover anger; self-pity may disguise hatred; and sadness, loneliness, feelings of rejection, remorse, alienation, anxiety, hostility, and vulnerability are all spin-offs from the Seven Deadly Emotions that you may experience in combination or separately around departure time or thereafter.

How these emotions affect you will determine the way you separate from your spouse and the timing of that separation:

If *fear* is the predominant feeling surrounding your desire to separate, you may divorce by *never* leaving home! Clients have come to me for counseling, tortured by the fact that they have announced to their spouses that they are leaving on a specific date and have already made separate living arrangements. The announced day arrives, but fear of the consequences of leaving keeps them rooted in the marital home. It is not unusual for a client of this type to set a new date for leaving and fail again to do so when that date arrives. Two people can live in chronic misery for years with this black cloud of leaving-but-not-leaving as an ever-present factor in their relationship.

If *guilt* predominates, you may delay the timing of your departure by first trying to appear to be the "good" person in your spouse's and children's eyes, so that they won't condemn you when you separate. But if you are already irrevocably alienated from your spouse, all you will do is prolong the pain of separation rather than mitigate it, for your spouse will be confused and embittered by the double signals you send out: on the one hand, your total dislike of the marriage, and on the other hand your insincere attentiveness to him or her, will combine to make for a lethal separation, and your children's anxiety about this situation may escalate to unbearable heights.

When *anger* has the upper hand, separating may occur without any thought of timing or where you will live or even what you will do next after you leave. A towering argument (perhaps like many before) may this time become the breaking point and you may leave your house or apartment in fury, not even knowing this will be the last time you will live there.

Should *hatred* swamp you, you are liable to pick a time for leaving that will inconvenience, shame, or hurt your spouse: the week before a vacation he or she is looking forward to; the month before an early retirement; the time he or she may be preparing for a visit with parents. Or you may inflict the torture of a thousand cuts: setting a date for leaving, announcing that fact to your spouse, then making sure he or she sees you screening the newspapers for a separate rental apartment.

When *self-pity* is paramount, you may arrange for your separation under the pretext that it is your spouse who wants to separate. By making life miserable for your spouse because you are totally alienated from him or her, you may cause your spouse to become angry and frustrated to the point where he or she demands the divorce. This will enable you to believe you have been victimized and therefore to assume no responsibility for the breakup. Self-pity can then become your way of life.

Self-flagellation is the mirror image of self-pity, and involves seeing yourself as an ineffective victim of external events over which you have no control. Should this emotion predominate, you may stew in the juice of an agonizing marriage for years and then pick the most inappropriate occasion to announce your desire to divorce, if your spouse does not announce it first. The straw that breaks the camel's back may be the next time there is interference by your spouse's relatives in your marriage, or when once again your spouse's involvement with friends, career, or hobby makes you seethe in isolation. Feeling furiously helpless and ineffective in the face of these external events, you may blurt out suddenly in the midst of a dinner-table argument that you are going to separate.

When a sense of personal *failure* predominates, you may try to avoid a direct announcement to your spouse of your decision to separate. You may leave a letter in place of talking with your spouse, and try to vanish in a separate apartment. You may avoid telling your children about why you are divorcing. You may vaguely announce your desire to separate, and then disappear from your house unexpectedly some days later, without informing your spouse. Indeed, the first news your spouse may hear that you are permanently separating may come from your lawyer some weeks later, which will embitter subsequent encounters with your spouse when the nuts and bolts of the divorce must be dealt with.

Who leaves and who is left? In the most frequent type of divorce situation, it appears as if one person wants out of the marriage while the other doesn't. The reaction of the partner is often one of shock and surprise: "I never knew you felt that way." "I thought we had a good marriage." "Why do you act this way?" "What have I done to deserve this?" "You can't leave just like that, after all I've done for you." "You mean all the years we've been together amount to nothing?" These are typical reactions of the spouse who hears I-want-a-divorce news from his or her partner and then feels like the victim in a ghastly melodrama.

To the person who is left, it seems clear enough that he or she is the victim and the spouse the victimizer. However, a closer scrutiny of this appearance will unearth quite a different reality: your surprise and shock (if you should feel like such a victim) may very well be a fear reaction to the fact that you must now assume total responsibility for the direction of your life on your own, rather than a desire to hold on to the marriage. The feeling that you could not make it on your own may be overwhelming you, so that maintaining your marriage may appear to you to be much more precious than it really is.

When you look behind the curtain of your fear, you may discover that instead of being the victim, you feel that your marriage, as it currently exists, is even more agonizing than your spouse believes it is. Reread the list of emotional divorces that I have outlined above, and see if you can identify with any of them. You may discover that you have left your marriage in your feelings even longer ago than your spouse claims to have done. This will enable you to divest yourself of the black garments of self-pity and wounded pride that could inhibit your dealing constructively with your separation. Otherwise you may wind up playing the role of the embittered victim in future years, which could wreck your chances for any kind of happiness in your life as a single person.

Even in cases where a couple mutually agrees to a legal divorce, there is usually one spouse who wants to hold on to the marriage more than the other one does. And the same kind of fear of the future in which one feels incapable of surviving emotionally and physically on one's own may be operative. Should you find yourself in this situation, the sooner your acknowledge this reality beneath the appearance, the sooner you will be able to make positive things happen in your life after you have started living alone.

If you are to experience divorce as an opportunity for self-renewal, a second chance to improve the quality of your life, it is of paramount importance that you recognize the profound impact that the Seven Deadly Emotions can have on your life as a single person.

I have called these emotions "deadly" because they can destroy the possibility of your dealing skillfully with your new single life experiences should you allow them, separately or in combination, to permanently seize control of your personality and define your actions toward your former spouse, children, relatives, and friends, and within the new situations that you will find yourself in as a divorced person. To permit this to happen is self-destructive. Many divorced men and women who come to me for counseling have fanned the flames of these emotions for as long as ten or twenty years after their divorces, and have lived chronically bleak and bitter lives as a consequence.

When Does Your Marriage End?

Although your emotional divorce from your spouse may have begun long before your actual breakup, the ending of your marriage, in your emotions, may take place long after you and your spouse have gone your separate ways. Every day, clients who come to me for counseling after they have been legally divorced for many years discover that they are still embroiled in the battles and bitterness of their past marriage to the extent that they cannot experience any happiness in their present lives. Here are some of the typical ways in which that can happen:

- The question "How long have you been divorced?" will elicit a flood of four-letter words about an ex-spouse, and a detailed list of his or her basic rottenness. As if it's almost an afterthought, my client will then say, "Oh yes, I've been divorced twenty years." Here, fierce anger is a living testament to a dead marriage.

- "I'll get even with that bitch if it takes every cent I have and even if I have to go to the Supreme Court to get custody of my kids," says a client divorced seven years, who has just instituted a fifth court case against his ex-spouse. He still seethes in the remembrance of his wife's leaving him.

- "That bastard will never see my kids again, regardless of the custody stipulation," says a woman whose husband left her for another woman five years ago. Her vengeful need to "get even" has become her lifetime occupation.

- "My ex is having a ball and I'm starving to death; he's not going to get away with that," says a woman divorced five years, who yesterday deliberately defaced the body of her ex-husband's latest model car.

- "I told my friends that if they ever talk to my ex, our friendship is ended. They're either for me or against me," says a woman who broke off many friendships after her divorce six years ago and now finds herself almost totally isolated. She is quick to find deceit in any new possible friends, since she demands total dedication to her interests from them.

- "All women are deceitful bitches. You can't trust any of them," says a man who discovered his wife had had many affairs during their marriage. That marriage ended twelve years ago, but he is still carrying that image of "all women" inside himself today, and it has made a shambles of every one of his new relationships since his divorce.

- "My wife called me a wimp when she left me, and said no woman in her right mind could be attracted to me. But I sure showed her! I've laid so many women since my divorce that I can't remember all their names. So why am I so unhappy?" The man who tells me this has been divorced for fourteen years, but is still trying to prove to his ex-wife that he is right and she is wrong. The battles of his long-deceased marriage still rage in his head.

- "I keep asking myself, 'How did I fail?' I thought I was a good wife, a good mother, a good housekeeper, yet he left me. Maybe if I'd lost twenty pounds and looked sexy again, or if I had been less critical of him, it would have been different." These are the words of a woman trapped in the land of what-might-have-been ten years after her divorce.

In all of the above examples, the battles of dead marriages remain very much alive in the hearts and minds of these unhappy men and women for years after their divorces have been registered in the law courts. Self-renewal as a single person is impossible to attain so long as bitterness over a past marriage dominates one's feelings and actions in the years after a legal divorce.

The fact that you are living separately from your ex-spouse is only a deceptive cover for the reality that you may still be married to your marriage if you allow remembrances of past marital anguish to blind you to present opportunities for increasing your chances of happiness. They exist, if only you will see them. Those opportunities will be dealt with in detail in subsequent chapters; for the moment, however, it is important to remember that your divorce *can* provide you with the opportunity to improve your own self-image, to make new friends, to have a better relationship with your children, to turn yourself on with new hobbies and interests, to achieve greater job fulfillment, and to attain a new love relationship that will last in a happier way than your past marriage. In seeking these new opportunities, you can also attain greater spiritual fulfillment, as well as a sense of bonding with your community and the world that you never realized was possible for yourself.

However, none of these bright possibilities can be attained if you allow yourself to be controlled during and after your divorce by the Seven Deadly Emotions and your previous marital experiences. Most divorced persons who continue to be unhappy are not aware that they are being controlled in this manner, and that nobody is doing the controlling except themselves. All they know is that they are unhappy, but they feel they *should* be happy, since they are now living alone.

Counseling with a capable, empathic divorce counselor is the step you should take if you find yourself in this dilemma. Once you become aware of the barriers *within yourself* that are preventing your making positive things happen in your life, then and only then will you become capable of tearing down those barriers and dealing skillfully with your present state of affairs.

Understanding the Emotional Upheaval in Your Divorce

Divorce, like a dormant volcano suddenly reactivated, erupts emotions that may have been hidden, repressed, denied, or even unsuspected within oneself. Perhaps you yourself, after a heavy session with your soon-to-be ex-spouse in a lawyer's office, have observed in astonishment, "That wasn't really me in there. I'm a warm, kind, understanding person, yet there I was, having a tantrum like a little kid, yelling, using every four-letter word in the book, expressing anger such as I never felt before, rage and even murderous hatred at the person I shared my life with for so many years.

I never cry, yet tears streamed from my eyes. That can't be me, can it?"

Oh, yes it can. You would be less than human if you did not experience intense, uncomfortable, often socially unacceptable emotions in the process of breaking up. For divorce, as I have previously noted, involves a loss of one of the most essential conditions for leading a fulfilling life: the loss of the most important adult in your life, apart from your parents, who was at one time the one you considered to be your only loved one and your very best friend, who cared as much about you as you did about him or her. Such a profound loss stirs up feelings that you have been betrayed and abandoned by the spouse to whom you entrusted yourself.

That feeling of abandonment is felt *as if* you were being abandoned by your parents, *as if* you were a little child whose survival depended upon your parents accepting and taking care of you. When those feelings grip you, fear for your very survival, physically and emotionally, wells up within you and that fear will explode into anger, murderous feelings, guilt, anxiety, self-righteousness, and bitterness. In fact, the intensity of these so-called negative emotions is a direct indicator of how very important and meaningful your marriage was to you, rather than that it was all a meaningless mistake. If your marriage was only an insignificant event in your life, you would never experience the intense, disturbing emotions that you may be labeling as foreign to your conception of who you are. These "negative" emotions indeed are "you," but a "you" who had no need to call upon these emotions when your marital relationship was a taken-for-granted, permanent facet of your life.

If you label such emotions as "bad," you are misreading their significance. *None* of your emotions are either good or bad in themselves; they are signals alerting you to important things about yourself and offering you the opportunity to act constructively on what they are saying. The Seven Deadly Emotions discussed above are not bad in themselves. They will inevitably appear in one form or another during the early stages of any divorce, since they arise as a consequence of mourning the death of a relationship. What will make them "deadly" is the way they can stunt your life permanently after your divorce if you attach yourself to them, refusing to let go of them.

Your divorce will begin to become a journey of self-renewal, a second chance for an improved life, once you learn the meanings of your "negative" emotions. Here are some guidelines for doing so.

1. Accept these uncomfortable emotions as part of yourself. They have always been part of you, but are only overwhelmingly evident in extreme crises, such as divorce or the death of a loved one.

2. Recognize that experiencing these emotions is part of the healing process of mourning the death of your marriage in the initial stage of your divorce, but can be self-destructive if you continue to be attached to them after that initial stage is experienced.

3. Consider these emotions as neither good nor bad in and of themselves. They are a part of yourself that must be understood, rather than wallowed in or feared.

4. Recognize the time for letting go of these emotions; you own them and therefore have the power to dispense with them. The time for letting go is when they no longer serve the appropriate function of mourning the death of your marriage. That typically will occur sometime within the first twelve months of your breakup.

5. Apply the W. C. Fields principle: "If at first you don't succeed, try again. Then stop. No sense making a damn fool of yourself." When you become aware that acting toward your ex-spouse continuously with anger, hostility, fear, or a desire for vengeance doesn't get the positive results you may want, or make you happy, you have allowed such emotions to seize control of your life far beyond the mourning stage of your breakup.

6. Focus on whether you would rather be "right" than happy, because you cannot have both. Feeling permanently self-righteous will cancel out your possibility of leading a happier life as a single person. Self-righteousness affords you the same kind of temporary fix that cocaine or alcohol does, with lethal day-after consequences for your life.

7. Seek outside help from a good divorce counselor when you find yourself unable to break the grip of any of the Seven Deadly Emotions by yourself. It is the *strong* man or woman who seeks out counseling, rather than the weak one.

The approach to your breakup that I have outlined in this chapter can provide you with ground to stand on, once you embark on your divorce. It can enable you to deal constructively and skillfully with the many *new* problems you will be faced with as a newly single person. Understanding how divorce might affect you *in your emotions* is the beginning step in the process of your self-renewal. Without such understanding, you will not be able to utilize your intelligence and survival abilities to their fullest extent, which will result in your repeating the past rather than improving on it. As a consequence, you may continue to harbor illusions about your divorce that will prove to be a permanent barrier to your moving your life forward.

The sooner you eliminate these illusions from your thinking and deal with the realities they hide, the sooner you will be able to chart your life on a the-best-is-yet-to-come road rather than on one that ends in a blind alley.

Avoiding the Seventeen Key Illusions About Divorce

I have identified the seventeen most harmful illusions about divorce (derived from my personal divorce experience and those of the men and women I counsel) and the realities that lie behind these illusions; they are listed below. You must come to terms with them in order to free yourself of any tendency toward self-victimization:

Illusion 1 "Divorce is a legal piece of paper signifying you are no longer married."

The Reality The reality is that divorce is a process over time, with no set ending date. That legal piece of paper is only one stage in the divorce process, which involves mourning the death of your relationship, letting go of the past, and living in the present. You will move through this process at your own speed; each person has his or her own readiness time for becoming truly divorced. You will recognize that time when you feel yourself a person of value and worth in your own right, not as part of a couple, and when you no longer wallow in past regrets. You will *never* be truly divorced if you continue to allow the hurt remembrances of your breakup to continue to flare angrily in your heart and mind years after you and your spouse have separated. All too many men and women carry their ex-spouses inside themselves long after their divorce papers have yellowed with age.

Illusion 2 "All my problems will end once I divorce this turkey I'm chained to."

The Reality Many unpleasant surprises may await you, once you divorce the person you believe is the cause of all of your mental and other problems. When you begin living alone, you will discover this is not true. You may feel temporary relief and then find yourself out of the frying pan and in the fire: the problem of finding a place to live; hassles over the children's custody and when you can visit them; new money problems; friends seeming to avoid you; putdowns from relatives; unexpected eruptions of guilt and remorse; the difficulties of establishing new relationships with the opposite sex; the split-up of your relationship with the person you may have left your spouse for. Until you begin taking personal responsibility for your contribution to the breakup, and begin to identify your own self-defeating behavior so you can eliminate it, you will tend to repeat the past rather than improve upon it. In other words, you will simply be exchanging one set of problems for another.

Illusion 3 "I was unlucky in choosing my spouse. Now that I'm divorced, my luck will change."

The Reality Luck has nothing to do with it. The unrealistic expectations you had in your mind about marriage, your failure to see your spouse as a separate person apart from your own needs, your lack of skill in resolving your mental problems, your tendency to become a resentment collector, your inability to communicate openly, without anger, your hurts and desires: these are some of the major reasons a marriage turns into irreconcilable differences. Unless you deal with these issues, your belief in good luck the next time rests on the same solid foundation as a belief in Santa Claus.

Illusion 4 "I'm really not normal. This divorce is making me crazy."

The Reality You are normal if you are experiencing some off-the-wall behavior and out-of-control feelings (bursts of anger, sieges of depression, difficulties at work, self-pity and sadness, attacks of loneliness). A divorce is the most wounding experience in your life, apart from the actual death of a loved one, and the disarray within you is part of the healing process of mourning the death of your marriage so you can make way for your own self-renewal as a single person. Practically all men and women in the initial stages of divorce experience this kind of disarray, saying to themselves, "This is not the real me, I never felt or acted this way before." In fact, you would be abnormal if you forced your behavior and feelings into a straitjacket, giving the outside world the impression that everything's cool, when everything isn't. Denying the hurt that you feel will set the fuse for a time-bomb explosion later on. In the long run, allowing a wound to fester is far worse than dealing with it at the time of its happening.

Illusion 5 "Everyone will now think of me as a failure because I'm divorced."

The Reality Even as late as a decade ago, there would be some truth to this fear. However, today this is no longer true. Divorce is now widely seen as a normal though painful life event, since one out of every two marriages end in divorce. Each year, two and a half million American men and women get divorced, which signifies that every person you meet has been touched by divorce—if not their own, then that of someone in their families or among their friends, co-workers, or acquaintances. You will discover that most people will react to your divorce nonjudgmentally.

If they themselves have also been divorced, they will often share that fact with you and give you the encouragement you need to get on positively with your life as a single person; but, if you view yourself as a failure, you will be certain to fail in attempting to create a better life for yourself. There is something seductive in self-pity and hopelessness, but if you remain in that sea of despondency for too long, it will drown whatever possibilities of happiness that life might present to you.

Illusion 6 "I made a mistake, marrying the person I did, and now I'm paying for it."

The Reality If you label your marriage a mistake, you are liable to run scared the rest of your life, always looking over your shoulder and waiting for your next mistake to catch up with you. Such an attitude will inhibit you from living your life constructively as a single person. If you focus on your past marriage as a mistake instead of as a *learning experience*, the future will indeed look permanently grim to you. Consider, however, the good advice we give to our children. We are always telling them it's okay to make a mistake, provided they *learn* from the mistake. Your life will become brighter when you ask yourself what you have learned from your past marriage, and how you can correct the errors of judgment, the lack of insight, and the unskillful way you dealt with your marital problems.

The objective of a divorce should be to help you become a better person, more skillful in handling life's problems. You can only do this by learning from your past marriage rather than putting a negative label on it.

Illusion 7 "Now that I'm divorced, there is another person out there who will make me happy."

The Reality No other person can make you happy. It is naïve to believe that another person can be your permanent entertainment factory. Usually the other person in such a relationship is expecting the same from you! And if not, that person will feel resentful over the fact that you are demanding something no person can give. The best relationship occurs when two people are already happy in themselves as single persons, but wish to become *happier* by being *interdependent* with one another, sharing hopes, dreams, adversities, and successes in a kind and loving way.

The greatest single cause of divorce is the insidious, unspoken demand of couples that each person should make the other happy. They are feeling empty and miserable inside themselves, and refuse to face the fact that they must each make an effort to make positive things happen in their own lives, which they can then share with each other, enhancing their happiness together in the process.

Illusion 8 "The person who asks for a divorce usually has another lover waiting in the wings."

The Reality Today this is frequently *not* the case. The belief that it is only the man who wants the divorce because he already has another woman on the side is often not true. Now that women have a more confident sense of their own worth and their ability to earn their own living, they are refusing to be taken for granted by men and to remain in devastatingly unhappy marriages. There is a trend today for women to demand divorces from their husbands. Their reason is not that they have found another man, but that they need a divorce in order to find themselves, since their marriages are demeaning them as human beings. This trend toward leaving a marriage for self-discovery rather than for another lover is also present in men who want a divorce, although it is currently more prevalent in women. The old belief that men want a divorce while women want to stay in the marriage is undergoing a fundamental change in today's times.

Illusion 9 "I'll be free of harassment now that I've got my divorce papers."

The Reality A legal piece of paper will not curb the explosive feelings of a spouse who believes he or she has been rejected or betrayed. Attempted harassment can continue long after the divorce is finalized on paper if your ex-spouse is determined to "get even," to hurt, inconvenience, or embarrass you. Such an ex-spouse is intent on regaining his or her pride by fanning the flames of righteous anger, believing it is better to be "right" than happy.

Phoning you in the middle of the night, barging into your house unexpectedly, refusing to allow your visitation rights to the children, delaying or neglecting spousal support payments, and shadowing you at home and at work are only some of the almost endless forms of harassment you can experience long after your legal divorce has ended, if your ex-spouse has a vindictive streak. (Of course, you don't have to put up with any of this. Your lawyer should apply for a restraining order.) The more confidence you gain in taking charge of your own life as a single person, the less effect such harassment tactics will have on your daily activities. The game takes *two*—victimizer and victimized—and you don't have to participate.

Illusion 10 "My children will hate me because I want a divorce, and they may never want to see me again."

The Reality Even though you and your spouse no longer love each other, the children will continue to love *both* of you. A divorce will initially shatter the sense of security the children feel in living in a two-parent household (although living in separate households may increase the security the children feel, if your spouse was alcoholic, violent, or screamingly argumentative most of the time). The uncertainty they may feel now that Mom and Dad are living separately may appear to you as an expression of hostility toward you. However, the hostility is really an expression of their fear for their survival, their fear that you are abandoning them forever.

Beneath that fear is their fear that you no longer love

them, not that they hate you. The way you and your ex-spouse handle your divorce will determine the way in which your children will relate to you. They will continue to love and respect both of you when they see you taking positive charge of your lives as separate persons, when neither parent bad-mouths the other, when you have reliable and flexible visitation rights which assure the children that although Mom and Dad are living apart, the distance is only geographical, and that your love for them and their love for you has never left their home.

Illusion 11 "Men are hurt less than women by a divorce."

The Reality Pain is pain, whether experienced by a man or a woman, and divorce is one of the most painful experiences any human being ever incurs. To claim men hurt less is to imply that men are less human than women. Speaking personally as a man whose divorce was one of the most anguishing experiences in my life, I know the depths of pain a man can feel when love ends. I have seen the guilt, fear, anxiety, loneliness, vulnerability, and self-flagellation in the eyes of countless men I have counseled at the time of their divorce, and can empathize with their suffering. Pain is always a subjective experience, and each person expresses his or her pain in individual ways.

Men may not express their emotions in the same way women are accustomed to doing so, but the emotions they feel are the same as women's. Usually, men wall up their pain inside themselves, but it is always ready to explode into visibility at unexpected times and in indirect ways. Your divorce will be your opportunity to bridge the understanding gap that exists between men and women. You can lay the foundation for that bridge by becoming aware that men want the same thing as women: love and affection. And when men feel in a divorce that they have lost these two essential elements in their life, they bleed equally with women suffering that same loss.

Illusion 12 "We're going to have a 'friendly' divorce, with no hard feelings toward each other."

The Reality If you haven't invested your heart in your marriage, truly believing you were marrying for life, if you were married for just a few months or just for money or to escape a bad family life, if you married without love and commitment to each other, then you may have a "friendly" divorce. But most people don't marry for those reasons, and you probably didn't either. Therefore, you will be in for an unpleasant surprise if you believe you can have a friendly, unemotional divorce. Should you try to present that image, it will turn out to be a fine piece of playacting designed for relatives', friends', and neighbors' consumption, but hardly an accurate reflection of your own and your ex-spouse's real feelings about yourselves and each other.

You would be less than human if you did not feel some hostility toward your ex-spouse, since your falling out of love is a consequence of your former partner's inability or refusal to satisfy your need for love and affection. And you would feel rejected and angry because of that rejection, since your spouse also no longer loved you. No hard feelings? Of course there would be some, initially, since you have been hurt and the person you were married to was the one who hurt you. The facade of we're-still-good-friends ordinarily cracks when you discuss money questions like spousal or child support, or when one of you has a new lover and the other seethes with a jealousy that he or she thought was nonexistent. Yes, a divorced couple can have friendly relationships eventually, but that may take years to materialize. And even then it will not be a typical friendship, since the person who was once the love of your life cannot be changed into just another friend. In the initial stages of divorce, acknowledging your real feelings of hurt, disenchantment, and alienation is normal. You can, however, minimize the hostility you feel by enriching your new life as a single person with new friends, new experiences, new hobbies, new job challenges that have nothing to do with your ex-spouse, but are of paramount importance in reinforcing your own sense of your self-worth as a separate individual.

Illusion 13 "My spouse wanted the divorce and I didn't. I've been rejected, and that means nobody will ever love me again and I'll be alone for the rest of my life."

The Reality Almost everyone who has been left behind
feels this way at the beginning of a divorce. However, subsequent events prove this to be the exact reverse of what
happens. In fact, four out of five divorced persons eventually find someone who will love them as they are and eventually marry them. That your spouse was no longer
responsive to you does not mean that there are not many
other persons of the opposite sex who will be attracted to
you. However, if you hold on to the belief that you are an
outcast because you have been "rejected" by your spouse,
you will send out signals to everyone you meet that you are
not worthy of being loved. And that will be your surest
guarantee of becoming that lonely person you fear you may
become.

Illusion 14 "Now that I'm single, my friends tell me to get
involved with singles organizations and divorce groups, but
I don't want to associate with losers, because that's all they
are."

The Reality The men and women in these organizations
are trying to move their lives forward as single persons.
They are trying to make new friends and learn more about
the advantages that single life offers them. You want the
same things they do, so they can make a contribution to
your life and you can do the same for them. To call them
losers is to call yourself a loser also, since you are no different
from them. You are setting up a barrier that will prevent
you from exposing yourself to new people, places, and hap-
penings when you start labeling others (and yourself!) as
losers. Try them and you might like them.

Illusion 15 "I'll never get married again. Marriage is for
the birds, and my divorce proves it."

The Reality If you feel this way, remember that when you
say "never," it means that is the way you are feeling *now,*
and that "never" may very well not be forever. You may
surprise yourself two or more years after your divorce, for
you may then want to marry again. You may then realize
that to run away from intimacy is to run away from the best

part of yourself. The love and commitment you make the next time around will not be a replay of your past marriage if you learn how to love again in new ways rather than simply repeating the old habits that led to the divorce court in your past marriage.

Your old marriage may have been "for the birds," but that doesn't mean a new marriage will not be quite different from and better than the old one, provided you let go of your belief that any new marriage *must* be a duplication of the one you left. On the other hand, you may be one of a very small minority of persons who have never been comfortable with married life and discover in the divorce that single life is permanently preferable for you. Are you one of them, or are you only temporarily disenchanted? An open mind about your future will enable you to find out.

Illusion 16 "I'm too old to change. My divorce should have happened when I was in my thirties instead of in my fifties, because the best of my life would have been ahead of me instead of in the past."

The Reality Your age will prevent you from improving the quality of your life after your divorce only if you allow your thinking to be controlled by outmoded notions of what you can and cannot do. The good news is that all of us are now living at the beginning of an age revolution. All previous conceptions about how your chronological age should control your self-image, beliefs, attitudes, and behavior have been proven false by modern scientific findings in psychology, physiology, and biology.

It is no longer exceptional to see men and women in our society proving by their actions that age has little or nothing to do with the impediments we ascribe to it: marathons are run by people over sixty as well as those in their twenties; sports once reserved for the young, such as skiing and flying, are now embraced by people over forty; exercise and good nutrition can maintain good health and normal blood pressure at seventeen or seventy; good looks can last a lifetime if we cultivate inner as well as outer attractiveness; intelligence and creativity can increase with age, since the brain is a use-it-or-lose-it instrument; long-standing, self-defeating habits such as smoking can be broken; new careers can be started at any age.

Divorce in one's forties or fifties can be a beginning as well as an ending, provided you recognize that it's not how old you are but who you are that counts.

Illusion 17 "Divorce is better than marriage."

The Reality Divorce and marriage are no answers in themselves to life's problems. They are simply arrangements in society that are there for the using when you need or want them. You can be miserable in a marriage or you can be happy. You can be happy in divorce or you can be miserable. Divorce and marriage are what you make of them. Like two equally empty houses, it's how you furnish each house that will determine its quality. Furnish the house shabbily, keep it gloomy, dust-ridden, and dirty, and it will be a terrible place. Pay attention to it, enhance its attractiveness, and it's a fine place to inhabit. As a divorced person you have an opportunity to inhabit a place you can feel comfortable living in. That place is inside yourself. By tending to that place with greater self-awareness, insight, and skill, you can like the life you might be living as a single person.

I have indicated that divorce is inevitably a very painful, uprooting experience that shatters the habits of your previous way of life and has profound emotional repercussions on your personality. However, when you regard these as the necessary dues that must be paid if you are to *improve* the quality of your life now that you are single, you can cope constructively with the new realities that enter your life. Since your goal is the freedom to direct your life in a way that will make for your greater happiness, it is essential for you to recognize that the travail you will initially undergo is the toll that must be paid for that opportunity. For there is no such thing as a free lunch, as the saying goes. The higher the goal, the greater the effort that must be expended to reach it. When you clear away the trees of illusion and confusion, you will be able to see the forest you can safely journey through to arrive at your goal. To understand the psychological consequences of divorce as I have outlined them above will not enable you to escape entirely the fear and disarray that your breakup will initially trigger inside you. However, this psychological knowledge can help prevent you from victimizing yourself, so that you will not act against your own best interests when any of the Seven Deadly Emotions or the Seventeen Key Illusions about divorce attempt to define the ways in which you act and think during the time you are divorcing.

At no time in your life is clear thinking more necessary than when you are involved in your divorce proceedings. Yet this is the very time that your emotions are spreading clouds of darkness over your thought processes. And the darkest clouds are liable to appear when you deal with the laws and lawyers that might be involved in your divorce case. However, as Melvin Belli demonstrates in the next chapter, you may have more power than you realize to minimize legal expenses and court hassles.

3

Melvin Belli's Advice on How to Take Skillful Charge of Your Legal Divorce

≡

At the same time that you are beginning to experience and come to terms with the emotional, psychological, and social aspects of your divorce, which Mel Krantzler discussed in the previous chapter, you will also have to begin to deal with its legal aspects. This is where I can be of help to you.

For starters, put your mind at rest: you needn't become the victim of some lawyer who might bankrupt you by charging outrageous fees for handling your divorce. By the time you have read all the chapters in this book, you will have learned to deal skillfully with every aspect of your divorce, including the legal ones. This means that the lawyer you choose to represent you will be working in the most effective, reasonable way to protect your interests because you will be skilled in knowing how to use him or her to your maximum advantage. This can happen if you first absorb and incorporate into your behavior the psychological findings and guidelines Mel Krantzler has shared with you in his chapters in this book on how you can prevent yourself from becoming a helpless, walking-wounded divorce victim. You can think clearly about the legal issues in your divorce, and work effectively with your lawyer to achieve your best interests, only if you diminish the emotional upheaval inside yourself that your separating from your spouse might entail. That's why Mel Krantzler's chap-

ters are so important for you to read as you concern yourself with the legalities of divorce. Otherwise you may wind
up with a divorce settlement that is more like your shoot-
ing yourself in the foot than coming to an agreement you
can live with.

In this chapter, I will give you the basic orientation on
how to handle the legal aspects of your divorce. In my
subsequent legal chapters, I'll show you the ways in which
you can avoid the specific pitfalls you might fall into when
dealing with property distribution, alimony, child support,
child custody and visitation, and tax consequences, along
with many other concerns that could crop up in your divorce.

But at this point I would like to present you with this
thought: one thing that my living on this earth for nearly
eighty years has taught me is that there are no easy answers
or escapes from life's major problems, of which divorce is
certainly one. But answers there are, because there are
ways of dealing with your problems skillfully and constructively *or* unskillfully and destructively. Whatever maturity
I possess is not the result of my living seventy-eight years,
but of my learning to deal more skillfully with what life lays
on the table before me as the years pass. That's the challenge your divorce offers you.

I think that the easiest and clearest way to explain the
legalities of divorce, and how to make your divorce lawyer
work for you, is the question-and-answer format I have used
in each of my chapters in this book. In this chapter, and in
all the subsequent legal chapters, I will present the most
frequently asked questions about divorce that my clients
may have in mind when they see me in my office the very
first time, and the answers I give them. The questions are
those you yourself undoubtedly are concerned about, and
my answers may save you a lot of unnecessary anxiety, grief,
and money. Let's begin at the beginning:

Whether to Divorce, When It Begins, How Long It Takes, and Whether It Can Be Prevented

I'm thinking all the time about getting a divorce, but haven't yet decided what to do. What would you advise?

First try to get a good marriage counselor, and if such counseling for both of you fails, then consult with a good divorce lawyer. The emotional and psychological trauma most people suffer when thoughts of divorce are persistent prevents them from thinking clearly about the main divorce issues, i.e., property settlements and providing for your needs, financial and otherwise, and those of any children you may have.

The consultation, *which, for the first visit, is generally free,* will at least result in your having a clearer understanding of these issues as they relate to your present situation. More important, however, should your thoughts about divorce become reality, you will be infinitely better prepared to deal with the divorce process than those people who consult a lawyer for the first time *after* the divorce has begun.

My wife and I are separated, but are still trying to work things out. What can I or should I do in this state of limbo?

Unfortunately, if you have children and don't ultimately get back together with your wife, you may already have created some major problems for yourself. First, if you are the "outspouse" (the one living away from the family home), it's really unlikely that you'll be awarded temporary custody of your children in the event of your divorce. In addition, you may have established a permanent pattern of financial support for your wife and children (for instance, maybe you're already giving them $700 per month, in addition to paying all of the family's bills). If so, I guarantee you that you'll have great difficulty convincing the judge at a "temporary support hearing" that you can't continue the pattern while your divorce proceeds, should your reconciliation attempt fail.

Your best bet, therefore, is to get some competent legal advice, and to get it now. You may want to get a *decree of legal separation* (a divorce in every respect except that you're still legally married after the decree), a subject that is discussed a little later in this chapter. But in any event, you'll probably need to "crystallize" your assets and liabilities (record on paper, as of a specific date, preferably one as close to the date upon which you separated as possible, what you own and where it is located, and exactly what is owed to whom, and for what). The point here is that working on a reconciliation is *not* a good reason to ignore things that you may already have done or are doing, for this could adversely affect your best interests later on, should your reconciliation attempts fail. You may regret letting such things slide by, and I can promise you right now that I won't take any pleasure in being able to say "I told you so."

When does the legal process of divorce begin?

It begins whenever you or your spouse formally requests a court to dissolve your marriage. You're probably more familiar with the term *filing for divorce*. They're both the same thing. The form of such requests often differs from state to state. In California, for instance, they're called *petitions for a dissolution of marriage*. In other states, however, such requests may be called *complaints for divorce*. Whatever their form, these requests are sheets of paper, given to and filed with a court clerk, that typically set forth certain statistical information relative to your marriage and your requests in regard to dissolving that relationship. The statistical data may include any or all of the following:

- The date and place of your marriage (critical to a determination of whether a particular court has jurisdiction to dissolve your marriage).
- Your name and that of your spouse.
- The names and ages of any children born of your marriage.
- The nature and extent of property owned by you and your spouse.

Common requests are that the court divide your *marital property* (this can be, and generally is, accomplished by having a court *confirm* the settlement you and your spouse have already agreed upon), and that the court make *orders* securing a reasonably good future, both financial and otherwise, for you and your children, if any. In some states you may even request the court to restore the wife's maiden name at no extra charge.

How long does the legal divorce process usually take?

Both of you become single persons again when the court grants you some form of a final decree of divorce. This can take six months in some states; in others it can take twelve or eighteen months from the date upon which you or your spouse formally request the court to dissolve your marriage.

However, you can fight in court as ex-spouses and single people for years afterward with regard to various issues in a divorce that has already been granted. The latter situation occurs when the court *bifurcates* the process; this means that the court separates its task into two parts, the first of which is to make you and your spouse single people again, even though you still have property or other issues to be resolved. The court retains the power to make orders concerning the marriage *after* the final divorce decree is granted, orders that you must abide by. You can, however, appeal the court's decision to a higher court on some legal or factual ground.

Who gave a court in the state and county of my marriage the right and power to dissolve my relationship, anyway?

You gave it the *power* to do so when you got your marriage license and certificate. Despite their simple form, these documents essentially constitute the formation of a legal contract that the state and county affirm with a seal. When you gave your county and state the power to affirm your marriage, you also made their courts the *sole* legal means to dissolve it, unless you moved out of your state after you married.

As to the *right* to dissolve your marriage, either you or your ancestors did that, either by enacting the divorce laws yourselves or doing so through elected representatives. If you don't like the current divorce laws, I encourage you to work to change them.

My friends tell me that my spouse can get a divorce even if I object. Is this really true?

Yes, whether fortunately for you or otherwise, it is emphatically true. I say this because it's a 95 percent sure bet that you live in a state where *no-fault divorce* is now the order of the day. This means that your spouse can get a divorce without being required to prove that you are guilty of some act of marital misconduct. In fact, he or she can divorce you without having to prove much of anything at all. All your spouse has to do is to tell the judge that your marriage is beyond salvation, in his or her mind, and that he or she wants out. Bingo! Divorce granted. I'm not trying to be glib or funny. It's just about that easy.

Conversely, it's just as true to say that if you think you're going to use your spouse's marital indiscretions to "get even" in the divorce, you are dead wrong. In no-fault states (at last count, all but the states of Illinois and South Dakota had adopted some form of no-fault divorce system), it is no longer legally important that your spouse was to blame for the marriage failure. And he or she is no longer going to be punished by the system for the horrible things you may believe were done to you by him or her.

This fact makes television programs like "Divorce Court" of concern to me, especially when I consider the nearly national exposure that some of these programs command. They perpetuate the myth that "fault" is still the *main* focus of divorce proceedings *everywhere*. They make it appear that it is still generally a question of who is proven to be the "bad" or "guilty" spouse that mistreated the "good" or "innocent" one.

Such programs also promote the notion that whether you "get" him or her in the divorce or he or she "gets" you is a function of who can sling the most mud. These programs may be entertaining, but don't assume that they accurately depict what generally happens in real life today, because it's not true anymore.

Nowadays, "fault" is really only an issue in child custody proceedings, and even then, only if the "fault" concerns the children's welfare. As an example, an insanely jealous and violent spouse might be legally prevented from seeing his or her children after the divorce, at least until and unless he or she changes his or her ways. Or he or she might find that his or her "visitation privileges" with the children are legally and significantly curtailed and/or qualified in one or more ways.

Consequently, if your spouse really does want out of your marriage, his or her wish will eventually be granted wherever you live. So don't waste any of your time and energy trying to prevent a foregone conclusion.

Although I believe that, on balance, no-fault divorce has much to recommend it, it does create inequitable situations. For example, it allows the courts the legal latitude to make unreasonable demands on women who have been in long-term marriages as homemakers, by insisting that they become financially self-supporting without providing adequate spousal support for a long enough time to obtain the necessary skills. It appears that the pendulum has swung too far, in that no-fault divorce assumes an illusory economic equality between the sexes rather than recognizing the real fact that women in general are still severely discriminated against in our society, both economically and in career-advancement opportunities.

The Characteristics of a Good Divorce Lawyer, Where to Find One, What to Expect, and How Much the Divorce Will Cost

What characteristics should a good divorce lawyer have?

A good divorce lawyer will have eight general characteristics, as follows:

> 1. He or she must be both sensitive and objective. This means that your lawyer should be sensitive enough to understand the nature of

your particular divorce. For example, he or she should be willing to listen to and respond to all of your feelings about yourself, your spouse, lawyers, the legal system, and the law in general. However, that sensitivity should be tempered by your lawyer's objectivity in getting you to channel your feelings into the most positive resolution of your situation in relation to your future happiness.

2. The lawyer will be straightforward with you about what you will be charged for, how you'll be billed, and at what rate or rates, so that there won't be any surprises later on.

3. Your lawyer will not intimidate you with legal jargon. He or she will be sensitive enough to explain, in terms you understand, what legal words mean and what legal procedures are all about.

4. The lawyer will be listening for the questions you're afraid to ask for fear of being thought naïve or stupid, and elicit those questions from you in a nonthreatening way.

5. The lawyer will not promise you the world and will work to minimize your costs by avoiding unnecessary court battles. Beware of "barracuda" lawyers who fan adversarial flames. However, be just as aware of don't-make-waves lawyers who sacrifice your best interests by not fighting hard enough for them.

6. The lawyer will communicate with you frequently, so that you don't feel your case is being neglected or placed on a back burner.

7. The lawyer will have a general familiarity with the divorce law of your state, and considerable experience with how that law is procedurally applied by the county court in which your divorce is generally processed.

8. Finally, the lawyer will be sensitive to minimizing your legal costs by encouraging the use of nonlegal procedures such as mediation and, where possible, face-to-face and private meet-

ings between you and your spouse to resolve
those issues capable of being resolved by the
two of you.

Can one lawyer represent both me and my spouse?

I definitely tell my clients that you both can't possibly use
the same lawyer. It's like the old saying that a ship can
have only one master. A good divorce lawyer can't realistically serve your best interests and those of your spouse at
the same time. When I was in the Soviet Union, I addressed one of the Collegiums (their equivalent of a bar
association) and the one thing they couldn't understand
about our legal system was why the district attorney can't
represent both the state and the defendant. They told me
that our system is like a circus. The state hires both the DA
and the public defender, one to prosecute you and the
other to defend you.

What the Soviets don't understand is that the lawyer-
client relationship is a very personal and ethical matter. And
this is especially true of divorce work. I'd hate to be representing both parties, because no matter how well I knew
both of them and what would be good for them, what I
thought might not be true, and there would therefore be
repercussions later on. One might say to the other, "You
know, I think you should have gone to another lawyer. I
know you love me and I love you and that Henry [the
lawyer] is a good friend of ours, but we should have had
independent lawyers."

What I'm trying to say is that your relationship with
your lawyer should be as close as that between you and your
priest or doctor. It's a very personal relationship in which
the lawyer should be available to you; he should be the kind
of person you like and be respected by his peers and the
courts in front of which he or she practices, and, above all,
be *loyal* to your best interests. Don't ask for an attorney to
do something, therefore, which is virtually impossible for
him or her to do. And don't be a party to a triangular relationship like that *even if* the lawyer says it's okay and is
willing to do it.

Where can I find a good divorce lawyer?

There are at least six possible sources of information:

1. Your local Yellow Pages. Many such directories separate the lawyers' names by categories of practice, one of which will be divorce. Look for such statements as "practice devoted to divorce work," "family law practice," or "practicing divorce law for over ten years." However, each lawyer should be scrutinized carefully until you are satisfied that divorce cases represent his or her specialty. The way in which he or she responds to your inquiries in your initial interview (see page 82 for information regarding the initial interview) will determine for you his or her possible trustworthiness and ability.

2. Your local bar referral services. These organizations, both public and private, typically provide you with a list of names, addresses, and telephone numbers for some divorce lawyers in your area. While they are generally bound by ethics not to recommend one attorney over another, these agencies will at least give you some names, and perhaps some statistical information as well, related to the number of years of practice or areas of specialty.

3. Your own experience. I realize that you may be loath to do so, but if you sit for just half a day in a courtroom where a number of divorce cases are being heard, you'll more than likely find a good variety of experienced lawyers to choose from. As a spectator, you can watch and examine their performance anonymously. If you see one you like, you can catch him or her in the hallway and make a consultation appointment. If you're shy, you might be able to get the lawyer's name either by checking the court calendar list that in many states is

posted outside the courtroom setting forth the
name of each case and the attorneys representing each party, or perhaps by asking the
court clerk for the attorney's name.

4. Other, non-divorce lawyers whom you know
and trust. He or she may be able to recommend a good divorce lawyer.

5. Recommendations from members of divorce
support groups. Such organizations as Parents
Without Partners can be marvelous places to
find an attorney. You'll get what may be an
excellent list of names, and added benefits as
well. You'll meet people with divorce experiences similar to your own, and you will also
have a relatively safe environment within
which to work on your internal self while getting positive feedback.

6. Family and friends. I have deliberately left
this source for last because I want to urge caution. *Any* of these people *may* be a good source
of information. However, the fact that a
friend's recommended lawyer may have done
a great job for your friend is not necessarily
valuable information upon which you should
rely in evaluating that lawyer. We repeat the
following phrase over and over again in legal
circles: "Each case must be decided upon its
own merits, and no two divorce cases are exactly alike." The attitudes of friends or family
members are more often than not subjective,
based on what the lawyer did for them or how
they feel about the attorney they're recom-
mending. Even if the facts of your divorce
case and those of your friend or family member seem identical, their "good" attorney may
be totally wrong for you. Once again, however, you may at least get the names of one or
two lawyers to interview.

As a general rule, try to see first those attorneys who
appear to have the most experience. Whether you ulti-

mately hire such an attorney or not, you'll be better off for having at least started there.

What can I reasonably expect from my attorney?

You can and should expect at least three things from your lawyer:

1. You should expect him or her to be "you" in any courtroom situation or in any lawyer-to-lawyer confrontation. That means that the lawyer represents *your* knowledge of the acts of *your* marriage and *your* choices concerning property division and child custody, support, and visitation. Don't, however, expect your lawyer to do any of these things without a lot of your help.
2. Your lawyer should not be your therapist or confessor. Your lawyer is not generally trained for either job, and it's not what you hired him or her to do. And avoid at all costs getting involved with your attorney on anything other than a lawyer-client basis.
3. Your lawyer should represent your best interests, *always*, but understand that he or she can only get for you what the laws and procedures of your particular state allow. Those laws differ drastically from state to state. Consequently, you should expect your attorney to inform you about the particular characteristics of your state's divorce laws and procedures.

What is a divorce lawyer's typical fee?

There's no such fee because no divorce is typical. A lawyer can charge by the hour ($150 to $250 per hour is common these days), or can charge a lump sum (typically this is only done in simpler cases, generally ranging between $1,000 and $2,000, depending upon the complexity of the issues). Absent violently antagonistic spouses, unethical attorneys, a custody battle, or complex property division questions, most divorces probably cost between $1,500 and $5,000. There are simply too many variables to give you a better estimate without knowing your specific circumstances.

I'm a woman who would probably feel more comfortable revealing my life to a female attorney, but I wonder how she'd do in a male-oriented process. What should I do?

You should first of all interview that woman. If she's sharp, skillful, and understands how the system works, she will probably do very well, even if the other principals in the case—your spouse, his lawyer, and the judge—are all men. Hire her if it will enable you to take more skillful charge of your divorce.

Your attitude reflects a woman's traditional point of view with respect to divorce—that it is primarily the loss of a relationship and you are sensitive primarily to that loss. But don't allow that sensitivity to keep you from doing the best you can to protect your material loss as well, and don't get trapped into believing that a female attorney can't compete in a man's world. They can and do compete, very successfully I might add. For that matter, don't think that you should necessarily hire an older male person to be your lawyer because you believe he'll tend to be more sensitive to your relationship loss than a younger person might be. This may or may not be so. Choose an attorney who is knowledgeable and experienced, and whom you like as a person. Everything else will work itself out just fine.

Should I look for an attorney to represent me who's been through his or her own divorce?

It probably can't hurt, though you shouldn't make it your sole or main criterion for hiring an attorney. As you know, divorce affects everyone in different ways. For instance, if the lawyer you'd like to hire is a man, the fact that he went through his own divorce may not in itself have made him aware enough of his own internal feelings to be of any help to you when it comes to understanding the relationship loss you feel. He may still be thinking about the "bitch" who "took him for everything he had"!

We've got three children and nothing but debts. How can I afford the cost of divorce?

A more appropriate question might be, "How can I afford *not* to get a divorce if I am in a bad marriage going nowhere but down?" It's really a choice between your possible positive future and your clearly negative present. Not really much of a choice at all, is it? And besides, there are a considerable number of options available to you. There is, first of all, the unlikely possibility that you can do your own divorce for nothing but court costs (filing fees and the like), which vary depending upon where you file and generally range from $35 to $200 (see the discussion of do-it-yourself divorce on page 88.)

If you seek positive ends, you probably won't pay much more than $1,500 in your situation even if you require an attorney. Also, you may be eligible for public services lawyers, if your state has them as most states do. There are always loans to pay your fees and costs. You may also be in a situation where your attorney will be able to effect a court order requiring your spouse to pay some or all of your fees.

If you still don't think you can afford it, many states have statutes that will enable you to get divorced at *no* cost to you. You will have to be nearly destitute, in most cases, to get the benefit of such laws, but you may well be in just such a situation in your case.

What if I hire a lawyer, and he or she turns out to be wrong for me later on? Can I change lawyers in midstream, and should I do so if I'm not satisfied?

You *always* have complete freedom to change lawyers *at any time* in the divorce process. If you are shy about discharging your lawyer, just find a new attorney and let him or her perform that part of the process for you. Furthermore, your prior attorney has an ethical obligation to cooperate in the transition. However, you will more than likely be required to pay for your former attorney's time and to reimburse him or her for any court costs or other expenses that he or she incurred on your behalf.

The earlier you make the change, the better, because judges generally don't like for divorcing people to change lawyers midway through a case; they presume it's the client's fault rather than the lawyer's. Watch out, however, if you find yourself changing lawyers more than once, as it may reflect something you need to look at in yourself as opposed to your having simply been unlucky twice.

In deciding whether to change, be mindful of my comments about judges' typical perceptions. But don't let that consideration stop you if you've got a bad attorney-client relationship. You and your lawyer are "married" while he or she is representing you. If you have *any* serious doubts about the workability of your relationship, you will probably have great difficulty being as honest and open as you'll need to be. And you may, just as likely, have difficulty trusting that lawyer. So don't settle for a bad lawyer-client relationship any more than you would for a bad marriage relationship. That's what brought you here in the first place.

The Initial Interview: Its Importance and What to Do in Preparation for It

How can I best prepare myself for the initial interview in my divorce?

Above all else, learn everything you can about the nature and extent of your property, so that you can tell the lawyer how and when each piece of property was acquired, how much you believe it is worth, and whether you want to keep it or not. Specifically, identify everything that you or your spouse has *any* interest in, whether it be a household item, an antique, a bank account, a credit card with a large balance due, or some stocks and bonds. This goes for assets as well as debts. Reduce all this data to written form. Furthermore, learn to understand the nature of your own and your spouse's relationship with any of your children, so that you may inform the lawyer as to what you think is reasonable with regard to child custody, support, and visitation. Finally, write down all questions you want the lawyer to answer.

I have a mile-long list of questions to ask at my initial interview. What questions do I really need to ask?

Focus on priorities. Get those questions answered first that
are most important in determining whether the lawyer is
right for you. *Why* do you want the divorce? Beyond these
questions, ask any others, in order of importance, until your
needs are satisfied. The following questions are offered
merely as a guide, but, I believe any good lawyer should be
able to give you at least some answer to each of them:

- Will you be charged by the case or by the hour?
- If by the case, ask for the approximate cost,
  based upon the facts you supply, and ask what
  the services will cover. (A minimum of $750 is
  probable, and unless there's a great deal of property involved, $1,500 to $5,000 might not be
  unreasonable, depending upon the circumstances; in any event, get it in *writing*.)
- If by the hour, find out what you will be charged
  for, at what rate or rates. (Hourly rates vary generally between $75 and more than $200, depending largely upon what the lawyer believes
  he or she can and should receive; have the lawyer spell it out to *your* satisfaction, and then get
  it in *writing*.)
- Will you be charged for the lawyer's travel time
  between his or her office and the court or elsewhere, and if so, at what rate or rates? (Typically,
  you will be charged at the lawyer's regular
  hourly fee.)
- Will you be charged for secretarial time? (Generally, you won't and shouldn't be charged for
  this. If you are, complain loudly that this should
  be included in the lawyer's fee.)
- Will the lawyer be the sole attorney handling
  your case?
- If not, when can you meet the other members of
  your "team"?
- How long has the lawyer practiced law, and how
  long in matrimonial law?
- In how many *contested* trials has he or she been
  engaged? (The answer may give you an opportunity to test the attorney's skill.)
- How much settlement negotiation experience

has the lawyer had, and how many property settlements has he or she effected?

- Will you be charged for telephone calls? (Typically, yes, and it can be expensive as we'll see a little later on. (See the discussion of how to keep from being ripped off by your attorney, at page 89).

- How much experience has the attorney had with tax implications attendant on property transfers and support payments and income tax filing?

- If you have children, what experience has the lawyer had with contested custody proceedings?

- How will you be billed, and at what time or times? (Typically, if you are being charged by the case, a retainer fee is paid up front, and the balance of the fee will be billed at the time of a trial or property settlement agreement; if by the hour, generally you will be billed on more or less a monthly basis. Request that the bills be monthly and explainable to your satisfaction.)

- Will the lawyer seek to have your fees and costs paid by your spouse? (Generally not, since you are always primarily liable for the fees you incur. However, your attorney may press for payment from your ex-spouse if your ex-spouse is employed and you are not.)

- How long will your case take to resolve? (Depending upon the circumstances, divorce cases take between two and eighteen months as a general rule.)

- What will the lawyer require of you as his or her prospective client? (Look for the attorney who will support your growing self-awareness and self-esteem by giving you lots of homework to do; remember, you're involved in a joint project with your lawyer.)

If you are satisfied with the answers to all of the above questions, then you might want to ask the lawyer any of your other questions. However, remember where we started from. Ask only those questions that you *need* answered. There may be times other than the present when you can more appropriately ask some of your questions. Some sample questions are the following:

- What are the tax consequences of your property and support resolution?
- What should you do with bank accounts and credit cards?
- Should you talk to your spouse?
- What problems does the lawyer foresee, if any?

When in doubt about certain questions, make an additional appointment to see the attorney. It will give you time to evaluate both your choice of lawyer and your remaining unanswered questions.

Will I be charged for my initial interview?

Generally, you won't and shouldn't be. This is true for those who have an interview just to "check out" divorce, as well as those who are actually looking to hire an attorney. The only exception here is where the lawyer has *specifically* advised you that there will be a charge, and you come to see him or her anyway.

Don't, however, take any chances. *Always remember to ask the question.* It may save you and the lawyer a lot of embarrassment later on. And don't give in to any temptation to feel guilty about receiving "free" advice. The main reason we lawyers generally don't charge for an initial interview is our belief that you will hire us at a later time because we gave you sound legal advice. Free initial consultations are part of our cost of doing business.

The Special Relationship Between You and Your Attorney: Why You Must Be Truthful

When a person takes the stand in a courtroom, he or she is sworn to tell the truth, the whole truth, and nothing but the truth. Do I have to act the same way toward my lawyer and, if so, why?

Absolutely so, if you want always to protect your best interests. You see, the process you are now entering is uniquely one of honest revelation. This is true largely because such family-related matters are what we lawyers call *fiduciary* situations (ones in which confidence and trust are of paramount importance). This means that *both* parties, and lawyers as well, have a much higher degree of responsibility to tell the truth than might otherwise be the case. You must, therefore, tell your lawyer everything and honestly.

For example, if you've been "shacking up" with someone, you'd better say so. You'll only have yourself to blame for bad advice if it's brought about because of your untruthful (or incomplete) answers to your attorney's questions. And remember, your lawyer is like a priest in that whatever you tell him or her can't be repeated. You'll feel a hell of a lot better letting the skeleton out of the closet, and maybe you'll find that because of some peculiarities of the law, the skeleton isn't a rattling one anyhow. If you have a venereal disease from having sex with someone other than your spouse, your lawyer may even be able to help you in this kind of extreme situation. On at least a few occasions I've been called upon to recommend the most helpful and understanding G.P. or gynecologist I know.

In addition, the proven lie or suppression of truth will, in most instances, result in a different disposition to the case than might otherwise occur. It could cause an alteration of the final property settlement after the divorce has been completed. This is true because of the court's continuing *jurisdiction* (power to decide) over the marriage, even after it has been dissolved, to rectify a fraud that was perpetrated by one party or the other. Such conduct can, and frequently does, result in an attorney's fee award to the other side. Consequently, give yourself your best shot by always telling the truth.

Alternatives to Hiring a Lawyer: Mediation, Legal Separation, and Do-It-Yourself Divorce

Is mediation a viable alternative to using the services of an attorney to get my divorce done?

It's a relatively new method that you might wish to consider. Normally, you and your spouse will confer with a person specially trained to *mediate* (listen to and help resolve) the breakup of your relationship. He or she will listen to both your story and your spouse's. Thereafter, the mediator will attempt to help clarify your disputes and resolve them amicably. Obviously, this is not a good method for those spouses who can't communicate anymore.

If meditation works, however, it can immeasurably speed up the divorce process and perhaps result in lower costs to both you and your spouse than you might otherwise incur. My one warning would be for both you and your spouse to have whatever written settlement you two can agree upon reviewed by independent lawyers of your own choosing, prior to your signing the agreement.

If you decide to try mediation, also remember to avoid some pitfalls inherent in the mediation process:

- If your marriage has a "domineering spouse" problem, the mediator might not spot it and, even if he or she does discover it, might not be able to control it in any event.
- The mediation process does not generally provide a legally enforceable "power" in either spouse to command the other's presence. This means that the mediation could continue for a long time and leave you nowhere should your spouse, at some point, decide not to continue.
- There is some possibility that the mediator may have a conscious or unconscious bias in favor of either you or your spouse. Despite these warnings, however, I recommend *any* method that increases your reconciliation opportunities, if there are good reasons to save your marriage, and that reduces your financial costs resulting from getting a divorce if you aren't able to work things out.

Can't I get a legal separation instead of a divorce?

You certainly can, if your state allows you to do so. The more important issue for you to decide, however, is *why* a decree of legal separation rather than a decree of divorce? In most states there are both. The process is identical, with the exception that one document provides for your separation while you remain married, and the other provides for your separation while also enabling you to become single again. Unless your religion is involved, there really isn't too much difference. Both proceedings divide property and provide for unemployed spouses and the children, if any, to ensure their survival. Both proceedings can and often do require the assistance of a lawyer. And, quite frankly, my experience has been that most proceedings initiated for legal separation end up being resolved as divorces anyway, perhaps after some time has passed. So why wait to do the inevitable? Avoid this solution unless your moral or religious beliefs clearly require it.

I hear a lot about do-it-yourself divorce. What is it, and can I use it to my benefit?

Do-it-yourself divorce is marketed to divorcing people as an easy way to avoid lawyers and their supposedly outrageous fees. Be wary of such claims, because there are just too many complications today, what with complex property transfers and their attendant tax implications, let alone the difficulties in arranging a divorce settlement if children or a nonworking spouse is involved.

Don't risk doing it yourself unless your case fits the following criteria:

- You and your spouse have been married for less than five years.
- You and your spouse don't have any children.
- You are both presently employed and capable of separately supporting yourselves.
- You have a combined net worth of less than $50,000.

Even if your situation fits these criteria, do-it-yourself divorce won't be right for you unless you and your spouse can also communicate with one another in rational ways. If you can't communicate with one another well enough to reach an agreement, you're probably going to have to consult with an attorney anyway.

If your situation doesn't fit the above criteria, you will need an attorney. For example, if you and your spouse have been married for more than five years, you may have spousal support issues to be resolved. (Spousal support, sometimes still called alimony, is money paid to the supported spouse, during and after the divorce, to help that person adjust to his or her new single state.) If you don't consult with an attorney, you may be coerced by your spouse into forfeiting your right to it, or you might not receive the amount you are entitled to under the laws of your state.

If there are children, you will need to look at the complicated issues of custody, support, and visitation that will be discussed in more depth in Chapter 8. I don't believe you'd be willing to risk your children's future welfare just to avoid an attorney's fee.

If there is a nonworking spouse, that person may be left in a horribly unequal position after the divorce without competent legal advice on such issues as your entitlement to rehabilitation support. (This will be discussed further in Chapter 6.)

And finally, if your combined net worth exceeds $50,000, there may be tax implications regarding the property transfers between you that neither of you are competent to evaluate.

How to Prevent Yourself from Getting Legally Ripped Off

The thought of seeing a lawyer about a divorce scares me because I've heard of other divorcing persons getting ripped off by legal parasites. I'm afraid that I, too, will get nothing and my lawyer will wind up with all of my money. Are you going to tell me that this can't or won't happen to me?

Unfortunately, it can and does happen, although not as frequently as you might be led to believe. The point is, you needn't be frightened of getting "ripped off" by a lawyer, if you take charge over your divorce by following these four guidelines:

1. Recognize that *you* hire the lawyer and he or she *works for you,* and not vice versa. If you've got a bad lawyer or one with whom you can no longer work, there is nothing preventing you from getting another, without inconvenience or extra cost to you.

2. Insist upon regular billings, preferably on a monthly basis, specifically setting forth, *in terms that are clear to you,* what you've been charged for during the billing period and what each performed service cost. Anything that doesn't seem reasonable to you should be clarified to your satisfaction.

3. Use your attorney's time wisely. This means to avoid using your lawyer as a therapist. We're not trained in that capacity, and it's not what you're paying us to accomplish. It also means to understand that your attorney is a businessperson as well as a professional lawyer. Unfortunately, time often is money. For instance, understand that a typical lawyer will charge for *every* telephone call from you that he or she answers. This can be critically important when you also realize that your forty-five-second telephone call can be, and often is, billed by an ethical attorney at up to as much as a quarter of an hour of his or her time. That's a bill to you of fifty dollars if your attorney charges two hundred dollars per hour! Therefore, get the maximum value out of each such call. Save up your questions and use the full quarter of an hour to ask as many of them as you can get answered in that time. Using your lawyer's time wisely means, furthermore, to ask your attorney only *legal* questions and not other kinds, such as what to do with the remainder of your life or whether

you should purchase some clothes that are on sale.

4. If your lawyer does most, if not all, of what you ask him or her to do, *including* those things he or she advised you against doing, realize that most of the cost of your divorce is within your control and can be expensive. However, you have every right to demand of your lawyer an adequate justification regarding any billing you might question.

I really want a divorce, but I'm afraid that I may end up just like a buddy of mine who just got divorced and lost everything. Both he and I are midlevel executives married for about the same length of time. Does the fact that we live in different states give me any assurance that what happened to him won't happen to me?

If you're looking for one-hundred-percent assurance, the answer is probably no, you can't be sure. However, the chances are far better than average that your divorcing experience will not be the same. This is primarily because *there is no general divorce law applicable throughout the United States.* Therefore, what happens in one state may not be applicable to the same set of circumstances in another state.

There are fifty separate sets of divorce laws, one for each state. Every state can, and frequently does, treat similar marital circumstances in different ways. Therefore, it is crucially important that you understand how your particular state handles your particular set of marital circumstances. That's where your lawyer can be of real help.

Besides, I seriously doubt that your buddy really did "lose everything." Men traditionally view divorce as primarily a material loss rather than the loss of a relationship. They tend to see it as a battle in which the loss of even a little of what they believe they deserve is viewed as a defeat, which they then interpret as "losing everything."

You should also become aware of how your divorce will be *procedurally* handled by the county court in which your divorce case will most likely be processed. These procedures differ, often drastically, from county to county *within the same state*. In child custody proceedings, for instance, one county may require an investigation of the custody issue, often taking six months or more, and a full written report and recommendation by the county's psychiatric staff, prior to having the judge decide the issue. And yet, in the same case in another county, perhaps very close by, the same issue is decided with simply a few hours of court time and testimony and *no* written report and recommendation *from anyone*. This can, and occasionally does, encourage "forum shopping," in which a spouse attempts, sometimes successfully, to effect a change in the marital residence (often the principal criterion for determining where the divorce case will be processed), to get what he or she believes will be more favorable treatment on some issue than would otherwise be obtainable.

Therefore, ease your own mind by learning what you can about your state law with regard to divorce in your type of situation, and the procedures for applying that law in the county where your divorce will likely be heard. In any event, make sure your lawyer learns and/or knows that law and those procedures *intimately*. In addition, you can minimize the chance that your divorce will come out like your buddy's by securing an excellent attorney in your own state who keeps you fully informed about your rights, and fights effectively for your best interests.

Special Problems: Physical Violence, Service of Papers, What to Do When You're Locked Out of the House

I've just been what I believe is called "served with divorce papers." What do I do now?

The most important thing is to realize that you probably have approximately thirty days before you have to do anything. So don't panic. You should consult with an attorney at your earliest convenience and get him or her to help you understand what the papers you've recently been served mean and what your options are, now that the divorcing process has begun for you. (There may be occasions when you are served with papers requesting something other than or in addition to a divorce, such as a request for a temporary restraining order, which may have a shorter time requirement—in which event, contact your lawyer immediately.)

What should I do if and when I find myself sitting on the lawn in front of my house some morning because my spouse, whom I am divorcing, has locked me out of the house?

You should take the following steps immediately:

1. Check with a lawyer or even your local police station to find out whether your spouse has any *legal* right to keep you out of the home, such as a valid restraining order entitling him or her to sole possession of the home, and, if so, get a copy of any such order.
2. Call your spouse (and pay particular attention to the fact that I did not say to create a scene at your front door) and ask what his or her intentions are in locking you out.
3. Consult with your divorce lawyer about how you can get a valid restraining order placing you back in the home and kicking your spouse out (and, if and when you get in, have the locks changed to prevent any future disturbance from your spouse).

Once you've accomplished these tasks, you'll be in a far better position to evaluate your next move.

I've been a victim of physical beatings by my spouse during my marriage. I'm also under constant stress from the fear of further violence. Friends tell me I should get a divorce, but I'm scared to death of what my spouse will do to me and the kids if I follow this advice. What can I do to stop the violence?

Nothing—I repeat, *nothing*—in your marital vows requires you to submit to physical violence, or to live in fear of it being done to you. There are few things in life that I find more tragic than married people who are unaware of this. Even sadder, however, is the married person who has been beaten by his or her spouse so often, and so fiercely, that the person becomes really unsure that he or she deserves any better. Well, I'm here to tell you that you do deserve better! And you don't have to submit to the fear of physical violence or to being threatened with it, either. An example of this emotional violence is the gun-crazy spouse who sits around in the evening reading gun magazines in your presence, after he or she has threatened to shoot you. Living in such a situation too long can do you more harm than you might at first imagine. At best, you may become paranoiac, suffering perhaps a great loss of physical health and emotional well-being. At worst, you might become tempted to take matters into your own hands and get your spouse before he or she gets you. Or you could discover that your greatest fears about physical violence being done to you by your spouse are fatally realized. Regardless of whether it's emotional violence being done to you, or actual physical beatings, or both, do not expect your spouse to change his or her ways. It is you who must decide whether and when the violence will end, and I recommend that you do so now.

Once you're committed to ending the violence, you'll need to do one of two things if you are to continue to remain in skillful charge of your situation. You will need either to remove yourself and any children you have from your marital home or legally to require your spouse to get out of that home. You have to do this because you must secure your own physical safety and that of your children if you are going to make the calm and rational decisions about your future that you now need to make. So put some space between you and your spouse.

If you decide to get out of the house yourself, and you don't have the money to rent a temporary place to stay, try asking your family or friends for help. Maybe they can loan you the money to get a place, or provide space in their homes for you to stay. Also, there may be a shelter in your area for abused and/or battered women, perhaps even a hot line to get such information. Some of you might be embarrassed to seek familial help because you feel that you'll be wrongfully imposing upon them or perhaps for fear of having to reveal your problems. But you might be very surprised to discover how many of them would welcome you with open arms and understanding hearts. Besides, you can live with embarrassment. Living in a violent situation, however, can get you scarred for life, or worse. And don't worry right now about how you'll survive on your own. Just believe that you will and worry about it, if at all, only after you've secured the physical safety of yourself and your children.

If there's nowhere you can go, you will have to consider forcing your spouse to leave. Unfortunately, outside of the legal remedies available to you in a divorcing situation, the only legal help you can get in most states is to charge your spouse formally with the crime of assault and battery. Pursuant to such charges, you can request that your spouse be kept in jail pending a hearing or trial and, in any event, that you be given police protection, if necessary, to keep your spouse away from you and your children. But check with any good criminal or divorce lawyer for other, perhaps less harsh, remedies. You may be living in one of the states that have enacted special laws to deal with family violence. Such laws may allow you to secure your spouse's removal without resorting to having him or her thrown into jail, and will keep him or her away from you and your children until the situation is resolved. Domestic violence laws are a rapidly developing trend in divorce practice, so don't hesitate to utilize them if they're available to you. They are there for your protection.

And finally, once you've said "never again" to the beatings and placed some safe distance between you and your spouse, then calmly consider how you want to proceed with a divorce and any other legal action to prevent further violence being done to you. An example of the latter is a lawsuit against your spouse to recover money damages for the physical injuries you've sustained and the emotional damage you've suffered. When you see a lawyer about your divorce, he or she should immediately get a temporary restraining order (called a TRO for short) against your spouse to protect you and your children from any further violence. And once it has been obtained, a copy of it should be given to your local police to alert them to your spouse's violent tendencies and to help ensure a quick response from the legal authorities, should your spouse be tempted to violate the order. How well the lawyer you've hired handles the crisis may well determine whether you want him or her to continue to represent you in your divorce. Such a restraining order is a court-approved piece of paper telling your spouse when, where, and under what circumstances he or she can see you and the children. Further, it provides notice to your spouse that a violation of the orders is punishable by fine and/or imprisonment. In most states, the TRO is available on a moment's notice, which is why your lawyer has no excuse not to act immediately, and can be gotten *ex parte* (meaning on the strength of your sworn statement alone, and without your having to let your spouse know in advance about your action).

Such an order will typically remain in effect until the court has a hearing to determine whether it should be continued in force and, if so, under what circumstances and for how long. At this hearing, your spouse will be able to offer evidence against the maintenance of such an order, so you should be prepared to further support your reasons for needing this device. (Such support can come from friends or family who have witnessed your spouse's actions, or from the police or other people who have personal knowledge of the situation.)

And remember, the restraining order is available both in cases of actual physical violence and of threatened violence as well. Speaking of the latter, I remember a case in which the husband was accused of holding a loaded .45 in his wife's mouth until she agreed to sign a property settlement agreement favorable to him. It's not just on TV that these things happen; they also occur in real life, so don't let them happen to you. In the case I've mentioned, the wife was able to get a permanent injunction (like a TRO, except that it generally lasts forever or until further order of the court) and a nullification of the property settlement agreement, because of the husband's conduct.

Being able to get a restraining order, however, is not

the only reason you'll probably be better off in your situation once you begin your divorce proceedings. Another reason is that your spouse's conduct will now be under the watchful eye of the court. His or her further expressions of violence can be used as the basis for severely and permanently restricting your spouse's visitation rights with his or her children, and will certainly affect the court's decision with regard to whether you or your spouse will be awarded their custody. In some states, your spouse's violent conduct can be a factor in awarding you more property than you might otherwise receive. This could happen in a situation where your spouse's violent attitude has carried over into his or her unwillingness to pay spousal and/or child support. The judge can simply award you more of the marital property to counter the possibility that your ex-spouse won't pay you a dime. In most divorcing situations, the restraining order, in its various forms, will provide you with ample protection from a violent spouse. However, if stronger measures are necessary, don't hesitate to sue your spouse for damages or have him or her put in jail as a penalty for being convicted of assault and/or battery.

Canadian Law

I'm a Canadian here on a visit, and I'm thinking of getting a divorce on my return to Canada. Can I assume that Canadian divorce laws are the same as those of your country?

The answer is both yes and no. Divorce issues relating to the granting of a divorce, the post-separation financial support of spouses and children, child custody, and access rights of noncustodial divorcing or divorced parents regarding their children, are dealt with in many of the same ways in Canada as they are in most states in the United States. Also, like each state in this country, each province in Canada treats issues relating to property in its own local and individual way.

On the other hand, Canadian law is different in that Canada has a single national divorce law (called the Divorce Act of 1985) that is applicable and enforceable throughout the entire country, unlike the United States, where we have fifty separate divorce law systems, one for each state. Here the issues involved in post-separation relationships between parents and their children (child custody and related matters, which will be discussed in depth in Chapter 8) can be decided one way in my state of California, and in an entirely different manner in some other state. For example, state courts in my country can reach radically different decisions on the proper level of financial support for a child of divorced parents.

In sharp contrast, in Canada today, a Toronto couple getting their divorce in Vancouver, after having moved into the latter province to live, will find that courts in both cities are subject to the same rules and procedures relating to divorce. What a great way to defeat the "quickie" divorce so readily available in some states in this country.

Now let's look at the following specific issues and how they are applied in Canada and the United States:

Grounds for Divorce

In the United States, there are few states that have exactly the same grounds for divorce. One state may have four or more such reasons, while another state may have only one. Furthermore, some states still have so-called fault grounds (desertion, mental cruelty, and the like) while others may have entirely excluded such grounds in enacting no-fault divorce laws. However, in Canada there is currently only *one* ground for the granting of a divorce, and that is "marriage breakdown." Such relationship deterioration can be shown in only one of two ways. First, it is shown if the spouses are proven to have lived separately and apart for at least one year immediately preceding the initiation of the divorce case, and are living separately and apart when the divorce proceeding commences. (This is similar to the principle common to our various no-fault divorce laws in the United States.) Or second, it is shown if the party responding to the divorce action is proven guilty of having engaged in adultery or mental cruelty. Either ground may be proven, as it may here in the United States, by a "preponderance of the evidence." This means the court decides that, on balance, it's more probable than not that ground for divorce has been proven. Even adultery or mental cruelty need only be proven by this ordinary civil burden of proof, rather than by the more stringent criminal burden of proof, i.e., "proof beyond a reasonable doubt."

Jurisdiction

Remember, from our earlier discussion in this chapter, that jurisdiction gives a court the power to decide the granting of your divorce, and is typically a function of your residence at the time the divorce action is filed. In the United States, each state has its own individual jurisdictional requirement. One state can force you to prove you've been living there for at least one year prior to initiating your divorce, while in some other state you need prove only three months' residency.

On the other hand, in *every* province in Canada, you now need only to satisfy one common requirement for jurisdictional purposes. That requirement is that either you or your spouse has resided in that province in which you intend to file for divorce for at least one year prior to being able to commence the action, and that one or both of you is residing therein when the lawsuit is actually begun.

Length of Process

The time realities of the legal process of divorce are the same in both Canada and the United States. In both places, it commonly takes between three and eighteen months to be finished with the divorce. Obviously, the length varies according to the number of issues and the liveliness of the debate.

One significant difference in this regard relates to the varying burdens imposed upon Canadian and U.S. divorce attorneys. Canadian law, as now determined by the Divorce Act, requires divorce lawyers to certify to the court at the time of trial that they have complied with the law's policy of promoting marriage. This means that Canadian divorce attorneys must satisfy the court that they have advised their clients of the Divorce Act's public policy, have recommended reconciliation between the divorcing spouses, and have suggested various reconciliation resources, such as a divorce counselor, to enable the parties to find reasons to stay married.

I'm aware of no such requirement in the United States, although I regularly give such advice anyway. Also, and more important, Canadian uniform divorce law mandates that family matters such as child custody and post-separation financial support for spouses and their children be handled in a nonadversarial manner. It suggests the use of mediators, rather than the court system, to resolve such matters. I wish I could say the same for the situation in the United States with regard to these family-related issues, but unfortunately I cannot. And it's all too often true here that our adversarial approach to deciding these issues fosters more harm than health.

Financial Support Issues

Your reading of the questions and answers contained in chapters 6 and 8 of this book should prepare you well for your Canadian divorce, because both countries have common principles. Those principles are the relative condition, means, and needs of both spouses and their relative abilities to support themselves alone after the divorce, and also the needs of children born to those spouses. And in neither country is marital misconduct an issue in support hearings (meaning that an adulterous husband will not have to pay more support to his ex-wife than he would otherwise be required to pay, so as to punish him for his infidelity).

At least in one respect, the Canadian system of divorce is presently more humane than ours is, by and large. The Canadian uniform law recognizes what our various state laws generally don't take into account, namely, the appalling financial circumstances of divorced mothers with custody of their children (the fastest-growing group of poor people in the United States today). The Divorce Act encourages courts in Canada to attempt realistically to set up two totally self-sufficient households where there was just one before the divorce.

And finally, the Canadian system tends to rely less on *support schedules* (statistical guidelines for determining the proper level of support) and more on a case-by-case analysis of generalized principles, like those set forth above, in determining how much money will be paid by one spouse to support the other, or to support his or her children. Our guidelines for support too often don't take into account how difficult it may be for a homemaker married for more than twenty-five years to find gainful employment now that she is divorced; it may, in fact, be impossible. Also, remember that in Canada, as in the United States, there are legally allowable procedures to modify such financial awards when a change of circumstances has occurred, to either a higher or a lower amount than was originally ordered by the divorce trial judge.

Child Custody and Related Matters

In both countries, it is the children's best interests that determine with whom the children will reside when a divorce is concluded. And in neither place is the past or present marital misconduct of either parent an issue in custody proceedings unless the conduct has a direct bearing on the children. (For instance, in both countries, a parent who is a child molester will have severely limited access rights with regard to his or her children until he or she has undergone psychiatric treatment and has been rehabilitated to the satisfaction of the court.)

Although Canadian divorce law does not mandate "joint custody" (see the discussion of this and other forms of custody arrangements in Chapter 8)—as, for instance, does my state of California—it is at least provided for. The Divorce Act says that custody may be awarded to one or more persons (in Canada, this can include grandparents as well). Furthermore, Canadian uniform law, like many divorce laws here in the States, does provide that children should have as much contact with each parent as is consistent with the children's best interests.

Canada has also enacted laws similar to those now operative in the United States to require a more or less uniform treatment of custody matters in interstate or inter-province disputes concerning conflicting custody orders. I'm glad to report that Canada is as vitally concerned with forum-shopping (to get more favorable custody treatment for one spouse or the other) and child-snatching as is the United States. (Some of these laws will be discussed in Chapter 8.)

Property Division upon Divorce, and Related Matters

These issues can be extremely complicated, and their treatment varies radically from state to state in the United States, as well as from province to province in Canada. Therefore, I will not make any attempt at specific comparisons, since there are simply too many variables to consider. Just to give you one example of this problem, property laws in Ontario have very individual rules pertaining to the matrimonial home, rules unlike any that I know of in the United States. (In that province, even though the matrimonial home may be owned solely by one spouse, both are equally entitled to possession of that home while the parties are still married.) You should check with an attorney in the province in which you intend to file your divorce action to get specific advice concerning property division.

I do, however, want to address a couple of points that are important when considering the generalized treatment of property-division issues in our respective countries. First, Canada's separate provincial laws generally divide only the *net value* of property acquired by either spouse during marriage, rather than the actual property itself. For instance, if you acquired property in your own name during your marriage here in the United States, that property could be held by one of our courts to be divisible marital property upon your divorce. In Canada, however, only the enhanced value of the property during marriage would be subject to division. The property itself would not be subject to division, but rather would be held to be yours outright.

The second point is that, in either country, the principle of a fifty-fifty split of property (whether physical or simply the *value*) acquired during marriage is pervasive. In the United States, community property rationales are largely responsible for this modern trend, but in Canada it is primarily the result of the Divorce Act's statement that marriage is an "economic partnership." This generalization means that the *effect* of the property division laws upon divorce in both Canada and the United States is quite similar, despite the divergences between the respective laws themselves.

Finally, it is worth noting that in both Canada and the United States, laws have been enacted to protect your economic interests in property you're awarded in your divorce, should you decide to remarry or live permanently with someone outside of marriage. You can, for instance, create a *premarital contract.* (See Chapter 10 for the specifics, but for now think of these agreements as ways to protect the property you were awarded in your divorce from the claims of a new marital partner.) In both Canada and the United States, such contracts will be enforced unless they were entered into primarily to give property and support in return for sexual favors.

In giving you this overview of the differences and similarities between Canadian and U.S. divorce laws, I've not discussed the similarities, if any, in divorce costs or lawyer's fees. Though they are similar, there are simply too many variables to answer such questions adequately here. However, if you review the earlier discussion dealing with what inquiries to make at your initial interview (beginning on page 82), you will be able to find out from your Canadian lawyer about costs and fees for your particular divorce, so that you can expeditiously handle these cost issues.

4

The Learning Process of Becoming Single

⬛

*T*he thirty-seven-year-old woman named June who came to me for counseling was weeping. Tears stained her worry-worn face. "I can't make it on my own," she said. "My husband left me four months ago, and all I do is cry. I've got to find a job or else I'll starve, and so will my two kids. My only career was marriage—we were married for fourteen years—and now I'm unemployed. I feel like I'm worthless, I'm nothing."

As we talked, I found out that June's ex-husband was the sales manager for a prosperous computer company. A divorce settlement, which had already been worked out, assured her of monthly child and spousal support payments of $2,500, as well as a half-interest in their $350,000 home. Certainly this was a far better settlement than most divorced persons receive.

So what was her problem? Was she crazy, to have such an unrealistic view of her situation? Not at all. In fact she was right; she was poverty-stricken and helpless. But she was experiencing *emotional* poverty and helplessness instead of economic disaster. She was "starved" for love and affection; she felt "worthless" because of the ending of her marriage; she felt "poverty-stricken" because her former husband, who had been the most important adult in her life, no longer cared for her. Her life felt like a yawning pit. This kind of emotional bankruptcy is far more difficult to face than economic bankruptcy, so it was not surprising that June transformed her feelings about her emotional deprivation into an unrealistic belief that she was ready to apply for welfare.

You are *normal* if you experience feelings similar to June's at an early stage in your divorce, regardless of your income level. In a divorce, it is the exception rather than the rule that a woman—or a man—won't feel some of the emotional terror that June was experiencing. And it should come as no surprise that men as well as women feel this way, since in their basic emotions they are no different.

Men are more accustomed than women to place a money value on their sense of how they value themselves, and consequently they find it almost automatic to displace their initial feelings of loss in a divorce to a loss of some of their income in their property, spousal, and child support settlements, and have visions of selling apples in the street. Yes, they have been "taken to the cleaners." But it is their former way of life, their married life, that has been taken to the cleaners, which is the underlying reason for the sense of terrifying emptiness they might feel. The hole in their pocket terrifies them not as much as the hole left in their lives, now that they are no longer married. Of course money, or the lack of it, is of great importance, but only insofar as it reinforces a happier or sadder life after divorce. In and of itself, money cannot define the feelings of self-worth and personal competency that only you can give yourself.

Those feelings can't be bought; they can only be earned by virtue of the effort you make to understand the emotional process of your divorce, and the internal resources you possess to make positive things happen in your life now that you are divorced. The psychological cost you have been paying is your strong motivation to change the self-defeating behaviors in your personality that create misery in your divorced life. And the cost has nothing to do with money, but everything to do with your willingness to take an in-depth look at your own feelings and behavior, rather than ascribing the cause of all your problems to your ex-spouse or a cruel society or the workings of a malevolent fate. In return for this cost that you must pay, you will receive the greatest travel tour in your life: a vastly exciting journey into self-discovery that will enable you to enhance your life as a divorced person.

You will discover the wide range of who you are, and be able to tap survival and achievement abilities you thought you never possessed when you were married.

The Normality of Divorce Feelings

With two and a half million people divorcing each year, divorce is so prevalent in our society that it can now be regarded as a *normal* life event. Equally normal are your experiences, thoughts, feelings, and behaviors as you live through the divorce process. Consequently, in the initial stages of your divorce, you may hear yourself saying things like these:

"I'm going crazy."

"Life isn't worth living."

"I feel dead, a walking zombie."

"I'm sad and cry all the time and don't know why."

"I'm helpless."

"I'd like to kill my ex."

"I'm not me anymore."

If these statements reflect your feelings, you are perfectly normal! You are experiencing a normal response to the normal crisis of divorce. For divorce has an emotional logic of its own. It is a quite different logic from the kind you are accustomed to, which is the logic of your intellect divorced from feelings.

Divorce is the logic of feelings experienced in a crisis situation—and the strange disarray of your emotions is part of the logic of the mourning process that you must live through if you are to attain the stability and happiness you are now yearning for. It is of primary importance for you to recognize this basic fact of divorce. For it is only on this foundation of understanding that the disarray you might be experiencing can make any sense and can give you realistic hope that the storms now buffeting you will eventually subside and a brighter horizon will take their place in your life.

Before you can reorganize your life, the old basis on which your life rested has to be shattered. *The emotional disarray you might be experiencing is an inevitable and necessary preliminary to your self-renewal as a single person,* for there is no such thing as being "suddenly" single. In the initial stages of divorce, the physical everyday presence of your spouse is no longer a taken-for-granted fact of life. But he or she is still very much present, along with the married life you had, in your mind and feelings.

Living without your spouse requires you to respond in a single-person way to the new demands of single life. However, that is impossible if you are still perceiving the world and responding to it as a married person. To be truly single is to realize that you can survive well both physically and emotionally on your own. You must prove this to yourself, not to anyone else. You do so by the ways in which you respond positively to the challenge that living singly affords you.

That challenge is for you to take personal responsibility for the shape and direction of your own life, to stop blaming others for your unhappiness, and to begin to make your own efforts to make positive things happen in your life. However, this state of being single has to be *earned* by you, and cannot happen to you overnight. You begin to earn your singleness through the process of mourning the loss of the person who was once the most important adult in your life.

Learning to Become Single Through the Mourning Process

If you have experienced the death of a loved one, such as your father or mother or another close relative, you might recall how you mourned that death, grieved and yearned for the presence of your loved one, and felt angry and resentful at the injustice of it all.

Life seemed empty and different without his or her presence. After the shock subsided, you renewed yourself, accepting the fact that that person no longer physically existed, and readjusted your way of life in accordance with that reality. You went through the process of mourning the physical death of a loved one. To cry and feel abandoned, to be angry and resentful, to feel shaken and helpless were *healthy* things for you to do.

Mourning a death is the natural and normal way we let go of a no-longer-present relationship (and a way of life that was to a greater or lesser degree dependent on that relationship), so that we can live more alertly in a present that demands new adjustments in our behavior. In fact, it is the person who doesn't mourn such a severe loss who is liable not to be normal. Such a person's inability to grieve may result in severe physical, emotional, and behavioral consequences.

The Mourning Process of Divorce

Since divorce is the process of experiencing the death of a relationship, mourning that death is equally as essential as mourning the death of a loved one, if you are to move your life forward as a no-longer-married person. That process has been clearly outlined by my colleague, Dr. William M. Lamers, Jr., whose chart illustrating the process is reproduced on page 109.

Protest This is stage one in Dr. Lamer's mourning process chart. This is the "Oh no, this can't be happening to me!" stage. In the inner segment of this stage, the *emotions* resulting from the loss of the marital relationship that are experienced are listed: shock, confusion, denial, anger at self, and lowered self-esteem.

In the outer circle are listed the *behaviors* that result from your experiencing these emotions of loss, such as crying, pain, weakness, nausea, sleep disturbances, loss of appetite (or voracious eating), and other physical changes such as constipation, vomiting, scrambled thoughts, splitting headaches, back pains, menstrual period irregularities (periods

LOSS → RECO

DETACHMENT

Decreased Socialization

No New Friendships

"Bland" Expression

Absent Spontaneity

Apathy

Indifference

Loss of Interest

Desire to Withdraw and "Give Up"

Agony

Grief

Anguish

Depression

Shock

Confusion

Denial

Anger

Anger at Self

Lowered Self-Esteem

PROTEST

Crying

Pain

Weakness

Nausea

Loss of Appetite

Sleep Disturbances

Other Physical Changes

DESPAIR

"Urge to Recover" That Which Was Lost

Slowed Thinking and Actions

Continuing Physical Symptoms

© 1978 William M. Lamers Jr., MD

that once were predictable may now occur every two or three weeks or once every two months), and severe weight loss or gain.

Stage one is the *beginning* of your letting go of your past way of life as a married person. You are still too close to the person you were in your marriage to feel that your present state of living singly is a comfortable fit. Singleness is still more of a threat than a promise for a better life. You cry for, are sad over, and regret what might have been, yet never was, in your marriage. You are angry at the present uncertainty and unpredictability in your life and yearn for a more stable, predictable existence. Even your past unhappy marriage sounds like a more tempting alternative to the terror-inducing present; at least you knew what to expect in the marriage, even if that expectation was another day of unhappiness. Yet you know you can never go back to that old marriage. You are like the person who jumped on his or her horse and rode off in all directions at once, because *you are now in the time of your divorce when you are separated but still married in your feelings.*

Despair It is in this stage that you realize that the loss of your old way of married life is permanent; it can no longer be disbelieved or denied, yet you feel you cannot make it on your own. In this stage you grieve, mourning over the irretrievable loss of your marriage.

You feel depressed and despairing, engulfed by a sense that you are helpless because you fear you are worthless and have no conception about how you can move your life forward. As a consequence of this image you have of yourself as a vulnerable victim, you may become very distrustful of people and spend most of your time bathing in the warm water of self-pity. It seems to take ages even to dredge up enough energy to wash the dishes that have been piling up in your sink. You are still living more in the past than in the present, but now *you are divorced but not yet single.*

Detachment In this stage your despair gives way to apathy, for why bother doing anything anymore? Since life appears meaningless now that the marriage in which you invested your hopes and dreams has disappeared. Your behavior may take on an automatic, robotlike quality, like that of a zombie going through the motions of living but not really living. It's as if you put up a glass wall between yourself and other people, so that you feel isolated even in a crowd or at a party—a glass wall that protects you from ever being hurt by other people again.

In this stage you are finally detaching yourself at the emotional level from the feeling that you are still married. Detachment is a recognition that indeed the marriage has died, which means you must truly begin to think, act, and feel like the person you are, which is a single man or woman who must make it on his or her own. Your married self-image has disappeared. You are no longer living in the past, but have yet to begin to live in the present. *You are now in the time when you feel that you are divorced, but there is no future for you.*

Recovery Now that you have detached yourself from believing you are still a married person in your feelings, you begin to live more skillfully in the present reality of being a divorced person. You respond to the demands of single-person life in ways that are very different from the ways that were habitual to you in your marriage but are inappropriate now. You build a new self-image on your newly discovered belief that you are no longer a victim; instead, you are a person who has the ability not only to survive but to prevail over the new challenges that single life affords you. Your past marriage is seen as a learning experience that can become a stepping-stone to a better life rather than as a sign of your failure. You begin to prove to yourself that your self-esteem is based on how you live your life in the present, not on how you lived it in the past.

The numbed, shocked, crying, regretful, bitter, sad, depressed, apathetic, isolated person you may have been during the earlier stages of the mourning process has disappeared, except for infrequent and short reappearances. Your physical system no longer is attacked by the sleeplessness, digestive disorders, headaches, back pains, and menstrual irregularities that may have plagued you earlier in your divorce. Just as your life now begins to stabilize itself, your emotions and your physical condition respond in a similar manner. You are now living in the exciting time of *self-renewal as a single person.*

The Mourning Process as Your Key to Health

The degree to which you will have a skillful divorce that leads to happier horizons is dependent on your awareness and acceptance of your mourning process. The mourning process is your key to healing yourself. If you are unaware of the mourning process, you indeed may think you are going crazy rather than being perfectly normal. As one of my clients told me, "I felt as if they should put me in a straitjacket during the first year of my divorce." Fighting the mourning process by pretending everything is fine when it isn't, trying to hasten it, or denying its existence will only intensify the gloom in your life rather than lighten it.

Each of the stages you pass through may contain traces of the other stages. You will not experience everything listed in Dr. Lamers's mourning chart, but you will certainly live through significant aspects of these stages. Quite often there will be a one-step-forward-two-steps-back progress through these stages. Don't think of these stages as rigidly compartmentalized.

It is of far more importance for you to recognize that, as a divorced person, a process inside you is set in motion whereby your thoughts, emotions, and behavior may explode into disarray at the beginning of your divorce, then move through a stage in which you feel isolated and disengaged from everyone, including yourself, then progress to a stage in which the past is laid to rest and you begin to think and act skillfully as a single person. This is perfectly normal, for you are following the typical path that divorced people experience.

The Time Span of the Mourning Process

How long does the mourning process last? Each person experiences the process in his or her own unique way, so no set time can be given for everyone. However, it usually takes up to two years for the mourning process to spend itself to the point where you begin to feel a sense of yourself as a separate individual whose singleness is alight with possibilities for self-realization that you thought were impossible to attain at the beginning of your divorce.

You must guard against the danger of becoming stuck in one of the stages of the mourning process. For example, if you find yourself, month after month, remaining in the "Protest" stage rather than moving on to the next, it is time for you to seek professional help from a good divorce counselor so you can find out what's blocking you from moving forward. I have known men and women who have remained stuck in the "Protest" stage for a decade or longer, to the severe detriment of their lives. They have pretended that everything was fine when they knew that their hearts were bursting with sorrow and anger; and that sorrow and anger, dammed up inside them for a dozen years, turned into a heart attack or a stroke. Others have denied their own feelings to the point where they proudly stated that their divorce caused them no emotional difficulties whatsoever. They were so out of touch with their feelings that they never acknowledged the roaring volcano of hatred, bitterness, anger, and resentment that remained inside them. And a half-dozen years after their divorce, their denial of their mourning process took its toll in the form of suicide or psychotic episodes. Their stalled mourning process reactivated itself suddenly, explosively, tragically.

Recognizing the Arrival of Your Mourning Process

Mourning the death of your marriage may come in surprising ways. Some men and women mourn the deaths of their marriages long before they have actually separated or filed for divorce. Their protest, anger, despair, and isolation are played out within the declining months or years of their marriages. They discover that two can be lonelier than one while living together. Quite frequently, these are people who have slept in separate bedrooms and have had no sexual relationship with each other (or have experienced sex only as a form of obligation) for a long time. With couples such as these, economic considerations, fear of living alone, or "waiting until the children grow older" is the reason for remaining in the marriage long after that marriage has proved to be a hopeless shambles.

These are the people who, once they separate and divorce, feel an initial sense of exhilaration and a rush of freedom when they actually make the breakup happen. Yet traces of the unworked-through parts of their mourning process may erupt and demand resolution six months or a year or two after that breakup.

The Movie-Divorce-in-Your-Mind Some men and women impulsively rush into divorce, leaving a spouse without preliminary notice. Such persons suffer a stunning shock when the reality of living a single life clashes with the romantic expectations of freedom and love that they thought would be simply there for the taking in the divorced world. Stunned shock may occur a few weeks or months after the breakup, when the mourning process begins with powerful intensity.

The Another-Person-in-the-Wings Divorce Sometimes a spouse has another lover waiting for the breakup. The man or woman exults in a vision of future happiness after divesting himself or herself of the "turkey" he or she was married to. However, more often than not, the rosy future turns into a disenchanted and scary present after the breakup occurs. For within a year or less after the separation, the new relationship also breaks up.

The problems that existed in the marriage (such as failed communication, poor sex, lack of shared interests, or value differences) are not eliminated, but simply transferred into the new relationship. When the bloom is off this new relationship, the excitement and exhilaration that existed on leaving the marriage disappear and confusion, resentment, anguish, and fear take their place. The breakup of this new relationship will then trigger the mourning process, rather than the breakup of the old marriage.

The Civilized Divorce A couple may mutually decide that divorce is right for the both of them; "Let's be adult about our divorce and remain good friends after the separation" is the song both of them sing. And then something happens: one wants what the other considers the lion's share of the property, or spousal support is objected to, or who will own the house or get custody of the children becomes a clashing issue and the masks of sweet reason (which they indeed believed portrayed their "true" selves) fall off and rage, hatred, screaming, or coldness transform their civilized image of themselves into that of two children having tantrums. They become human beings in pain rather than Barbie dolls, and the mourning process begins.

The Left-in-the-Lurch Divorce When one partner in a marriage is suddenly told without warning that the other partner wants to leave the marriage immediately and move out of the house, this usually triggers off the mourning process immediately. The partner who is left behind is initially stunned. "It's like the sky fell in on me. . . . I never knew my partner even thought about divorce. . . . I thought we had as good a marriage as anyone else's," are the typical comments of the person who is left. The floodgates of the mourning process open up once the stunned disbelief begins to subside, and that process may then run its course, if not resisted but accepted for the healing value it possesses, in the first month or two after the separation.

Paradoxically, it is the person who experiences the left-in-the-lurch divorce whose potential for self-realization as a single person is often the greatest. Mourning the lost marriage occurs quickly after the breakup, and while the pain of separation and feelings of rejection are almost unbearable at times, the decks of the "rejected" person's life are cleared for a new self-image, based on increased competency and newly discovered internal survival resources, far sooner than is possible for the person who blithely persists in imagining divorce without high emotional payment.

The choice is yours: either connect with your mourning process and accept its developmental healing stages, or run away from the pain of that process, only to be shaken by its force when you least expect it. Since there is no such thing as a free lunch, you will either have to pay now or later. Paying now is a protective health measure; paying later is also a health measure, but at a time when additional damage has been done to your mental and physical systems.

The Disappearance of Your Taken-for-Granteds

The mourning process is the road you must travel to lose your married self-image so that your single self-image can take its place. This *emotional* loss is intensified and reinforced by the losses in your everyday life that you experience at the same time the mourning process is at work.

At the beginning of your divorce, here are the major everyday losses you might experience:

- Economic loss. Living in two separate households is far more expensive that living in one household. The stable combined income you counted on to pay the bills no longer exists.
- The loss of your home, condominium, or apartment. The rooms, furniture, and furnishings you knew so well have vanished, along with the community in which you lived.
- Social loss. Many of the persons you regarded as friends now seem to avoid you. The parties you were invited to when you were a couple have disappeared. Your phone no longer rings and there you sit lonely in your loneliness.
- The loss of *daily* contact with your children if you do not have custody. The everyday connection with your children that you once thought was often more of an inconvenience than a blessing now becomes a cherished memory.
- The loss (if you are the ex-husband) of the housekeeper, the dust-and-dirt remover, the dishwasher, the cook, the food and clothing buyer, the bookkeeper, the taxi driver for the kids, the laundry and sewing specialist, and the social arranger who was your wife.
- The loss (if you are the ex-wife) of the home-fixer and car repairman, the plumber, the electrician, the lawn-mower and weed eliminator, the major decision-maker on big-ticket purchases such as new cars or video equipment, and the person whose income provided the lion's share of the total amount you could spend and save as a family unit.
- The loss of your career. If you, as a woman, considered your marriage your career, that career no longer exists.
- The loss of your ex-spouse's family, if they regard you as the "culprit" in your divorce.
- The loss of your own family and relatives if they regard divorce as an unacceptable and terrible reflection on themselves, rather than as a normal

and painful experience that happens to millions of people.

- The loss of your sex partner. No matter how distasteful your ex-spouse might seem to you now, he or she was at least a nightly warm body in bed who assuaged your physical needs to a greater or lesser degree. Now the bed has become a lonely, cold, and deserted island.

- The loss of physical security. If you are an ex-wife, the presence of your spouse, even when you disliked living with him, afforded you a measure of physical security. He at least gave you the illusion of protection when a dog howled in the middle of the night, or when the wind ominously rattled the windows, or when an unexpected knock was heard at the door. That kind of security blanket has vanished, and nights alone now seem like a Hansel-and-Gretel-in-the-wilderness experience.

- The loss of your value system. This is the most important loss of all; your once taken-for-granted assumptions that your marriage was for life and that your spouse was your most trustworthy friend have turned out to be illusions. And the God you believe in seems cold and unconcerned about your pain.

All of these are major losses of what once were everyday, taken-for-granted realities. You may not experience all of these losses, but certainly a number of them will be present in the initial stages of your divorce. They will reinforce the tendency in the "Protest" stage of your mourning process, where you experience disbelief that this is happening to you; and the floodgates of anger, sadness, and bitter regret, along with sleep and appetite disturbances, may open up so that you believe you are in a sink-or-swim situation.

And, yes, you *are* in a sink or swim situation. At this time, life gives you the choice either of remaining a victim, doomed to believe that the best of your life has now passed, or that the best is yet to come, provided you *learn* to become single.

At this time in your divorce, the losses in your life are telling you that just being divorced does *not* mean you are single yet! Your mourning process is the time in your divorce when you clear the decks of your married self-image; for as a divorced person you have yet to think of yourself as a single person and begun to act on that realization.

For example, during the initial stage of the mourning process, if you are the ex-wife, you still may be locked into the time schedule for breakfast and dinner that existed when you were married. Out of habit, you may find yourself still preparing dinner at 6:00 P.M. (which was when your husband expected it), when there is no present reason other than that it seems appropriate to do so. Or you may overbuy food, since you are accustomed to buying for yourself and your spouse. And if you are the ex-husband, you may return after work to your new apartment at 6:00 P.M. because you always did so in your marriage, and then wonder why you are there, since no one is at the door to greet you!

Because the loss of your married identity is so enormous (far greater, perhaps, than you ever thought it could possibly be when you fantasized in your marriage about the happy divorced life you would lead instantly upon separation), letting go of that identity is a push-pull operation in the first year of your divorce. During that early time, it is a mistake to believe you are living "alone." For although the *physical* presence of your former spouse is no longer an everyday reality, he or she is likely to be ever-present in your thoughts and feelings—obsessively so—during the early stages of your divorce.

Images of your ex-spouse may dance in your mind at work and at home in sometimes poignant, sometimes hateful form. Dramatic remembrances of past togetherness and separateness, arguments and sadness may be replayed over and over again on the video recorder of your mind. And as in a mystery story whose plot is yet to be unraveled, the questions you ask yourself as the past is replayed are, "Why did this divorce have to happen? What have I done to deserve this punishment?" But no matter how often you ask yourself these questions, the answers never seem to be forthcoming.

And if you thought that once you separated, you could

divest yourself of further communication with an unwanted spouse, you might find yourself in for a shock. In fact, during that first year of separating, you may find yourself talking to your former spouse far more you did in the months prior to your breakup. There could be face-to-face talks in the lawyer's office or at a mediation or divorce counseling center about the economics of the breakup, spousal and child support, or discussions in restaurants or your former home about the division of the records, paintings, furnishings, and video and stereo equipment; or there may be communication by phone or letter over issues dealing with your children's welfare and visitation arrangements. Indeed, couples who had nothing to say to each other before the breakup often have very much to say to each other in their separation, in words that are poisoned with self-righteousness, anger, bitterness, accusation, resentment, and distrust.

Turning Your Losses into Gains

It is in the "Detachment" stage of the mourning process that you fully realize that these losses in your life can no longer be denied, nor can you still believe they are only temporarily nonexistent, nor can you imagine that they can be regained with your former spouse. Now your life is a stark sink-or-swim situation; there is no going back to the past, so you must move forward, or drown in fear of the future. Because you have had little or no experience in living, thinking, and behaving as a single person, the future seems too scary and difficult to cope with. Consider for a moment whether you have ever been truly single in your life. If you are a woman, you probably went from your parents' home to your married home; and even if you went away to college before marriage, you were always told by others what to do, and you always had the resources of your family to pay your way.

If you are a man, the steps from your parents' home to the armed forces and/or college, then to your own married home meant that other persons likewise determined the major actions in your life. And even when you work, your

job is part of a "family" in which your boss is the stern father
or mother telling you what to do and how much money you
will receive.

It is because you have had so little experience with
taking personal responsibility for the shape of your own life
and the value system you have lived by that the future
seems fraught with fear and terrifying uncertainty. For the
buck has now stopped with you; no one else but you can now
determine what you want and will do with your life. Choices
must be made by you, not by someone else telling you what
you must choose to do. Of course that's scary, and the natural survival instinct causes you to become immobilized, to
detach yourself from everything, to feel empty, incapacitated, and helpless. After all, when you can't go back-
wards and you can't move forward, what else is there to do
but remain frozen and abdicate all forms of decision-making, even as to whether or not to eat a meal?

Of course, this decision to become apathetic and disengaged from life is no workable decision at all. Something
must give; either you become more apathetic and waste
away into possible suicide, psychosomatic illness, or
psychotic behavior, or you move beyond divorce into the
realm of becoming truly single by taking personal responsibility for your new life and the actions you take to better
your condition. Fortunately, all human beings have a capacity for self-renewal in the face of shattering life crises such
as divorce. Built into the human condition is the thrust for
psychological and physical health. Consequently, at the
very lowest ebb of your feelings about yourself and your
surrounding world, the seeds of your self-renewal are ger-
minating; there is spring in the winter of your discontent.
In fact, your sense of emptiness, of believing that nothing is
worthwhile, is the source of your self-renewal!

Where Your Self-Renewal Begins

Begin with the feeling of "nothingness" about life that
you may be experiencing. This "nothingness" is like a rain
that sweeps away the dust and smog so that a glistening new
day can occur. It enables you to start from scratch and

reevaluate and reexamine everything you once took for granted. It enables you to find out for the very first time that the faulty assumptions, self-defeating behavior, limited estimation of your abilities and capacities, and distorted value system needed to be rained away into nothingness before you could create a better day for yourself. "Nothingness" affords you a second chance in life, a chance to replace your old perspective with a new one that is far more realistic and appropriate in allowing you to attain your wants and needs at this time in your life. The poet William Blake said it all when he wrote, "The eye altering alters all." For the word "alter" means not only "to change or make different," but also "to adjust to a better fit."

Applied to your approach to your divorce crisis, this means that the way in which you view your divorce will determine the way in which you deal with the problems it generates. And the outcome of your divorce will lead to a more miserable or a happier life, depending on the way you deal with your divorce situations as they arise.

If you view your divorce as an unmitigated disaster representing the end of any hope for personal betterment, you will create a self-fulfilling prophecy and guarantee your future unhappiness. But if you view it as a very painful but necessary prelude to your self-renewal as a person well able to act skillfully in taking more effective charge of your life, then your life after divorce will improve rather than deteriorate.

I am not suggesting that life automatically gets better if you view your divorce as a series of challenges to triumph over rather than as a series of disasters that will destroy you. On the contrary, all that your "altering eye"—your changed vision of your situation—can do is to provide you with the *opportunity* to better your life; you yourself will have to do the actual work to make it better.

This doesn't mean putting on rose-colored glasses to convince yourself that your divorce problems do not exist. They *do* exist—they are very critical—and denial of that reality can only lead to misery rather than happiness. There are no easy answers or solutions in a divorce, and some problems may never have an answer or a solution. But there are sufficient opportunities for you to resolve many of the critical problems in your divorce, provided you know how to approach those problems constructively and are willing to invest considerable effort in resolving them.

Similarly, the mourning process is a series of developmental stages that frees you to take positive action to solve your divorce problems; it is not a substitute for your taking personal responsibility to move your life forward. The mourning process releases you *emotionally* from still thinking, feeling, and acting like a married person. This enables you to respond in skillful ways to the demands of single life. You yourself must do the actual work that you now are able to do.

The sense of "nothingness" combines with the mourning process to provide you with insight to see your divorce situation in a new way ("the altering eye"), which in turn enables you to discover new solutions to seemingly hopeless dilemmas. Here are examples of how you can turn the losses you experience in your divorce, as enumerated on the following pages, into gains in your single-person life by utilizing your "altering eye."

Economic Loss Viewed with Your Altering Eye

The loss is real, but alter your vision of your situation and regard your condition as one of being broke, not poor. This is not a play on words; it expresses a fundamental shift in your attitude toward the stressful economic circumstances you face. To be broke implies that your situation is temporary and that you have the intelligence and capabilities to bounce back and improve your economic condition. To be poor implies a permanent state of deprivation, a hopeless state of affairs in which you will be doomed for the rest of your life. Your thinking shifts from believing you are a victim to searching for ways to overcome your current dire circumstances.

To improve your situation, you need to let go of the blame you place on your ex-spouse for the scary economic situation you are in, because it doesn't help you improve your lot, but only allows you to wallow in it. Instead, focus on what *you* can do with *your own* capacities and abilities to emerge from the economic hole you are in. When you begin to see yourself as an activator of new economic possibilities rather than as a passive recipient of misfortune, positive things can happen.

For example, if you are a woman who has had little experience in the outside world of work, there are a host of career training programs available to you at a community college in your area. These are two-year colleges that are usually cost-free or available at low tuition, which people of *all* ages can and do attend. They require no past educational qualifications. The excuse you might give that you are "too old" to go back to school is simply nonsense; you will find people from eighteen to sixty years old and older in your classes, since the educational concept of lifelong learning is now built into our national educational system. Such community colleges will give you tests to find out what your occupational interests might be, and what work capabilities you might have. Counselors are available to help you interpret those tests so that you can realistically choose a career that fits you and that you can succeed in.

The choices are great, ranging over careers in the helping profession, medical health services, hotel and restaurant management, landscape gardening, and the wide variety of computer industry positions. And since more and more jobs have become open to women, such fields as automotive repair and video and television repair are available. Or you may set your sights on a career you always wanted, but thought impossible to attain while in your marriage, such as that of a lawyer or teacher. This involves longer-range planning, since these require more time than the one or two years of study available to you in a two-year community college. State colleges are available at modest cost for you to achieve that goal.

"But this choice doesn't help me in my present situation," you might object. True, but there are intermediate steps you can take to attain your goal of economic betterment. To help you cut costs, you might return to live in your parents' home again. Parents will usually welcome a chance to assist a divorced child, and inconvenience themselves temporarily in order to do so. Sometimes you have to take one step back now in order to take two steps forward in the future. Accept the fact that returning home temporarily is the one step back that's needed for you to return to school and embark on a new career.

Other alternatives are part-time or full-time jobs that may not appeal to you (such as secretarial work or waitressing), but which you can tolerate if you know that these jobs will not become a permanent way of life. Working at them during the day and going to school at night might be difficult, but it is a temporary sacrifice for a brighter future. And if the very worst is happening, you won't starve. The welfare system and food stamps are available for help. To apply for them at a time of temporary distress is neither a sign of your personal failure nor a stain on your character. You yourself have paid for the welfare system through your taxes, just as everyone else has. The system was designed to aid people in temporary distress, consequently it is there for you to utilize when you have no other alternative available.

You will not be exceptional in doing so, for many divorced women who were economically secure when married have utilized this service as an emergency measure. Again, in this situation, if you view yourself as temporarily broke rather than permanently poor, it can make all the difference in the world, for you can use this economic help to relieve some of the pressure while you go to school and/or seek other jobs.

Telling your friends, neighbors, and acquaintances that you are looking for employment is also a sensible thing to do. You might be pleasantly surprised that simply telling people you are available for work (how else will they know you are in the labor market?) can lead to eventual employment.

If your bills are overwhelming and you are being dunned by creditors for missed payments, you can contact the Consumer Credit Counseling Agency in your area. This is a free, nonprofit service that is national in scope and is funded by department stores and banks to help clients maintain their credit standing and use credit carefully. Without any charge to you, you can meet with a credit counselor who will help you budget your income more skillfully and also help you work out payment plans so that your credit will not be impaired and your creditors will get off your back.

You will notice that I have said nothing about a Prince Charming or a lottery jackpot solving your economic problems, for these are illusions rather than solutions. The beginning of your economic betterment commences when you shed these illusions.

If you are a divorced man, much of what I have said about divorced women relates to you. None of your economic problems will be solved if you continue to thrash about in the muddy waters of your righteous anger, ranting against "that bitch," the ex-wife who "ripped you off" in the divorce settlement, as the cause of your economic impoverishment. Let the anger go. Acknowledge that your children need those child-support payments and that your ex-wife made a major contribution to the family's economic welfare. Recognize that you probably have a much better immediate economic future than does your ex-wife, since you have a job at which you are skilled, and can use that as a basis for moving on to a better job. If you are still obsessed with righteous anger against your ex-spouse, realize that the energy you expend in bitterness and vituperation could more profitably be used in advancing your career.

You may very well be blinded to opportunities to improve your present career or move on to a better one because you are still fighting the battles of your past marriage in your mind and feelings and behavior. How, for instance, can you get a merit pay increase if you work ineffectively and act like a sad sack on the job because you are still feeling the presence of your ex-spouse as a Frankenstein monster while you are performing your assignments?

And if you continue to believe your ex-wife is victimizing you toward a pauper's grave, remember that you are making yourself into a helpless victim. When you feel you are a victim, you will act like one, guaranteeing a place for yourself on poverty row. Let those feelings go and begin with a clear slate, with "nothingness."

Now positive things can happen. You may see that now is the time to seek out a better job with another company, or you may become more aware of possibilities for a transfer to a higher position in the company you now work for. Or maybe you are fed up with working for others and are sick and tired of always being told what to do. You may be ready to strike out as an independent entrepreneur, responsible to no one but yourself, now that you are a single person. Opportunities abound for you to explore these options if you will release the creative energies inside yourself that are being throttled by the righteous anger you are directing against your ex-spouse.

If you are unemployed, there is an opportunity for you to work at the unexpected: nonsexist jobs are a two-way street. Consider the possibility of applying for work as a *male* nurse or *male* flight attendant. As one male secretary has said, "I could really urge men to look at this as a serious career. You can support yourself, it's very fulfilling, and it has nothing to do with being gay."

Let the anger go. Begin with "nothingness."

The Loss of Your Home Viewed with Your Altering Eye

It may seem like bad dream from which you will never awaken, living in strange, uncomfortable quarters immediately after your breakup. This usually happens to the divorced man who leaves the house, apartment, or condominium he knew so well for so many years as a married man, only to find himself displaced into a tiny and gloomy rented place in another part of town where he has no roots. Alone now in a tiny apartment (exaggeratedly described by the landlord as "spacious two rooms") with walls so thin that you might think you were living with the people next door, you may feel as if the end of the world has arrived. . . .

I can still recall this feeling vividly, eighteen years after my own divorce. I didn't know where to start, but Gerard, a kind, unmarried friend, let me stay in his apartment during that first week of my separation. He then spread out the section of the morning paper that listed apartments for rent, and my search for a new place began. I wound up on the other side of town from where I had lived for over a decade in a spacious house in a quiet neighborhood.

My new residence was laughably called a two-room furnished apartment. Since I am six feet tall, my own presence seemed to take up the space of an entire room. The place was furnished in apple-crate shabby: a table that had seen its best days ten years ago; three chairs that groaned in pain when sat upon; a half-iced refrigerator that occasionally worked; a stove with two of the four burners unusable; and a closet spacious enough to harbor eighteen inches worth of clothes.

The neighborhood came equipped with police sirens and fire alarms that I could count on to appear as midnight friends who would outdo themselves on Friday and Saturday nights. But I was broke and the place was cheap. The loss of my own warm house overwhelmed me in those early weeks of my divorce.

However, divorce is full of surprises, many of them positive. The very depth of my despair turned out to be the beginning of new hope in my life. My new living quarters made me focus on what was really important in my life. Even if it were possible to return, was my old house important enough to offset a relationship that showed no hope of improvement? Could I settle for a life of mutual unhappiness in exchange for comfortable living quarters?

I then asked myself what "house" I had actually lost. It wasn't the house made of wood, brick, plaster, cement, and stone. What I had lost was the house *inside* myself, which made me believe that my identity and self-image were defined by the size of my external house and its furnishings.

And my shabby two-room apartment was an expression of the shabbiness of my illusions that the "good" life consisted solely of an accumulation of my furnishings in large living quarters that defined my status in society. Once I realized that I had the personal power to rebuild the house *inside* myself on a firmer foundation than the flimsy one my life had previously been based on, my two-room apartment began to represent a promise of a better life rather than a validation of a squalid present existence.

Shift your focus with your altering eye from the loss of your married house that you no longer live in to the gain that you can accomplish by creating a new single-person house within yourself, a house more richly furnished and spacious than the one you left behind. You can start by paying attention to your own physical and nutritional needs. The deadly sins of fear, destructive guilt, and self-flagellation are hard at work in the early stages of divorce, and often affect your physical condition.

You can refurbish your body by taking personal responsibility to do so. A regimen of daily jogging or a walking program every morning is a good beginning, and it costs you nothing but your own commitment to put it into action. Attention should be paid to your own nutritional needs. You don't need to be a scientist to know that a balanced diet that allows for an adequate supply of all the vitamins and minerals you need is a requisite for good health and good thinking.

If you don't act on that knowledge, don't be surprised that your attitude toward life continues to remain bleak and that your intellect is blocked from seeing alternatives that can help you extricate yourself from your divorce dilemmas.

In these modern times, many divorced women, rather than their husbands, are the ones who leave their old married homes. Or they may be forced to sell their houses and move to smaller quarters shortly after their divorce. They frequently tell me they have discovered that "less is more." In a recent counseling session, Judy, a thirty-seven-year-old divorcee, told me, "You know, Mel, I never would have believed it. Oh, how I cried when I had to sell my old house and move into my small apartment. But I've been freer in my new place than I ever was in the large house I left. I can decorate it the way I want to; I can invite the people I want to visit with me; I can think, write, and meditate when I want to, and not be accountable to a bitter man who is always judging me and putting me down. And I now know I'll get a larger place eventually, because I'm taking courses to upgrade my computer skills so I can get a better job."

Judy is refurbishing her inner house; perhaps it's time for you to begin on *your* house.

Social Loss Viewed with Your Altering Eye

It seems as if many of the friends you had when you were married have disappeared. Some may have "taken sides" with your ex-spouse and may be avoiding you because of that. Others may have eliminated you and your ex-spouse from their circle, so that the both of you have now become nonpersons when it comes to socializing with them. That part of town you lived in, which you knew like the back of your hand, is a memory rather than an everyday reality now that you are relocated. *Divorce* feels like just another word for *loneliness*.

Yet that very emptiness, that nothingness you might be experiencing, can become the beginning of a whole new world of friends as well as the first step toward creating new community connections for yourself. When you are "all alone by the telephone," stop feeling sorry for yourself and take a closer look at the nature of your relationships with the people you once regarded as friends and who now seem to have disappeared. This is your time for reevaluating your connections with them. Ask yourself how many of them were habitual acquaintances rather than true friends, persons you knew because they lived in the same neighborhood and had life-styles similar to your own, based on being married and having children.

These are the people you could exchange baby-sitting time with, go shopping with, invite to parties where other married couples were always present. They may go to the same church you went to, be fans of the same football or baseball team. And talking with them was on the level of "Did you see that TV movie last night and wasn't it good?" or "Why don't we go to that dress sale tomorrow?" or "Wasn't that Monday-night football game great?"

These were people with whom you never shared your innermost thoughts, or felt that they cared deeply for you. Losing them is really the loss of an old habit rather than the loss of true friendship. If these people have "taken sides" with your ex-spouse, it usually is because your ex-spouse has remained in the same neighborhood while you have relocated to another part of town, and your children and theirs are still seeing each other on a daily basis.

And even when they take the side of your ex-spouse, they may no longer invite him or her to their parties as frequently as they once did, if at all. That's because the guests at those parties were married couples, and consequently a divorced person is no longer part of that shared experience.

There are other still-married couples whom you care more deeply about, and who may no longer be in touch with you after your divorce. But their reason for not seeing you after your divorce often has nothing to do with rejection. They are *not* rejecting you; you may have frightened them by your divorce, since that may cause them to think about *their* marriage difficulties.

Quite often I hear divorced men and women tell me that their married friends have said to them, "We thought you had the best marriage of all of us!" If that is their state of mind, you can very well understand that their next thought is that they too might be on the brink of a divorce. To block this scary thought out of their minds, they then eliminate you from their social life. Consequently, when they "reject" you, it is *their* problem, not yours.

In other situations, it may very well be that there were married couples you knew prior to your divorce who were not really your friends as a couple. You may have liked either the husband or the wife, and tolerated the one because you had a friendship with the other. After your breakup, such a couple may have equally divided allegiances toward you or your ex-spouse. Such a couple may avoid seeing you simply because of that fact. Again, it is *their* problem, not yours.

When you look at your past married relationships in these ways, light shines through the darkness of your loneliness. You now possess the knowledge that can enable you to make positive things happen:

- You can acknowledge that you have experienced no real loss when your habitual acquaintances disengage themselves from you.
- You can help your true friends resolve their problem as to how to relate to you by reaching out to them and setting them at their ease. If they haven't called you, you can call them without any fear of rejection. Explain to them that you understand their confusion and tell them your honest feelings about your divorce. Suggest a visit for lunch to help them catch up on what has happened to you and to them during the time you haven't seen each other. You could be

pleasantly surprised by their reaction to your call.

- In situations in which you were really friendly with only the husband or wife of a married couple, call that one party up at his or her workplace, and suggest a meeting of the two of you apart from his or her spouse. You can continue to maintain your friendship on a one-to-one basis, rather than on the old couple basis. This has happened to me. Some of my friends from my first marriage days who are still married to spouses I didn't particularly like, and vice versa, are still dear friends. I see them apart from their spouses and we continue to have warm feelings toward each other.

- As for those married couples whom you liked but who no longer see you because you represent a threat to their shaky marriages, there is nothing you can do except to realize that it's their problem, and you cannot solve it for them. There is a certain sadness that goes with realizing this fact, but it is time for you to let go of your attachment to them so that you can focus your energies on making new friends. There may come a time in the future when they will reconnect with you, once they resolve their own marital dilemmas. While you can't put your life on hold until that day comes, you can derive some emotional sustenance from that possibility.

- Allow time to run its course and change the nature of your non-relationship with some of the friends you had when you were married. Your real friends will eventually make contact with you if you make yourself available to them. It may not happen today or tomorrow, but it will happen. As for the others, it's best to know, even though it is painful to acknowledge, that those relationships were really based on sand rather than rock.

Even under the best of circumstances, your relationship with your still-married friends will never be the same

as it was when you too were married. Some may envy your
freedom as a divorced person and your ability to involve
yourself in new sexual relationships while they are
"trapped" in their marriages; others will still be involved in
married activities and concerns. You may be concerned
with dating, battles with your ex-spouse, visits with lawyers,
new housing quarters, a new career, making new friends—
concerns that are foreign to your married friends. Where
once you had much in common with them, now you find
that you have rather little.

What this tells you is that as a divorced person you must
reach out and make new friends whose interests and concerns reflect the *present* state of your life rather than your
past life, if you are to assuage the loneliness that engulfs you.
And the possibilities of such friendships are enormous.

The divorced world encompasses millions of men and
women; there are 50 million single adults in our society,
most of them previously married, as you were. The men and
women in this divorced world are people like yourself,
eager for new friendships and searching for a new sense of
belonging. Where can you find them? They are right before
your eyes, once you begin to look through your new single
person's spectacles rather than the married spectacles you
once wore.

Your favorite newspaper will probably have a listing of
events designed for singles: notices of lectures announced
by churches and social organizations on how to cope with
single-life challenges; divorce-adjustment groups for the recently single; single dances; rap groups for children of divorce; singles clubs (theater groups, gourmet groups, music
groups, literary discussion groups); special vacations for singles, designed by organizations like Club Med; Parents
Without Partners groups, Big Brother and Big Sister groups,
designed to fill the gap of an absent parent; community
college courses in which you can indulge in your favorite
hobby or spark the beginnings of a new career.

All of these events afford you opportunities to make
new friends and explore new parts of yourself. They are
there for the taking when you are ready to take them, which
is when the mourning process has pretty well run its course.
Your friends and colleagues at work can give you sugges-

tions as to what to do and where to go, since many of them have already passed through the stages of divorce you are now experiencing. You will reach out to them only when you begin to see yourself no longer as a married person, but rather as a person who must create new connections for yourself.

If you yearn for community in your life, you can reconnect with people on a more compassionate and loving basis than you did before. I know of many divorced men and women who, while experiencing the agony and pain of their own divorce, have reached out to people in greater need than themselves. You will find many of those divorced persons volunteering their services on Thanksgiving or Christmas Day at the Salvation Army or St. Anthony's Dining Room or a nursing home, to bring some cheer to others in a far more desperate state than their own, and feeling much the better for it.

If living alone is too painful, consider the possibility of living in a "shared housing" unit. Shared housing is an idea that has caught fire nationally among divorced men and women. With rents for individual apartments skyrocketing, shared housing offers you an opportunity to lower your rental costs and involve yourself in a new kind of self-help community life.

Usually, shared housing entails renting a room in a large house that has a common living room and kitchen. Cleaning chores are allocated amongst the renters, who are all divorced people intent on establishing a new life for themselves. The sense of community can be great indeed. Shared housing is not for everyone, but it is an option you might seriously consider. It may well be a viable temporary solution until you can find a permanent individual residence.

With social loss comes self-renewal as you learn to become a single person. In the transition to the point of becoming comfortable with singleness, loneliness is perhaps the major problem that most recently divorced persons have to contend with.

Should you find yourself in this state, when you want to run away from yourself rather than face another evening in the threatening silence of the place in which you are now living, take a new look at what your loneliness is telling you.

You can begin to find a positive resolution to the problem of loneliness when you differentiate between loneliness and solitude. The *American Heritage Dictionary* defines *lonely* as "dejected by the awareness of being alone." On the other hand "solitude" is simply "the state of being alone" and has nothing to do whatsoever with feeling dejected. Sitting alone in your apartment may involve far less dejection than sitting together with your spouse when you were married and feeling miserable and absolutely isolated because of the terrible stresses in your marriage.

Now that you are living alone, you need not "live lonely." You can transform that time you spend with yourself into a time of constructive solitude: you can meditate, keep a journal of your daily experiences, reach out to friends by calling them, write letters, study toward advancing your career, indulge in new hobbies, reevaluate your goals and priorities, invite new friends over for dinner. Please note that you can make all of these things happen at little or no economic cost to yourself. Your motivation to stop wallowing in self-pity is your primary expense.

In a very real sense, living alone presents you with the possibility of knowing yourself at far deeper levels than you ever did before. Constructive solitude enables you to make friends with yourself, while loneliness perpetuates the belief that you are your own worst enemy. The difference between solitude and loneliness is the difference between viewing yourself as a person who has the ability to prevail over adversity and viewing yourself as a victim of a terrible fate over which you have no control.

The Loss of Daily Contact with Your Children Viewed with Your Altering Eye

If you are a noncustodial parent, your most poignant loss may very well be the absence of your children from your daily life. This often comes as a shock of self-discovery to the divorced husband who becomes a "visitor" to his children since his ex-wife has sole custody. When they were married, such men never realized how important and enriching was the daily presence of their children in their lives. At that time the children were often regarded as oppressive economic obligations, pandemonium-creators when one yearned for peace and quiet, a bottomless pit of needs and demands, and a reflection on oneself (an "A" report card meant that *you* were the achiever). Delight and satisfaction in your children as persons in their own right was foreign to your experience.

These realizations come to mind as you sit in your isolated apartment and flood your soul with regrets, destructive guilt, and self-hatred. How could you have been so stupid and ignorant? Even when you were home every night, were you really there for your children? You spent so little quality time with them while you were married, while you were distracted at home worrying about your job, your boss, the bills that had to be paid, and the growing hurts in your marriage. So self-centered were you that you squandered the time available for you to be present with your children. And now even that is gone. . . .

Yes, that way of life is all lost, but something different and even better can take its place. Consider the possibility that you have been given a gift when you are sitting in isolation and the pain of separation from your children overwhelms you. For that very pain can jolt you into a realization that your relationship with your children can now be improved upon rather than destroyed. As a divorced parent, you now have a second chance to relate to your children on a *human* basis, to engage them in activities and talk that will elicit from you, and from them, closer loving feelings than you ever expressed at the time you were married. By doing so, you validate the major importance of your children in your life.

The first step you must take to arrive at this new relationship with your children is to revise your conception of what a good parent is or should be. There may be many cobwebs in your mind that need to be cleared away: the cobweb that traps you into the belief that a "good" parent can only be a parent in a home where the mother and father live together; that your physical presence every day in your children's lives designates you as a "good" parent; that should you live in a city or state many miles away from your children, you are deserting them and therefore are a bad parent. None of these cobwebs have any basis in reality.

In fact, you now can be a better parent than you were

before by realizing that "less can be more," because even though you spend less time with your children, that time can be more enriching and gratifying than the far larger amount of time you spent with them in your marriage.

All your children ever wanted from you was your authentic self, the self that loves and cares for them and voices and demonstrates that love and caring in your behavior toward them. Children are quick to forgive and forget past hurts when you remedy those hurts by becoming consistent, open, and honest with them. Consequently, there is no need to flagellate yourself for the imagined or real pain you inflicted on your children in the past; it is how you relate to them now and in the future that counts most. There is no denying that the loss of your everyday contact with your children is very real and perhaps permanent. The dull ache of that loss may remain within you to a degree for years to come, but the present pain and anguish of that separation will be eliminated when you reconnect with your children as the compassionate parent you are now, rather than as the disengaged parent you were in the past.

5

The Universality of the Divorce Experience: Breaking Up in the Lives of the Rich and Famous

That the rich and famous are endless sources of fascination and admiration for enormous numbers of Americans in today's time is confirmed by the phenomenal success of *People* magazine and its many TV program clones: Rich is "better"; famous is "better"; happiness is being wealthy; happiness is being famous. That's what the college of media knowledge teaches us.

As a divorce counselor, I was curious to find out whether or not these teachings were true where divorce was concerned. Are the rich and famous able to resolve their divorce problems in an easier, less painful way than the rest of us because they can buy their way out of them?

I sought my answer by spending some time in Los Angeles interviewing a representative sample of divorced men and women who were typical of the kind that *People* magazine and TV regularly feature. I was not interested in media hype (the presentation of phony, happy images that magazines, newspapers, and television flood us with), but rather in their honest sharing of their divorce experiences so that readers of this book could be helped by their personal stories of what they have undergone. I am happy to report that I received precisely that from the celebrities I interviewed, and I am grateful that they have allowed me to share their unvarnished divorce experiences with you, as told below.

I asked them to focus on the particular aspects of their

divorces that affected them most significantly. Their remarks were candid and illuminating, as evidenced below.

Blossoming in Mid-Life After Divorce: Phyllis Diller's Story

Many men and women who are divorced in their later years despair in the mistaken belief that the best years of their lives are now over and that their future will become nothing more than an essay in hopelessness.

When I hear words to this effect from one of my divorcing clients, I like to relate to them the story of Phyllis Diller, whom I recently had the pleasure of interviewing.

Phyllis is a remarkable woman, a successful comedienne, actress, and writer who proclaims that she is in her seventies and feels even more alive to the challenge of life today than she did in her youth. She was born on July 17, 1917, in Lima, Ohio, and was thirty-seven when she created a comedy nightclub act that made her famous. Before that time, she was the working mother of five children, earning her living as a radio copywriter. She married for the first time at twenty-two and divorced her first husband fifteen years later. Then, at the age of forty-eight, she married again in 1965 and divorced her second husband ten years afterward.

"A good divorce is better than a bad marriage," she told me. She believes her painful divorces were the stepping-stones she needed to renew her life and grow as an individual.

"I grew up in Lima, Ohio, before coming to California," she said. "In that city, divorce was something you whispered about. My father waited until I was eight years old before he told me he himself had had a divorce before he married my mother. The way he told me, it sounded as if he had killed a judge in cold blood!

"I grew up believing the only thing that mattered in life for a woman was to be a good wife and mother. It was like I married marriage my first time around. I was twenty-two then, and didn't want to be an old maid. But within six weeks of my marriage I felt trapped and that we were mismatched. I even called my mother and begged her to bring me home. But my mother talked me out of it. She said, 'Hang on.' Well, I hung on because I had no support from anyone to do otherwise then. I remember going to my minister and telling him of my misery in my marriage. The minister asked me, 'Is he a drunk? Is he kind to the children? Does he beat you?' I said no, he's not an alcoholic, he's kind to the children, and he doesn't beat me. So the minister told me I didn't have any real problems. But I did.

"In my first marriage, I was *in* it but not *with* it. I became the working housewife, expected to take care of everything, the house, the money, the children, and my husband. Why did I stay in that marriage fifteen years? Because I had this terrible fear of making it alone. I was petrified at the idea that I could support myself and my children and live alone without a husband. Yet that was what I was really doing for so many years, because my husband was like a piece of furniture around the house. But a woman is nothing without a husband, even if he isn't really a partner to you, is what I thought.

"During all the years of my first marriage, my major satisfactions came from my children, plus my writing and my music. I suppose I made lemonade out of a lemon when one night I tossed out an ad lib about my husband, calling him 'Fang' in my act when I started to work as a comic. That got a lot of laughs from the audience. It caught on so well I expanded on my cracks about 'Fang' so they became an expected part of the act. My husband wasn't angry or put out by my 'Fang' remarks. In fact, he thought it was great. It was his main claim to fame.

"Despite my very low self-esteem in my marriage, I was forced to go to work and took my first job with a newspaper when I was thirty-two, and then worked as an advertising copywriter for a department store and a California radio station before I became a comic. I always had these abilities within me, so I suppose when I stifled them during most of the time in my first marriage, that was one of the reasons for my desperate unhappiness. I knew I was ready to really end my marriage back in 1953, when I was thirty-six, when a book changed me from a petrified child to a tiger.

"It was called *The Magic of Believing*. I read it continually for two years and became fearless. The secret in the book was to believe in yourself.

"I filed for divorce when I was thirty-eight. It was a no-contest divorce, and although there were economic differences, I tried to make it as uncomplicated as possible. I wanted a clean break without the long-lasting bitterness I see in so many divorces. In fact, today my ex-husband and all my children and myself live near each other in the same southern California city. The children see their father regularly, with the exception of my youngest son, who is still resentful about his father. Children are smart, they always knew I wasn't happy in my marriage.

"What actually triggered my divorce, in addition to my beginning to believe in myself and no longer being petrified at the idea of divorce, was my meeting the man who was to become my second husband. He looked as if he was all the things my first husband wasn't. He was the world's greatest lover, he was so handsome, and he was an actor and singer of talent. He was nice to the kids. But very soon, things went downhill. It was so bad that I filed for divorce during my first year of marriage, but then dropped it. I stayed with him ten years because of the companionship. But I wound up doing exactly what I had been doing in my first marriage.

"In 1975, I filed for divorce and have been single ever since. Does that mean I'm soured on marriage? Not on your life. I believe there is somebody out there for me."

Discovering Your Personal Identity Through Divorce: Lynn Landon's Story

In the early stages of a divorce, many clients who come to me for counseling cry out that they feel as if they have lost their personal identities. This is particularly true of women, who in the past have been programmed to invest their entire sense of self in their marriages. "Before, I was a married person; now I'm nothing," is the feeling that grips them. However, their very feeling that they are "nothing," that they are starting from scratch, can provide the basis for them to discover their personal identity for the very first time in their lives.

Lynn Landon is an outstanding case in point. She was married to TV star Michael Landon for nineteen years. "I met Michael at Paramount Studios," she told me. "I was working as an extra and somehow got on the set of 'Bonanza' for one day. Michael had been doing the show for about a year. We dated off and on for almost two years. At that time, it was love at first sight, which is something I don't believe in anymore. But there was a chemistry between us. I loved his warmth, humor, and intelligence. Michael and I started having children about a year after we were married. We had four children together. I didn't have any clues until the last couple of years before our marriage ended that our marriage was deteriorating. We were growing apart. At first you feel things are not the same, you know it by looking around. You say, 'Well, is there someone else?' I raised the issue with Michael and there was someone else and eventually I found out. I think all of a sudden he was reaching a certain age with all the responsibility, with all the work pressures, and I think all of a sudden he felt he needed something else.

"I know I misplaced myself somewhere in that marriage. I was being the kind of wife he wanted at that time. But it was what I wanted at that time also. In other words, he was number one, then the children, then our home and our social life.

"Our marriage ended when I found out there was someone else in the picture, and I knew the marriage was not going to work any longer. By then you start having arguments, yelling and screaming, and eventually one evening he left and from that time on that was it.

"When we separated, I felt I didn't want to live. I think you go through the part where you're numb, you can't think, you can't move, you're paralyzed. After numbness I think there are definite stages you go through—you go through a depression and then comes anger. I think anger is a very important feeling because at least you feel alive again. But you must get rid of anger in order to go on with your life. But during that time I started saying not too complimentary things about their father in front of the children.

And that is what I found to be so detrimental. I just realized I was hurting my children by doing that. They loved us both and they still do and the last thing I wanted to do was to hurt my children. I started to get well when I began to acknowledge that I had had a great marriage for a lot of years but now I had to go on by myself."

When you're divorcing a famous TV personality, your divorce is front-page news that can be a very painful experience. Lynn felt anguished when her divorce became a public event: "It was something very difficult to turn off. Turn the TV set on, and there it is in front of you. Pick up the paper, and there it is. If you happen to miss it, you can almost count on somebody calling you to tell you it's in the newspaper. So when you're trying to pick up the pieces and go on with your life, you have to face that all the time. It's like you're dragged back into the past all the time."

For the duration of her marriage, Lynn saw her identity as that of Michael Landon's wife. She told me, "I laugh now because I think for nineteen years my name was Michael. Now the real bitterness and anger is gone. I finally started growing and feeling better about myself. I also started going back to church, that was a big help. Christian church. I hadn't had church for so many years, since I was with my parents. I started looking around at who was happy and who had it together and I really couldn't find anyone. My manicurist, a very dear friend of mine, always seemed to have an answer for everything. I feel that my being a Christian is the basis for my life, the foundation, and I think God and Jesus can teach us how to live our life. I certainly don't have all the answers, but I do read the Bible every day. I've gotten a very peaceful feeling from it, and I was able to release all of the anger that I had, and my children are going to church and it's helped them tremendously. It must be a decision of yours not to be angry anymore.

"I'm still finding out who Lynn is. I haven't got that all together, but I'm enjoying a lot of things. I'm enjoying my children more. I'm enjoying my home and I'm enjoying more traveling and I'm getting more interested in my own investments. I've opened my own clothing store on Melrose Avenue. It's called Trio, and we're designing some of the clothes, and I'm enjoying that.

"I am very active in a divorce group I helped form five years ago. It's called LADIES, which stands for Life After Divorce Is Eventually Sane. It's designed to help women in all walks of life improve their lives after divorce. It all began when I was having lunch with Leslie Curtis, Tony Curtis's ex-wife, and I realized we shared a lot in common. Then I invited Patti MacLeod and Leslie and a couple of other women out to dinner and then I went on Marilyn Funt's TV show and said I'm really interested in women who had been married to celebrities or high-profile people. So then Marilyn Funt and Patti and Jackie Joseph called these people and we had the first meeting of the group which eventually became LADIES at my house. I think we were all looking for a way that we could step outside of our group and maybe help other women. So we all had this strong urge and it's still there. We're working now with Displaced Homemakers, the only government-funded group in the U.S. to help women get back on their feet, and we also are bringing this message to colleges around the country.

"I'm still learning who I am as a separate person. I found out I am capable in certain areas like running my own life and capable as a mother, and even without a mate, I'm capable in social areas. It's just that each day I learn one more new thing and apply it and it's making me feel better about myself. Right after my divorce, I did not want to admit to my age. I was capable of passing for a younger woman and that's exactly what I did. On the first trip I took with my daughters, I didn't allow them to call me 'Mother.' They went along with it and now I look back on it and see how ludicrous it was, but at the time that's how I felt because of this age thing. And now I'm fifty-four and I'm the best fifty-four I can be. But for a long time that was a big hangup for me.

"Fifty-four is only a number. I feel great. I'm having fun, what does the number have to do with it? If somebody else is hung up on the number, that's their problem, not mine. I think the more women aren't afraid of numbers, the better all of us are going to be. We've been told men get better as they get older, but for women it's the end of the world. I think women get better, too. I feel I have more to offer now than I did when I was twenty-five."

The Hurt of Divorce:
Marty Ingels's Story

I can always spark a lively discussion among the men and women in my divorce counseling groups by asking them, "Who bleeds the most in a divorce, men or women?" The women usually say they suffer the most while men become instant happy bachelors the day the divorce decree arrives. The men look hurt and vulnerable when they hear these remarks, for they know they are not true to their own personal experiences. Some of them are afraid of seeming to be wimpish or weak if they reveal that they have experienced heartfelt anguish over their divorces, and remain silent. Others, however, are vocal in their disagreement with the women's perception of the male divorce experience.

I interviewed the Hollywood celebrity Marty Ingels, who wanted to share his divorce experience with the men and women who will be reading this book. He did so in the hope of correcting the popular misconception that men experience divorce without pain and emotional disarray.

Marty Ingels, a well-known comedian who starred in the ABC comedy series of the 1960s, "I'm Dickens, He's Fenster," is now a highly successful businessman, president of a celebrity brokerage that packages major movie-star promotion projects. He is married to the Academy Award-winning actress Shirley Jones. But Marty Ingels's beginnings were not at all so wonderful. His first marriage ended when his wife walked out on him after nine and one-half years—and the kinetic funnyman still talks freely about the devastating crash that followed.

"I was twenty-seven when we were married. Jean was twenty-two. We clung together like two shipwrecked souls, more sure of the terror we had for what was out there than of our commitment to each other. So the marriage floated, strong and buoyant, as long as we both 'needed' it to hang on to. And Jean stopped needing first. She was no longer complete being merely the wife of comedian Marty Ingels, sitting in Johnny's and Mike's and Merv's audience. She was stronger now and ready to leave. She knew it. And gradually, I did too.

"And that's when the 'seizures' started, slowly at first—rashes, nausea, shortness of breath. Then worse—headaches, chest pain, dizziness, and panic so acute it was hard to carry on. And little by little I carried on less and less, dreading normal encounters, the simplest responsibilities, even the coveted audience exposures I had thrived on for so long. Finally, during an appearance on "The Tonight Show," sitting on the couch and before the whole damn world, it all came to a cataclysmic head and I fell totally apart. Grinding out one of my whacky stories, I suddenly felt—in the middle of a sentence—an uncontrollable trembling in my toes and my right leg. I tried to ignore it, but slowly it began traveling up to my knee and my thigh and the whole right side of my body, which was beginning to lose its feeling. At first I thought it would go away. I crossed my legs and sat on my tingling fingers—and of course, the audience merely giggled. Before long, 'pieces of the vision puzzle' started falling away, my hearing began to fade in and out, and all I could think of was getting off that stage before I lost consciousness. (If indeed I was gonna die, I didn't wanna do it on national television.)

"Always the comic, I mustered the strength to stand up and announce that I would be the first guest ever to use Johnny Carson's private bathroom, and off to the rear I staggered, the audience still laughing. I managed to make it to the curtain, which I held tightly on to, and swung myself around to the back stage, into the arms of the TV crew. Two of them carried me to my dressing room, then to the car and up the elevator to my apartment, laying me on a woolen blanket which was on the living room floor in front of the TV (a refuge I had used for as far back as I remember).

"Astonishingly, I lay on that floor, on that very spot in that small apartment building, for nine months, three weeks, and four days, crawling to the kitchen, crawling to the bathroom, and then back to my little fetal nest on the floor. Were it not for a young girl in the building (herself a shut-in for her kidney condition and the long and tedious home dialysis treatments) who brought me a home-cooked dinner every night for all those months, I would have expired on that dismal living room floor.

"There are lots of theories about what hit me so hard and so completely. 'Separation anxiety,' some of them called it. 'An emotional flashback to another time in your early life when you felt abandoned by someone you needed, now magnified a hundred times by your imagination and the unthinkable dread of it happening again.' For me, it just felt like something in my head had ordered all my body parts to quit working.

"And that's the way it was—a nine-month nightmare of agonizing sunups and sundowns, a premature death, if you will, triggered by the loss of someone I had foolishly viewed as an extension of myself, a virtual appendage. And I suppose there's a lesson there. To be sure, your *need* for someone must never become so great that you surrender to that person your security and your self-respect, and, in fact, your very *reason* for living.

"And that's my 'divorce story.' Fortunately, I got up one damp September morning as if it were marked in red on my calendar and started piecing it all back together, little by painful little—standing, walking, washing, shaving, even driving; not unlike the survivor of stroke, relearning his basic life functions one by one, the way a four-year-old child does.

"Now, of course, it has all turned around for me. Whatever force or spirit set me down to that bleak and lonely prison for so long has also chosen to see me through a full recovery to success, love, and, for it all, wisdom. And I carry with me always the bittersweet truth I learned so painfully: However strong and admirable your bonds of love and marriage and unceasing commitment, you must retain for yourself somewhere silently inside the most critical, most difficult, most valuable asset of all—the ability to let it all go if you must. If you can beat that one, you've got it all."

Overcoming the Legacy of a Single-Parent Childhood: Jackie Joseph's Story

Approximately half of all children, at some time before they turn eighteen, can expect to live in a single-parent household. Divorce or a parent's death will primarily account for that fact. In Jackie Joseph's case, the death of her father three months before she was born created that situation.

Jackie is a vivacious fifty-three-year-old woman. She is an actress, the star of the original version of the well-known film *The Little Shop of Horrors*, and is the ex-wife of Ken Berry, who was the star of "Mayberry RFD" and "F Troop," now considered TV cult classics.

"I never knew my father, he died three months before I was born," she said in our interview. "My mother also never knew her father. Her parents died when she was three years old, and she grew up in an orphanage in Chicago. She married my father at seventeen, and was nineteen years old when he died. She remarried when I was fifteen, but that only lasted a year, and she died in her fifties. She had to make it on her own, and had to be tough as nails in order to survive.

"Mom was a real survivor, and she was the only family I ever had. Because of that fact, I had absolutely no idea what a father or a husband was really like while I was growing up. My home life consisted of two women, Mom and me. Mom's one-year husband had been a shadowy negative figure in my life, so men were blank pages while I was growing up.

"So where did I get my ideas about what fathers and husbands were like? From the radio and the movies, that's where. There was no TV when I was a kid, so the radio was my educator. There were radio serials like "One Man's Family," which implanted in my mind that all fathers and husbands were kind, stable people who were always right. And the movies (that was in the late thirties or forties) showed women as perfect homemakers and loving mothers. So I grew up with the notion that 'father knows best' and that a married woman exists to make the man in her life happy by keeping a spick-and-span house, by not making waves, and by having lots of lovely babies whom I would sacrifice my life for.

"You could say the way in which I grew up trained me to be a people-pleaser rather than a person in my own right. I suppose that's one of the reasons I became an actress. I loved to act because acting was the place where you got approval for making people happy. And just like in the movies, my marriage to Ken Berry began as a backstage romance. We met when we were both performing in *The Billy Barnes Review of 1958*, which was a famous show in its time. He was and is a marvelous actor, singer, and dancer. He appealed to me because he was so kind and came from a loving family, something I never had. He grew up in Moline, Illinois, with an older sister. His parents never divorced, and his mother is still a good friend of mine.

"Ken and I were the same age, and we married in 1960 after being engaged a year and a half. We were twenty-six at the time. Of course, we didn't live together before we were married, since we were dating in 1958 and 1959, when such a thing was definitely a no-no. We wanted children and adopted a boy and a girl, who are now twenty-three and twenty-two, after our only natural child had died six days after birth.

"In our marriage, which lasted fourteen years prior to the time we separated, I was determined to be the greatest wife and mother, based on my imaginary knowledge of what they were supposed to be like. So I never made any waves with Ken. I never insisted on, or demanded, anything from him. I always tried to protect Ken, keeping the children quiet and out of his way. You know, 'Don't disturb Daddy.' Looking back, I now see I tended to single-parent my children because I came from a single-parent home. I regret doing that now, for all our sakes.

"Even though we were married for fourteen years, I don't think I ever truly got to know Ken. I still think of him as a very decent person, but he was such a private person. It was always difficult, if not impossible, for him to divulge his feelings. On the other hand, I always wanted to let everything hang out. But I learned early in our marriage that this made him uncomfortable. So I made sure never to discuss with him personal feelings that might be awkward. In all the time we were married, we never learned how to communicate openly and directly with each other. We were like two different trains going on two different tracks.

"Since I was a people-pleaser, I always assumed, when anything went wrong in our marriage, that it was my fault. I would always try to guess what Ken was thinking or feeling, but never checked it out with him. I made a million guesses, always blaming myself if he seemed sad or unsatisfied. I probably guessed wrong most of the time.

"When Ken left and we faced a divorce, it was like he was taking my self-image with him. I gave it to him—he didn't ask for it! I felt absolutely worthless and was in therapy for three months. The jolt of my divorce made me realize I had been quite a wimp, a pale, uninteresting woman in my marriage. My identity had been wrapped up with only being a wife and mother who happened to work once in a while. Painful as it has been, I've begun to rebuild my self-image since my divorce on a healthier, more realistic foundation. I now believe I don't have to marry again just for the sake of obtaining an identity for myself. There's been no hatred between Ken and me since the divorce. We've maintained friendly relations and never fought over our divorce settlement. I've seen too many divorces where hatred destroys an entire family. I'm building a future for myself by accepting myself as I am, not trying to please everybody at the expense of my own self. I now see that a good marriage is a two-way street in the nurturing department. In my marriage, I never felt I deserved to be nurtured by my husband; now I think that would be very nice.

"I'm beginning to see men more realistically, neither as saviors nor as monsters, but as people who would make nice companions. I enjoy going out with men and women now; I was a hermit, nursing my wounds, at the time of my divorce. In fact, I believe there might be some men out there who might be admiring me. That's a great step for me.

"Out of my own pain, I've come to see that there are millions of other divorced women needing economic and emotional assistance. So I've become very active in helping divorced women. I serve as publicity director for LADIES, which I helped found five years ago. This organization works to help divorced women become self-supporting through participating with the Displaced Homemakers Network. I'm very proud of the award I received recently from the Los Angeles Division of the National Council for Jewish Women for helping divorced women, and I'm a program director for the State of California's Department of Education, Vocational Education Division. The LADIES are media links between the 'new bereft' and the service-providers that are available.

"I'm learning to like being a person in my own right. That doesn't rule out my being married again. But should I ever marry again, it will be a marriage of two equals rather than one in which I allow myself to be unimportant, and invite being treated as the 'insignificant other.'"

Adult Children of Alcoholics and Divorce: Gary Crosby's Story

The interpersonal relationship problems experienced by adult children of alcoholics have been the focus of national attention in recent years. Since there are at least 25 million adult men and women who grew up in alcoholic households in our society, this attention is well-warranted. The most widespread and dangerous drug in our society is alcohol. Ironically, this drug is not only socially acceptable, but it is also not even regarded as a drug in the minds of most people. Yet this drug causes more physical disease, deaths, and divorce than the combined total of all the other drugs ingested by men and women in our society.

The impact of alcohol on marriages has been enormous. Consider the fact that one in ten adults is an alcoholic, and that these men and women are for the most part married or have been married. The effects of alcoholism on marriages are devastating. Anger, violence, mistrust, irresponsibility, untrustworthiness, joblessness, chronic illness, and early death are only some of the disastrous consequences of this drug addiction. Alcoholism becomes the loaded gun that blasts many marriages into divorce. Children of alcoholics tend to replicate the divorces of their parents in addition to which they are twice as likely as children of parents who are not alcoholics to become alcoholics themselves.

Actor Gary Crosby has been outspoken in alerting the general public to the problems of adult children of alcoholics, and to the ways in which alcohol abuse destroys marriages. Gary is the eldest son of the great popular singer

Bing Crosby. His mother, Dixie Lee, was an actress, a singer, and an alcoholic.

Growing up in an alcoholic environment, Gary experienced a great deal of pain, bewilderment, and uncertainty. He never knew what to expect from his mother. He told me that as a child, "One of the rules when you came into the house was to kiss Mom hello. So when you came in you started talking to her the minute you walked in, before you got to her bedroom, so you could tell if she was drunk or not, or what kind of mood she was in, because when you leaned over to kiss her, you might get hit in the face or you might get kissed. And if you guessed wrong, you would wind up with your ears boxed.

"When she was drunk she was maudlin, blue, sad. She wasn't a happy drunk, she was miserable. She had given up her career when she married. She was real happy to get out of her career. She always said she was scared to death; she never did get over stage fright. She always said she'd looked forward to being a mother and a housewife. She was a wife of the old school who believed that what her husband said was law, and no matter what he said, you did it, and we'd better not talk against him and nobody else had better talk against him. So there wasn't a whole lot of communication going on in that house. I loved my mother and I hated the fact that I wanted to stay away from her. As a kid I thought, 'She's so great when she doesn't drink. Why does she do that?' She died of stomach cancer at the age of thirty-nine, when I was seventeen."

Gary felt his mother and father were mismatched. He told me, "My parents were always trying to put up some kind of front, but there was always some underlying tension; they didn't talk, there was no communication. When there was communication, it was always on Dad's level, which was light banter. I was talking to one of Dad's directors once; he wanted my input. We discussed him as we knew him, and at the end of the discussion, we were sitting there looking at each other and we came to the conclusion that what we were looking at was really a tragic thing. Here was a man who was the personification of love to women and men throughout the world during his time, and he could do all that giving on radio and TV and in theaters, he could write

the most beautiful love letters, but to look someone straight
in the eye and tell them he loved them—he couldn't do it,
he couldn't show it. If he loved you, it would have to be
shown in a joking way, a throwaway. My mother needed
more, she needed constant love and affection, and it was a
shame that she wasn't married to someone who could give
her that."

When Gary grew up, he in turn created unhappy marriages for himself, which ended in divorce. He also became
"a full-blown, raging alcoholic and speed freak." He was a
person who was always "angry, full of rage and negativism
and cynicism."

Gary hid the pain of his divorces. As he told me, "We
men are so hung up with that macho image that we can't
show hurt and we can't show pain. That's the way we act,
but to the ladies I say, please, don't believe this. Our hearts
and our souls can ache just as bad as yours do. And many is
the night we'll sit with tears running down our faces and not
be able to talk to anybody. We suffer real good.

"If you talk to guys about divorce, they say, 'The goddamned broad did this to me; she and her lawyer are taking
me to the toilet.' And that's the way you cover up. You talk
real tough about your ex-wife, and inside you're like a little
boy, just crying, and you don't want anyone to see it. So you
cover it up with a lot of tough talk."

Gary's life began to change when he was forty-eight: "I
had to have a triple bypass for smoking and anger. The
doctor said, 'if you don't change your attitude, you're going
to die.' It was then that I got into the Alcoholics Anonymous
program."

He has become an outspoken advocate of Alcoholics
Anonymous, believing it has changed his life for the better,
and given him a spiritual underpinning he never possessed
before. He told me of his new approach to life: "Now I don't
want to be a big star in show business, I want to be of service
to people. I found out I was never equipped to be a big star.
I just don't have the ego; I don't have that I-gotta-be-on-top-
and-screw-everybody-else. There are things you have to do
that would gag a maggot, and I can't do them. I didn't think
it was that way in the beginning, but now I know. I look at
it this way: I sing and I act and I'm good at both of them.

God gave me these talents. Now if He wants me to use them,
I'll use them. If He has other plans for me, I'm not going to
go anywhere with my plan versus His. I never wanted to be
number one. I just wanted to work enough to be comfortable financially, and I wanted to work a lot and I wanted my
fellow actors and singers to say, 'Yeah, he's good, he's a pro.'
That's what is important to me."

Divorce as Rediscovery of the Ex-Spouse: The Patti MacLeod Story

Do couples who divorce ever remarry each other? Yes,
they do, but very infrequently and for a variety of reasons.
Sometimes it's because making it alone as a single person
seems too scary for each of them. They are like Hansel and
Gretel, fearfully tiptoeing through the perilous woods of the
singles world, and they return to each other as if each were
the safety net for the other. Learning little from their divorces and not improving themselves as persons in their
own right in their single state, they remarry each other
because they fear the new. They do not improve the quality
of their previous marriages, but simply return to the safety
of the chronically familiar pain that defined their relationships before they broke up.

On the other hand, there are couples who, after their
breakups, remarry each other because they have used their
divorces as learning experiences in which they have become wiser, more loving and caring individuals. They chose
to remarry each other because they are now free to create
a *new* marriage rather than a repetition of the old one, a
marriage in which they can skillfully relate to each other in
a kinder, more loving way, nurturing each other as individuals as well as growing as a couple. An outstanding example
of this type of remarriage occurred when Gavin MacLeod,
the popular star of the "Love Boat" TV series, and his ex-
wife, Patti, remarried in June 1985, after a separation and
divorce that had lasted four years.

I interviewed Patti, who is an excellent actress in her
own right, during the time of her divorce. She recalled at

that time that "when Gavin and I met, it was like God put us together, a magical thing happened. He lost one hundred pounds—he had weighed 265 pounds. He also stopped drinking—he was an alcoholic, which I didn't know when I met him—and he had gout and smoked three packs a day.

"I was a health nut, and all he needed was someone to say, 'You can do it, you can have some self-esteem, I love you, you don't have to be unhealthy.' He was like a sunflower, he was on a roll, and we were doing it together and he gave me all the credit. He said, 'I couldn't do it without my Patti.'"

But Gavin suddenly left Patti one day in 1981, without a word of explanation: "I heard," she said, "this robotlike voice on the phone saying, 'I want a divorce and I want it now!' He didn't want to see me or talk to me. After seven years of marriage, he just said good-bye. My head was spinning, I couldn't believe it. I didn't know which way to turn. It was the most painful experience of my life.

"I believed that Gavin was going through some terrible thing: chemistry, male menopause. My joke was that I made it through my menopause without a a hot flash, but I couldn't make it through Gavin's. I also really thought that if I had been better, Gavin wouldn't have left me. After he left, I just wanted to die, I didn't know what was going to keep me together.

"It took me two years after the divorce until I started working again. I was in heavy therapy for those two years, for four or five days a week. It was so beneficial to me, and I would recommend it, for first of all you have to heal yourself."

Part of the healing process was the recognition that Gavin had left for reasons other than that she was the cause of his discontent with the marriage. She said, "Gavin had been married for eighteen years before he met me, and immediately after his divorce he started going with me. Like many married people, he thought there was something out there he was missing, and when a person sets his mind on leaving, he'll use any excuse to do it."

Gavin later confirmed Patti's explanations. He said, "I felt pressure to explore, to find out what was on the other

side of the fence. I thought at the time that if I continued
to talk to Patti, I'd probably be back with her before I knew
it. I felt I had to be alone. I discovered that once I could have
anything I wanted, it really didn't mean that much when I
got it! I preferred being with Patti."

A few months after I interviewed Patti, I spoke with her
again, on February 1, 1985. At that time, Patti told me of an
exciting "miracle" that had happened: Gavin had contacted
her and they were now working on a whole new relationship. Both of them were much more understanding and
patient with each other. They were correcting their misin-
terpretations and misunderstandings of each other. Gavin
had always thought Patti was too controlling: "When I asked
him about things, he would think I was telling him what to
do." Patti told me, "He used to be a very angry man, but
now he's much more humble and showing his love, which
he was formerly afraid to do. We're still living in separate
houses and we've had fourteen-hour marathons of talking to
each other. He said he felt I had been controlling his life, but
now he knows I don't want to control anyone's life. We're
not rehashing the past, because the big thing is forgiveness—forgiveness by both of us, plus a willingness to change
for the better, is necessary if we're going to get together
again.

"A cut on your arm doesn't heal instantly, so I don't
expect our relationship to do so, either. However, we pray
a lot together and he's letting go of his workaholism and I'm
letting go of my former belief that it is my responsibility to
make everything right in his life. I've learned that I'm only
responsible for my own life, and that just by giving people
their freedom and space and loving them and having patience, positive things will happen. All the garbage will drop
away."

I heard from Patti again in June 1985. She said, "When
I joined the born-again Christians' organization, Born Again
Marriages, I believed that God was going to heal our marriage. And it's true. Gavin and I will be married again on
June 30. Forgiveness is the key. What happened in the past
isn't necessarily what's going to happen now. You have to
believe that when you reunite, it's the first day of a whole
new relationship. Now there's a lot of communication be-

tween us. We speak frankly but with kindness and understanding. I appreciate the importance of God and church and family, and I've never been happier."

Do celebrities have an easier time in their divorces? I think the six interviews you've just read answer that question eloquently. These interviews were not exceptional; I could have duplicated them many times over with similar tales of bitterness, hostility, pain, anguish, loss of the sense of self, difficulties in handling their children, and fury at the "rip-offs" of unscrupulous lawyers.

Ironically, many public people have a *harder* time in coping with divorce, since they have lived in their spouses' famous shadows for much or all of their married lives. As Lynn Landon said, "I know I misplaced myself somewhere in that marriage. . . . I think for nineteen years my name was Michael." They were terrified at the loss of their sense of self when they were divorced.

Fame did not cushion them from feeling a terrible sense of loss and failure when they divorced. Nor was it very different for the men involved; witness the profound disarray that Marty Ingels and Gary Crosby experienced. All of them were forced to reexamine their values and rediscover what was most important and valuable in life. Wealth, status, and fame counted for little in the face of the shattering emotional impact of their divorces. And many were shocked to find out that their friendships, more often than not, were built on sand. They now found that what was most important was creating a closer, more loving relationship with their children, finding spiritual and religious enlightenment, helping others in the process of helping themselves, and learning to be kinder, more caring individuals.

They have rebuilt their self-images, acknowledging the need for support groups and therapy assistance to help them do so. Just like the average divorced person, these celebrities had to take personal responsibility for their self-renewal.

None of us, rich or poor, famous or average, is exempt from experiencing the pain inherent in the divorce process. But every one of us is afforded, through our divorce experience, the opportunity to grow.

6

Melvin Belli's Advice on How to Protect Your Economic Interests When Divorcing

≡

*I*n the previous chapters you have learned how to see yourself as a single person of value and worth, who no longer needs to be married to validate that fact. In other words, you no longer see yourself as a victim or a seeker of vengeance. This new outlook is absolutely necessary if you are to protect your economic interests in the divorce settlement and not harm your children or your ex-spouse in the process of doing so.

When you regard yourself as neither a victim nor a bully, but rather as a decent human being who wants to deal fairly with your former spouse (and children, if any), you can then skillfully resolve the economic issues in your divorce. Listed below, in question-and-answer form, are the economic issues you may have to contend with and resolve, along with my suggestions as to how to do so without hostility or the panic belief that you are being ripped off or robbed:

Protecting Your Economic Interests: The General Considerations

Now that I'm divorcing, how can I insure and protect my economic interests?

If you are to fulfill your desire, you will need to do the following three things:

1. Realize, now, that you and your spouse have separate, distinct, and competitive economic interests.
2. Develop a complete understanding of all the things you and your spouse own, and all of the debts that either or both of you are obligated to pay.
3. Begin considering what you believe would be an equitable division of this negative and positive property (a fair settlement, considering all of the particular circumstances of your marital situation).

You can complete the first task above by not making one or the other of two common mistakes made by divorcing people. The first error is more generally, though not always, made by women. This is because women typically view divorce as the loss of a relationship before they think of it as a division of property. The mistake is to be reluctant to stop thinking in terms of "our property" and to move on to a mind-set that is crucial to have in a divorce setting if you are even to begin to protect your own economic interests. Maybe these women persist in their thinking because "it's not feminine to do anything else." Or perhaps they have always thought that "property decisions" were the exclusive province of their husbands.

In any event, and regardless of how you may have thought in the past, you must realize that in a divorce an "our property" mind-set can only cause you grief. As hard as it may be for you to change, if you are to take skillful charge of your divorce, you must move on. You need to see property clearly as "your things" and "your spouse's things." Otherwise, you will be giving your spouse a club with which to beat you silly. I trust that the following example will provide a meaningful illustration of this problem.

I once had a female client who, when divorce became inevitable for her, spent the majority of her time trying to figure out what had gone wrong with her marriage, and

why. In the meantime, unfortunately, her husband was selectively removing things from their home. Apparently he
didn't see anything wrong with not having to divide things
that he considered *his* property, even though all of these
things had been purchased by both of them during marriage
and were presumptively, therefore, to be equitably divided
in their divorce.

Sadly, my client was too long reluctant to change her
mind-set before coming to see me. As a consequence, when
it came down to the property settlement agreement, a substantial amount of their property had disappeared, and I
had insufficient evidence to prove that her husband had the
things in his possession or under his control, or even that this
property had ever existed at all. I did have my client as a
potential witness, but, unfortunately, she hadn't done too
well in completing the second task above, either, i.e., to
know what you own and who you owe. As a result, my client
wasn't sure of the specific things that were taken by her
husband, or of the property's value. She could only speak in
terms of "a large number of guns and rifles," or "a tremendous amount of professional tools." I hope this sad case will
spur you into avoiding my client's mistake.

While you men may have little difficulty refraining
from getting into an "our property" mind-set, beware of
making a second and equally unfortunate mistake. Most
men, you see, can easily get psyched up to protect their own
separate economic interests. They are generally more prop-
erty-oriented than women, and can tend to look upon divorce primarily as a loss of their property and secondarily
as the loss of a relationship.

Consequently, men tend more easily to avoid coming
to grips at all with what they perceive as a secondary concern. They are blinded by their property preoccupation and
never feel the emotions that were probably a huge part of
the underlying cause for the marital difficulties. As a result,
men more commonly make a second mistake, which is to let
the protection of their economic interests interfere with
their taking appropriate responsibility for ending their marriages equitably. While loving feelings for your wife may
have long since vanished, you should be aware that the clear
trend of modern divorce law is to place both "new"

households in a situation where each can prosper more or less equally well. This is all the more true when there are children to consider. So do yourself a big favor by being manly enough to make a clean break of your relationship (one that fairly gives *both* you and your ex-wife the best opportunity for a new life). You can't begin to build a positive future for yourself as long as you perpetuate the negativity of your past.

You can accomplish the second task above—to know what you own and who you owe—by doing what I'll call "crystallizing your property," and doing so as of a specific date. In most cases, this date will be the one upon which you separate and begin living apart from your spouse. For those of you who aren't yet separated, but who are seriously considering a divorce, that date should be as soon as possible. By crystallizing your property I mean that *you must make a written record of everything you and your spouse own and owe,* including, but not limited to, the following:

1. Every *single* item (such as a house, a car, or a boat) or *collection* of items (such as a set of workshop tools, some wedding silverware, or a bedroom set) that has a value of more than $500. Your written record should include the date upon which the item was purchased, the purchase price, any amount still owed against the item's purchase price, its approximate value at the present time, how "title" is held (is it in your name, your spouse's name, or both?), and some sort of specific identification of the item (e.g., "1988 Ford Taurus station wagon, license number 123TSC").

2. Every item under $500 in value that has *strong* sentimental value for you. (List the same information as in category 1, above.) The items that don't fit into either of the above classifications can be listed as "miscellaneous household furniture, furnishings, and effects." Generally, the latter get fairly well and evenly divided early in the divorcing process. The husband gets a few chairs, some silverware, his

personal clothing, and a bed, perhaps, and the wife gets a similar amount of the same things. A really useful thing to do with regard to this property is to list all of it as best you can, and then get a friend to examine all of the items against your list so that he or she can state, under oath, if necessary, that all of the things on your list were in the home on the date you made your list.

3. *Positive intangibles*, such as checking and savings accounts, stocks, bonds, CDs, insurance policies, and money market funds. You should list a specific identification of each item: its account, certificate, or policy number, the bank branch location of checking and savings accounts, the account balance or value of the item at the present time, the current location of each such item (is it in your possession or within your control?), and how title is held.

4. *Negative intangibles*, such as outstanding loans and credit card accounts. Specifically identify each item in this category by its loan or account number, the date upon which the loan was made or the account opened, who is legally responsible for paying the debt, the current loan or account balance, and who has possession of any credit cards.

I can readily empathize with all of you who think that this second task is a lot of work, because it is. I can also empathize with those of you who find this task overwhelming because you've never involved yourself in such matters before. However, your attorney is going to ask you to get this information in any case, so you might as well do it now as later. And the sooner you do it, the better. You will be well rewarded for your work by finding that you are in a much better position to deal with a division of this property when divorce occurs. And don't reveal your work or its results to your spouse. Your lawyer will thank you for your cooperation later on. Your "secret" work may prove useful in foiling your spouse's attempt to get more than he or she deserves. *Also,* ensure the safety and secrecy of your lists by entrusting them to a best friend.

When you have substantially dealt with how to avoid "our property" type of thinking, and when you know what *you* own and owe, you will have gone a long way toward ensuring the protection of your economic interests now that you are divorcing. You will eventually have to begin thinking about how to divide the property, but it is not critical that this necessarily be done right away.

However, if you can begin to do it now, you will benefit both yourself and your lawyer. You will benefit by stretching the time in which you can consider just what a "fair" division of your property is, and how you can best effect a corresponding result. And it will benefit your attorney by giving him or her an earlier and clearer understanding of what you want and/or can settle for than would otherwise be the case.

Now that my spouse and I are getting divorced, what do I need to do about our bank accounts and the things in our safe deposit box in order to protect myself?

With regard to your safe deposit box, the best thing you can do is to fix the box's contents at a specific point in time, and to try to do so without making your spouse aware of your actions. This means two things. First, you must get into your box and make a written record of all its contents. Second, you must then have a bank officer or friend compare the box's contents against your list, attest to the latter's accuracy, and sign and date the list, stating that it is an accurate description of what is in the box. Then, if your spouse should secretly take some of that property and hide it, your attorney can utilize your list to rectify your spouse's illegal actions.

Bank accounts are more troublesome, but don't panic. You are not legally helpless. If you have a joint account, either you *or* your spouse can withdraw all of the funds in it *without* the other's legal consent. Therefore, at the very least, you should get the bank to confirm to you, *in writing,* the account balance as of a specific date, and thereafter to be prepared to explain every withdrawal you make from the account. Your action cuts both ways. It is both a shield to protect you and potentially a sword in the hands of your spouse if you don't act responsibly.

Individual accounts, however, are another story. Typically, if you or your spouse has an account solely in your name or his or her own name, only *that* individual can deal with the funds therein. But if you are aware that your spouse has one or more of these accounts, and you think that one or more of these accounts contain funds that you believe to be *marital property* (property subject to division between the marital partners), you can still protect your economic interests by providing your lawyer with all information known to you about the nature and location of such accounts. Although you may not be able to gain legal access to information concerning the deposits to, withdrawals from, or balances in these accounts, your attorney will probably have a variety of legal methods at his or her disposal to secure all three pieces of further information.

During my marriage, my spouse took care of all our family finances. Now that I'm divorcing, I'm not sure that I'll know what to do with whatever I get. What should I do?

In the first place, you can get your lawyer to recommend you to a competent financial adviser. Such counselors are persons or companies professionally trained to assist you in working out sound plans to ensure your present and future financial security. They can help you to establish budgets and show you how to live within them. They can also aid you in resolving any kind of credit problem you might have now or in the future. Finally, they can advise you on how best to go about promoting your future by utilizing your current property holdings as investment capital. These professionals run the gamut from simple credit counselors, who can help you to resolve some immediate financial problem, to sophisticated financial advisers, called *certified financial planners,* who are more suited to the divorcing situation in which the parties are concerned with developing a current and considerable property base.

Although certified financial planners used to be a small number of financial advisers to the rich and famous, the inflated value of everything in this society has caused an explosion in the number of financial planners available today at competitive prices to deal with an increasing number of people, including those who are divorcing, who have considerable property to invest. Such counselors typically provide you with a plan for investing in a whole range of vehicles designed to promote your greatest financial security and development.

However, if money is a problem for you, get your lawyer to assist you in finding a nonprofit consumer counseling service in your community that can help you. Even if your attorney can't recommend someone he or she personally knows to advise you, your attorney should at least be able to help you search for one of these agencies. These advisers, such as the Consumer Credit Counselors (a national nonprofit organization supported by business concerns willing to work with responsible consumers who want to clear up their credit problems), don't charge you for their services. This means that, at no cost to you, help can be gotten now to assist you in arranging a sound set of rules governing your immediate financial situation and helping you to resolve any current crisis you might be in.

Furthermore, and again at no cost to you, you'll be getting competent help to assist you in developing a sound strategy for ensuring your future financial security. I really like this group of counselors because these people place great emphasis in their work upon your taking responsibility for your situation. They also expect you to take charge of developing and protecting your own future financial security. They won't do it for you, because they have respect for your own self-worth and abilities. If you haven't yet done so, acknowledge these things in yourself. Also realize now, if it hasn't already become abundantly clear to you, that your spouse's handling all the family finances really handicapped you in dealing with your new single status.

However, the disability isn't permanent, and you have tools to heal yourself, so get on with it and don't ever again allow anyone to handle your financial matters for you. You are fully capable of doing that for yourself.

Finally, if you have sufficient resources to pay for financial advice but can't get a personal recommendation from your attorney, ask the latter to put you in touch with any competent estate planning attorney. Such lawyers regularly consult financial advisers, particularly certified financial planners. They do so because the estate plans (post-death property transference) of their clients often require competent financial advice to promote asset growth so that the estate plans these lawyers have drafted will effectively provide for heirs of clients after the latter have died.

When interviewing any of these financial planning professionals, you can utilize some of the questions we discussed in the section of Chapter 3 relating to your initial interview with your attorney (beginning on page 82). All you need to do is change those questions to fit your present situation.

I've decided to divorce, but I'm worried about our joint credit card accounts. Am I responsible for my spouse's charges now that we're separated?

Generally not. But that doesn't mean you don't have to take charge of the situation to insure a favorable result. Although you might not be responsible for the debts under the divorce laws of your state, your creditors can probably still sue you for all of your spouse's post-separation debts, because you authorized him or her to charge on your own accounts.

In most if not all states, creditors are not in any way obligated to honor the legal decisions made in your divorce unless either you or your spouse has made those creditors parties to your divorce action to the extent that your state law permits such an addition. Therefore, so far as any of those divorce court decisions concerns a creditor's contract with you and your spouse, the creditors may, but need not, abide by the court's decision.

In some situations, however, you may be responsible and liable for your spouse's charges in any event, because most states hold that purchases, even post-separation ones, for the necessities of life, such as food or clothing, are the joint responsibility of both spouses, at least until the divorce is final. Here's what you can do to protect your economic interests. First, close out all joint accounts that your creditors will allow you to close. And get them to send you up-to-date statements as of the date of your request and as of the date of your separation. Although I would not suggest or advise it, some desperate spouses have been known to call their creditors and report the cards missing or stolen. Then, while they're in the process or making the report, they slip in a mention of their pending divorce coupled with a casual request that the cards be reissued in the sole name of the reporting spouse. Second, for any accounts you either can't or don't want to close out, at least do the following:

1. Get the creditors to send you statements of account of both the date of your separation and the date of your request.
2. Inform your creditors, preferably in writing, that your accounts are the subjects of a pending divorce proceeding between you and your spouse, and that you do not intend to be held liable for any post-separation debts incurred on those accounts by your spouse (understanding, of course, that you may be held liable for certain of those debts).
3. Request new statements from those creditors, at least every month, after your original request (this will aid you and your lawyer in quickly isolating and possibly resolving any problems).
4. Be prepared to explain any of your post-separation charges, in detail, and get your attorney to question your spouse about every one of his or hers.

The above measures should protect your economic interests in most situations. And don't allow yourself to be stalled in your circumstances. We don't like to do it, but you can pay your attorney to do all of the above work for you, if you can't handle the matter right now. Furthermore, uncooperative creditors can be persuaded to comply with your requests by being legally required, commonly in the form of a *subpoena duces tecum,* to supply you with copies of all your account records so that you can review and copy any material you need for your case.

You have stated elsewhere that it is very important to be completely honest with your attorney in revealing all your marital circumstances. I'm afraid to do so in my divorce, because I believe that a portion of the funds used to purchase our marital home was derived by my spouse from illegal sources. What should I do?

You should follow my previous advice and tell your lawyer everything. First of all, whatever you disclose to your attorney is completely confidential. Lawyers are under strict ethical and legal obligations to remain silent concerning all communications from their clients (with the possible exception of some *future* criminal conduct), particularly here, where the information, even if true, is related to some past event.

Even if you had been a participant in the illegal scheme, your attorney would be duty-bound not to reveal the information even to law enforcement officials, because your story relates to an already completed act rather than to an event that will or may occur in the future. In such situations, you are very fortunate to be living in this country, because you're innocent until proven guilty, and there is no legal requirement for you to help the state convict you of any crime, particularly here, where you weren't even a knowing participant.

Second, if you're not honest, you will severely handicap your lawyer in dealing with any of the many problems associated with your situation in the event that your spouse's past conduct is discovered via some other means. Therefore, the only way for you to take skillful charge of this situation is to arm your lawyer with every fact of which you are aware concerning the transaction, and let him or her advise you.

The price you could pay for refusing to do so could be staggering. You could, for instance, be charged with being an accessory after the fact to the crime your spouse committed, and perhaps be charged with suppression of evidence as well. Don't risk it. The property's not worth going to prison for, and your lawyer can't do anything to protect you from past events that he or she knows nothing about.

Spousal Support and Related Issues

I hardly ever worked outside my home during marriage. Now that I'm divorcing, what rights, if any, do I have to receive any kind of financial support from my spouse? Are my chances poorer today than ever before?

The right, if any, would be to receive what is typically called spousal support. Generally, such support is awarded only in approximately 15 percent of the divorces occurring in America today—about a one-in-seven chance that you'll have any award made at all. And spousal support is getting harder and harder to get, in all but a small number of cases, so you probably would be better off downplaying your expectations in this regard.

The one-in-seven rate is about what it was twenty years ago, so this situation hasn't changed much. What has dramatically changed, however, is the duration of such awards, both in term length and amount, even in those few cases in which such awards are made. For that reason, you might want to think twice about readily agreeing to settlements on this issue that are not to your advantage. Although I would ordinarily discourage litigating issues in open court, spousal support may be one of those questions that should be answered by a court after a hearing of all the facts, rather than by a settlement that can all too often result from fear caused by ignorance and lack of total candor on the part of all participants, including the lawyers.

First let's look at whether you might be among that 15 percent who do get some level of support for some length of time. Broadly speaking (and remember to check out all of these generalizations with your lawyer, because states can differ drastically in their treatment of the issue), spousal support is awarded, if at all, in longer-term marriages of, say, more than ten years, and particularly in which one spouse has been a homemaker throughout the marriage rather than a wage-earner.

In a few states, such as California, a judge is required, when awarding spousal support, to consider the contributions made by one spouse to the education and training of the other. The amount of such awards varies drastically from state to state and from case to case, so check with your attorney in this specific regard.

I wish there were some way I could make this information more palatable to women, or say it in a gentler way. However, I would feel less than honest if I were to paint too rosy a picture of this subject. For there is a real danger that the present system is fostering the rapid development of a new class of poor people, namely divorced women and/or mothers.

The picture becomes even bleaker when one considers that the developing trend in resolving spousal support issues is to shorten the duration and lower the level of such awards. This is an unfortunate by-product of modern divorce, and one that can be critically paralyzing to say, a forty-five-year-old woman who was married for twenty-five years but never worked outside the home.

This woman typically finds herself in a no-win situation at some point. If she finds a job after her divorce, it often results in reduction of the support, and consequently may jeopardize her ability to sustain the employment and/or improve upon it. Conversely, if she doesn't find a job, she gets accused of not trying hard enough to become self-sustaining, and the ex-spouse still tries to get the support reduced.

This illogical Catch-22 situation is typically justified with such flowery statements as "It's not supposed to last forever," or "It's healthy and positive for a divorced woman to learn to stand on her own two feet." It's a sad comment on our system that it functions this way at present. But it does. So take skillful charge of the situation by alerting your attorney to as many facts as you can relating to your training, skills, hobbies, interests, and past standard of living, as well as what results, if any, you've had in finding work utilizing your knowledge and skills.

Don't ever allow yourself to be pressured into settling this issue too readily. Instead, do all of the following. First, thoughtfully consider your attorney's advice about what *generally* happens in divorces like yours. Second, consider the merits of any proposals made by your spouse concerning the issue. Third, get your lawyer to inform you which judge or judges are most likely to preside over the trial of such a so-called permanent award (the word *permanent* is used in this case simply to distinguish this type of award from "temporary" support given while the divorce is going on), and how they typically resolve spousal support issues. Fourth, consult with your attorney about the best strategies to employ to ensure your greatest economic gain now and in the future. Fifth, after carefully discussing all of the above with your attorney, make a well-reasoned decision concerning whether you should accept any proposed settlement or instead take your chances in court.

For this reason, it is critically important in cases such as yours, where support is likely to be granted, to have a lawyer representing you who has had a considerable amount of experience in spousal support cases. Look for one who is familiar with most, if not all, of the judges who might preside over your divorce trial and how those judges think. Also, seek a lawyer who has not refrained from going to trial if he or she reasonably believed it was worth it and the client agreed.

Finally, if it is awarded to you, use whatever you get wisely, by utilizing the income to help you to attain a place where you can take care of yourself. There are an increasing number of strong women who have endured in such circumstances despite the worst kind of decisions. Be among them to whatever extent you can. You'll feel better for it.

Further, get competent tax advice on all aspects of the proposed spousal support resolutions, so that you can get maximum use out of whatever support you receive.

At the present time, my kids and I are all covered by my husband's insurance policies, both health and life. Now that we're getting divorced, I'm scared to death that we won't be covered by his insurance any longer. Are my fears realistic?

Probably less so than you might imagine at the moment. First of all, in many states your attorney will be able to secure the result you desire, by way of a court order if necessary, to require your spouse to maintain at least health insurance on both you and your children. The legal vehicle for such a requirement will commonly be called a *child support* or *spousal support* or *family maintenance* order. Those of you who have been married for less than ten years may have a more difficult time obtaining such an order, but check with your attorney. It may be available even in this latter situation.

Property Settlements

Hidden Assets and How to Find Them

I've heard legal experts caution divorcing people to look out for "hidden assets." Is this a subject about which I need to be aware, now that I'm starting my divorce?

It's certainly possible, and in any event, "hidden assets" are a problem with which all divorcing people should have some familiarity. The term refers to property owned by both you and your spouse, or either of you individually, that literally gets "hidden" from discovery. The concealment can be either innocent or knowing; most commonly, it is the latter.

The problem with such hidden assets is twofold. First, such property is typically of a type that would ordinarily be divided between you and your spouse if its existence was revealed. An example of this situation might be a bonus that your husband gets his boss to delay giving him until after the divorce is final, in an attempt to keep you from finding out about it and requiring your share of it because it was "earned" during marriage.

Second, such property, whether divisible or not (some property, such as an inheritance, is awarded solely to the inheriting spouse, whether the property is acquired before or during marriage, and therefore is not divided between you and your spouse), might cause an increase or a decrease in the amount of a support order for you and/or your children if such property was discovered. This could occur in a situation in which a wife gets paid in cash for working at a job her husband doesn't know about and then requests and gets the court to grant, or her husband to agree to, a higher support order than the wife would otherwise have received. Don't, however, let the existence of this issue either scare you or cause you to worry. Instead, act now to protect your economic rights. There are a number of ways such property can be "uncovered," once you know what to look for and when. Here is what to look for:

- Property such as a house, a boat, or some stock that was purchased by your spouse with his or her income earned during marriage, but that you don't know about because he or she "takes care of finances," and the property is located in another city or state or kept by your spouse in a "secret" place.
- A bonus, stock option, or salary increase that was earned during marriage by your spouse, but that isn't paid to him or her until after the divorce is final, as part of a scheme by your spouse, in which his or her employer is either an innocent or a knowing participant, to keep you from discovering it and, therefore, getting your share of it.
- A savings account or money market fund that your spouse opened without your knowledge, as a custodial account in the name of one of your children. Your spouse may have deposited in such an account income he or she earned during marriage, which, but for his or her ruse, would be divided between you. These custodial accounts give your spouse, and *not* that child, all of the deposit and withdrawal rights. And such accounts are hard to discover because the interest on them generally does not have to be claimed on your spouse's tax returns.
- A phony marital debt to one of your spouse's friends that your spouse "retires" with his or her income earned during marriage, thus preventing you from getting your share of the income. (Your spouse subsequently gets the friend to se-

cretly reimburse him or her, after your divorce is final.)

- "Salary" paid to a nonexistent employee in your spouse's business, the checks being sent to a post office box until after the divorce, at which time your spouse tears up the checks; or money paid to a real person who performed either overvalued services or no services at all, and who gives the checks back to your spouse after the divorce is final.

The above summary is by no means a complete listing of repositories for hidden assets; for this reason, you should generally discuss this whole issue with your attorney, regardless of your particular circumstances. It doesn't hurt to ask, and you might have a problem you weren't even aware of. Furthermore, you should specifically discuss the hidden-assets issue if you are in any of the following situations:

- If you are in any way unclear about precisely how much money your spouse makes or has made during your marriage.
- If your spouse is a part owner of any type of business, whether the enterprise is a sole proprietorship, a partnership, a corporation, or any other kind of arrangement.
- If your spouse is commonly paid in cash for the work he or she performs or has performed during marriage.
- If you are one of those spouses who leaves all financial matters to his or her spouse, and has always done so.

In most divorces where there is even an inkling of a hidden-assets problem, you will commonly have a variety of methods at your disposal to uncover such property. It is most important, however, not to discuss your investigation with your spouse or unnecessarily tip him or her off to it. Diligent and secret work by my clients has more than once foiled the attempts of their spouses to get more than they rightfully deserve.

Once you've really geared your mind to playing detective, you can utilize a number of different research tools when looking for hidden assets. Any or all of the following may be appropriate:

- Old tax returns can be reviewed.
- Checking and/or savings account record books can be studied in depth (you might find large and unexplained withdrawals).
- Employers can be required to tell you and your lawyer a great deal of information that your spouse might be reluctant to reveal. (The employer probably won't perjure him- or herself to protect your spouse's schemes to thwart your legitimate economic rights.)
- Financial statements that your spouse has filled out from time to time to get loans can be a marvelous source of hidden-assets information, because the borrower spouse may inadvertently list some or all of these assets to beef up his or her financial picture.
- Securities or commodities accounting statements can be investigated for unusual or unexplained purchases or sales that your spouse might not think you'll discover because he or she controlled the account or accounts during marriage.

Utilization of these tools, and others that your attorney can tell you about, will generally go a long way toward ensuring that you get some share of all property in which you have an interest. It will also help you uncover all property that might have a bearing on the amount of a support order.

If you discover what you think are *most* of any hidden assets by using the above tools or others that you think of or that your attorney recommends, don't worry about discovering *all* of them. Do, however, remember to do at least two things. First, get your attorney to make sure that all of the property divided between you and your spouse, or awarded separately to either of you because it is not properly divisible, and that has a value of more than $500, is *specifically* listed in the divorce decree or property settlement agreement *at the property's agreed-upon value*. This technique may help you to recover the value of assets that were undervalued in the divorce as a consequence of one of your spouse's schemes, but of which you later discover the *true* worth. Or the procedure may prevent your spouse from successfully arguing at a later date that the item of property you don't discover until after the divorce is final was part of some general language in the settlement agreement or divorce decree, such as "husband gets all boats in his possession."

Second, to the extent that such language can lawfully be inserted into the decree or property settlement agreement in your state, make sure that your lawyer includes what we typically refer to as "boilerplate language" to protect and preserve your economic interests. Such language typically says that both you and your spouse have revealed all property that is properly subject to being considered by the court in your case. It further states that any property that either should be divided between you and your spouse or should be considered by the court in determining the proper amount of support to award, and which is not discovered until after the divorce is final, may be considered and/or divided by the court at a later time.

Having done these two things, though you may not have recovered all of the hidden assets in your divorce, you will at least have preserved your rights with respect to them, should you be able to discover their existence sometime in the future, but after your divorce is final.

Getting the Property You Want

When I came home last night, I found that a lot of our property had apparently been stolen. I was just about to call the police when I discovered a note from my spouse telling me that he'd taken his stuff and was suing for divorce. Today, on the phone, he had the nerve to act like the missing items never existed at all, even though I just

*know he walked away with them. What can I do about
this situation?*

Maybe nothing or perhaps everything. This question presents the problem of *disappearing* assets as opposed to
hidden ones, which we've just discussed. Typically, in
these cases, one party believes that property subject to
being divided between the divorcing spouses has been
"stolen" by the other spouse, the latter naturally claiming
that the property either doesn't exist at all or has apparently disappeared.

The result, in your situation, depends upon how well
you've done your homework. If you began to make a written record of all of your possessions when divorce became
imminent for you, and completed it before your spouse left,
you now have in your possession the evidence either to get
all of the disappeared items back or to use as a sledgeham-
mer to pound out a divorce settlement more favorable to
you than to your spouse.

If you didn't do that homework or didn't complete your
list before your spouse left, then you have a more difficult
situation, but not an impossible one. First, sit down right
now, or as soon as you can, and make a detailed list of the
items that are gone. Second, search out every document
that would prove or otherwise suggest that the items existed
and, even better, when the property was purchased. Third,
if the items are of great monetary value, consider hiring a
detective to bird-dog your spouse until the detective discovers the whereabouts of such property or confirms its conver-
sion into money or some other liquid asset. Fourth, if
anyone you know can testify to the existence of any of this
property, and to its having been in the house before your
spouse left, get them to your attorney so that the latter can
take their sworn statement.

You might want, however, to think twice about asking
your children to testify to any knowledge they have. Is
recovering the property more important to you than the
harm your children might suffer in such a situation? Finally,
and most important, make sure that your belief as to the
existence of any property you don't recover is clearly set
forth in any court decree and/or divorce settlement. In this

way, if you thereafter discover the property's whereabouts, you can eventually gain your share of it.

Avoiding the Five Emotional Divorce Traps

How can I avoid letting my emotions get in the way of making sound decisions concerning my economic interests now that I'm divorcing?

I urge you first to reread Mel Krantzler's section in Chapter 2 on "Understanding the Emotional Upheaval in Your Divorce" (pages 53–56), which provides you with the groundwork for eliminating any tendencies you might have to endanger your long-term economic interests. Specifically, you can then avoid the following five emotional divorce traps that all too many divorcing persons unfortunately fall into:

1. You feel guilty about leaving the marriage, and feel you must pay heavily for your guilt.

   You may be falling victim to this trap if you're thinking about agreeing to extend support orders for a longer time than might be legally required under the circumstances, even though your spouse might not really need it; if you are tempted to give your spouse a greater share of your joint property to the point where you may be bankrupting yourself; or if you are relinquishing the spousal support you are entitled to. Don't. You can't buy away your guilt. Instead, work on your guilt feelings with an appropriately trained counselor and resolve, with the help of your attorney if necessary, to make the necessary and appropriate decisions without guilt blinding you to what is reasonable and appropriate.

2. You have always left "money matters" in your spouse's hands and might tend to do so in a divorce settlement (even though your economic interests are different now).

This is the situation in which my client doesn't prepare the lists I ask her to prepare, or provide me with documents so I can look for hidden assets, because money matters have always been handled by her husband and she doesn't see any need to alter the situation, even though her husband will probably try to screw her out of every dime he can.

Recognize that you and your spouse now have separate, distinct, and perhaps competitive interests. Otherwise your husband may laugh all the way to the bank, thinking about the property he got away with because you left money matters to him. Start right now to begin to view yourself as capable of handling your own money matters, and resolve to work your hardest to make sure you get everything to which you're entitled under the divorce laws of your state.

3. You agree, on your spouse's suggestion, to have the same lawyer, without knowing that that lawyer may be working in your spouse's interests, and at your expense.

These are the "Why should we pay for two attorneys?" and "Let's get Joe [the "family" attorney who's really your spouse's lawyer] to handle the divorce for us" pitfalls. Be advised that an ethical lawyer can seldom, if ever, provide competent and loyal advice to *both* spouses in a divorce proceeding. And such lawyers can be disbarred for soliciting such business.

If you find yourself in this trap, extricate yourself from it by acting now to secure the services of another attorney. Or, at the very least, get whatever you're inclined to agree with reviewed by independent counsel of your own choosing, before you sign anything. The price you may pay for not doing so may swallow up any money you think you're saving by using only one attorney to get the job done more cheaply and/or amicably. Besides, it's really high time that you, and not your spouse, made the decisions affecting your future.

4. You settle too quickly for less than what you are entitled to, because you want to get your ex-spouse out of your life as soon as possible.

How can you possibly build a strong and healthy future for yourself if you start out your post-separation life by being in such a hurry to get on with it that you forget to, or avoid, taking appropriate precautions to ensure that you begin that life with all you are entitled to. I fully realize how the tedious and objectionable harassment of your spouse can upset you. I also know, however, how expensive your avoidance can be. Give yourself a break. If you had the good sense to end a bad relationship, at least take the time to tie up all the loose ends so that you can more appropriately begin your positive and rewarding single future.

5. You just don't know how you'll ever cope with the complexity of your divorce. I call this the "helpless victim" trap. This is the situation where a spouse "doesn't know where to begin to look" for the documents wanted and/or needed by his or her attorney, or who doesn't want to explore the possibilities of reimbursement alimony as a consequence of laboring to put his or her spouse through some professional school, because the argument for it seems so flimsy or complicated. All I can do for you, if you find yourself in this trap, is to tell you that you are a unique and valuable person who is fully capable of mastering any situation you resolve to master, despite your feelings that you might not succeed. If you must fail, do so only in the eyes of society, your friends and/or relatives, your ex-spouse, or your children. But don't fail yourself!

One of my clients was a tiny middle-aged woman who wept for an hour the first time she consulted me because she just didn't see how she could ever cope with her spouse's leaving her for another woman and suing my client for a divorce. It wasn't easy for her at first. But that little lady had become a lioness by the time her divorce was concluded. And today she is a happily remarried and marvelously successful and independent new woman.

Work really hard to discover where your "helpless" feelings lie, and then resolve with the assistance of all your counselors to begin turning those feelings of self-pity and lack of worth into joyful emotions of pride and high self-esteem.

Sentimental Attachments

I've got a strong sentimental attachment to some of the things my spouse and I purchased while we were married. Now that I'm divorcing, I'm afraid that my spouse will use my feelings for this property to blackmail me in the divorce. What should I do?

You can do at least three things, the first of which you may already have done, which is to realize that you have such feelings. You'd be surprised to learn how many people don't even realize how attached they've become to some property they've acquired during marriage, only to discover that they have become obsessed by it during their divorce.

A "special" pet, a set of dishes, a fishing rod, or a lounge chair may be the focus of such feelings. And they have been the undoing of more divorcing people than I care to imagine. Give yourself credit for understanding your feelings by realizing that it's really okay to have them. You are not weird or bizarre because you feel the way you do.

Second, you can carefully examine just how strong your attachment really is. For instance, is your attachment so strong that, if you had to, you would be willing to pay ten times the present value of your "favorite" thing to buy it, if you didn't already own it? Maybe not. Divorcing people in your situation commonly are blinded to realizing that although their attachment is really okay, getting the property they want may come at a very high price if their spouse becomes aware of these "special" feelings and tries to use them to his or her own advantage. Therefore, focus clearly upon how far you're willing to go to get what you want.

Finally, if you still find, after due consideration, that your attachment to some piece of property is strong, then you need to act almost indifferently about your favorite thing's disposition. If you haven't already let the cat out of the bag, don't let your spouse know about your feelings. It just doesn't make any sense to give your spouse a weapon to force you into seeing things his or her way. Then, try as best you can, on all occasions when you are in spouse's presence, not to tip your hand unnecessarily until you have secured a favorable settlement with regard to this property and at a reasonable price.

Personal Injury Awards

My spouse, whom I'm divorcing, got badly injured recently and is suing for damages. What legal rights, if any, do I have, if and when my spouse wins the lawsuit?

Probably none, but be sure to review all of the accident circumstances with your attorney. In many if not most states, divorce laws would require that any money recovered by your spouse in the lawsuit be awarded *solely* to him or her in your divorce. You have no interest in such property.

This result is in accord with the general rules pertaining to damages recovered in personal injury lawsuits. Such damages are deemed to be personal to the successful litigant, and thus are his or her *sole* property. Some states differ slightly in their treatment of this matter. In these states, the money recovered by your spouse would be held to be "the property of the marriage," and thus subject to division between you and spouse if, and only if, the injury occurred after the date of marriage but before separation. Otherwise, such money would be held to be the sole property of your spouse, following the more common rule.

However, if your spouse was totally incapacitated and could not work as a result of the accident, you probably have a claim, in all states, to some portion of the proceeds if there are outstanding sums due under a valid spousal and/or child support order which haven't been paid. And you may even have a right to some interest in those damages as security against a permanent disability preventing your spouse from further work.

Speaking of lawsuits in a general divorce context, it would not be a bad idea to have your attorney check court records to make sure that neither you nor your spouse has been sued or has claims pending in lawsuits of which you are unaware. Then, if any actions are found to be pending, they can be appropriately dealt with in the divorce.

Social Security and Pension Benefits

Now that I'm getting divorced, will I be entitled to share in any social security benefits my spouse receives after the divorce is final, including any survivor benefits?

Generally, yes, if you were married to your spouse for at least ten years prior to the divorce and have yourself reached a certain age. But check with your lawyer for more complete advice relating to your specific situation. With regard to social security retirement or disability benefits, you must fulfill the ten-year marriage requirement and be at least sixty-two years old.

As to survivor benefits (these are benefits paid to a surviving spouse or, in some cases, to more than one spouse), you must again meet the ten-year marriage requirement. But in this case you need only have attained sixty years of age to be able to collect. However, unlike the situation with regard to retirement or disability benefits, you must also be unmarried at the time you apply for these latter benefits.

A parallel issue in these situations is the availability of the above benefits as a source of money to satisfy valid spousal and/or child support orders. Under federal law, such benefits are always subject to being garnished to satisfy such orders. However, the government is typically not obligated to give priority to one claim over another. This means that benefits are garnishable on a first-come-first-served basis.

Thus, if your ex-spouse had other wives and/or children, benefits will be paid to whoever moves the quickest, regardless of whether that person was the first or last wife or child. If your spouse had other wives and/or children before marrying you, or you later discover that he or she remarried after your divorce, you may need to move swiftly to protect your economic interests in such benefits, so be prepared to do so.

My spouse was employed by the same company throughout our fifteen-year marriage. Will I get any of my spouse's pension benefits, now that we're getting a divorce?

Yes, you will generally be entitled to some portion of whatever benefits accrued to your spouse from the time you were married until the date of your permanent separation. And this general rule is applicable to all types of pension benefits, including both private and public types. You should, however, check with your attorney for specific information related to your particular set of circumstances.

Furthermore, you generally have an option to take your proportionate share now of the present value of those future rights or to have your share valued now but not distributed to you until your ex-spouse retires and begins receiving his or her pension benefits, thus allowing you to share in the increased value of your proportionate share when those benefits ultimately begin to be paid. (This procedure is called the "time rule.")

Of course, the trade-off in the latter event is that you risk being awarded a larger piece of nothing, should your spouse not reach retirement age before he or she dies. As you can readily imagine, there is a lot of room here for a variety of bargaining strategies. Therefore, to take skillful charge of your economic interests in your spouse's pension benefits, first get your lawyer to advise you as to whether your state follows the general rules with regard to the distribution of such benefits upon divorce, including whether you have the options presented by the "time rule"; and then, on the advice of your lawyer, adopt the strategy best suited to protecting your long-term interests. Finally, when you have done both of the above, choose your option, make your decision, and move on to the next issue in your divorce.

Are These Settlements Forever?

Now that the economic settlement in my divorce is final, does that mean it's "cast in stone" so that I can't thereafter change it?

The court always retains the power to make modifications of child-related issues and spousal support, even after the divorce is final, as long as the children are minors or the spouse is still entitled to receive support. And be sure to protect your economic interests in any situation entitling you to spousal support. Instead of agreeing to remove it from the court's power to change the amount, request instead that it be set at least at one dollar per year. This will allow you to have the divorce judgment modified to enable you to increase the level of support at any future time, provided you can justify it by showing a substantial change in either your own financial situation or your ex-spouse's, or both.

Furthermore, the court always retains the power to modify the divorce decree if you or your spouse can demonstrate that the decree was obtained by the other spouse through fraud. The fraud here lies in engaging in an intentional act, such as "hiding" assets, designed to obtain an unfair advantage over the other spouse in the divorce.

Finally, the court can retain the power to modify the decree in whatever manner you and your spouse agree to, such as to deal with divisible property not discovered until after the divorce is final or to ensure the proper and equitable windup to a family business or the sale of property.

Therefore, take skillful charge of this situation by having your decree include language protecting your right to modify the decree according to whatever issues you or your attorney believe might arise in the future.

Taxation Issues and What to Do About Them

Do you mean to tell me that even though I've got the standard marriage—spouse, a couple of kids, a house, and little else—I still need to look out for tax problems now that I'm divorcing?

It's quite possible today, because even in the seemingly simple situation you've described, a divorce can and probably will have major tax implications for you. Tax issues formerly surfaced only in the divorce cases of wealthy individuals such as company presidents, entertainment figures, and sports stars. Most other divorcing couples didn't even know what a tax issue was!

Unfortunately, that situation has truly become a thing of the past. More and more often in the past ten years or so, tax considerations have come to touch the lives of divorcing couples in all but the lowest of income brackets, and most of you aren't in this latter category. Tax laws seem to be perpetually changing. Sadly, these laws seldom change with everyone's best interests in mind. Act now to protect your economic interests.

First of all, understand the full significance of the oft-quoted maxim, "The only things that are certain are death and taxes." Now that you're divorcing, there are a number of tax events that will happen, whether you like them or not, because the law requires their occurrence in the situation you've chosen to create by seeking a divorce. For instance, in most states neither you nor your spouse will be able to obtain the favorable tax benefits accruing to married spouses filing a joint tax return.

Another example is that you *or* your spouse may soon be paying some form of financial support to the other person. In either event, a variety of tax consequences are unavoidable. Under *current* federal law, spousal support is considered to be taxable income to the recipient spouse *and* a tax deduction to the paying spouse. Such, however, is not true of child support payments. And generally, *only one of the divorcing spouses* will now be able to *legally* take a tax deduction for each of their children, because the deduction *cannot be split.* Most commonly today, that deduction, by law, is given to the custodial spouse unless there is evidence sustaining the noncustodial spouse's claim that he or she is paying a significantly greater level of support for the child than is the custodial spouse. This is what we lawyers sometimes refer to as a *legal presumption.* And your lawyer can tell you how much it can cost to successfully overcome such a presumption in your divorce. But only six years ago the legal presumption was just the other way around! And if these considerations weren't bad enough, pause to reflect that *each state can have different tax laws with regard to filing your state income tax returns.*

A third event likely to occur in your situation is a *taxable transfer* of an interest in the family home, resulting in a capital gains tax. This may be delayed, but it will eventually have to be paid.

Because of the incredibly complex nature of some of these tax considerations, you should be aware that many, if not most, tax consequences can be structured to promote a healthy economic future for whichever spouse gets the best tax advice. And always remember that, because you're divorcing, you will now have separate tax considerations from those of your spouse, and those interests may be competitive. It's your individual life now, and you have no further legal, ethical, or moral obligation to be concerned in any way with the promotion of tax benefits favorable to your spouse.

Don't, therefore, buy into the tax proposals of your spouse or his or her lawyer until you've reviewed them with *your* tax adviser. And don't sign any such proposals until and unless you and your advisers conclude that those proposals include satisfactory benefits to you. While the tax laws are purposely designed to get every possible penny the government can get, they also, by their very nature, pro-

vide you with a variety of tools to cushion their effect upon
you if you creatively use these laws to promote your best
economic interests.

From what has just been discussed, it follows quite naturally that you should take skillful charge of promoting the
most favorable tax situation for yourself by getting competent tax advice. I say this with full knowledge that such
advice does not come cheap. But consider it as an investment in your best economic future, and remember that tax
advice concerning the protection of your property interests
may be tax deductible. You would be well advised to pay a
relatively minor fee now, rather than risk monumental ones
later on, should you have to fight an unfavorable tax decision
by the IRS because you initially considered tax advice too
costly and unnecessary in your situation.

You will already know whether your lawyer possesses
such tax expertise because you will have remembered to
question him or her on this subject at the initial interview
(see pages 82–85). If your attorney doesn't have the requisite experience, get him or her to recommend a tax specialist to you to explain both the federal and the state tax
implications of any proposed settlement agreement in your
divorce. And remember to *keep asking questions* until you
understand the situation to your satisfaction. That's part of
the tax service you're paying for, so get it.

Further, get your tax adviser to suggest the most
beneficial means to save you the most tax dollars now and
in the future. Then incorporate that tax advice, through
your attorney, into appropriate settlement proposals of
your own. You can enable yourself to better evaluate the
advice you get by reading readily distributed and free information provided in your place of residence, such as IRS
Publication 504, "Tax Information for Divorced or Separated Individuals."

Taxes may be a tangled thicket, but they don't have to
scare you. You are fully capable of taking skillful and immediate charge of the situation. Do so now, and you will be
much better able to reduce or eliminate any unfavorable tax
consequences that may occur because you are now divorced.

I'm going through a divorce and my spouse just called to ask me to sign our joint federal and state income tax returns. What should I do in this situation to best protect my economic interests?

Resist any pressure from any source whatsoever to force you into making a snap decision that you might regret having made later on. And review the whole issue with your attorney *before you sign anything.* In the general situation, you will probably have a little more money, or slightly less debt, in your new and single future, by cooperating with your spouse in perhaps one of the final acts of your marriage. This is because typically, though not always, married spouses filing a joint tax return pay less overall taxes than would be the case if either spouse were to file an individual return.

Credit and Creditors

During my marriage, all of our credit was in my husband's name. Now that I'm getting divorced, I've begun to worry about getting my own credit established. What should I do?

You should realize that your situation is common to lots of divorcing women, and for that matter to all of us, both women and men, when, for the first time, we seek to establish credit. Furthermore, under certain circumstances that I'll discuss later on, you may be in a better position to secure that credit than most first-time credit-seekers who are single. So stop fretting. Anxiety won't solve this problem. Your determination to establish credit, however, will. Therefore, take skillful charge of your situation by understanding the basis upon which creditors will grant you credit, what you can do to make extending that credit to you more likely, and what to do if it's denied.

First, consider how most creditors will determine your credit worthiness. Generally speaking, potential creditors will evaluate your credit application with reference to the "five *C*'s" of credit, namely, character, capacity, capital, collateral, and conditions, the first three of which are typically most important. *Character* is mostly a question of whether you've lived up to the terms of other credit agreements you've had. *Capacity* refers to your ability to pay for the credit you want to get. For example, how much money is regularly available to you, and what is your potential for increasing that income level? The third C is for *capital;* this is some proof of your ability to pay off any debts you now incur. The proof they're looking for is a secondary source of debt repayment, such as a house, a savings account, or stocks and bonds. *Collateral* alludes to whether you have any property you're willing to pledge as security for the repayment of your debt. For instance, are you willing to give a potential creditor a *secured interest* in some property which you own? *Secured* means that the creditor can legally cause a liquidation of the property pledged as collateral for a loan if the latter is not repaid in a certain amount of time. And finally, *conditions* refers to external circumstances that may affect your ability to repay your debts. Such circumstances may include the seasonal nature of your job, if any. More appropriately, considering your current situation, what is the likelihood of your enforcing a spousal or child support order that you used as a partial basis for your credit application? These "five C's" form the basis upon which you either will or won't be extended credit.

Now that you are aware of how your potential creditors will evaluate you, here's how to make their extending you that credit more likely. The following suggestions are not steps that must necessarily be taken in any particular order. Start by opening a checking and/or savings account in your maiden name. This is useful because such accounts are financial records in your sole name. It's like establishing a financial "presence" or credibility in the minds of the credit extension community.

Second, if you are in the classic divorce situation for the particular problem we're now discussing, you probably didn't work for wages outside of your home, in which, you may sadly remember, you worked for peanuts. Such situations are what I call "marital slavery." Like the blacks of the old South, you have worked gratis for "the man," namely your husband, and you've been raised to believe that that's okay because your husband is providing you with the security of his interest in you, his concern for you, and his financial support of you.

Sadly, you've probably now discovered that you can't bank on that "security," because divorce can eliminate all of it. And unfortunately, your divorce, like the Emancipation Proclamation that supposedly "freed" the slaves of the old Confederacy, will not, in and of itself, prepare you for what to do to get credit in your future.

However, if this describes your current situation, don't punish yourself, but instead utilize your resources and move on. Even if it's only part-time, get a job! And don't allow foolish pride or other obstacles to stand in your way or be the basis for any self-pity in your current circumstances. All you need do right now is to establish, in the eyes of a potential creditor, that you'd make a good credit risk. Your willingness to seek and secure employment, even if only as a housekeeper for fifteen to twenty-five hours per week, is an indication of that credit worthiness. Whatever job you get, it is not forever!

Don't let the boring drudgery or low pay of some jobs be your excuse for not doing all that you can to make credit extension more available to you than it would otherwise be. You, and no one else, will be the ultimate loser. Couple your efforts to find and get employment with legally securing a valid and enforceable support order, which I'll discuss in Chapter 8. A job and a checking and/or savings account should enable you to get a gasoline credit card or perhaps a Visa or MasterCard account with a low credit limit. Remember, once you can establish even a small and short credit history, and even with only one creditor, you will find getting more and other credit a lot easier.

You might also consider getting a friend or a family member to co-sign on a small purchase you might want or need to make. Co-signature means, however, that your friend or family member is obligating himself or herself for your debt if you don't pay, so please utilize my suggestion responsibly. With this co-signing assistance and your determined and successful efforts to pay off the debt on time, you will, again, have begun to develop the basis for additional credit later on.

Third, if you did earn money for work you performed while married—and increasingly, both members of divorcing couples these days have had to work to make ends meet during marriage—you are probably in "fat city," even though all marital credit is in your spouse's name at the present time. For instance, you may be able to convince one of your husband's creditors that your earnings helped to retire your spouse's debt to them. If so, the creditor may look upon your past efforts as considerable evidence of your "character." The latter, in combination with your evident "capacity" (which your previous work for pay has also demonstrated) and the creditor's familiarity with your husband, may cause the creditor to more readily issue you credit in your "sole" name than would perhaps be the case with a new creditor lacking any knowledge of you or your husband.

But in any event, the character and capacity that you can certainly now demonstrate should be sufficient to get you some credit. A valid and enforceable support order might also help, because such income to you would be additional indication of your capacity.

And don't frustrate your efforts by making a big deal out of getting credit. One small loan that you successfully get credit for paying off on time is all you need to begin establishing your own separate credit. A good repayment record with that one creditor will produce more and other credit.

In the event that you are initially denied credit, don't give up. Your future is too important for you to do that. There are federal laws, which your lawyer can explain to you in greater detail, that require creditors, in evaluating your earnings during marriage, to give those earnings the same weight they would give to your husband's income in any evaluation of his credit worthiness. And it is illegal for a creditor to discriminate against you because you're a woman or because you're divorcing or divorced.

Further, you are entitled to have any denial of credit explained to you in writing. So don't be afraid to assert your rights. You are a valuable and uniquely beautiful person. Don't let getting credit be a stumbling block to your future happiness. Review any denial of credit with your attorney if you are in any way unclear about it, or believe that the denial was improper. And keep plugging away until you have succeeded in securing, developing, and protecting your credit rights.

As a result of my divorce, I'm now overwhelmed with bills, and creditors are nagging me all the time for payments. What can I do?

Don't, under any circumstances, allow yourself to respond to your debt problems as if you've failed in some way by going through a divorce that resulted in your current debt situation.

You may remember from reading my introductory comments to this book, in Chapter 1, that I am no stranger to poverty or the situation in which you currently find yourself. So please believe me when I tell you that you can master this situation by utilizing the following tools to take charge of your situation:

The first such tool is to use letters to put a stop to any further harassing phone calls. With regard to such calls from collection agencies, under federal law, you can prevent them from contacting you almost entirely. You can do so yourself or through your lawyer by sending the collection agency a letter notifying the collector that you are aware of your debt obligation but that you are asserting your right under 15 United States Code 1692c (called the Fair Debt Collection Practices Act). Pursuant thereto, the collection agency must cease any form of communication with you except at the specific times and places and for the specific reasons set forth in the federal law. Thereafter, it is illegal for the collection agency to contact you except in the following cases:

> 1. To inform you of a specific legal step being taken against you, such as filing papers with the court or garnishing your wages (this means that the agency legally requires a portion of your income of other property to be paid to it instead of you, but this can generally only happen after the creditor has obtained a judgment against you, and you have a right to participate in that proceeding).

2. To call you periodically to inquire about your current financial situation.

With reference to calls from creditors other than collection agencies, such as department stores, you can utilize the above tool with some slight variations. Again, either on your own or through your attorney, send a letter to harassing creditors in this second group, informing them that you are aware of the debt and the payment terms. Inform them also that you fully intend to take care of the obligation, but that, as a result of your divorce, there will be a temporary alteration in the amount and perhaps the timing of your payments. Further, let them know that in the near future (give a specific date if you can) you will present them with a formal plan for paying off their claims within your temporary reduced capacity to do so.

And finally, request that they call you at a certain phone number that you designate as the number where you can be reached for a defined and limited amount of time (typically between 6:00 and 9:00 P.M.), and that you would prefer any further communications concerning the obligation to be discussed between those hours. The lesson to learn here is that properly phrased words, in writing, and sometimes with the assistance of law (which is just some more words in writing), can enable you to exert tremendous power in this situation. That power, properly used, can provide you the time necessary to get a greater degree of control over your financial situation so that you can creatively resolve your problems.

When dealing with debt collectors of any kind, remember that it is generally illegal for them to engage in any of the following practices:

- To use profane or obscene language of any kind.
- To threaten to harm you or any member of your family or any of your friends.
- To threaten to expose you publicly as a person who doesn't pay his or her debts.
- To send you "fake" court forms or government documents.

- To contact your employer except to verify your employment or for purposes of collecting a debt by way of, for instance, garnishing your wages.
- To threaten to get your unemployment or welfare benefits stopped (this could not be done in any event).
- To claim to be a lawyer, unless he or she actually is, or to suggest this in any way, such as by using a lawyer's stationery.
- To pretend that a lawsuit has been initiated against you when this has not, in fact, occurred.
- To threaten to take away any portion of your income or other property, that is unless a court judgment has been obtained against you.
- To call you at your place of work if your boss forbids this.

But remember, illegality doesn't prevent some people from trying anyway. Therefore, protect your economic interests by remembering what your creditors can and cannot do.

As you are restoring some semblance of peace and quiet, you can begin to create a second tool, namely to develop a debt payoff plan to deal creatively with your debt crisis. Since you and your creditors have a common desire, namely, to see your debt paid off, all you really need do to gain almost complete control over this situation is to develop a plan that is reasonably within your current and foreseeable financial capacity to carry out.

Your first task in developing your plan will be to assess your current financial situation and what prospects you have for improving it in the future. Then you will need to devise the means for you to resolve the situation over time. You can do this yourself or by consulting and working with one of the many public service agencies, such as Consumer Credit Counselors (see discussion of this nonprofit organization on page 165), to assist you. Most of these groups will help you at no cost. They will act as an intermediary between you and your creditors in arranging an appropriate plan.

When you have made your written proposal, you will

have effectively shown your creditors that, while you are temporarily down, you are not permanently out. If any of them are thereafter foolish enough to sue you, they will have to demonstrate to the court why your payment plan is unreasonable or won't work.

Your willingness to take charge of the situation and put into effect a plan to deal with it responsibly will carry great weight in the eyes of most judges. Therefore, don't get angry or frustrated in your debt crisis. Instead, discover your power and use it.

Finally, don't ever allow your situation to make you feel as if you just want to chuck it all and go bankrupt. The label "bankrupt" will follow you everywhere for ten years, a long-lasting stigma that, after all you've just been through in your divorce, you certainly don't need. Consult with any decent bankruptcy lawyer in your area and get him or her to explain to you what options you have, short of all-out bankruptcy.

The federal bankruptcy laws provide tremendous legal protection to people who want to reorganize their debt payments and take care of them, rather than simply opting for a full-blown bankruptcy. Get that information from the lawyer and proceed. Remember always that your current situation is only temporary—that is, unless you want to make it last longer by not doing all that you can do to change it. And these situations can last a lifetime. Please, don't allow it to happen to you.

Can credit agencies, landlords, or employers discriminate against me just because I'm divorced?

Legally they cannot, since there are numerous federal laws against such discrimination, and many states have supplemented that law with what are often more effective enactments of their own. For instance, if you were turned down for a job by an employer who asked you if you were divorced and who then decided not to hire you because you were divorced, you would have the legal right to sue that employer under federal antidiscrimination laws.

So take skillful charge of this situation by being vigilant in any of your contacts with these people. If you are denied

credit, a rental home, or a job you've applied for, and you
feel even the slightest inkling that you have been discriminated against because of your divorced status, then
you can assert your rights by arranging the necessary time
to consult with an attorney. If we lawyer-legislators have
done nothing else beneficial for divorcing people, we have
at least done our damnedest to take the historical stigma out
of being divorced by enacting some decent antidiscrimination laws.

And many of these laws have sharp teeth, too. So respect yourself enough to not be abused by this problem.
Divorce does not mean you have failed in any way, so why
should you allow yourself to be punished for having the
enormously good sense to put an end to a bad relationship?
You can prevent this from happening to you by using these
antidiscrimination laws to correct the problem and then to
protect your economic interests and rights.

*Three years after my divorce, I remarried. Sometime there-
after, my new wife and I wanted to buy a house but discovered, to our surprise, that my credit was lousy. Upon
subsequent investigation, I found out that my ex-wife had
overcharged on charge accounts that were in my name, but
to which she was a joint signatory. These over-limit accounts are wreaking havoc on my credit rating. What can
I do?*

To the extent that you are able, the best thing you can
probably do to protect your economic interests is to pay off
all the overcharged accounts and then request a clear credit
rating. And do so, communicating to your ex-wife, in writing, that you intend to recover from her any debts incurred
on your accounts after your permanent separation. Of
course, typically in such cases, the ex-wife has blown whatever property she received in the divorce, so your letter
may net you nothing.

But there is little else you can do, short of a malpractice
claim against your attorney, which isn't a likely course in
this situation. It won't help you at all to assert that the
creditors should seek recovery from your ex-spouse; you
authorized your ex-wife to charge on the accounts. Further-

more, why should these creditors go after what is probably
a judgment-proof debtor (i.e., one who is not worth suing
because such a person doesn't have anything with which to
pay a judgment recovered against him or her), when they
have you firmly on the line, so to speak?

Also, you may have an even more serious problem if
you did not inform your attorney of the specific existence of
each such account, and did not have each one set forth in
the property settlement agreement or court decree. If you
did not take care of these potential problems, you may be
barred from reopening the divorce to recover anything
from anybody, including your spouse, or at least you might
be required to bring an independent action to recover these
debts. And the latter lawsuit has almost no chance of going
anywhere.

These are really tragic situations. Unfortunately, they
are often the result of the best of intentions. In the present
case, for instance, the husband probably had little or no
balance on any of his accounts at the time of his divorce.
Furthermore, probably out of some lingering guilt, this ex-
spouse left the accounts open and his ex-wife still a signatory
on them either by mistake or, more likely, because he
wanted to ensure that his ex-wife would have credit if she
needed it for emergencies.

And there is probably no one to help him now other
than his new wife, who isn't likely to be too keen about their
property being used to satisfy the debts of his ex-wife, especially because her new husband made a mistake in his divorce from a prior spouse by not taking care of business.

Don't let such a thing happen to you. Take skillful
charge of this situation by creatively resolving such issues at
the time you divorce. Blindly trusting that "things will all
work out for the best" is a mistake that may end up costing
you a bundle. If you truly want to provide your ex-spouse
with some "emergency" money, then help her establish
credit in her own name—even paying on some credit balances to those accounts, if you must—but get her name off
your individual accounts and close out all joint accounts as
well. And do all of these things before the final decree is
entered, not ten years after the fact, when it may be too late.

7

Your Children Are Forever: Bridging the Divorce Communication Gap Between You and Your Children

I often lead group discussions on divorce with high school seniors who are taking family life courses. Many of these teenagers are personally concerned about divorce, since they have witnessed the breakup of their own parents' marriages. Others are intensely curious about the subject, since they have friends or know other students who are living in a one-parent household, and they wonder if their parents, too, will ultimately divorce.

When I ask them what they learned most from our group discussions, they invariably reply, in the words of Laura, a bright seventeen-year-old who lives with her divorced mother, "I thought that only children hurt when there's a divorce. I didn't know that grownups hurt, too, because I thought they just got divorced, you know, like getting a car license."

This is the generation gap at its widest: the communication gap between children and their divorcing parents. It can be, and is, experienced by children of every age, as well as by their parents. If you are a parent when you are divorced, bridging this gap between your children and yourself must be given top priority if you are to lead a happier life as a newly single person than you would if you remained married. You are not alone in dealing with this enormously important issue; *more than one million children* each year *become children of divorced parents, since most of the two*

*and one-half million adults who divorce each year are also
parents.*

I see evidence every day at my counseling center of the
devastatingly painful results of gross misunderstandings by
divorced parents about how children are experiencing the
breakup, as well as how their children misperceive what
their parents are going through:

- Baby Mary, at fourteen months old, cries continuously and refuses to eat, in sharp contrast to
  her behavior prior to her parents' divorce.
- Judy, age five, refuses to sleep in her own bed as
  she did prior to the divorce, and insists on nest-
  ing beside Mommy. Then she often wakes up in
  the middle of the night, screaming that gremlins
  are attacking her.
- John, age nine, was an A-student whose grades
  are now all D's and F's. Since Dad left, John
  often stays home from school, complaining of
  headaches or stomach aches.
- Mary, age fourteen, formerly gentle and passive,
  defies her mother by frequently staying out with
  friends until one in the morning, then returning
  home with alcohol on her breath. Her mother
  discovers marijuana joints in her room. "So
  what?" Mary says. "You have no right to tell me
  what to do, now that Dad's left."
- Larry, age sixteen, has been caught shoplifting,
  and his mother and father, who have been divorced a year, must appear with him in juvenile
  court. He had attempted to sell a stolen VCR for
  money to buy some cocaine. His mother and
  father are involved in an ongoing court battle
  over who gets ownership of the house.
- Beth, age eighteen, formerly a careful driver,
  has been involved in a series of car crashes in
  which she was the driver. The latest one occurred after her mother was taken to the hospital, raving drunkenly that she was going to get
  even with that "sonofabitch husband" of hers
  who recently filed for a divorce.

- Terry, age twenty-one, refuses to visit either his mother or father during his college vacations. His parents are still calling each other names three years after their divorce, and both insist that he take their side of the argument. All Terry wants to do is to escape from both of his parents.
- Maureen, age thirty-five, hasn't seen her father since her parents' divorce when she was eight years old. She doesn't dare to, because her mother has told her repeatedly, "Your father is a no-good bastard, and if you ever visit him, you'll never see me again."
- Robert, age forty-four, writes a harsh rejection of his father's invitation to attend his remarriage ceremony. Robert says bitterly, "My old man is one mean prick. After what he did to my mother, I'll burn in hell before I attend his wedding to another woman." The hurt over his parents' divorce, which occurred twenty-five years ago, still flames in Robert's soul.

If you multiplied the examples I have just given ten thousand times, you would still barely scratch the surface of the parent-child estrangement that can and does occur as a consequence of mishandling divorce issues. I have not even mentioned the tragic teenage suicides resulting from depression caused by parental battles over custody rights, or the psychological or physical violence that divorcing parents impose on each other. (Some five thousand boys and girls age fifteen to nineteen commit suicide each year; for many of them, the agonizing divorces of their parents are a contributing factor in their deaths.)

Nor have I mentioned the one million children who run away from home each year, or the "kidnappings" by non-custodial parents who refuse to return their children to the custodial parents. (Melvin Belli discusses the legal aspects of these situations on page 274 and page 306.)

I have drawn your attention to these tragic examples to alert you to the lifetime scars you might inflict on your own children's psyches should you act toward them in inappropriate ways during and after your breakup. I speak as a divorced parent myself, who divorced when my two daughters were teenagers, and who learned the hard way about how to correct the errors I made in relating to my children during and after my divorce.

Now comes the *good* news. Your children *can* lead healthy, happy lives after your divorce; they *can* survive without being scarred for life; they *can* have good, loving relationships with *both* you and your ex-spouse until the time you leave this earth; they *can* grow up to be tolerant, mature persons who will be able to establish lasting marriages for themselves, rather than fear commitment of any kind; they will *not* turn gay or lesbian; they will *not* turn out to be antisocial vandals, fit only to wear prison uniforms. Best of all, *you* can deepen and enrich your own relationship with your children as you prevail together over the crises in your divorce.

However, none of these positive results will happen automatically. They can only come about if you and your spouse deal constructively with the issues in your divorce and jointly agree to cooperate as parents after your divorce in your children's best interest. Indeed, children are forever. Your children are not divorced when you divorce your spouse: they remain to be nurtured and cared for by *both* you and your former partner, despite your present distaste for each other. Even if your children are adults at the time of your divorce, they will mourn the death of Mom and Dad's marriage, and will need your attentiveness to their hurt, resentful, angry, bitter, guilty, mixed-up feelings.

Disposing of Stuff-and-Nonsense Beliefs About Children of Divorce

You've probably been exposed to many magazine articles, books, newspaper reports, and television documentaries that either assert or imply that children of divorced parents inevitably suffer lifetime damage as a result of the breakup of their traditional family households.

These media representations of children of divorce may very well be true to the individual cases they focus on (although even in those instances, hyped-up overdramatizations of "problem children" are the rule rather than the exception). However, even when true, they present a misleading impression of what will and must happen in *your* particular divorce with *your* particular children. For the belief they leave you with is that most if not all children of divorce are as traumatized by divorce as those they talk about. Pseudoscientific surveys in books and magazines attesting to the horrifying effects of divorce on children, which assault your eyes with elaborate statistical tables, may look very convincing.

But no long-term study of thousands of children of divorce from all classes and races in all sections of this country has ever been made! In fact, the study given the greatest national prominence as the most authoritative in the field consisted of a tiny sampling of 131 primarily white, middle-class children from an affluent California county.

My work over many years on the firing line of helping children and their divorced parents overcome the very difficult, very stressful involvements they experience with each other when a breakup occurs, has convinced me that you and your ex-spouse are the best determiners of whether or not any long-term damaging effects to your children will result from your divorce. At the start, please throw out of your mind any preconceived notions you might have about what divorce *must* do to *all* children. Otherwise, you may perpetuate a self-fulfilling prophecy; if you believe your divorce will permanently damage your children, you will behave toward them in such negative ways that you will guarantee that damage.

Whenever you hear someone say, "Surveys show . . ." listen with skepticism; absorb whatever kernels of truth the surveys offer, if any, but don't automatically apply those findings to your specific relationship with your specific children.

Do the same when you observe what has happened to other children in your friends' or relatives' divorces. Avoid the "comparison trap," since each family is unique, including yours. The way you and your spouse raised your children prior to the divorce, and your family life-style, are yours alone, not clones of any other family.

A Fresh Look at Yourself as a Divorced Parent

The parent-child relationship is the greatest guilt-manufacturing industry ever invented by human beings. You are guaranteed seven-days-a-week, round-the-clock, lifetime employment in this industry once you have children. "What have I done wrong?" is the universal theme parents play on their own heartstrings whenever children behave in what appear to be self-destructive ways, regardless of the ages of the children.

Perhaps the ultimate guilt-manufacturing story is the one about the ninety-year-old couple who visit a lawyer because they want a divorce. "But you've been married for seventy years. Why do you want a divorce now?" the puzzled lawyer asks them. "Well, we've disliked each other ever since we were married," they reply. "But we had to stay together for the sake of our children and wait until the last one died!"

This story elicits a laugh because the couple's behavior is so absurd, but at the same time touches the guilt in every parent. But it is also a tragic story, since the couple led self-punishing, unhappy lives and probably destroyed their own children's potential for happiness by demonstrating that life was a terrible chore, and marriage an abomination.

How You Can Use Guilt Constructively

Guilt, as Lillian Hellman once said, is often used as an excuse for not thinking clearly or constructively. It can also be used as an excuse for wallowing in self-pity and helplessness in order to get sympathetic attention from others so as to avoid taking personal responsibility to remedy a painful situation. If this is happening to you with regard to your children in your divorce, you can take corrective action that will enable you to have the better and deeper relationship with them that you long for.

But before that can happen, it's necessary for you to think clearly about the nature of the personal guilt that may be pervading your relationship with your children. You are not a bad person who has done something purposefully harmful if you feel guilty about any of the negative interactions between yourself and your children that may appear now that you are living with each other in a single-parent household.

To feel guilty about harming someone is a human response. In fact, the most dangerous individuals in our society are the persons known as psychopaths or sociopaths, who have no sense of guilt whatsoever for any of the cruelties or crimes they deliberately create. Guilt can be a humanizing factor that prods us into becoming kinder, more caring persons, rather than self-centered me-firsters who callously ignore the reality of other people's psychological and economic sufferings.

It's important, however, to separate *constructive* from *destructive* guilt in your own feelings and behavior toward your children. Constructive guilt arises when things are going wrong with your children and you do not automatically label yourself a bad person, but instead label this situation as a challenge to your ability to resolve it in as positive a way as possible. As an adult, you have the responsibility to initiate a positive solution, since your children have far less of the experience and problem-solving capacities that you possess.

On the other hand, destructive guilt allows for no solution to the situation. If you are in the grip of destructive guilt, you may automatically label yourself a bad person who caused the problem. And since nobody likes to believe he or she is really bad, you may then try to escape from that painful label by becoming self-righteously angry at your children, placing all of the blame on them, which in turn makes them even more defiant than they originally were, or you might shift the blame to "that rat," your ex-spouse. Another way you may run away from feeling like a bad mother or father is to deny that a problem exists when it is right before your eyes, or rationalize it away by believing it's only a "passing phase" rather than the real problem it is. And if you have a tendency to wallow in destructive guilt, you may say to yourself, "Yes, yes, yes, I am a very bad father or mother. Pity me, I'm helpless. God is punishing me for my divorce by having my children turn out badly." Instead of resolving difficulties with your children, you escalate those difficulties when you adopt such attitudes.

Here is a specific example of how you can deal with your guilt constructively or destructively in a typical situation. If your child (say he or she is ten years old) was always an A student who never cut classes before your divorce, but now gets D's and frequently misses school, what can be done about it? If you become overwhelmed by destructive guilt, you might view your child's school performance change as a failure on your part to be a good parent. You would view your child's performance as a reflection on yourself, believing others might fault you as a bad parent because of those low grades. You might then become self-righteously angry at your child because you don't want to think badly of yourself, and blame the problem on the child. Threats and punishment may flow from your anger. Or you may say to yourself, "It's just a passing phase that will soon end, and she [or he] will return to normal." If you are a guilt-wallower, you might go to extremes by doing all of your child's homework in the frantic hope that he or she will get good grades again.

You might also become excessively permissive, perhaps allowing your child to stay up far beyond the normal bedtime hour to watch television because "the poor baby" has a divorced parent. The upshot of all these well-intentioned reactions on your part will be that your child will *continue* to cut classes and receive D's. Destructive guilt never works.

On the other hand, constructive guilt directs you to focus positively on the problem at hand and its underlying cause, rather than on an obsessive concern about yourself and your "failure" as a parent. Constructive guilt permits you to acknowledge that out of unawareness you may not have paid sufficient attention to your child's school difficulties, and that now is the time to do so. Instead of viewing your child's poor performance record at school as a reflection of your own poor performance as a parent, you would concern yourself with what your child is feeling about the divorce, about himself or herself, and about school.

You would enable your child to feel free to express

everything with you (including possible anger toward you), without condemning or attacking him or her. It may very well be that your child still feels he or she may have been responsible for the divorce, and is depressed and fearful, which contributes to low grades and absenteeism. You would then clear up your child's distorted view of your divorce. Your child might also tell you that some of his teachers say derogatory things about divorce, so that he or she feels like an outsider, which frequently results in a what's-the-use attitude toward going to school.

As the concerned parent, you might then contact the school counselor and principal and inform them of your divorce. (A parent harboring destructive guilt would probably avoid notifying school officials of his or her divorce, out of a misguided belief that this would shelter the child from negative school reactions.) Your talks with school officials might reveal that many other students also come from divorced households, which is typically the case in schools throughout the country.

You could then suggest that the teachers themselves be alerted not to present a negative attitude about divorce toward students whose parents are no longer living together, and that they should neither pity nor demean such students. You could also ask the school counselor to notify you of any difficulties your child is experiencing, and discuss with the counselor ways in which both of you can assist your child.

You might get involved with the PTA at school and with other divorced parents, and have some group discussions about how to assist the children, since these other parents probably are facing similar problems. From this PTA group might arise the suggestion that the school itself should institute a program for the children of divorce to air their concerns, a type of program that other schools have already initiated.

You can assist your child with difficult homework, but you should not take over doing all the homework, and you should enforce reasonable home discipline instead of over-indulging your child. If you indeed have been neglecting your child because of the many pressures and demands that your divorce has imposed on you, you should reorder your priorities to pay more sensitive, kind, and caring attention to your child's feelings and behavior. The problem is now on its way toward a positive solution, which is exactly the function of constructive guilt.

Parents, whether married or divorced, never lose traces of personal guilt about the way they have brought up their children. That comes with being a parent and lasts a lifetime. Constructive guilt is necessary and is simply a reflection of your love for and concern over the welfare of your children, whom you brought into this world and feel responsible for. You want the best for them, and may feel that your best is not enough. You would be less than human to feel otherwise.

But that does not mean you must express your guilt feelings over your children's welfare in overprotective or punitive and angry ways, nor should you try to escape from your guilt feelings by neglecting your children or placing all the blame on them or your ex-spouse for their negative behavior. Consider that to be responsible for your children's welfare means to respond with ability to your children's needs. That's what the word *responsibility* means.

How can you, as a divorced parent, "respond with ability" toward your children? First of all, relax. Let go of the notion that you can control the destiny of your children. Parenthood has been called, quite rightly, "the impossible profession." You are neither a saint (the modern version is called super-mom or super-dad) nor a sinner (the "bad" parent who has spawned "rotten" kids).

You, like every other parent, are just a normal, well-intentioned, fallible human being who is capable of remedying many of the errors you may have made in dealing with your children. But you cannot do so if you psychologically flagellate yourself or your children when errors occur. In subsequent sections of this chapter, I will deal with the major dilemmas that divorced parents are confronted with, and indicate how they can be constructively resolved.

For the present, it's important to keep in mind that you will *never* be able to shape your children according to your image of what you want them to be. They are listening to their own distant drummer, not yours. This should not surprise you; just remember your own relationship with your parents, and recall how you became what you wanted to be, not what they imagined for you. At best, all that you can provide your children with in their earlier years is secure ground to stand on, from which they can confidently embark in their subsequent journey through life as independent adults.

That secure ground is within your capacity to create for them. It does not depend on whether or not you are divorced, nor on an accumulation of wealth and material comforts. In fact, this most important gift that you can give your children costs you nothing but your ability to respond skillfully to your children's basic needs.

Unconditional Love: A Necessity for Your Children's Emotional Health

The paramount need of your children, from the very moment of their birth, is to feel that they are unconditionally loved by you and your spouse, and that this love continues throughout *both* of your lifetimes, no matter that you are now divorced. To love your children unconditionally means you love them for who they are, not for what they do. Do not confuse unconditional love with overindulgence and excessive permissiveness. The latter are reflections of a divorced parent's feelings of helplessness and lack of control, while unconditional love is a reflection of your feeling that whatever difficulties you might be experiencing in your divorce are capable of being overcome, and that you are transmitting that sense of security to your children.

You communicate unconditional love to your children when you create reasonable rules for the managing of your household and for their behavior, and consistently discipline them in an appropriate way for infractions. You do so in an *authoritative* way rather than in an *authoritarian* one. To love your children for who they are means to respect and pay attention to what they are feeling, to generate a sense of growing self-worth and competency in them, to allow at all times for open communication so that they are free to express their deepest and most painful feelings and concerns without fear of your condemnation of them, to encourage their thirst for independence while recognizing their continued need for nurturing and guidance.

But loving them for who they are does not mean that anything goes, that they are free to do harmful, destructive things to themselves or others. On the contrary, it means you are establishing the kind of relationship with them that will elicit the best qualities inherent in your children: personal integrity, sensitivity toward and cooperation with others, self-discipline, and motivation to learn and achieve by competing with oneself rather than at the expense of others.

The way in which you handle your divorce will significantly determine whether or not you will be nurturing those qualities in your children. When you make skillful efforts to make positive things happen in your own life, no longer using someone else's behavior as an excuse for not doing so, you become the role model for your children to do the same.

Creating a Positive Role Model for Your Children

You are your children's most important soap opera. They tune in to the TV channel of your daily behavior and feelings throughout your divorce twenty-four hours a day, for you are the principal person whose actions affect their ability to survive either securely or fearfully, now that you are no longer living with your ex-spouse. They watch the plot that you and your ex-spouse create in your divorce. What will happen next? Will Mom and Dad bad-mouth each other in the children's presence? Will they force the children to "take sides" and make them agree that their divorced father or mother is a "bastard" or a "bitch"?

Will the children become hostages to one parent, who refuses to allow the other parent to spend time with them? Will the next day bring the children to court, to testify against one of their parents in a bitter custody dispute? Must the children become informers, telling scurrilous tales one parent wants to hear about the ex-spouse? Will tomorrow be happier than today?

You and your spouse create the script, and your children hang on to each new development as if the quality of their lives depended on what you did in your divorce to yourself, to your ex-spouse, and to the children. And it does, because you and your spouse are your children's most influential role models. Consequently, the way you handle the parts you play in your divorce will affect the ability of your children to handle stress and pain and change in their own lives now and in adulthood.

Do you want your child to respond like a victim to his or her own life's future crises? Then act like a helpless ingenue or wimp in your life as a divorced person. Like a defeatist? Then act like a despairing doomster. Like a resentment-collector? Then act like a bitter complainer. Like a distruster of everyone? Then act like an everyone-is-out-to-get-me paranoid. Like a denier of difficult reality? Then act like a pain-escaping alcoholic, drug-user, or workaholic wearing an artificial-happiness mask. Like a future many-times divorced person? Then act like a permanent plunger into short-term affairs, proclaiming that commitment equals disaster. Like a self-centered me-firster? Then act like a contemptuous user and exploiter of others. Like a guilt-ridden apologist for ever being alive? Then act like a martyred wreck. Like a timid loner? Then act like an incompetent bumbler afraid to take chances. Like an I'm-always-right-even-when-I'm-wrong person? Then act like an angry prosecutor vengefully determined to extract the last ounce of blood from your ex-spouse.

You would be less than human if you did not *at times* feel and act in some of the ways I have noted above as you ride out the storms of your divorce. However, experiencing twinges of these reactions on your part is quite different from perpetuating any of these self-defeating behaviors as the permanent way in which you live your life as a single person.

When you might overhear a friend saying to someone about you that you are always the complainer, martyr, or helpless one, then it's time for you to reevaluate what you are doing to yourself, and the effect this has on your children.

You can utilize constructive guilt to avoid or escape

from any of these self-defeating traps by becoming aware of your own way of behaving and feeling during and after your divorce. No permanent harm will be done to your children, provided that you begin to function as the capable person you *really* are, and then establish new and better ways of relating to them, whether your children are preschoolers or adults at the time of your divorce.

And if there has been an estrangement of many years' duration between you and your children because you have perpetuated self-defeating behaviors long after the divorce occurred, your relationship can be vastly improved when you take constructive action to eliminate the iron curtain of unintended hurts, miscommunication, and resentments that have accumulated between you. But before this can happen, we will have to journey together to understand what children want and need, and how they experience their relationship with their parents in a divorce situation.

A Fresh Look at Your Divorce Through Your Children's Eyes

The central thing you need to keep in mind throughout your divorce is that your children love *both* you and your ex-spouse. This is true of all children of divorce, whether the children are five years old or fifty. Even in those extreme cases in which a parent is truly a villain (a vicious alcoholic, an uncaring parent, a cruel authoritarian), the love of the child for that natural parent remains alive and hopeful. The bond between a natural parent and a child may become very tenuous at times, but it is never broken. When a child says, "I hate Mommy [or Daddy]," that is usually an expression of the pain of a child who feels a lack of reciprocated love from his parent, rather than a statement that the parent is rotten and must be dispensed with.

This permanent love that a child feels for both parents arises out of the very nature of human existence. Your child first emerges from the womb as a miracle of welcomed delight for you and your spouse. But that child also emerges as a Mount Everest of personal needs and demands that must be fulfilled if the child is to survive, let alone flourish.

You and your spouse have life-and-death control over that newborn baby. He or she will die or waste away if both of you don't provide sufficient food, physical care, shelter, and constant attentiveness to guard the baby against self-inflicted or external harm. Moreover, it is essential for your child to feel that he or she is loved and wanted forever. You and your spouse reassure your child that this is the case by providing a basic sense of security for him or her through the consistency and predictable regularity of your nurturing. Attention only to physical needs is not enough; your playtime with your baby, the hugs and kisses, the loving way you talk to your infant (your words may not be understood, but the feeling behind those words is communicated and internalized in your child) all combine to convince the child that he or she has the two most special people in the entire world, who can always be counted on for love and concern.

You lay this *emotional* security foundation in your child during the first three years of his or her life, when your child is most vulnerable. In fact, very young children have even been known to die for lack of this kind of emotional security (there is a medical term for this sad situation: *infant marasmus*). Such infants are frequently found in orphanages, where they may be provided with adequate food and physical conditions, but do not have one very special person they can count on for love and affection. The infants become listless and depressed, and lack the will to eat or live.

You and your spouse are undoubtedly typical parents who have provided this emotional security for your own children in those early years of their lives. Your divorce cannot take that basic fact of your children's existence away from them or you. This means that the love bond between you and the children (and between your ex-spouse and the children) remains very strong regardless of the alienation that might occur during or after the divorce. Of course, if you are like most parents, you may feel you never did provide enough of the kind of emotional security for your children that I have talked about, in these beginning three years of your children's lives. Calm yourself in the knowledge that *every* parent feels that way.

Of course, knowing what we know now, we could have done better then. But we did the best we could, given our knowledge at the time—and we *did* create the love bond that will never die, even when it might seem it has. You will find this to be true once you begin to make the effort to bridge the divorce communication gap between you and your children in ways I will outline later in this chapter.

In his or her earliest years, your child's entire world consists of your family: you, your spouse, and whatever siblings and other relatives might be present. You and your spouse are the Rock of Gibraltar that his or her world depends upon for physical and emotional survival. The most excruciating nightmare a young child can have is the fear that he or she might be abandoned for being "bad," and then thrown out of the house to starve and die, which would then occur because he or she is too inexperienced and vulnerable to survive alone.

Mom and Dad's togetherness in the same house, and their overriding concern for the child's welfare, afford assurance that this will never happen. The nightmare remains only a nightmare. But when a divorce occurs, the nightmare can be experienced by the child as a waking reality.

"What's Going to Happen to Me?"

The consequences of a divorce are the equivalent of a major earthquake in a child's mind and feelings. As an adult, you may also feel such tremors inside yourself once your divorce begins, but you have the learned experience and the developed intelligence to survive the shocks and move your life forward. Your children are still novices in coping with the major life crises that adult flesh is heir to. Left to their own imaginings and fears, your child could believe the following kinds of distortions of reality expressed by the children I counsel:

"I caused the divorce because I didn't eat my spinach and my report card showed two C's the night Daddy left."

"Mommy left the house, that means she hates me."

"Now that Daddy left, he will never want to see me again, ever."

"I'll starve because Mommy says she has no money because Daddy left."

"My friends will think I'm bad and won't play with me because my Mom and Dad no longer live together."

"The teacher will punish me because my parents are getting a divorce."

"Now that Daddy has left, Mommy might leave the same way, then what will happen to me?"

"Mommy tells me Daddy is a very wicked person because of the divorce. Daddy tells me the same about Mommy. If both of my parents are wicked, I must be wicked too, because they both made me."

"I hate being put in the middle. I love my mom and I love my dad. It makes me feel terrible when they force me to take sides."

"My grandma and grandpa don't love me anymore because they never visit me now that Mommy and Daddy are divorced."

"Mom and Dad don't care about me. They spend more time seeing their lawyers and fighting in court then they do with me."

"Just you wait and see. My mom and dad will get together again and it will be just like it always was. I'll show them I'll be good. I'll clean my room, eat everything on my plate, and get all A's on my report card, then there won't be any reason for them to stay apart."

I could multiply these poignant examples by thousands of similar cries for help from children of divorce that echo in my counseling office. All of these examples have one thing in common: they are all self-centered remarks. They all arise from the desperate need of the children to feel secure in the face of a crisis that has shattered the stability of their personal world. Their sense of personal security was rooted in their assumption that Mom and Dad would be living together in the same household forever.

Children see divorce through the tunnel vision of "What's going to happen to me?" Since they are too young yet to survive on their own, their own security is their over-riding concern. When their basic home life is fundamentally disrupted, as happens in a divorce, terror over their own survival in this new situation can flood their souls. It matters little to a young child that Mom and Dad are divorcing because they can no longer get along or love each other. All the child cares about is his or her own security. Parents can carefully explain to their child the reasons why they are divorcing, yet the child may respond by saying, "Yes, but why can't we still stay together like it was?" The unhappiness of the parents takes second place in the child's mind to his or her own threatened security.

It is perfectly natural for young children to feel totally self-centered, since they are still too vulnerable to survive on their own. Your child primarily views you as the permanent service industry created solely for the purpose of attending to his or her basic needs. A child does not view you as a separate person with needs of your own that are unrelated to his or her own welfare.

Children's Self-Centered Divorce Fantasies

A child translates everything you do in terms of the effect it has on his or her own welfare and happiness, rather than yours. Even a child's eagerness to make Mom and Dad happy is fundamentally a consequence of the need of the child for approval and *continued* parental attention to his or her welfare. When a child grows to adulthood, very significant traces of this belief that parents were created solely for his or her own welfare remain embedded in the child's mind.

Paradoxically, very young children also believe they are all-powerful, the center of the universe, the person who magically makes things happen. After all, when they cry for food, it's quickly given; when bored, they are entertained; when the diaper is full, a fresh, clean one takes its place; when tired, they are placed in bed; when lonely, they are hugged, cuddled, kissed, and talked and sung to; when in harm's way, they are snatched to safety; when anxious, they are reassured by warm body contact.

A very young child interprets his or her own great vulnerability as a sign of tremendous personal power, since the parents are always present to fulfill his or her wishes and commands. It appears to the child that he or she has magical powers; desire seems to become reality because he or she wills it. This belief in one's own magical power to transform reality is very apparent in preschoolers and in children of elementary school level. It repeatedly arises in a divorce situation. So do not be surprised should your child assert during your divorce that he or she will make it all better, that Mom and Dad will be together again because your child will make it happen by being a good boy or girl.

I have previously noted that the desire for a fairy-tale ending to your divorce, in which you and your ex-spouse are reunited into a happy household, may never die in your children's feelings. Twenty or thirty years after the divorce, it can still smolder at an unconscious level as an ember of regret and resentment, while at a conscious level that hope has long since eroded away. No matter how miserable and anguished you were in your marriage, a fact that made your divorce inevitable, the children's desire for the security of Mommy and Daddy living together and taking care of them can remain chronically embedded in your children's hearts.

It can take the form of resentment or hostility or distancing or anger or sadness on your children's part whenever they find themselves placed in the middle of any dispute between you and your ex-spouse. And when you date new people or involve yourself in a living-together arrangement or a remarriage, your children may have very mixed feelings about your doing so: on the one hand, they may be happy that you are now happier; on the other, they may see this as a threat to their dream that you and your ex-spouse will eventually reconcile.

This is a fact of divorced life that you will have to live with. No happiness pill has been invented whereby your children's longings or your own guilt (which your children's longing may trigger) can be entirely eliminated. Your major challenge is to recognize the existence of this fact and diminish its negative impact on your post-divorce relationship with your children.

Children, as one of my clients remarked, have "built-in shit detectors." They have a radarlike sensitivity that can pick up the disturbances in your relationship with your former spouse even before you yourself may be aware of them.

In my counseling practice I continually hear expressions of surprise from divorced parents who say, "My kids tell me that long before my divorce, they knew we were a very unhappy couple; in fact, they knew we were unhappy before we ourselves did!" This really should come as no surprise if you realize that young children know that their very survival depends on the security their parents create for them. Consequently, they intuitively "read" their parents' actions for clues that indicate whether or not the family ship is sailing smoothly. If their radar sensitivity was at work prior to your divorce, it is working at maximum level after your divorce. However, young children are apt to totally misinterpret the signals they receive from you because they do not as yet possess fully developed reasoning power and still believe the earth revolves around them. Thus, when Mom or Dad, during the divorce, seems helpless or insecure, children believe they caused this behavior in their parents and feel guilty for doing so. Their guilt may then turn into anger or depression when they discover that they themselves cannot eliminate their parents' helplessness or insecurity, since making their parents capable and secure is the only way they feel they can rid themselves of their guilt. They might then label themselves "bad" and "failures," believing themselves unwanted and unloved.

You have a powerful tool to correct these possible attitudes of your children, and the disturbing behavior that may result from them, when you become aware of their existence. Then you can exorcise the goblins that may be invading your children's psyches. You can also take heart in the fact that children are much more resilient than parents give them credit for. They will not be traumatized for life if you exhibit helplessness, insecurity, unhappiness, anger, frustration, hatred, or despair during your divorce. These feelings come with breaking up and reordering your life as a single person. Stiff-upper-lip denial of that reality will only be experienced by your children as a fraudulent attempt by you to impose a sense of security where none exists, and will only compound the children's feeling that they are indeed in a helpless situation. As long as your children are assured that such out-of-control outbursts on your part are temporary and fleeting responses to difficult life situations (such as a confrontation with your ex-spouse, finding a decent child-care facility, worrying about getting a job), which you yourself correct by proving yourself capable of handling these situations in a constructive way in the long run, no real harm is done. It is to your children's advantage to see their parents triumph over adversity, to understand that life is not all fun and games, but rather a mixture in which adversity plays a prominent role. It is the child who is raised "under glass," sheltered from all harm, who experiences the greatest difficulties in adult life, who lives with resentment because he or she was promised a rose garden but received thorns instead. To prevail over a major life crisis is to provide your children with one of the most helpful legacies you can ever give them. It demonstrates that they, too, can prevail.

The Divorced Father Rediscovered

Divorced fathers, with rare exceptions, dearly love their children.

Unfortunately, in all too many divorces this obvious fact is not the taken-for-granted reality it should be if the children are to experience their parent's divorce as a temporary disruption that is a prelude to a new stability, rather than as a permanent trauma. Nothing causes more anguish in children, or more self-destructive behavior, than a belief that now that Daddy no longer lives at home, he no longer loves them.

That this belief is totally false is beside the point, for, from a child's point of view, you and your ex-spouse may be acting toward each other during and after your divorce in ways that would encourage that line of thinking. And our society's way of dealing with divorce perpetuates the idea that fathers are rather disposable persons as parents after a breakup.

It is still relatively exceptional for a child to live in the new household of his or her father after the divorce, rather than with the mother. Judges in disputed-custody cases still tend to decide in favor of the child's living permanently in the mother's home, with the father receiving visitation rights. The very nature of this arrangement generates an impression that fathers are outsiders and that only mothers experience a permanent love bond with the children.

Too many divorced men at my counseling center have shared with me, in voices trembling with despair and with tears in their eyes, their love and longing for the lost daily contact they once had with their children, for me to believe that fathers are unloving parents once they live apart from their children. Such men do not miss their former wives, but they do feel lost and empty because their everyday relationship with their children no longer exists. It is the little things they recall. Quite often it is the poignant remembrance of helping their kids with their homework that will bring tears to their eyes.

More and more men these days are allowing their true emotions to emerge. Our society is just now beginning to acknowledge the falsity of the sanctioned macho image that men have been programmed to model themselves after. If you were a "real man," according to that image, you would not reveal or even possess any tender, caring, sensitive, loving emotions. "Real men don't cry." "Women hug and kiss their children, men shake hands." "Women are natural-born homemakers, men are natural wage earners." The list of clichés that were once accepted as holy writ is now slowly but surely being shredded and dumped into the ash can of history. Yet many men still believe that to acknowledge that they are vulnerable, that they hurt badly and yearn for a continuation of the reciprocated love between themselves and their children, is to make them seem less like a man (a "feminine" man, God forbid!) in the eyes of other men. Women, in turn, make their evaluation of what men are really like from what men reveal of themselves. So it is small wonder that all too frequently in my divorce seminars, women will state that what they learned most from the sessions was that men had feelings too!

For men to come out of the closet with their true feelings, validation by society is needed. They are beginning to get that validation from the women's movement, and also from those prime reinforcers of what is acceptable in society, films and television. The film *Kramer vs. Kramer* was a watershed event, since it validated divorced men's love for their children and educated *both* men and women to the fact that men can take profound satisfaction in nurturing their children.

In television, the miniseries "Breaking Up Is Hard to Do" further reinforced this aspect of men's lives. We can expect more films and television programs of this nature to appear in the future. Men's groups, taking encouragement from the women's movement, are burgeoning throughout the country; they are involving more and more men who seek their freedom from the sexual stereotypes they were trained to live by.

If you are a divorced father who has lived by the rules of the old stereotype of what a "real" man should be, there may be some surprises awaiting you, once you begin to live apart from your children. Like other divorced fathers, you may find yourself crying for the first or second time in your life, if you find your children refusing to visit you. Or you may discover that you miss intensely the kids you felt were so bothersome and loud when you were married; their noise now seems like music to your ears compared to the deadly silence of your new apartment. Or, for a moment, your guard may drop when you become overwhelmed with joy at seeing your child again, and you may surprise yourself by hugging and kissing him or her, something you never did before. (And you may be equally surprised should your child express delight and tell you how much he or she has always hoped you would do precisely that!)

Many divorced fathers discover a deeper, more meaningful relationship with their children *after* a divorce. While in the marriage, such men all too often ignored their children because they saw their home as a sanctuary, a respite from their grinding work day. "Don't disturb Daddy," was the whispered warning to the children by the wife in that unhappy household. The wife tended to the needs of the children; the husband tended to the TV set. Or the father would pay lip service to the children, asking them perfunctorily, "What did you do in school today?" "What's your report card like?" "Did you get on the basketball team?" Divorce shatters that empty routine. When a father begins to live apart from his children, he may very well become aware of how barren his relationship to them really was when they had lived together. In the depths of his soul he suddenly realizes how centrally important his children are to his life, the children he once took for granted like the furniture. He may then painfully regret the time he squandered in never truly knowing who his children *were;* he only knew what they *did.* Now he can no longer squander time, for time is precious since he no longer sees his children every day. The time he *now* spends with his children becomes quality time during which he tries to connect with the person who is his child, and not merely the performer of duties. His child's joys, sorrows, hopes, fears, uncertainty, anger, frustration, confusion, and desires now become touchstones of their relationship.

Nurturing his children in times when dependency and guidance are required soon becomes second nature to such a father. Telling his child he loves him or her, and reinforcing the words with hugs and affection, takes the place of the old macho image. In turn, this permits his child to feel secure enough to express *all* of his or her concerns, which this father can truly hear, perhaps for the very first time.

This deepening father-child relationship after a divorce can prove to be one of the most important benefits resulting from a breakup. The price for this benefit is very high. It is paid for in tears of regret and anguish at time squandered; it requires a lonely confrontation with your old parental image and the arduous substitution of a better one. The price is very high because your goal is such a precious one. In human relationships we get what we pay for; the cheaper the price, the shoddier the product.

Guidelines for Bridging the Divorce Communication Gap Between You and Your Children

Since the love bond between you and your children *never* disappears, you *always* have the opportunity to bridge the divorce communication gap that may exist between yourself and your children. Bridging this gap can enable you to have a better, closer relationship with them. In fact, your relationship with your children during your unhappy marriage may have been the seedbed of many of the difficulties you are experiencing with them now; your divorce, then, could be the magnifying glass of the kind of overprotectiveness, estrangement, or alienation that long existed between you and your children, which you never noticed when you were married. Your divorce can jolt you into an awareness that focused attention must now be paid to the ways in which you may have been relating to your children ineffectively and how you now can relate to them more skillfully and work together as a team rather than as antagonists.

Should you, in moments of frustration or despair, yearn for the time when your children lived in the two-parent household you once had, stop for a moment and think of how your then-spouse and your children were really relating to each other. Was it a happy time? Or did your children, long before the divorce, experience parental overprotectiveness? Did you give them smother-love because you needed the love your spouse denied you, and therefore burden your children with excessive affection?

Did your children experience alienation and estrangement in your marriage when they saw Mom and Dad often not speaking to each other, their parents feeling self-pity and isolating themselves from the family? Did your children witness vicious put-downs and countless bitter arguments between you and your spouse while married? Did your children see Mom and Dad battering each other, so that plate-throwing and bruised faces and bodies became their image of what married life was all about? Did your children frequently see Mom or Dad in a drunken stupor, or raging with alcoholic violence, so that the children felt they had no one to depend on except their own vulnerable selves?

Did your children find Dad always ignoring them, always glued to the TV, while Mom busied herself elsewhere, so that it seemed their parents were like two ships passing in the night? If so, you will be putting the cart before the horse if you believe your divorce is the cause of your children's seemingly odd and negative behavior now that you are living singly. Your children's behavior in your divorce is really the consequence of how they were conditioned to react to stressful circumstances during your marriage.

If you should recognize yourself or your spouse in any of the instances noted above, this does not mean you were a "bad" parent. All it demonstrates is that you, like every other parent in this world, were not as skillful as you could be relating to your children. Now is the time to become more skillful. Parenting is a process by which you learn through trial and error to become more able; there is no gene you can inherit that comes labeled as the "skillful parent gene."

Nine Guidelines for Connecting Positively with Your Children

As a divorced parent, you can begin to improve your relationship with your children by applying the following guidelines:

1. The past cannot be remedied, but the present and the future can. Consequently, forgive yourself for the unskillful ways you dealt with your children in the past and take personal responsibility to correct your relationship with your children now.

2. You and your ex-spouse are the natural parents of your children, which means your children love *both* of you. You may dislike or detest your ex-spouse, but your children do not feel the same way. Therefore, do not impose your own attitude on your children; allow them to continue to love their noncustodial parent without making them feel guilty for doing so. You have a right to your own feelings; permit your children to have an equal right to their feelings.

3. Your children desperately want to have a good relationship with both parents. Capitalize on that fact by allowing frequent flexible and continuous visitation rights to your ex-

spouse. Every barrier you erect to prevent your ex-spouse from seeing the children will generate anger, hostility, resentment, or depressive guilt in your children.

4. Your children's love for you and your ex-spouse is a well that never runs dry, no matter how you have raised them in the past. They forget past hurts in the presence of new, more mature and insightfully attentive behavior toward them on your part. Your acting with confidence on this fact can establish a better relationship with your children after your divorce than you may have had during your marriage. Trust in the resilience of your children.

5. Accept the fact that you and your ex-spouse are the most important transmitters of the basic values your children will continue to live by, and you are the role models for them in the way they will react to the crises that will inevitably occur later in their lives. By your behavior, in your divorce, you educate them into becoming persons who see themselves (like their parents) as victims of society or as self-assured persons (like their parents) who make the effort to bring positive results out of adversity.

6. Practice empathy with your children. Empathy means putting yourself in your children's place in order to understand why they behave the way they do. You know how your own life crises affected your own feelings and behaviors as a child. When you were unhappy and insecure in your childhood family (because Mom and Dad may have felt sad or angry or helpless or hopeless when faced with the loss of a job, the death of a loved one, endless squabbling over never having enough money, and so on), you probably acted out your unhappiness and insecurity by becoming angry or unruly or depressed or defiant. Apply that

knowledge to your own children and use it to
remedy similar occurrences in your children if
they appear during and after your divorce.

7. Recognize the cries for help in your children's
behavior during and after your divorce. The
younger your children are, the less formed is
their ability to communicate their needs verbally to you during and after the divorce.
When preschool children feel unloved, neglected, or insecure, they "talk" out their feelings to you by their behavior: they may
regress to an earlier stage of their development and once again suck their thumbs or be
afraid of the darkness; they may lose their
appetites and wake frequently during the
night crying anxiously, where once they slept
soundly without a whimper. Older children
can communicate with you verbally about
their hurts and insecurity if you will take the
opportunity to initiate open communication
with them, but they will also "talk" to you
through the changes in their behavior: elementary school children may "tell" you they
are sad and depressed over the divorce when
they suddenly exhibit behavior such as a lack
of interest in school, getting poor grades in
courses where they previously excelled.
Adolescents may "tell" you that your relationship with them needs constructive changing
when they suddenly begin to cut class frequently, when they become verbally abusive
to you or sexually irresponsible, night-owl
defiers of your home curfew rule, or when
they start imbibing alcohol, cocaine, or other
drugs after they find themselves living in a
single-parent household.

8. Do not label your single-parent home a "broken" home. The word *broken* implies that it is
an imperfect, deficient, wrong kind of home,
which communicates to children that there is
something bad about themselves since they

live in such a home. Call it a "readjusted" home instead, one that allows for ongoing loving relationships between the children and your ex-spouse, even though your ex-spouse is no longer living with you. A home is not a physical place but a psychological state of security. In Robert Frost's words, home is "the place where, when you have to go there, they have to take you in."

9. Recognize that your children's fundamental need for security after a divorce remains the same as it was during the time you were married. Your children, above all else, need to feel that Mom and Dad will always provide them with the emotional and physical security they need to develop into confident maturity. Their security does *not* depend on the state of your income or the place you live, but on whether you and your ex-spouse demonstrate by your behavior in your divorce that both of you are fully competent to weather the storms of change that divorce entails.

Bridging the divorce communication gap between you and your children begins when you incorporate these nine guidelines into your way of thinking and behaving toward your children, thereby enabling you to give *focused attention* to your children. By focused attention I mean viewing your children as persons in their own right, whose emotional reactions and behavior resulting from your divorce necessarily differ from your own.

Adults tend to attribute the stresses and strains of this time in their lives solely to the divorce. Children, on the other hand, see their situation through the tunnel vision of their own need for security. Unlike adults, children do not have the capacity as yet to survive physically or emotionally on their own. Consequently, they translate the behavior of their parents toward them as signals informing them as to whether or not they can count on Mom and Dad to provide security. They are primarily concerned with their own welfare because they require the kind of parental nurturing that is essential if they are to become secure adults.

The inevitable self-centeredness of children, that obsessive concern with "what's going to happen to me?" existed in your marriage as well as in your divorce. In fact, to younger children, divorce is only an abstract word, not a condition of life. They do not see their parents as separate individuals with a host of needs that have nothing to do with them personally. For children, parents are simply the extensions of their own needs, and exist solely for the benefit of making their lives secure.

Understanding the Many Ways Your Children Communicate with You

Armed with this knowledge, you can begin to communicate with your children in a more constructive way. Communication means much more than just talk. Children state their concerns in their behavior toward you. And what they *don't* talk about is often more revealing of their state of mind than what they say. *How* they talk to you may tell you more about their concerns than what they talk about. By utilizing focused attention, you can translate these many forms of communication your children are giving you into a more in-depth, positive relationship with them. The divorce communication gap narrows when you focus your attention on the causes of your children's seemingly "weird" or "strange" or changed behavior after your divorce and act to eliminate those causes.

If your once-active children suddenly become moody, silent, and listless, they may be mourning the breakup of their two-parent household. It's your responsibility to help them talk about their feelings about the divorce, rather than avoiding the subject and hoping their behavior is just "a passing phase." Your children will feel much more secure when you assure them it's okay for them to feel the way they do about the divorce, and that you too feel that way sometimes. By reassuring them that you are doing everything possible to make a good family life for them, and that they did not cause the divorce, you can relieve them of much unnecessary anxiety.

If your children spend most of their time with their friends or their gang and seem to avoid coming home, consider the possibility that they may be angry with you for preventing them from seeing their noncustodial parent. If you have been placing roadblocks in the way of your ex-spouse's desire to see the children frequently, your children will more likely act out this resentment by defying your authority rather than by confronting you directly with their anger over being placed in the middle of a never-ending battle with your ex-spouse. It's okay to tell them you were wrong, that sometimes parents do improper things under stress, and that you will remedy this situation. Your children will respect you more for your honesty than they would for your self-righteousness.

If your formerly conformist teenager suddenly takes to alcohol, cocaine, or other drugs, he or she may be trying to kill the pain of the breakup of their family household. You will get nowhere by calling your child a "rotten kid" or a "juvenile delinquent." You will begin to remedy this situation when you allow your child to express his or her pain directly and tap into his or her constructive interests and objectives. You become the role model by getting your own life together in constructive ways.

Your teenager may become sexually very active after a divorce, and even argue that since you may be sexually active now, why should he or she be denied this right? Recognize that in our present society most teenagers *are* sexually active, whether they live with two parents or in a divorced household. However, sex for a teenager who has witnessed a stressful divorce in their family may be a way, just like drugs, to dampen the pain they feel about the divorce. When you address their pain and discuss alternative ways of dealing with it, you begin to help them act more responsibly where sexual involvement is concerned. And by confronting their challenge to you as to why they can't be as sexually active as you are, it is appropriate to acknowledge that you, as an adult human being, have needs for love and affection that include sexual intercourse. However, such restrictions as you place on your children's sexual activity that they may not sleep with a partner in your house or apartment, for example, result from the fact that this is a reasonable rule of *your* house. And as long as they still rely on your support, that rule has to be respected. When they are adults in their own homes, they are free to do as they wish. You cannot prevent them from having sex outside your home, but you can educate them to the profound meaning of the sexual experience and help minimize their sexual indulgences as an attempt to alleviate or deny the pain they are feeling about the divorce.

Your child may communicate with you by the anger or defiance in his or her voice over some minor issue like washing the dishes. However, the anger or defiance may have nothing to do with the dishes, but everything to do with the child's feeling betrayed by the divorce, which undermined his or her sense of security. Don't act like another child by returning one shout with another. Acknowledge to your child that it's okay to feel angry, since all feelings are okay, but that, angry or not, the dishes must be washed. Then, at a later appropriate time, engage your child in a discussion that will address the *real* causes of the anger and defiance, so that your child can be reassured that you are creating a new stability and continuing security for them in your new life as a divorced person.

The indirect ways in which your children communicate to you their basic underlying fears and misconceptions regarding the divorce are like a detective story. You are the sleuth who must unravel the clues they strew in your path. The clues take the form of denial of the pain, confusion, sadness, or anger over the divorce (when asked how they feel, their answer always is "I feel fine."); defiance of authority ("Now that Dad's left, why should I listen to you?"); regression to an earlier stage of development (bedwetting or fear of the dark, which was nonexistent prior to the divorce); assuming too much authority ("I'm the one who's going to take care of Mom, now that Dad's gone"); escaping the pain (through sexual irresponsibility or drugs); avoidance (by substituting friends or partying for home life); or disengagement (refusing to see either parent if the adult child is living away from the places where his or her parents are located).

You can assuage these behavioral disturbances, so that divorce will be a passing phase in your children's development rather than a lifetime scar on their personality, when you create a stable home environment in which your children see you taking positive charge of your life. A place where they can comfortably share with you *all* of their feelings, no matter how scary some of those feelings may seem to them, since you are not judging their feelings but are helping them understand why they may be feeling the way they do.

How to Survive as a Divorced Mother Without Losing Your Mind

All children regard their parents as service industries, created by God only to pay attention to them and fulfill their needs. In a child's very early years, that is an accurate view of the parent-child relationship, since children are indeed so very vulnerable at that time. However, it is the function of good parenting to create the conditions for a child to grow in independence while the parents provide the nurturing appropriate to the child's age.

However, children at *every* age find it very difficult to give up the belief that parents exist only for their benefit. Indeed, adult children often become shocked when their divorced mother becomes sexually involved with men. It is as if their mother has violated the fundamental rule that a mother must be a mother and nothing else in life. Somehow they assume it's perfectly all right for a divorced father to engage in new sexual activity, but a mother, never!

The divorce communication gap narrows when you begin to educate your children to the fact that you are more than just a parent, important as that fact is. Divorce offers you the opportunity to discover the widest range of who you are, apart from your identity as a mother. You are *also* a person with a need for love, friendship, affection, career, and personal time for yourself, including hobbies and social activities. In other words, you are a human being, which includes but does not limit you to the role of mother.

And since you are human, you have your ups and downs, moments of happiness and despair, achievement and defeat. Should you try to shield your children from these basic realities of who and what you are, in the belief that you are not entitled to fulfill your own needs, your children will sense the anxiety and destructive guilt you feel behind your mask of silence. And because of that fact, they in turn will become more insecure rather than less so.

Relieving Your Children's Anxiety by Dealing with Their Hidden Issues

If it is true that your children are more vulnerable than you are to dramatic change in their life situation, it is equally true that they have more ability and intelligence to weather that change than you may be giving them credit for. When you openly share with them the reasons why you are feeling and behaving the way you are, you provide them with the psychological security they need to develop normally and healthily as members of your newly restructured household. Children feel terribly insecure and fearful when you avoid sharing feelings or information with them. What they may imagine from your silence is infinitely more terrifying to them than the realities from which you may be trying to protect them. Their imaginations run wild; they translate everything you leave unsaid as a sign that you are abandoning them. You can eliminate this basic fear when you initiate open discussions with them about hidden issues.

Your children could be relieved of their anxiety when you tell them you are now dating because this is what mothers do after divorce; and that mothers need companionship and affection from other adults. You can reassure your children that dating does not mean you love them less or are leaving them; on the contrary, it means you will become a happier, more contented person when you are with them.

Your children will feel more secure if you tell them you are working because that is what you have to do to provide their food and home and the fun times you have together. You reassure them that going to work is not a trial run for abandoning them permanently, but instead is the way in which Mom shows her love and caring for them.

Inform your children that leading a good life after the divorce requires teamwork and demands new responsibilities from everyone in tending to household duties. Children welcome being part of a team that will make life happier for a parent; they like to know that they are needed, and feel more secure once that need by a parent is voiced. The alternative of trying to become a silent-suffering super-mom by overburdening yourself with chores they could help with communicates to your children that you are inse-cure, unhappy, and uncertain about your future, which means they themselves become fearful for their own future.

When you tell your children that you are taking a course at the local college or engaging in a political cam-paign or meeting new friends at a social gathering, because these are the kinds of things mothers do to make life more interesting for themselves, your children will understand and accept these activities as a normal part of your new life as a divorced person. They will *not* accept them if they believe that you are leaving for an evening in order to escape from their presence, so you should explain to them why you are involved in these activities, and that they have nothing to do with your wanting to leave them perma-nently. Your neglect to voice the reasons for your activities may be the result of your feeling guilty about doing some-thing solely for yourself instead of for the children. Leaving the children at home, then, becomes your "dirty little se-cret," which could activate abandonment fears in their minds.

If your divorce has resulted in a decrease in your stan-dard of living, necessitating the elimination of some previ-ous pleasures your children enjoyed, don't hide from them the reasons for this situation. Share with them the reality that this is a temporary condition and that you are doing everything you can to change it for the better, such as im-proving your job skills and taking career courses. Things like this happen in life, but can be overcome. Give your children substitutes that don't cost money, such as local community recreation programs and library showings of children's movies. Parks and playgrounds are free and made for enjoy-ment. Feeling sorry for yourself or trying to create a false appearance that everything's okay will only create in your children's minds the fear that the wolf will be permanently at their door, and that fear for their future will be their lot in life.

How you talk to your children is just as important as what you talk to them about. They will hear your guilt if you keep apologizing for your present state of affairs, which may make them think they are the cause of your feeling guilty. They will hear your anger if you keep raging at the injustices in your life, and believe they are the causes of your anger. They will hear your constant silent suffering and believe you are rejecting them. They will hear the righteous indignation in your voice should you tell them your ex-spouse is the cause of all of your present problems, and they will feel that you are a victim who can't solve those problems by yourself, which places them in jeopardy. They will hear the sadness in your voice and then feel that they are helpless, just as Mommy is.

However, as long as you feel competent within yourself to solve the problems you face as a divorced mother, you will demonstrate that fact in your sharing of family difficulties with your children in a panic-free, assured tone of voice that will communicate to them that these setbacks will be overcome. They will be reassured that this is indeed the reality they can expect, when they see you making the effort to make positive things happen in your family life. Your words and the way you say them combine with your deeds to create the psychological security your children need when you are divorced.

Eliminating the Super-Mom Syndrome from Your Life

The demands upon a divorced mother's time seem insatiable. There never seems to be enough time to accomplish all of the tasks thrust upon her. If you are like millions of other divorced mothers who hold an outside job, your working day may very well begin at 6:00 A.M. (preparing breakfasts and school lunches for the children, arranging the clothes they will wear, dropping your school-age children off at school or your preschoolers at a day-care center), then working from 9:00 A.M. to 5:00 P.M., at which time you return to the day-care center to shuttle your children home. Your school-age children are already home because arrangements with other mothers were made to pick them up after school. Now that you are home, further work is in store for you: there is dinner to be made, homework to be done with some help from you, laundry and dishes and dusting and the changing of bedsheets, plus a host of other home chores.

Oh yes, somehow the marketing for the house has to be done, otherwise there will be no meals the next day. By the time you get to bed at midnight (or even later), you may feel fortunate if you have squeezed out an hour of free time for yourself after you put the children to bed. Weekends are the time to work at the household chores you neglected earlier in the week, plan some joint activities with the children, search for a baby-sitter if you have a Saturday-night date, and wind up exhausted on Sunday. Then get ready for a new week of more of the same. . . .

Your concern for your children's welfare is a black cloud that hovers over your head while you are at work. You may feel guilty for working rather than spending your working hours with them. Or you may feel resentful toward your children because they may jeopardize your job, which you desperately need to make ends meet, when you are notified at your office that one of them has just become ill or had an accident. That requires you to take time off from the job, which your boss may not tolerate if it happens frequently.

The problems of finding responsible baby-sitters at the times you need them, or a reputable day-care center you can afford, are ever-present concerns. You may shudder when you read headlines and see TV news programs that report revelations about child sexual abuse at some day-care centers. Will the fears, the pressures, and the exhaustions ever end?

Yes, they will, but not if you panic or expect them to disappear overnight. In the very beginning stage of your divorce, your may feel as if you are living through an earthquake, as I mentioned in Chapter 2. Your emotional and physical survival may then appear threatened, so that all of your energies become focused on how you can regain a sense of personal security in your life.

In that stage, when self-centeredness is required, you may be unaware of the impact your behavior is having on your children. Consequently, the sooner you create positive new arrangements and habits in your life, the sooner you will be able to construct an improved relationship with your children, rather than resenting them as impossible burdens in your time of distress and feeling guilty for thinking such a terrible thought. The light at the end of your tunnel becomes visible when your fear that you can't survive on your own diminishes, which then allows you to apply the following guidelines to your restructured family:

Eight Guidelines to Benefit You and Your Children

1. *Teach your children that the changed family condition is not a disaster but a difficulty you can overcome if you all work together in a new way.* This may mean additional household responsibilities for the children, such as preparing some of their own meals and taking greater responsibility for cleaning the house. You may very well have underestimated your young children's abilities to cope with some of the household work you thought you "must" do. By emphasizing that your household is a cooperative enterprise necessitating their teamwork, you can make the children an important part of your life rather than an encumbrance during your divorce. On the other hand, do not overwhelm your children with responsibilities for their own upbringing, and be realistic as to what they can or cannot do on their own in terms of their age and experience.

2. *Eliminate any traces of super-mom thinking from your mind that might make you overburden yourself with responsibilities that otherwise could be diminished.* You can't do everything by yourself. That is no crime, but rather a reality of your everyday life. Remember that you are not alone in your divorce. There are many other women in your commu-

nity who are facing the same problems; seek
them out and work out carpooling arrangements whereby they can take your children to
school or a day-care center part of the time.
Check with your friends or your minister,
priest, or rabbi or the family service agency in
your area for a good child-care center; join the
Parents Without Partners organization in your
city, which has a host of positive activities designed for children; alert your neighbors to
the fact that your children may be home on
their own for a few hours after school while
you are at work, so that they can contact you
should an emergency arise; contact your children's school counselor for recommendations
for good baby-sitters, in addition to friends at
work or in your neighborhood. Resources are
there for you to use, once you free your imagination to think constructively rather than
fearfully.

3. *Wipe out any fears you might have that your
children will become homosexual because
their father is no longer an everyday presence
in the house.* A child's sexual preference is
determined in the first year or two of life, according to modern findings. As long as your
children have ongoing contact with their father, their confidence in their own gender is
reassured. Should that contact not exist, their
continued identification with their own sex
can be reaffirmed by caring connections with
their relatives of the same sex. Little is yet
known as to what causes homosexuality, but
divorce is acknowledged *not* to be one of the
causes.

4. *Don't use your children as an emotional
crutch during your divorce.* They are your
children, not your confidants, advisers, protec-
tors, or substitute therapists. Should you treat
them as if they are your adult friends, as nur-
turers who can help you assuage your sorrows,

as people who can solve your emotional problems, as grownups ("My child is now the man
of the house."), as givers of adult affection
("My child is my best beau."), you will be overburdening them with inappropriate adult responsibilities that their age, their experiences
in life, and their special mother-child relationship are not designed to handle. You could
reap a harvest of anger, guilt, hostility, confusion, and alienation from your children,
should you impose these responsibilities on
them. In the very early stages of your divorce,
some of these inappropriate actions might
occur. However, no harm is done if you
change your behavior toward them as soon as
possible, which you can do once you demonstrate by your actions that you are assuming
positive control over your own life so that you
don't need your children to give you the security that only you can give yourself.

5. *Should you feel you are at the end of your
   tether and plagued with problems that neither you nor your friends and relatives can
   help you to solve, seek out a good divorce
   counselor for assistance.* It is the strong person, rather than the weak one, who seeks
   counseling. Sometimes we are too close to our
   own problems and fail to see the forest for the
   trees, and we need the help of an objective
   observer. Even if you have little money, such
   help is available on the basis of ability to pay
   from your local family service agency or religious organization, such as Catholic Social Services or a Jewish family agency.

6. *Release your children from becoming hostages to the war that may still be going on
   between you and your ex-husband.* Nothing
   will destroy whatever serenity and stability
   may exist in your household more than endless battling over custody and visitation rights.
   Separate the bitterness or even the hatred you

may still be feeling about your ex-husband from the need of your children to maintain a loving relationship with their father; you may no longer love him, but they do. If you put roadblocks in the way of their being able to communicate and visit with him regularly (because you want to hurt him for all of the wrongs you believe he inflicted on you, or because he is behind on child support payments), you will be harming your children and yourself far more than you will be hurting your ex-husband.

Your children then will become defiant or depressed, or will distance themselves from you. And if you demand that they tattle on their father when they visit with him, or if you bad-mouth him in their presence, you will generate mistrust and anger rather than cooperation and love. Vengeance toward your ex-husband may appear as a tempting plum to you; it is, however, a poisonous fruit that your children will find difficult to stomach. Cooperation with your ex-husband in arranging generous visitation rights will afford you the benefit of additional free time for yourself, time you urgently need for filling the cup of your own needs.

7. *Make certain your new dating relationships will not generate sexual fears and conflicts in your children.* One of the questions I am frequently asked is, "If I decide to sleep with a new boyfriend and he wants to spend the night, how can I explain this to my children?" If you feel guilty about this, it will not be good for either you or the children. If, on the other hand, you feel that what you are doing is appropriate to your needs and that the children can expect this from time to time, tell them so very simply and openly, and the situation will resolve itself. What disturbs children is promiscuity, the confusion and disturbance of many or even several men wandering in and out. If

there is a very special friend or lover in your life, explain to the children that he is someone you like very much, and that you hope they will get to know him as a friend. The children are then free to love their father as a father and to like the person you are attached to as a friend. Reassure your children that any new man in your life is not taking any love away from them, since children believe that any affection you may demonstrate to someone else means a lessening of your love for them.

8. *Don't eliminate your children's relatives on your ex-husband's side from their lives.* Grandparents in particular are enormously valuable enrichers of your children's lives. To deprive them of experiencing the grandparents on their father's side, because you are still bitter and angry about your ex-husband, will hurt your children and your relationship with them.

You also benefit from the time and attention they give the children, since it enables you to have more of the precious free time you need for yourself. And if you are avoiding these grandparents because you think they have automatically taken your ex-husband's side in the divorce, you may very well be mistaken. In addition, they love their grandchildren regardless of what has happened between you and your ex-husband. When you reach out to those grandparents (and your children's uncles and aunts on their father's side), you might be very pleasantly surprised.

Father Is a Forever Word

I cannot emphasize too often that ex-husbands, with very few exceptions, dearly love their children. That love and their desire for an ongoing connection with their children doesn't die when they leave the home and move into a separate place after the breakup, as is the case in more than 90 percent of all divorces.

However, the very nature of divorce, whereby a mother usually receives legal custody of the children, makes it appear as if the father is an outsider who no longer cares for his children, since he becomes a "visitor" rather than an everyday presence in his children's lives. The term *visitation rights* reinforces that misconception. And when an ex-wife who has legal custody abuses that fact to prevent a father from seeing his children regularly and often for a generous amount of time, the father as outsider becomes an imposed reality. I have observed the cruel situation in which an ex-wife will call up her former husband and tell him their son won't be able to see him that day, which had been agreed to, because he came down with a cold or a stomachache or some such physical ailment. All of this is untrue, of course, and is simply a way for her to "get even" with her ex-spouse.

Another device often used to "get even" is for the ex-wife to send a telegram to a father the day before he is scheduled to see his children, when he has booked a plane flight from another city where he now lives, saying plans have been changed or the child is too ill to be visited. Again, all a fiction, of course. Preventing visitation until delayed spousal support or child support payments are made is another typical device designed to make a father feel as if he is a bad or unwanted father.

And if the ex-wife insists on the children taking her side in the bitter disputes she has with her ex-husband, the children, to avoid the wrath of their mother, may be taught to "hate" their father and refuse to talk with him on the phone, respond to his letters, or see him in person.

Actions such as these inflict enormous pain on fathers, who respond all too often with rage or despair to these barriers that prevent them from seeing their children. I have seen such fathers batter their heads against a legal wall in countless lawsuits, trying to obtain their rights, and go broke in the process. I have seen fathers weep inconsolably when they tell me their children no longer want to see them. With this type of conditioning, many fathers actually begin to believe they are unwanted by their children and are bad fathers.

Although many ex-wives claim that their ex-husbands no longer love their children, they really know better than that. If that were really the case, why then deny them generous visitation rights? If fathers really didn't love their children, eliminating visitation barriers would provide proof of the fact, since uncaring fathers wouldn't take advantage of such rights. The very fury that fathers exhibit when denied such rights is a testament to their deep love for their children.

Fury, however, only compounds the problem rather than resolving it. If you are a father experiencing the pain and rage of deliberately malicious attempts to separate you from your children, your heartbreak will only be compounded if you engage in new court battles ("If it costs me every dime I have, I'll take my case to the Supreme Court if necessary!"), refusal to pay legally due child support ("I'll make that bitch hurt by not paying her the money; she wouldn't use it for the kids anyway!"), or child-snatching ("I'll take my children to another state or country. Let that cruel slut try to find us!"). Your frustration and rage may very well be justified, but acting on the basis of these feelings is not.

Substitute Love of Your Children for Vengeance Against Your Ex-Spouse

Consider the consequences of acting out of the need for vengeance. Creating new court battles will place your children in the intolerable position of having to take sides with either you or your ex-spouse. And since your children love you both, they will feel guilty, resentful, and depressed because they are forced to choose between the two of you and become informers. And should you gain a court "victory," it would be an economic defeat that might result in your own impoverishment (court costs and lawyer's fees in contested cases can create terror in your soul) and hostility from your children, because you have traumatized them in the law courts.

Delaying child support payments or refusing to pay them at all is an attack against your children rather than your ex-spouse. To deprive them of the basics (food, cloth-

ing, and shelter) only intensifies their divorce trauma and
will leave in them a legacy of bitterness toward you that will
be difficult to erase in future years.

Child-snatching is the ultimate trauma for your children. What better training could you give them to become
insecure, paranoid adults than to condition them in their
youth to be ever on the run, guarded in their actions, and
fearful of the cop that might appear on their doorstep when
they wake up in the morning? And how can you live with
yourself or happily renew your life as a divorced person if
your waking hours are overwhelmed with the worry of escaping legal action for your deed and covering up your
tracks?

Consider, first of all, what you will be doing to yourself
and your children if you embark on these courses of action.
The satisfaction you derive from such vengeful acts will turn
into dust and ashes, as so many divorced fathers have told
me.

What, then, is the alternative? The bitter reality is that
there is no easy, instant alternative solution to the problem.
If divorce were simply a situation in which two human beings could sever their marital relationship on the basis of
reason and intelligence alone, without blame-laying, and in
which the best interests of the children were of primary
concern, bitter custody and visitation battles would never
occur in the first place.

But that would be like asking human beings to act like
computers or robots, devoid of feelings. And since divorce,
by its very nature, is, at its deepest level, a profoundly disturbing complex of emotional experiences, it is inevitable
that some leakage of vengeance and anger and hatred occurs in the divorce process where children are involved.
However, it is one thing to acknowledge the existence of
these feelings when they arise; it is quite another to allow
your decisions with regard to your relationship with your
children to be swayed by those feelings.

The goal you long for—a loving, ongoing relationship
with your children after the divorce, without hassles
created by a vindictive ex-wife to prevent that from happening—may be a long time in coming. However, it will
never come if you pursue that goal through custody dis-

putes, denial of child support, or child-snatching. I have known more than a few well-intentioned fathers who have done exactly that, making their pursuit of what they regarded as "justice" a lifetime goal. Ten or fifteen years later they find themselves embittered and hopeless, their careers, their love life, and their children's affection for them sacrificed to that pursuit.

How can you have the relationship you want with your children in the face of unremitting attempts by your ex-wife to prevent it from happening? Since tit-for-tat vengeance is not the answer, the alternative solution resides in the answer Herman Hesse gave in his novel *Siddhartha*, about what can be done in a situation that seems impossible of solution: "Think. Wait. Fast" was Hesse's answer.

Think When you find yourself overwhelmed with feelings of righteous indignation and blind anger, *notice* what you are feeling and remember it's okay to feel the way you do, but not to make any decisions on these feelings then. Allow time for the feelings to diminish to the point where they don't overwhelm you.

Then think about alternatives to your seemingly no-win situation. You can try to educate your ex-spouse by phone, by letter, or in person, in a non-angry, nonthreatening way to alert her to the best interests of the children, informing her that it is them she is hurting the most by denying visitation rights. She may be more receptive to this approach if you are not withholding spousal support or child support payments to "get even" with her. If this does not work, you can still maintain contact with your children through letters and tape recordings, even if phone calls are prohibited by your ex-spouse.

You can continue to visit with your ex-wife's parents if you have a good relationship with them, and they in turn might have a softening influence on their daughter. You can also get involved with father-oriented organizations, such as the recently founded National Organization for Men, that perform an educational function, alerting your community (and your ex-wife) to the need for a more empathic understanding of your father's rights. And you can, above all, set aside whatever hatred you may still have for your ex-wife, so that you can truly separate your actions from what might be vengeance rather than a concern for your children's needs.

Are you withholding child support payments because you want more visitation rights, or because you want to punish your ex-wife? Would you agree to joint custody in the best interests of your children, or are you insistent on your own individual custody simply because that makes your ex-wife furious? By appealing to one of the best aspects of your ex-wife, her dedication to being a good mother, you can suggest that she set aside her possible enmity toward you (and vice versa) in order to go into joint counseling with a good divorce counselor so that you can work out arrangements that will be most beneficial to your children's welfare.

Wait Even if the above actions turn out to be initially fruitless, remember that today is not forever; people and situations change with time. Refrain from demanding of yourself instant rectification of what you perceive to be an injustice. Frustration and despair will be the consequences of your unrealistic insistence on an immediate solution to a situation for which no immediate solution is possible. However, keep in mind that a long-range solution *is* possible. Your ex-wife's using the children as a weapon against you is quite probably a reflection of the fact that she is desperately unhappy with her current situation in life. She may be plagued with inadequate income, underdeveloped skills that leave her with bleak job opportunities, and little time to make new friends and seek out a new and gratifying love relationship. The unhappier she is with her general plight, the angrier and less receptive she will be to any of your positive suggestions about dealing with the children. You have a stake in making her less fearful of her life as a divorced woman, which you can do by seeing to it that regular spousal and child support payments arrive at the agreed-upon time. If she can begin to make positive things happen in her own life, this in turn will soften her need to blame you for her sad situation. In time, your ex-wife, if she is like most other divorced women, will renew her belief in her own self-worth and find a job or a career as well as a fulfilling emotional life with friends and a new love relationship. When that happens, time will soften the battle between you, provided you too are getting on with your own life. In the light of such a development, working out constructive arrangements regarding the children can become a reality rather than a fantasy.

Remember also that your children have minds of their own. They are not clones of you or your ex-wife, nor are they puppets that can be manipulated at will. They may not *say* they don't like for Mom and Dad to bad-mouth each other in their presence, or being brought into court, or being forced to be "loyal" to one parent at the expense of the other, or being denied the right to see their father, but they *feel* the injustice of these things intensely. And as they grow older, they will often assert their own wants and needs rather than what their parents think they want or need. I have seen many instances in which teenaged children, whose parents may have been divorced when they were elementary school students or preschoolers, assert that they would like to live with their fathers in their teenage years, despite years of hearing negative comments from their mothers. The children in this case become the catalyst for creating a situation in which a new and better relationship with their father can occur. A mother in this case finds it very difficult, if not impossible, to ignore her child's cry for his or her father.

Fast Fasting is not the same as starving, though it seems that way when you are deprived of your fatherly desire to see your children at the time you wish to do so. However, it is of paramount importance for you to take a long view of your situation. Yes, when all else fails, you may be deprived of your children, but understand that this is a temporary deprivation, not an eternal fact. Accept the inevitable pain of temporary loss; that pain will diminish in time, even though it will not leave you. But also get on with the rest of your life. Fulfill your life with rich new experiences in the world of work, in community organizations, in hobbies, in making new friends, and in a new love relationship that will improve upon the past rather than repeat it. And all the while, your children will save your letters and cherish your tape recordings and gifts, even though they may make no immediate response, owing to fear of their mother's anger.

Patience and continued contact in any possible way with your children will pay off in the long run. Always remember that no matter what you or your ex-wife say about each other, your children love you both. You may have left them physically, for months or even years, but in their hearts and minds you never left home. Your eventual physical renewal of contact with them can become a foreordained reality by virtue of that fact.

How to Become a Real Father, Rather than a "Pretend" One

I have discussed the pain of actual physical separation between divorced fathers and their children. However, there is another special kind of pain that exists even when generous visitation rights are freely exercised and when custody has been agreed to. That is the pain fathers feel in missing the *everyday* experience of their children's presence. Now that they can no longer be taken for granted as an everyday part of your life, a feeling of enormous loss can engulf you. Oh, how you miss the joy and delight of just being with your children. The minor annoyances you once felt vanish from your mind; tenderness, affection, warmth, and love flood in their place. An overpowering yearning to know your children better, now that you are divorced, becomes top priority, where once it never entered your mind. You are now determined to make the time you spend with them quality time during which you get to know them as the individuals they are, rather than as fixtures around the house. Pretend-time is over; the loving father who expresses his love for his children emerges in place of the distant exasperated parent in a falling-apart marriage.

The very loss of daily contact with your children and the pain attendant on that loss (a pain that will never end, but will grow less sharp with time) may become a blessing in disguise. It can shock you into a realization that you never knew your children except as surface images. Now is your opportunity to really listen to them, to find out who they are as separate individuals, rather than as display pieces that positively or negatively affect your own self-image. The fol-

lowing six guidelines can assist you in bridging the divorce
communication gap that may exist between yourself and
your children:

1. *Don't fall victim to the belief that you are a
   bad father because you are no longer an everyday presence in your children's lives.* Even if
   you were to remain married, your children
   would eventually leave home permanently,
   often around the age of eighteen; you would
   then see them far less frequently than before,
   yet that would be no reflection on your image
   as a good father. When you spend regular and
   frequent time with your children after the divorce, and when you phone and write to them
   frequently, your love for each other is reinforced. There may remain some ache in your
   heart and in your children over the lack of
   daily physical contact with each other, but
   that ache will greatly diminish as your divorce
   lengthens into years, provided you strengthen
   the emotional bond with your children during
   that time.

2. *Eliminate the movie-father image of what a
   good father should be like.* Traces of past TV
   programs and movies you grew up with may
   remain imbedded in your mind. The old "Father Knows Best" TV series encapsulates that
   parental image: the always-wise, ever-com-
   passionate father, present every day at the
   breakfast and dinner table, radar-alert to his
   children's needs, doing the right things at the
   right times, typified who the father was on
   that show. Well, that kind of father only exists
   in TV land or in the old Andy Hardy movies,
   and is the product of the fevered imaginations
   of well-paid scriptwriters who long for a childhood they themselves never had. As a divorced father, you will corrode yourself with
   destructive guilt if you believe you are a bad
   father because you don't measure up to this

image. In the real world, all fathers (and mothers) are fallible human beings, doing the best they can to help their children develop into decent, intelligent, caring human beings. They do this through trial and error, just as you are trying to do. If, out of unawareness, you have been an unskillful parent in the past, once you become aware of how to act more skillfully with your children, your relationship with them can vastly improve. To become skillful means to dispense with the absurd notion that a good father must be one who is physically present every day with his children. In fact, the most emotional and physical harm is done to children in homes where divorce has not occurred and where the father is home every night. The everyday presence of a bitter, angry, authoritarian, or depressed father in a painful marriage is no blessing to his children.

You are a good father when you demonstrate *by your behavior* toward your children that they know in their hearts and minds that you love them, care about them, and are always accessible to them in ways that allow them to share their deepest feelings (fears, hopes, dreams, confusions, hates, and uncertainties) without being judged. You will always be there for your children, no matter where you are living now. In the country of your children's minds and hearts, you will always be present. Give "Father Knows Best" the burial it deserves.

3. *See your children for who they are, not what you imagine them to be.* Your daughter may physically resemble the ex-wife you now dislike. Your son may exhibit some of the behaviors of your ex-wife, such as a tone of voice that "drove you up the wall." It is inevitable that your children will exhibit traces of both you and your ex-wife, but that does not mean they

are clones of either one of you. Being skillful
means not reacting negatively to these surface
similarities, for to do so will distance you from
the children you want to get closer to. Our
children are themselves; to react to them as if
they were the ex-wife you now may feel bitter
about will make them feel as if there were
something wrong with them. They should not
be put into the agonizing position of thinking
they must give up the mother they love in
order to gain your love. Your children were
made from *both* you and your ex-wife. To attempt to split them in half, to deny their
mother's heritage, will generate hostility toward you. Unconditional love is the behavior
they need from you.

4. *Remember that nothing (except love) lasts
forever, and that includes alienation from
your children.* The brainwashing your children may have received from your ex-wife
that you were a "bad" father, and that therefore you are not entitled to see your children,
may result in their *temporarily* not wishing to
see you. This "temporary" state may sometimes last for years after a divorce, but eventually your children, as they grow older, will not
only desire but may even demand to see you
again, no matter what your ex-wife wishes.
The blood bond between you and your children will triumph in the end, so never lose
hope. It is a fact that adopted children, who
have experienced the ultimate form of rejection by their natural parents, will usually try to
seek out the parents who created them once
they are in their teens or in early adulthood.
If that happens in adoption situations, it can
and will happen in the infinitely less traumatic
situation of a divorce estrangement between a
father and his children. Your children will return to you eventually, provided you refuse to
play the tit-for-tat game of revenge against

your ex-spouse. Let your children always
know where you live, where you travel, what
you are doing, and that you love them; tell
them by letter, by phone, by computer, by
gifts, by birthday remembrances, if you cannot do so in person, that you are always available should they wish to see you. Their positive
response may be neither instantaneous nor
soon, but it *will* come.

5. *Always remember that children want you to
be yourself, not a "Disneyland Daddy."* How
best to spend the precious limited time you
have with your children? You will turn that
time into disaster if you try to become a permanent entertainment industry for your children. Your children do *not* want to be taken
to Disneyland every time they visit you, nor
do they want to be force-fed all the junk foods,
games, and gifts that are not readily available
in their custodial home. What they want is
involvement with a caring father who tells
them he loves them no matter where they are
living now, who is affectionate, who listens to
them, who feels comfortable rather than self-
conscious with them, who takes them walking
or shows them where he works, who makes
dinner at home for them and engages their
help in doing so, who shows them what his
normal, everyday life is as a divorced person.
They don't want *things,* they want the human
being that is you.

6. *Squeeze any self-hatred or destructive guilt
from your soul.* You may have done harmful
things to yourself and your children while you
were in your very stressful marriage. Now that
you are divorced, you may still be carrying the
guilt of your past behavior with you into your
present relationship or nonrelationship with
your children. For example, you may have
been the authoritarian father, quick with the
slap in the face or the strap on the behind. Or

you may have been an alcoholic father who treated your children abominably when drunk. Or you may have been a womanizer, so immersed in extramarital affairs that you paid little or no attention to your children.

Your divorce may have spurred you to reevaluate the way you lived your life and related to your children in your marriage, so that you are now changing your life-style in order to become a better person to yourself as well as to others. However, you may burden yourself with guilt in the process of doing so. Such guilt is helpful if it reinforces your desire to change your ways and act in a more loving, caring way toward your children. It is destructive, however, if you wallow in guilt over being the "rotten" person you once were and believe that your children will forever hate you because of the harmful things you did to them. You may then think your children are better off without you, and believe it's best for them if you don't interfere in their lives or ever see them or try to contact them. Many divorced men I have counseled tell me this is how they have acted toward their children after the divorce. Out of the best of intentions, they have widened the divorce communication gap between themselves and their children a million unnecessary miles.

Your children are far quicker to forgive you than you give them credit for. They will delight in seeing you in a new light. Indeed, they have loved you no matter what harm you may have done to them in the past: the most difficult thing in the world to break is the love bond that exists between a child and his or her parent. Indeed, you would have had to be a monster of monumental evil to sever that bond. You need to forgive yourself, first of all, for the past harm you did, and remedy that harm by behaving differently toward your

children now. The past cannot be remedied,
but the present can be lived differently.
Reconnect with your children by letter or
phone call, say you want to see them again. Do
so even if you've spent months or years avoiding them. You always have a second chance
with your children. Take that second chance
now.

Speaking Out About the Unspeakable: Divorce and Suicide

The old saying goes that where there is life there is
hope. The reverse is equally true: where there is hope there
is life. And where there is no hope, there is death. Divorced
men and women have very high suicide rates. Those men
and women who do not utilize their divorces as opportunities for self-renewal, for creating better lives for themselves
than existed in their marriages, are most prone to attacks of
severe depression and hopelessness. They are the people
who may kill themselves when they project what they see
as their bleak present into a future that will never improve.
Or they may choose, without being aware that they are
doing so, an indirect form of suicide: an overdose of drugs,
a car crash while driving in an alcoholic daze, or overexpo-
sure to disease resulting from severe dietary deficiencies
and sleeplessness. When life becomes meaningless, actual
death or death-in-life is sought as the alternative.

Hopelessness of this kind can have a profound effect on
your children as well as on you yourself. You and your ex-
spouse are the role models for your children. The eyes
through which they see the world are the eyes you give
them. If they see Mommy and Daddy triumphing over adversity, they know they can triumph too, with a little help
from their parents while they are young, and on their own
when they become adults. On the other hand, a heavy daily
dose of gloom, doom, and hopelessness from their parent
invites them to consider destroying themselves. If the most
important adults in their lives can't cope with adversity,

how can they do so, small and vulnerable as they are, and dependent as they are for their survival on those same adults? For that reason, children of divorced parents are more likely to consider suicide than are children in most other situations.

In the past twenty-two years, the suicide rate for adolescents, as well as for preadolescents ten to fourteen years old, has *tripled*. Five thousand adolescents will kill themselves this year, while half a million boys and girls will attempt to do so. It is estimated that twenty thousand boys and girls, four times more than the records confirm, actually commit suicide each year, since parents try to keep the real reason for death from the eyes of the neighbors and the public at large. Adolescent suicide is a national phenomenon affecting all classes of people, wealthy as well as poor, in all sections of the United States.

The increase in adolescent suicide parallels the increase in divorce during the past twenty years, which is all the more reason to pay close attention to how you are presenting yourself to your children during your divorce. Are you contaminating your children with your own feelings of panic and hopelessness? Do you see a child of yours, formerly outgoing and friendly, withdrawing from friends, giving away prized possessions, becoming uncommunicative, refusing to eat regularly, having bouts of sleeplessness, locking himself or herself into self-isolation, experiencing a devastating change such as the loss of a lover or an unwanted pregnancy or school grade failures? Then it's time to deal with these issues urgently by talking with your child to find out if suicide has been on his or her mind, and if so, to seek professional counseling, as well as getting your child involved in a peer counseling group at school that talks about suicidal feelings and how to overcome those feelings.

If children think about suicide because they feel hopeless in the face of personal dilemmas they believe are unsolvable (but really are solvable once you can get them to talk about their problems), their sense of hopelessness is enormously compounded by the state the world is in today. The pall that hangs over every child's head is a sense of hopelessness about even having the opportunity to grow up, since the world itself might commit suicide in the next decades. Adults may very well refuse to acknowledge this appalling fact, but children are well aware of it. *A recent study shows that seventy percent of teenagers fear that there will be a nuclear war in the next ten years, and that they will not survive that war.* Given this bleak future, feelings of hopelessness about one's current problems can trigger into suicide when those feelings fuse with the lethal belief that the world is going to blow up anyway before they become adults.

You may be among the more than two-thirds of American adults who believe that if the United States and the Soviet Union keep stockpiling nuclear weapons, it is only a matter of time before they are used. You are also likely to be among the 80 percent of the public who want a bilateral nuclear freeze. In taking these positions, you are protecting the mental health of your own children by giving them hope rather than despair when you actively involve yourself in the political process to prevent the world from blowing up. You and your ex-spouse, regardless of your divorce differences, have the joint responsibility to give your children the opportunity to grow into adulthood. To evade or deny that responsibility will only accentuate your children's profound anxiety and loss of faith in adults. If you and your ex-spouse can say to your children, "Yes, the world is a perilous place to live today, but we are doing everything possible to prevent a nuclear war from happening," your children, reassured by that fact, can tell their friends that a nuclear war will not happen because Mommy and Daddy are doing everything they can to make sure it doesn't happen.

8

Melvin Belli's Advice on How to Protect Your Children's Welfare in Your Legal Settlement

≣

You are getting divorced because you and your spouse can no longer live together without hurting or possibly hating each other. Living in separate households doesn't end that hurt or hate, but may escalate it instead. If both of you fan the fires of vengeance by moving the battles of your dead marriage into a divorce court, your children are the innocent bystanders you will harm the most, because revenge-seeking will cause you to make inappropriate and detrimental legal decisions concerning the child-related issues we're about to discuss.

Sometimes the children are not even innocent bystanders, but are rather the direct, though still innocent, recipients of an angry divorced parent's violence. You may remember the headlines of the case in which a parent, enraged over his divorce, "got even" with his wife by setting his own son on fire, thereby physically damaging the child for life.

Don't use your lawyer or a judge to solve the problem of your relationship with your children, the emotional and psychological aspects of which Mel Krantzler discussed in the previous chapter. If you do, you may prove yourself "right" in your divorce lawsuit and wind up broke and unhappy as a consequence of "winning" the case.

If, on the other hand, you would rather be happy than right—if you want to make a better life for yourself after the

divorce and become a more concerned and loving parent—
you will act in a more grown-up way. You will ask yourself,
"How can I make my children feel more secure physically
and emotionally, now that their mother and father no
longer live together? What actions on my part will prevent
my children from feeling that they have to take sides, so that
they can feel comfortable in loving *both* parents? Can I get
my ex-spouse to see that we're using the children to hurt
each other? Can my ex-spouse and I separate our anger
toward each other from our mutual love for our children, so
that the children won't feel angry or depressed over Mom
and Dad's bitterness?"

The most sensible—and least expensive—approach is to
work out these problems between you and your ex-spouse
with the aid of your lawyers. If they are good divorce lawyers, they will try to get the two of you to reconcile your
differences, rather than make you angrier with each other
in order to stretch out the divorce and charge you heavy
fees for doing so. In case you cannot agree, your lawyers will
recommend a good divorce counselor or a mediator, or
both, to help you see that while you couldn't cooperate with
each other in your marriage, you *can* cooperate with each
other in your divorce concerning your children's urgent
needs, because of your mutual love for the children.

A good divorce lawyer will try to help you avoid court
battles, and resolve the child-related issues of your divorce
through negotiation instead. About 90 percent of all civil
cases (a divorce is a civil case, i.e., a legal case concerning
the rights and obligations of private individuals) are settled
out of court, which shows that most lawyers seek fair compromises for their clients.

However, in order to skillfully negotiate the child-
related issues of your divorce, it's important for you to know
what the law has to say about the legal issues of children's
rights, child support, and custody and visitation rights. Here
are the questions my clients most frequently ask me about
these issues. My answers, I can assure you, come from the
heart because they're the result of my personal experience.
(See Chapter 1, in which Mel Krantzler and I discussed our
divorces.) I can assure you that if I had paid attention to the
answers I will be giving you in this chapter, I would have

saved myself an enormous amount of unnecessary grief and anguish in my own divorces.

Kids in the Middle:
The Legalities of Child Custody

Now that my spouse and I are getting a divorce, with whom will the children live?

Maybe with you, maybe with your spouse, or perhaps with both of you. There is no quick or simple answer unless you and your spouse can mutually agree on all of the issues relating to your question. To make reasonably intelligent decisions in this regard, you'll need to be conversant with the legal jargon applicable to your question, because you have just raised the subject of *child custody*. This phrase is a legal term referring to the decisions that must be made in any divorce situation involving children, concerning with whom the children will reside and for how much of the time prior to their reaching the age of majority (generally eighteen years of age).

Child custody can be temporary or permanent, and there are both *legal custody* and *physical custody* to consider. Furthermore, both legal and physical custody may be either *joint* or *sole*, and in addition there is a hybrid form of arrangement called *split custody*. But don't panic. None of these concepts is terribly difficult to understand, and being well-versed regarding their meaning will enable you to take skillful charge of the issue of child custody in your divorce.

We need first to consider the major categories of custody, i.e., *temporary* and *permanent*. The former means exactly what it says. Generally, your children will "temporarily" live with either you or your spouse while your divorce proceedings are in progress. Therefore, if you want your children to live with you, don't move out of the family home (unless you take the children with you) until this issue has been decided either by your agreement or a court order, because if you can't agree on the subject, the court will generally award temporary custody of your children to whomever they are living with at the time the order is made.

Furthermore, temporary custody often has a direct bearing upon permanent custody, owing to the court's reluctance to disturb unnecessarily the continuity of children's prior living arrangements. *Permanent custody* refers to your children's primary home after the divorce is concluded, and is permanent only until and unless the court order is subsequently modified.

Don't forget that no order concerning your children is written in stone, because the court's concern is for the promotion of your children's "best interests" (generally speaking, their health, safety, and welfare), and those interests are constantly changing. The court is always willing to consider whether its order concerning permanent custody needs to be changed to meet your changing situations, and those of your ex-spouse and your children.

Now let's look at *legal custody*. This term refers to a parent's right to make all of the critical decisions concerning how the children will be raised, including what schools they will attend, in what religion (if any) they will be raised, and what basic values they will be taught at home. A decision will have to be made at some point in your divorce as to whether you, your spouse, or both of you will be entitled to make the above decisions. And don't take the matter lightly, because more than once I've seen divorcing parents make a snap decision concerning legal custody, only to regret having done so later on, when their children are not being raised the way these parents wanted and/or believed their children would be raised.

Legal custody may be joint or sole. If the former, both you and your spouse will decide the vital questions concerning you children's future. Therefore, you must either be in agreement on all of the answers to those questions, or flexible enough in your respective viewpoints to allow the children to benefit from the divergence between you.

If at all possible, I highly recommend joint legal custody as the type best calculated to assure your children of the fullest benefits of parenting by both you and your spouse, even if the two of you can no longer live together as husband and wife. And be as creative as you can. If one of you really has strong religious convictions that don't offend the other, perhaps the former can be charged with directing the children's religious upbringing while the latter can be allowed to make all of the decisions relating to which schools the children will attend.

The other type of legal custody, called sole custody, means that after the divorce only you or your ex-spouse, but not both of you together, will be entitled to decide what schools and churches the children will attend, and what basic home values the children will learn. This latter type of legal custody relegates one parent to the status of little more than a relative or friend, and consequently should only be adopted either when one parent clearly does not want the responsibility of making these important decisions in his or her children's lives, or when the circumstances make sole legal custody the only intelligent choice, such as when one parent is emotionally disturbed or mentally unbalanced.

Joint and *sole* have similar meanings to those set forth above when used in conjunction with *physical custody.* Sole physical custody means the children live with one and only one parent, while the other parent has what lawyers call *visitation rights,* which are discussed elsewhere in this chapter. Conversely, joint physical custody means essentially that your children continue to reside with both you and your ex-spouse, except that they do so now in separate households instead of under the same roof.

Just physical custody, which is treated in greater depth in the next question in this chapter, can be an extremely beneficial arrangement for your children now that you and your spouse are divorcing. However, it is generally a very expensive and complicated arrangement because it requires two complete "family households" where only one was needed before, and involves frequent movement between households, which can be both confusing and stressful for all concerned without a great deal of cooperation and understanding between you and your ex-spouse.

Finally, there is a custody arrangement that has characteristics of both joint and sole legal custody and both joint and sole physical custody. This custody arrangement is what attorneys refer to as *split custody,* and it is a true hybrid, because it refers to a situation where all of the children live with each parent for a portion of each year, or one or more live with one parent while another or others live with the second parent. This type of custody is generally adopted only when the parents live a great distance from one another, and in any event it shouldn't be chosen unless the child or children clearly prefer the arrangement. I say this because in the case of a child living with each parent for a portion of each year, the arrangement means a constant upheaval in that child's life. Also, split custody is not conducive to allowing children to build lasting friendships or to maintain educational and perhaps religious continuity.

Whichever custody arrangement is considered appropriate by you and your ex-spouse, I highly recommend that you make these decisions yourselves, to whatever extent you can, rather than letting the court decide. I say this because your children will be the ultimate beneficiaries of whatever decision is made, and neither you nor your ex-spouse may appreciate the court's decision. Your children will benefit because they will be spared the acrimony typically expressed in a contested custody proceeding, and so will not become the ultimate victims of that war.

Also, they will thereby be assured of the continued loving understanding and attention from both you and your ex-spouse that is vital to their well-rounded and positive development. Furthermore, I urge you to do so because the judge, even if he or she is well-meaning, can't possibly know your family situation as well as do the two of you, and may not, because of this limitation, make a decision that anybody is happy to live with. Worse yet, the judge may make a decision that, while pleasing to one parent, causes the other parent to be bitter, which can, and often does, result in tragic consequences (such as child-snatching, which will be discussed later in this chapter).

Don't, however, under any circumstances, attempt to arrive at an agreement about child custody if you and your ex-spouse can't be civil to one another in your discussions, or are using your children as weapons against each other. I counsel you in this regard because only recently, in my home state of California, a divorcing couple met in a restaurant to talk about who should get custody of their five-year-old daughter, but the discussion turned into a continuation of their bitter court wrangling. Tempers flared, and shouts, arguments, and accusations followed swiftly, all in their child's presence. The angry husband grabbed his daughter and whisked her away in his car, with the wife screaming that he had no right to do that. She raced after him in her own car and in her anxiety and fury, she caught up with her husband's car and rammed into it, overturning the car. Both parents came out of the wreckage unscathed, but their daughter was killed in the crash. Now both parents have "joint custody" of the memory of their dead child, and "joint custody" of the guilt of their deed, which will remain with them for the rest of their lives.

What form of custody is in the best interests of my children, now that I'm divorcing?

Any form of child custody can be in the children's best interests, provided that it ensures the fullest possible access to these young people by both of their natural parents, and perhaps other important relatives as well, such as grandparents. Remember, when considering best interests, we're primarily looking at health, safety, and welfare. If you seek to use the legal process to promote the above solution to child custody in your divorce, you will almost always find that the future is positive and bright, both for you and your children.

Also, work to ensure that both parents are granted first-class status, whatever the actual custody award. No parent should ever be made to feel like a visitor with his or her own children. It is demeaning to the noncustodial parent and clearly, therefore, it is not in your children's best interests. The above "full parenting" concept is probably best embodied in the growing legal preference for joint custody, shared custody, or co-parenting in your state's laws. Consider it carefully, however, because such custody can be extremely expensive, and stressful as well, if both parents don't give one another full cooperation in the enterprise.

Joint custody is the expressed custodial award preference in more than thirty-five states, and is probably the best concept we currently have to work with. These states generally hold such custody to be in your children's best interests because it allows for both parents' full involvement in making those crucial decisions in your children's lives, such as what school they will attend. Joint physical custody may, in addition, be awarded when it is shown to be appropriate to do so. For either to occur, however, both parents should try to fulfill the following requirements:

- They should be capable of speaking to one another in a civil manner.
- They should not, in any way, seek revenge on the other parent.
- They should be solely concerned for their children's welfare even if both spouses hate each other.

I am a strong believer in any child custody solution that moves in the direction of allowing children to continue to have the fullest and richest possible experience with *both* parents. Children are entitled to continue to be nurtured by both parents, even if those parents no longer desire to nurture one another. Therefore, I emphatically support the concept of joint custody, particularly joint legal custody. I'm in favor of joint physical custody as well, but only if all the following criteria can be met:

- Both parents can afford it (it typically means two family homes instead of one).
- The parents live close enough to one another that the children don't feel as if they're going on a trip every time they move from one residence to the other.
- The arrangement enables your children to maintain continuity in their school and social contacts.
- The parents can arrange it so as not to make their children feel as if they're constantly moving through a revolving doorway.

If physical custody is awarded to only one parent in a joint custody decision, then taking skillful charge of the situation demands that you work out flexible and meaning-ful arrangements guaranteeing, to whatever extent is possi-ble, that the other parent's noncustodial visitation rights (which are discussed elsewhere in this chapter) operate to encourage and provide for as much contact with the chil-dren as possible, unless to do so would be detrimental to your children's best interests. After all, your children are ethically entitled not to be adversely affected by the deci-sion you and your spouse have made to divorce one another. And you are fully capable of making any custody and/or visitation arrangement work, if only you are willing to com-mit yourself to the proposition that your children's happi-ness must ultimately be part of your happiness as well.

Are mothers more likely than fathers to be awarded child custody if the father contests it in a court proceeding?

No, even though mothers are typically awarded the *tempo-rary* custody of the children at the outset of the divorce. When the issue of *permanent* custody must be decided, later on in the proceeding, and the father contests the origi-nal temporary award, then fathers win over 60 percent of the time. And contested custody proceedings account annu-ally for approximately 7 percent of the more than one mil-lion divorces occurring in America. Part of the reason for the statistics I've just cited is legal, and part is the result of disturbing new practices being adopted by combative par-ents. On the legal side, many states today are nonpreferen-tial in deciding which parent is best suited to be the custodial parent (and thus charged with being the prime influence in the life of a child). This means that modern-day courts are opting to award custody to whichever parent can demonstrate that he or she is better suited for the task, regardless of sex.

I'm happy to report that this increasing trend is largely a justifiable response to the many divorced fathers who lob-bied for the changes. Many of these parents were denied custody in their divorces, even though they may well have been better child-nurturing parents than their wives, or at least as good. And the reason was all too often because custody was almost automatically awarded to the mother.

Unfortunately, however, the disturbing fact is that

today's largely nonpreferential attitude is also providing many parents (sadly, most are males) with an excuse and an opportunity to utilize custody proceedings as a tool to extract a more favorable property agreement for themselves or to reduce their spousal and/or child support obligations. This kind of emotional blackmail is ultimately not in the children's best interests.

Tragically, also, such parents generally have more money to fight such battles and can more easily demonstrate their financial stability and potential for further economic growth. To the extent that you can do so without damaging what you perceive to be your children's best interests, the way to take skillful charge of this situation is to resolve the custody issues in your divorce *without* going to court. Such battles are costly, and are emotionally and psychologically damaging to both parents and children.

Ironically, this is particularly true with regard to those smug parents who think they won't suffer from their misuse of the process; custody battle scars can last a lifetime. Additionally, such contested custody cases seldom serve a positive purpose. But, by the same token, don't be afraid of going to court if you truly believe it's in your children's best interests to do so.

"Winning," however, is not the real issue in such matters. All too often a parent may subsequently find out that he or she won a court battle only to lose the war later on. A tragic result of such winner-loser contests can be what recently occurred in California, where the mother of one such "loser" shot and killed the "winner" of the child custody case right in the middle of an open courtroom monitored by several armed bailiffs. Most important, please consider that contested custody proceedings almost never serve your children's best interests.

And finally, for those caring parents among you, your real ace in the hole against any attempt by a noncaring parent to force you into a concession on some property or child/spousal support issue is to fully realize that custody awards can always be modified upon sufficient showing of "changed circumstances." This means that a truly noncaring parent, unequipped to be a good nurturing parent, will seldom enjoy the fruits of his or her victory for very long in divorces occurring today.

Can other people be awarded custody and/or visitation rights besides the natural parents themselves?

Twenty or even perhaps ten years ago, an award of custody and/or visitation rights to anyone other than the two natural parents would have been an unlikely event. Today, however, most if not all states in the union have laws entitling at least grandparents legally enforceable rights of visitation with their grandchildren. These are rights that can be effectively enforced whenever grandparents' access to the children of their children's divorce is denied or frustrated by their grandchildren's parents.

This has occurred primarily for two reasons. First, and most important, it has been legally recognized that the grandparent-grandchild relationship can be uniquely beneficial to the children, and clearly, therefore, it's in your children's best interests to allow such contact.

Second, it has occurred because of the "double whammy" of an increasing divorce rate and an exploding upsurge in the number of parents who work outside of their homes. The combined effect has created a tremendously real need for additional parenting assistance from caring people, and particularly those caring people related to the children by blood.

Whether, in addition to visitation rights, grandparents or others can be awarded physical custody of the children is a more difficult question to answer. For this to occur, both of the natural parents would need to have been found by a court to be legally unfit to be custodial parents having the physical custody of their children. Death, criminal behavior, problem drinking and/or drug use, and psychological or emotional imbalance of the parents are probably the only four circumstances making such an award of custody to, say, a grandparent, likely to happen.

But I encourage all relatives of children to share as much of yourselves with them as you possibly can. They desperately need, and can always use, any and all the help they can get, whether from custodial or noncustodial par-

ents or other persons who know and love them, and who
want them to survive the battlefield of your divorce.

*If my spouse and I can't agree about who's going to get child
custody, how will the issue be decided?*

Whether it is temporary or permanent custody that is at
issue, child custody will, in all cases, be determined by what
is in the children's best interests. Not very long ago, it was
predominantly decided that it was in the children's best
interests that the mother be awarded custody in either of
the above proceedings.

Those were the days, however, when the man was typically the sole breadwinner and the woman was the homemaker and mother. It was presumed—although, sadly, it
was not always true—that minor children, particularly those
of "tender years" (generally those under the age of ten),
were better off living with the parent who by experience,
training, and temperament was better equipped to be the
prime nurturing force in the lives of children.

Many courts today still seem to follow this reasoning,
even though there are now credible statistics that fathers
can be extremely good at nurturing their children, especially sons. More important, however, the legal trend is emphatically moving in the direction of finding that the
children's best interests are better served by allowing the
fullest possible contact with both natural parents. A number
of states are similar to California, which establishes in its
Civil Code Section 4600, paragraph (a), that the children's
best interests are more readily served by such full contacts
with both parents. This section states that

> the Legislature finds and declares that it is the public policy
> of this state to assure minor children of frequent and continu-
> ing contact with both parents after the parents have sepa-
> rated or dissolved their marriage, and to encourage parents
> to share the rights and responsibilities of child-rearing in
> order to effect this policy.

Your state may treat the matter differently, however, so
be sure to check with a good local divorce lawyer to find out

what your state says about custody in relation to promoting your children's best interests. In close cases in which both parents seem equally well suited to the parenting task, such things as who is more likely to allow and/or promote more frequent contact with the noncustodial parent may be the single determining factor.

The procedure for dealing with the child custody issue, in the absence of agreement between you and your spouse, is by a court hearing (which proceedings, by the way, are public in most states). Temporary custody proceedings tend to be short, with the judge usually leaving the children where they reside at the time of the hearing (generally, with the mother), unless such a ruling would be detrimental to the children's best interests. This would be the case where, for instance, an alcoholic mother takes her children with her when she separates from her husband and it is with her that the children reside at the time of the custody hearing.

However, the permanent custody proceeding is an open-ended affair, and the investigation process is much more thorough in most states in this proceeding than in a temporary custody proceeding. And many states' courts have a whole battery of psychological social workers to aid the court's judges in making their determination. Such personnel may perform an exhaustive review, over a number of months, before submitting their report to the judge who must thereafter make his or her determination. These reviews will typically involve interviewing persons other than family members, but you, your spouse, and your children will almost always be scrutinized under a legal microscope as a matter of regular practice.

So don't be too surprised if your children's teachers and doctors and your neighbors are consulted. Also, most courts will allow your children to express their preferences, if the children are mature enough to do so (generally, they must be at least seven years of age), and will tend to favor your children's wishes in regard to custody if the latter are over twelve years old.

Therefore, you can best take skillful charge of this situation by remembering to think in terms of demonstrating honestly to the court that you are always sincerely motivated by the desire to promote your children's best inter-

ests. Don't utilize such proceedings vindictively to punish
your spouse for the marital breakup, or as a tool to exact
some concession from your spouse on some property issues
in your divorce. Such attitudes are never in your children's
best interests, and they will always come back to haunt you.
Furthermore, your children will be the ultimate victims of
your expressed negativity, and you can't possibly promote
a positive and happy future for yourself or for them by
engaging in such tactics now.

*My ex-spouse and I can't agree on who is to have custody of
our two children. What's the next step?*

I recommend that you first be sure, in your own mind at
least, that all mutually desirable methods of reaching an
agreement on the issues have been exhausted, including,
perhaps, utilization of a mediator. Assuming you have done
that, your next step is to file a formal request to the court
to have the issue determined for you and your spouse (by
way of example, in my state such requests are called either
an *order to show cause* or a *notice of hearing*). And be
aware, before you commit yourself to a court proceeding to
determine this issue—or any other issue, for that matter—
that neither you nor your spouse may be entirely pleased
with the court's judgment. Few clients ever are.

In reviewing this area, it is desirable to be the *requestor*,
the person making, rather than responding to, such a request. I say this because in most states the requesting party
will have the first opportunity to present evidence relevant
to who should be awarded physical custody of the children,
and why. This will normally, and immediately, place the
other, or *responding* parent in an almost defensive position
in which he or she may be compelled to respond to, and try
to offset, the thrust of the requestor's evidence, before making out his or her own case for being awarded custody.

This is a type of situation in which it can be critically
important not only to have a good divorce lawyer, but also
to have one who has extensive experience in a particular
area of divorce work (in this case, child custody), plus having
well-established contacts with court clerks in your county
and in others nearby. You could probably call such an attor-

ney at nine o'clock in the morning and be such a requestor by one o'clock in the afternoon of that day, or perhaps even earlier. A less experienced practitioner might not as quickly recognize the importance, in your situation, of being the first to get to court. Instead, this attorney might attempt to get the papers filed the next day or even later, only to find out that your spouse's lawyer got there first, and now you, rather than your spouse, will occupy the defensive position.

Also, to the extent that you can do so, try to limit the issues decided in the court proceeding by agreeing upon a resolution of all other child-related issues, prior to filing your request to be awarded the physical custody of your children. Otherwise, any or all of the following may also be decided by the court, perhaps not to the liking of either you or your spouse, and irrespective of what decision is made by the court with regard to "physical" custody:

- How legal custody is to be awarded (normally joint, but perhaps sole or split).
- What the visitation rights will be, and how such rights might differ, if at all, depending upon which spouse becomes the visiting or noncustodial parent.
- What *indicia* (characteristics of parentage) the noncustodial parent will have; for example, will this parent have a parental authority to obtain independent (sent to you directly, rather than copies of copies received from the custodial parent) duplicates of records concerning the children's welfare and education?
- What the level of child support will be, and by how much, if any, it will be allowed to go up or down as a function of which parent ultimately is required to pay such support.

The importance of these additional child-related issues is a further reason for having a lawyer with tremendous experience in such matters. Such a lawyer may know better what your potential trade-offs are (optional positions you can take regarding each of the above issues), and how to utilize those trade-offs to your best advantage in the context of serving your children's best interests. If any of the issues being discussed here are unresolved when you get to court, they too will have to be decided, so you'd better have a well-trained and highly effective advocate for your position. And even then, consider well that the judge, not you and your spouse, will decide the issue or issues. Unfortunately, he or she often decides the issues in ways other than you and your spouse might have agreed to if you'd only taken the time and made the effort to resolve them yourselves in the first place.

When and under what circumstances is a child custody order modifiable, who pays for the proceeding, and how much does it typically cost?

As with child support modifications (which we'll discuss in a subsequent question in this chapter), child custody can always be modified when the parents agree to do so, and may also be altered whenever there has been a sufficient change of circumstances to warrant such a modification. The expense will be inconsequential in the former case, and in the latter will typically run between $500 and $1,500. However, a hotly contested proceeding can be a lot more expensive.

Who pays for the modification, without agreement between the parents, will largely be a function of the parent's relative abilities to pay, but most often each parent will pay his or her own costs and lawyer's fees. I urge you, for the sake of your children, not to put them through perhaps a further custody battle on top of the original one, unless you truly believe that the other parent's continued custody status would be detrimental to your children, or you can provide a substantially better quality environment for them than your ex-husband or ex-wife can presently provide.

Furthermore, children's lives will never have to be disturbed by a modification proceeding if parents take precautions now to see that the original custody order provides the fullest possible access to the children by both parents. If you are willing to do this when the original order is made, the permanent residence of the children will always be a minor consideration when compared with your shared responsibility in continuing to raise the children, even after you and your spouse can no longer live together as husband and wife.

Tragically, custodial parents, be they male or female, too often forget that a custody award, either by its nature (such as a sole legal and physical custody order) or by the way these parents conduct themselves in regard to it (seeking, regardless of the type of custody, to prevent and/or frustrate the other parent's contact with the children), may cause not only a continuing series of additional custody battles, but perhaps a child-snatching as well.

Unlike child support modifications, if you and your ex-spouse can't agree on a custody change, the court's focus will be less upon financial circumstances than upon the relative parenting skills and abilities of the parents and, most important, upon what is in your children's best interests. Bear in mind that if you seek to modify custody because some event or personality change has occurred in the custodial parent's life, making his or her continued custody status detrimental to your children, in your opinion, you may be required to show that these changed circumstances make the custodial parent unfit to be allowed to continue in his or her present custodial capacity. Don't do so unless your evidence is clearly convincing; if you do not heed this advice, your children may be scarred for life by seeing one of their parents destroyed before their very eyes. Or you may only prompt the present custodial spouse, whose place you now take, to become an avenging angel should you find yourself being the responding party to his or her request to modify custody again, in the future.

If you seek a custody change because you truly believe that you can now provide your children with a qualitatively better life, you'll need extremely convincing evidence in this regard, and you'll also have to show that you have done nothing to diminish the present custodial parent's ability to provide a high-quality environment for your children (by, for instance, failing to pay a sufficient amount of child support or not paying the support at all, whatever the set amount). Courts do not as readily change custody orders as they do child support judgments, because of the tremendous upheaval in a child's life that a modification of custody can—and generally does—cause.

As to the specific circumstances that a court might consider determinative of a necessary custody change, there are a number of situations to consider. Obviously, if the custodial parent has taken to heavy alcohol or other drug use, the court will probably find it necessary to order a custody alteration, because such changed conduct is clearly detrimental to your children's best interests. Similarly, if the custodial parent is using the family home for sex orgies to celebrate his or her new singleness, or the custodial parent is sexually molesting the children or being otherwise physically abusive, a custody modification is most likely in order.

However, other things remaining relatively constant, the fact that you have remarried and can now provide what you believe to be a more stable home environment, both financially and otherwise, than the present custodial parent who is perhaps still unmarried, and a working mother or father to boot, will generally not be sufficient to warrant a custody alteration.

The gray areas are situations such as the custodial parent's newly revealed homosexual preferences, or perhaps an interracial relationship entered into by the custodial parent subsequent to the original award. In these types of cases, constitutional rights issues are raised and the courts will generally handle such cases very delicately. This is because the events, in and of themselves, do not generally mean that the present custodial parent is now unfit to continue in his or her custodial status, and may not necessarily make you a better candidate to succeed him or her as the custodial parent.

And always remember that the promotion of your children's best interests will forever outweigh your need to be made the custodial parent, so don't pursue a custody modification unless, on balance, the former rather than the latter is your primary motivation.

I'm a divorced mother with sole custody of our two children. I've just been offered a really good job, but taking it would require my leaving the county in which my divorce oc-

*curred and in which the children's father still resides, and
moving out of state. Do I have the right to take the children
with me without having to get their father's approval first?*

You do, unless your state and/or county laws and procedures preclude you from doing so (not likely) or unless your
divorce decree specifically prevents it. Check with any good
divorce lawyer in the county where your divorce occurred,
and you should easily be able to get your question specifically answered.

I have emphasized looking to a local attorney (one who
practices in the county where your divorce occurred) because the issues raised by your question will ultimately be
decided according to your state law as applied and/or supplemented by the procedures followed in the county in
which the divorce occurred. You should, therefore, consult
a lawyer who is likely to be familiar with all of the above
laws and procedures.

However, in exercising your right to leave—which, by
the way, is part of your federally guaranteed right to
travel—you should also be prepared to do the following as
a part of making your decision:

- Pay the transportation costs necessitated by
  your move, incident to the exercise of your ex-
  husband's visitation rights (more likely if your
  move is voluntary; if the move is compelled by
  your employer, the result will typically be to
  split the costs).
- Provide your ex-husband with longer periods of
  visitation, offsetting the reduction in such visits
  naturally occurring as a result of your move
  (typically, this can mean a substantial portion of
  vacation periods).
- Provide legal assurance that your ex-husband
  will be continually advised of any change in your
  residence (there can be penalties if you fail to do
  so).
- Be able to substantiate that the move is not in
  any way prompted by your desire for revenge
  against your ex-husband.

- Relate how the move will foster the protection and enhancement of your children's best interests.
- Assist your ex-husband in obtaining "independent" evidence of how his children are doing in their new home state, such as medical and school records.
- Allow your children who are over seven years of age to stay with their father, if they and he desire it.

You may not be required to do any of the above, but taking skillful charge of this situation demands that you be at least prepared to do so, for at least three reasons. First, all of the above may be required before you make your exit. Second, it's the best way I know of to secure your ex-spouse's support for your move. This will undoubtedly save you money down the road in custody and/or visitation battles occasioned by your refusal to seek such support. (Support differs from approval in that the former may simply mean that your ex-husband isn't unduly disturbed by your desire to move, while the latter means not being able to take the children with you unless your ex-husband says it's okay.) Third, and most important, it's in the best interests of your children to do so.

This phrase, "the best interests of the children," governs all decisions in child-related issues, whether they arise from a divorce proceeding or from circumstances such as your own. And since the "best interests of the children" standard is the one by which a court would be required to evaluate your move, you'd be well advised to have taken care of dealing with the issue prior to any attempt by your spouse to prevent you legally from leaving the state with your children.

If you follow these suggestions, you will virtually ensure that you'll be able to leave the state with the children, knowing that you won't be hassled in the future for doing so.

Is a noncustodial ex-spouse legally permitted to take his or her children to live with him or her in a state other than that of the custodial parent?

Definitely not, unless the divorce decree specifically permits it (such as pursuant to the exercise of visitation rights or because of a split-custody arrangement), or unless the custodial spouse consents to it (and such approval should always be in writing).

This question generally arises in those situations in which the noncustodial parent believes that he or she is entitled to overrule the previous decision made by the divorce court with respect to custody. Such parents reason that their status as a mother or father gives them the right to take their children anywhere they please, regardless of what any court has to say on the subject.

Whatever the rationale, the answer is always that you don't "own" your children, and you therefore have no right to transport them around the country like so much baggage. Furthermore, you cannot do whatever you please in regard to your children because your divorce made the court a guardian of your children's best interests until those children reach adulthood.

If you are a divorcing or divorced noncustodial spouse who feels compelled to ignore my advice, please consider the following before taking a step in a direction you'll almost certainly regret:

- It is not in your child or children's best interests to do so, even if they really want to be with you; and this is because, among other reasons, your children will probably be forced to be ready to leave your new residence on a moment's notice in the event that your whereabouts are discovered by your ex-husband or wife seeking to enforce his or her custodial parent's rights.
- Any attempt you make to get legal custody changed by the courts of the state to which you move will most probably not succeed because all states have adopted some form of the Uniform Child Custody Jurisdiction Act, and this law would likely require the court to which you submit your custody change request to deny it based upon your divorce court's previous ruling on the matter.

- You'll be potentially chargeable with a crime called child-snatching, which is a felony in most states, and for conviction of which you could do serious jail time. (The Parental Kidnapping Prevention Act makes available a parent locator service designed to track you down.)

All of the above points make it exceedingly likely that your attempt to leave the custodial parent's state with the children will meet with the worst of consequences for all concerned. Is your need to be a custodial parent really worth placing you and your children in a situation where you and they are forced to be always on the run? Equally important, is it really worth going to jail for, and perhaps being thereafter legally precluded from seeing your children at all?

Finally, if you are a custodial parent who has already lost his or her children to a fleeing ex-spouse, you should immediately initiate a contempt proceeding against him or her. This court process allows you to prove that your ex-spouse has engaged in conduct that is in violation, or contempt, of a valid and existing court order entitling you to custody, and, if successful, possibly to prevent any further contact between your ex-spouse and the children. (Typically, your ex-spouse will be required to pay your attorney's fees and any court costs incurred by you in seeking the contempt citation.) However, enforcing such a judgment may require you to travel to your ex-spouse's new state, if he or she ignores the contempt proceedings you initiated in the state where you currently reside and in which the children formerly lived.

My spouse has come out of the closet, now that we're divorcing, and has admitted that she is gay. Can she get custody of the children under these circumstances, and if not, can I prevent her from seeing our children?

The fact that your wife has admitted to being lesbian or to having bisexual tendencies would, under the laws of most states, be theoretically only one among many factors that the court would review to determine what is in your children's best interests regarding custody and/or visitation. However, as a practical matter, in most states your wife would have tremendous difficulty being awarded physical custody of the children. The most common reasons would be either the potential for general social ostracism or the distinct possibility of enormous emotional and psychological damage that the children might suffer as a result of harassment by their peers.

This does not mean, however, that gay parents can't be truly loving and child-nurturing people. They can be, and many are, just such parents. Nor does it necessarily mean that gay parents are never awarded custody of their children; in point of fact, it has been known to happen.

Furthermore, in most states, and irrespective of the custody issue, she will at the very least be entitled to visit with the children, even if you are successful in getting the court to limit those visitations significantly, and perhaps not to allow them at all without court supervision. This is because, as a matter of current public policy in most states, the general rule is that unusual or uncommon sexual needs and conduct do not necessarily render a parent unfit to see his or her children or perhaps even to be awarded physical custody of them under some circumstances, such as when the other parent is a criminal.

What About Visitation Rights?

Are visitation rights the only rights a noncustodial parent has with regard to his or her children, and what are "reasonable rights of visitation"?

Not long ago, these so-called visitation rights would truly have been all the rights available to a noncustodial parent. Fortunately, that's no longer true today, by and large, thanks to the developing national trend toward some form of joint custody award. We'll discuss these additional rights and responsibilities shortly.

Visitation rights are what I call access-to-children rights. They theoretically guarantee the noncustodial par-

ent that he or she will be able to have the children live with
him or her for, typically, short periods of time, normally no
more than two days in succession, and perhaps not including overnight visits if the children are under two or three
years of age.

They are normally not spelled out in the court order
beyond a descriptive phrase, such as "reasonable rights of
visitation." This is done for the laudable purpose of allowing
you and your ex-spouse maximum flexibility in arranging
times and places to promote the fullest possible contact with
the children by both parents, as evidenced by your oral
agreement. However, if necessary, such rights can be
specifically defined in the court's order. You should make
sure to do so in two specific instances: When, from past
experience, you have good reason to believe that your right
to see the children will be frustrated by the custodial parent;
and when you believe it necessary to have the verbal agreement you've made with your ex-spouse concerning times
and places for visits etched into the court document as a
legal reminder of the oral agreement, in the event that
some future attempt is made to disturb your opportunity to
see the children.

Such rights can include any or all of the following in a
commonly quoted phrase: "Reasonable rights of visitation
to the noncustodial spouse on alternate weekends from 9:00
P.M. Friday night to 7:00 P.M. Sunday evening, and on alternate holidays, birthdays, and vacation periods including one
and one-half months during the summer." Within reason,
however, you and your spouse can work out whatever
schedule you deem appropriate to further both your happiness and your children's best interests. And I highly recommend that you work this out with the other parent so that
your children feel as comfortable with the arrangement as
possible. You'll all be happier, in the long run, for having
done so.

Whatever schedule you work out, make sure that there
is sufficient specificity to it, even if you don't have the agreement committed to writing. Otherwise it will be tremendously difficult for you or the judge to determine later on
whether or not your reasonable rights of visitation are being
frustrated. And remember, many courts will not specify in

their orders what reasonable rights of visitation are unless you, through your lawyer, request such specificity, and upon grounds that the court will recognize as valid reasons for doing so.

Also, please consider the legal fact that visitation rights and child support are not dependent upon one another. Nonpayment of child support is not a legally sufficient ground for refusing a nonpaying father the opportunity to provide other forms of sustenance to the children, such as his personal presence, understanding, and compassion. Likewise, frustrated visitation rights are not a legally sound basis upon which a father can refuse to pay child support, or to pay anything less than the full amount.

Finally, such rights can always be modified at any time a change of circumstances warrants some qualifications of those rights. A suddenly abusive parent, or one who has begun to drink heavily, are typical of the kinds of changes that can cause alteration of these rights. Though these access-to-children rights might not seem like much sometimes, in some states you may have little else. Please don't get bitter if that's all you get in your divorce.

You can't imagine how important to your children those few moments with you can be until you stop complaining about the fact that you don't have more of them. You can find out just how important and special those moments can be if you are willing to learn to use them to get to know your children as young people and to let them know you as the adult you either already are, or are now going to be. All the fancy gifts you could ever buy them and all the exotic places you could ever take them (sadly, perhaps to expiate the guilt you may feel at having failed them as a parent) can't hold a candle to forty-eight hours spent with your children in a totally thoughtful and creative manner, doing nothing more than the ordinary kinds of things they might do if they were at home.

So use whatever time you're awarded as creatively as you can. Your children will want to come back to spend time with you again. And they'll do so not because you buy them lots of presents but rather because you are the loving parent they always wanted to believe you were, and now know you are going to be. Your ex-spouse will eventually come to realize it too, as he or she discovers that while you may not have made a good husband or wife to her or him, you are amply demonstrating your generous capacity to love your children.

He or she may even agree to expand those rights, and perhaps to include as much time as you would like. And your ex-spouse will do so not by force, but rather by desire, in his or her certain knowledge that you are fully entitled to the additional time because of your demonstrated concern for your children's best interests.

In addition to visitation rights, noncustodial parents can find themselves with some or all of the following rights:

- Not to be noncustodial parents at all, if you can afford, handle, and work out a joint physical custody arrangement.
- To have medical records and dental reports regarding your children sent to you.
- To be notified by the school your children attend about important events in the school year, and to receive copies of your children's report cards.
- To be consulted by the primary custodial parent prior to major events occurring in your children's lives, such as orthodontic work and music lessons or other creative classes.
- To be made a part of the decision-making process determining where the children go to school or church.

Take on as many of these additional responsibilities as you can get in your divorce in your state. And follow through with whatever rights you get, because the whole purpose here is to promote and protect not your own best interests, but rather your children's.

Can I legally prevent my ex-spouse from seeing the children?

Yes, but only if further contact between your children and your ex-spouse would not be in your children's best interests. Situations that can be legal grounds for eliminating or

significantly qualifying visitation rights are extreme mental
or emotional instability; repeated evidence of violent conduct, especially if directed against the children; serious
criminal activities, particularly relating to use of dangerous
drugs or physical violence; a serious drinking problem that
is out of control; and any evidence of child molestation. If
any of these or other such circumstances exist, it is not only
your right but your parental obligation to seek to curtail, or
terminate if necessary, further contact with the children
until the other parent has rehabilitated him- or herself. Because the benchmark in such situations is always what's in
the best interests of your children, the following will generally *not* be sufficient to affect the other parent's visitation
rights:

- That you "hate his or her guts" and believe the
  other parent is horrible and should not be allowed to see the children.
- That the children don't want to see him or her
  (children, as you know, often change their
  minds).
- That the other parent is "shacking up" with
  someone (unless, that is, they are flaunting their
  sexual conduct in front of the children).
- That the other parent hasn't been paying support or has been continually late in doing so.
- That the other parent is gay, unless you can
  specifically demonstrate how his or her sexual
  preference would adversely affect the children.
  (There are not as yet—and I don't believe there
  will ever be—any reputable statistics suggesting
  that contact of some sort between children and
  their gay parents is fundamentally detrimental
  to the children. As I have said, some gay people
  have been awarded custody of their children
  and have made excellent custodial parents.)

And remember always that the law seeks to promote
the greatest possible contact between children and their
natural parents. So be prepared to demonstrate specifically
that you are not motivated by revenge and that you have

the children's best interests at heart, if and when you seek to prevent contact between your children and their noncustodial father or mother.

What can I do if my ex-spouse's visitation rights are exercised in conflict with our children's welfare and proper development?

This question typically arises because of the following type of problem: The children arrive at the custodial mother's home at 11:00 P.M. or later on a Sunday evening, exhausted from their weekend with a "Disneyland dad." One or more of the children throw up the following morning from having eaten too much junk food with their father over the weekend, and the child or children are now too sick to go to school. The answer to this kind of question is always the same. Your children's best interests always outweigh the exercise of any parental right. Therefore, if you can, seek to work out procedures with your ex-spouse that will prevent this state of affairs from happening in the future.

If that doesn't resolve the problem, seek informal assistance from the court-appointed family services personnel in your county. And finally, if informal means won't do the trick, you will probably have to initiate a modification proceeding to request that the court restrict visitation hours to specific times or otherwise qualify your ex-spouse's visitation rights.

In this latter extreme, if you've resorted to it only after exhausting all less formal methods, you'll probably get the court to order exactly what you want and you'll probably also be awarded fees and costs in the proceeding as well.

Although my ex-wife and I have joint custody of our children, there always seems to be some new reason why the children are not allowed to spend any time with me. What can I do about it?

Your situation reveals one major weakness in many joint custody awards. The problem is often that such awards do not provide any specific rules governing such matters, leaving you seemingly incapable of showing how your parental interests are being frustrated. The best way I know to deal with these situations is to discuss the problem thoroughly with your ex-wife, to the extent that you are able to do so. Remind her that the legal intent of joint custody awards is to foster the greatest possible continuing contact with the children by both of their natural parents.

I can think of no valid reason for you not to be able to see your children, even if they are sick (provided, of course, that they don't require hospitalization), unless your children themselves don't want to see you. Except in such cases, your ex-wife has no legal right to prevent you from seeing them or frustrating your efforts to see them either. She may be playing games with her parental responsibilities and your parental needs to see and be with your children. If you find this to be the case, your best bet is to tell her you don't want to play any of her games with the children's lives.

If your discussions don't result in an immediate resolution of the problem, you should then consult with a good divorce lawyer who specializes in custody matters. Don't fool around with an amateur, because the modern trend toward joint custody awards is largely an expression of society's desires to focus greater attention on the *quality* of the children's lives and their time with parents, rather than on the *quantity* of such time or on whether the children have beds to sleep in, clothes to wear, and three square meals a day. In such situations you will need an attorney specially equipped to portray to the judge how the quality of your time with the children is limited by the quantity of time you're prevented from seeing them.

Try to stay out of court if you can. The law is not really well suited to resolving emotional situations, because it operates in the context of legal generalities and exceptions to the rule. It punishes conduct, not thought, and unfortunately conduct can be misleading. But if you can't otherwise resolve your situation more favorably for you and your children, don't hesitate to use the court's full strength to protect your own and your children's best interests. Courts, in my view, are a last resort, but they are there to protect you in these situations, so use them if you have to.

My ex-spouse is trying to cut off my visitation rights by accusing me of molesting our daughter when she has been with me. I have not and would never do such a thing. What can I do?

These cases are truly awful for innocent parents; in more than 50 percent of such cases the allegations of sexual abuse are never substantiated. The reasons are many, but typically such allegations arise because Dad or Mom has a new girlfriend or boyfriend, or because the accusing parent feels he or she got "screwed" in the property settlement agreement and now wants to get even. There is never, and I repeat, *never,* under *any* circumstances, a valid legal reason to accuse a parent falsely of such conduct.

If you ever find yourself in the position of the person asking this question, here's what you can do: First, get yourself one hell of a good child-custody lawyer, hopefully one familiar with these kinds of cases. Second, it would be extremely helpful to get a child psychologist or psychiatrist (preferably one who has interviewed both you and your ex-spouse, both with and without the child present) to testify in your behalf. Third, be open and honest about any and all contact you've had with your children at any time, both during and after your marriage. And finally, to the extent that you are financially able to do so, or can find a public-interest law firm to handle your case free, be prepared to appeal any decision that is unfavorable to you, if you are truly an innocent parent. I believe we must eliminate all "divorce games" concerning children, particularly one such as falsely accusing Daddy, or Mommy, of being a child molester.

Adults can recover from the divorce games they play with one another. Children are seldom as fortunate. And all of you parents need to examine your motives carefully in seeking physical custody or in trying to prevent the other parent's access to his or her children. Your children deserve and are entitled to the loving care and nurturing of *both* of their parents. Don't destroy that for them by playing games with their lives.

I'm a custodial parent who's worried about my children's visits with their father because he's begun to drink heavily. What can I do?

If you and your ex-spouse are capable of communicating on a civil basis, discuss the subject with him in light of his drinking's possible detrimental effect upon the children's best interests. And I would give the same advice, by the way, on any form of drug use as well. If discussion doesn't resolve the matter, your next option is to utilize whatever psychological and emotional assistance is available to you through the courts of your state. In California, such services are provided through "conciliation courts."

If the problem persists, you will have to consider the expense and complications of a modification proceeding to qualify your ex-husband's visitation rights, until and unless he changes his behavior. Don't ever let problems of this type go unchecked. You have many good options available to help you deal with it, and the problem will not go away by itself. And frankly, your children's welfare is just too important to put off confronting the issue now, and doing so openly and honestly. If talking about the problem is not possible in your situation, you'll have to "do it by the book" and file a modification proceeding seeking to correct the problem, perhaps obtaining a temporary restraining order as well, if necessary.

An indirect aspect of the problem we're discussing here is whether to encourage your children to spy on the noncustodial father or mother, and report back to you on the results of their clandestine operation. This is a sensitive subject today, in part because of a series of incidents reported in the media involving children informing on their parents for drug use. Such events smack of the horror of George Orwell's *Nineteen Eighty-four*. Don't ever encourage your children to be spies. It's not in their best interests to do so, and personal alcohol or drug use is a matter that I believe is more positively resolved by encouraging your children to raise such issues with you first, so that collectively, in conjunction with whatever psychiatric assistance is necessary, the family can resolve such matters privately and in a way that will be truly beneficial for all concerned.

On occasion, I have allowed my ex-husband into my home to help get the children's things ready for their visitations

*with him. If he uses these incidents as opportunities to
harass me, what can I do about it?*

If it's verbal harassment in front of the children, you should
instruct him that you're no longer obligated by the tie of
marriage to tolerate such treatment, and that if he does not
grow up and at least try to act like an adult, you will use
whatever legal means are necessary to end his foolishness
for the best interests of the children and your own piece of
mind. And please remember to do so out of your children's
presence yourself, as it's necessary for you to practice what
you preach.

If the problem persists, then, and only then, consult an
attorney and do whatever is legally necessary to follow
through on your commitment to your own and your children's happiness. (You may, for instance, be able to get a
court to modify your husband's rights, to prevent him from
coming into your house.) Also, to the extent that you can,
avoid giving your ex-husband the opportunity to engage in
such conduct in the first place by reducing the incidence of
contact with him in your home.

If, rather than verbally harassing you, your ex-husband
is using these occasions to invade your privacy, such as by
looking into things that are none of his business, or by opening your mail, remind him that it is illegal for him to do so,
particularly now that you're divorced from him. Such conduct by your ex-husband is fodder for a lawsuit against him
that could cost him dearly, and may subject him to criminal
penalties as well.

The shock effect of your determined and assertive attitude may well cause your ex-husband to see the error of his
ways. (If not, you'll probably then want to consider hiring an
attorney.) I find this conduct totally inappropriate for adults
and believe that it must be nipped in the bud so as to prevent such conduct from becoming a dragon that some legal
knight has to slay.

*My thirteen-year-old daughter hasn't been getting along
with me lately, and has requested to go live with her father.
What can I do to prevent it?*

In the first place, you probably can't prevent it, so why waste your energy trying? Second, and more important, it's probably not in your daughter's best interests for you to try. (Neither is it really in your best interests, if you'll think about it for a moment.)

Taking skillful charge of this issue demands that you be willing to allow her to experience whatever it is she believes she is going to experience by living with her father, and provided, of course, that the father is a willing and responsible participant in the plan. Your daughter will realize soon enough which parent she really prefers to live with, and which one she prefers to visit.

To the extent that both you and your ex-spouse are financially able and willing to do so, I highly recommend that you allow your daughter to move back and forth between you, and to do so freely, provided that she is at least responsible in her number of such requests. You will thereby enable her to have a potentially larger and more well-rounded experience.

I have said you probably cannot prevent your daughter from leaving. This is true for a number of reasons. First, no matter how you feel about it, if your daughter really wants to go badly enough, she'll find some way to do so. Children almost always do, and I sometimes wonder how many teenage runaways are just such children.

Second if the issue is raised by her father, or, for that matter, by your daughter in a modification of custody proceeding, most courts would legally allow your daughter to do what she has expressed the desire to do, because she has reached an age at which she comes within a group that many if not most states find mature enough as a matter of law to be allowed to make such decisions themselves. Such a result will almost always occur, at least provided that the currently noncustodial parent is willing to take over.

You need not panic, however. Custody can be modified again if the circumstances warrant a change. And you might even prevent any court appearance at all by perhaps simply negotiating a trial period for her with your ex-spouse.

I firmly believe that children are rightly entitled to the fullest possible exposure to and nurturing by both of their natural parents, and that it is our responsibility as parents to encourage and promote such a result. Thankfully, this also seems to be the modern trend in the law, so you'd do well to come to grips with the concept.

My ex-spouse is living with the woman he left me for. Under such circumstances, do I have to allow my children to visit with their father?

Yes, you probably do, and generally, unless your children are three years old or younger, probably for overnight periods as well. However, always remember that the issue will be decided according to what is in your children's best interests. If you can establish that he and his new lady are parading their sexual activity in front of the children, you can almost certainly cause his visitation rights to be significantly curtailed and perhaps even totally eliminated, depending upon the circumstances, because such irresponsible conduct is simply and decidedly not in your children's best interests.

On the other hand, if he is living with this woman more or less as husband and wife, and treating his children in as healthy a way as he did when the two of you were married, then in spite of the fact that this other woman may, in part, have caused your marital breakup, the latter alone is not a sufficient legal reason, in any state that I know of, to prevent him from seeing his children.

Within the above two extremes, the legal issue you raise would be decided on a case-by-case basis according to what the judge believes would be in your children's best interests. States can differ greatly in their treatment of this area, so check with a good local divorce lawyer when you're ready to find out the answer in your specific case. If your ex-husband is at all a kind and loving parent, he will most likely handle any visitations under his present circumstances with delicate responsibility, if that's any consolation to you. And if he's not, then don't condone his infidelity by making a bigger deal out of it than it already is, either in your life or those of your children.

Instead, simply make the court aware that visits with the children in your ex-husbands's present situation would be detrimental to their best interests. That action will also, in many states, ensure that his future visitations are monitored by family counseling personnel under the court's authority as well. So understand that you are not without power in your situation. But please remember to exercise such power as you have to promote and protect your children's best interests, and not to seek vengeance upon your spouse.

What can I do about a "Disneyland daddy"?

There is very little that you can do to legally prevent such conduct. For those of you who are unfamiliar with the phenomenon of the "Disneyland daddy," the term typically concerns noncustodial fathers who seemingly are always taking the children somewhere special and/or buying them extravagant gifts. However, it's important to remember that such tendencies can afflict custodial parents as well. In any event, the answer is fourfold:

1. Avoid trying to *compete* with such a parent, even if you are able to do so (it's just not in your children's best interests).

2. Attempt to make your "Disneyland daddy" (or mommy) aware that there are other, more appropriate ways to assuage the guilt that probably lies at the heart of their tendency to spend extravagant sums of money on their children, and to help them understand that, in any event, it's not in the children's best interests to continue to be this type of parent.

3. Trust that your children will eventually figure out that their best interests are more surely promoted by your love, as evidenced by your willingness to listen for and respond to their needs for generous warmth, understanding, and compassion, than by any or all of the presents they receive or places to which they're taken by the other parent (they're a lot smarter and wiser than you may sometimes give them credit for).

4. Get help from the court's family services personnel if the problem does not resolve itself.

Also, don't aggravate such a problem in your situation by complaining about it to the children or trying to push them into believing that despite their "Disneyland parent's" generosity, he or she doesn't really love them. You probably won't get (and wouldn't want) your children to believe this, and both actions will tend to focus attention upon the problem rather than resolve it.

Our divorce has been a tumultuous affair, and has gone on now for two and a half years. When my ex-husband comes to get our daughter on his visitation day, she hides under the bed and refuses to visit with him. What should I do?

Here is a perfect example of how horribly children can be affected by their parents' divorce. Your child has undoubtedly concluded that Daddy is the "bad guy" in your "Divorce Court" drama. For her, spending any time with her dad is like rewarding the bad guy for being bad. Also, if she goes to see him now, she will carry with her the guilt of having punished you, the "good guy," and consequently she hides to avoid confronting what to her is an unresolvable dilemma. This situation becomes even more tragic if the father is really a caring and nurturing parent, because your daughter is depriving herself of part of the very understanding and compassion that she needs to surmount the problem.

What you must be willing to do, if you are to take skillful charge of this situation, is to honestly acknowledge in your own mind what kind of parent dad really is. If he has the capacity and willingness to care for and nurture children, then you must sit down with your daughter right away and explain to her that Daddy is not really the bad guy; it only seems that way because you and he have been arguing about property matters that do not concern her. And along the way, make sure she realizes that she is responsible neither for your breakup nor for the battle that is now raging. If necessary, seek counseling to aid you in your efforts. You must resolve such matters as quickly as you can if you are to start your daughter on the road to recovering from her emotional trauma. Furthermore, avoiding the issue or, worse yet, taking a secret and vengeful pleasure in your daughter's present attitude, because it seems to punish your ex-spouse, may simply create a horrible and avoidable series of child kidnappings that are not in anyone's best interests.

If, on the other hand, you have legitimate reasons for believing that further contact between your spouse and his child would be detrimental, then you must get your lawyer to bring these matters to the court's attention, so that appropriate orders can be made to protect your daughter's best interests. And, for her sake, please be careful here. Sexual or other physically abusive tendencies, problem drinking or drug use, severe psychological or emotional imbalance, and well-documented evidence of parental neglect are legitimate reasons. That he has a new girlfriend or is a "money-hungry bastard," or simply that you "hate his guts" is not a sufficient legal justification for denying your ex-spouse access to his daughter by your refusing to work with her to resolve her dilemma regarding her dad, for which you may be in some way responsible.

My son, who is fifteen, now wants to live with his father, although I have had legal and physical custody since my divorce eight years ago. I have no objection to my son's desire, provided that his father is agreeable. Before my son leaves my home, must I go to court for legal approval of his moving out?

Probably not, unless your state has some very peculiar rules in such cases. However, it would definitely be in your son's best interests if his father were to have some legal document transferring your legal rights and obligations to him. Your ex-husband might not, for instance, be able to gain access to his son's medical and/or school records without some proof that he is the child's custodial parent. As noted elsewhere, parents can always agree to modify the terms of a child custody and/or visitation order.

In any event, your ex-spouse will probably want such an amendment, in part at least to curtail any further child support obligations he may have to that child. The legal costs for dealing with a resolution of your problem are minor if you and your ex-husband are in agreement, and such a resolution is in everyone's best interests, so I would encourage you to make one. Then take the substance of the agreement to an attorney to prepare the agreement properly, under the law, and get it filed with the court.

Child Support: What It Is, How Long and How Much

What is "child support"?

This is a legal term referring to court-ordered payments of a specific amount of money for the care and maintenance of children with permanently separated parents. Such support is ultimately paid to the separated parent who is declared or ordered by law to be the custodial parent. It is paid by the other parent, who is adjudged to be the visiting or noncustodial parent.

The basis for child support is the joint responsibility of parents to provide for the needs of their children. The legal reasoning behind court-ordered payments of such support is the law's paramount concern for the welfare of children and the prevailing notion, whether fact or fiction, that many separated parents who don't have the physical custody of their children either forget or ignore the fact that they still have a legal responsibility to provide for their children's needs, requiring, therefore, that they be forced to remember.

Considering the basis of child support, it's really no different from the money that parents pay, routinely and without fail, to a baby-sitter who takes care of the children while Mom and Dad, or either of them individually, are out for the evening. Likewise, such support is the same as the money that one parent, who is a traveling businessperson, sends to the other parent to cover the family's needs while the former is away.

Unfortunately, the emotional and psychological trauma normally resulting from a permanent separation or divorce "blinds" many parents who are ordered to pay such support to the logic of the above comparisons and legal reasoning. Later on I'll discuss this "blindness" in more depth, and its tragic results, which are reflected in the fact that, according to national statistics, less than 50 percent of the parents ordered to pay such support do, in fact, pay the full amount, much less on time, and approximately 25 percent of such parents pay nothing at all.

Taking skillful charge of the issue of child support in your divorce demands that you be mindful of what has just been discussed, as well as the following general characteristics of all child support proceedings, whether they result from a divorce or from any other child-related proceedings, such as a lawsuit to establish that a man is the natural father of a child born to an unwed mother. First of all, there are four primary ingredients in any child support order:

1. That such support is periodically paid (normally monthly, but it can also be paid weekly and bimonthly).
2. That the support is paid at a level established by the court as a result of either the parents' agreement memorialized in a court order or the judge's independent decision when the parents can't agree, and sometimes even when they do.
3. That the support order remains in effect until the child dies, reaches majority (typically eighteen years of age), or becomes emancipated (moves away from the custodial parent to live alone and becomes capable of supporting him- or herself), whichever event occurs first.
4. That the child support order is subject at any time to modification by the court, to meet the changing needs of the children and/or the ability of their parents to pay such support. (Child support *may* include provisions for the payment of extraordinary medical and dental expenses as well.)

Second, under federal law, child support is neither taxable income to the receiving parent nor an allowable tax deduction to the paying parent. States may, however, treat these matters differently in regard to their own state income tax, so check with your attorney in this latter regard.

Third, the parent receiving such support is presumptively entitled to the tax deduction for dependent children. This seemingly odd rule is a consequence of the fact that the receiving parent is the custodial parent, as well. This presumption means that the receiving parent is the sole parent entitled to take the deduction unless the paying parent can qualify as an exception to the general rule. For instance, the paying parent may be able to prove that he or she has an agreement with the other parent to share the exemption, such as by alternating years.

Finally, child support is always ordered by the court, whether or not you and your spouse have agreed upon the amount. As mentioned earlier, this is because of the law's paramount concern for child welfare. By making child support an order of the court, the parents are legally assured of easy access back to the same court, and to the courts of other states if necessary, to change the order if altered circumstances warrant such a modification, and to have the court enforce its own order (typically by contempt proceedings resulting possibly in wage garnishments or jail time) when the terms of such an order are violated.

Considering the "blindness" I mentioned earlier, if you were to ask one hundred noncustodial parents whether they loved their children and cared about their children's welfare, I'm quite confident that well over 98 percent of them would tell you that they did. You might well wonder, given such a fact, why statistically less than half of them pay the full amount of child support that they're required to pay, and twenty-five of them don't pay a dime.

At the outset of this discussion I called such statistics tragic, because I firmly believe that more than ninety-eight out of one hundred noncustodial parents are decidedly concerned about their children's welfare and do love them very much. Also, I said it was tragic rather than blameworthy because I want to impress upon you the importance of paying such support, particularly now that you are aware of what's behind all the words we lawyers use (which more often than not confuse the issue), rather than to blame those people who haven't paid it or have paid less than they should.

Some people who are obligated to pay such support don't pay it, or pay less than required, because the other parent frustrates or denies the former's visitation rights. This act of revenge, which is discussed elsewhere in this chapter, is illegal. And you now know that such an act also reduces the income necessary to support the very children you so much want to see. The answer to your problem isn't to stop paying support; that will only aggravate the situation. Rather, the skillful way to deal with such practices is always to be on time fulfilling your obligations, and to bring the other parent's illegal activities to the attention of the court. You might be pleasantly surprised at how far a court is willing to go for such demonstrably responsible adults.

Others who are so obligated don't pay it, or pay less, because they seriously believe either that the children don't really need the money or that the real problem is that the custodial spouse won't go to work. For these people, I would direct your attention to the equally tragic statistic that divorced custodial parents (typically, although not always, mothers) are the fastest-growing group of poor people in America today.

Please believe me when I tell you that rarely does a divorced mother or father with dependent children—even a parent who works outside of the home—make sufficient income to meet the constantly expanding needs of his or her children without the aid of the child support of the other parent. I frankly don't believe that you could be callous enough to avoid the implications of the above statistics, even if you don't believe what I've just related to you largely from my own experience.

Still others don't pay, or pay less than required, because they believe total financial responsibility is the price the other parent must pay for being awarded the physical custody of the children. To anyone inclined to believe such fables, I would ask the following: How would you like to be legally prevented from seeing your children except at those times the other spouse sets aside for visits by non–financially supporting relatives and friends? I suspect you wouldn't much like such a situation. Remember, you can't divorce your children. Even if you wanted to do so, the law wouldn't allow it, because a child is entitled, under the law, to be nurtured and loved by both natural parents.

Finally, there are those people who don't pay, or pay less, because they quite frankly don't like being ordered to do anything, especially something that they would readily do in any event, such as caring for and maintaining their children.

To you noble people—and I don't use the term facetiously—I apologize for the legal realities typically associated with child support situations. Such laws are not meant to affect you adversely. Don't, however, allow the law's mistake in not being able to find some way to recognize your commendable attitude, to blind you to the importance of following through on your commitment. After all, the required support is only a minimum. You can pay any amount that you believe is necessary under the circumstances, so long as it exceeds that minimum.

I hope that in taking the legal mumbo-jumbo out of the subject of child support, I've convinced you of the very real and compelling necessity that it be paid, and on time. You will be in a far better position to have any child-related orders modified in the future if you have fully met your obligations in the past, and you will gain the added satisfaction of having dealt with this new and court-created parental responsibility, in addition to the other such responsibilities you are presumably already fulfilling.

How is the level of child support determined, and does paying such support fulfill all of my parental financial responsibilities?

The amount or level of such support is determined by considering the separate financial circumstances of each parent and the relative needs of the children born to those parents. And the level is set either by the judge, after a full hearing, presumably one incorporating all relevant financial information, or by the parents' agreement.

In the latter situation, which I highly recommend to your consideration, the court must still review the issue, guided by the same principles it would apply in determining the level itself. However, in the court's subsequent order, it will ordinarily abide by what you've agreed to, unless the agreed-upon amount is drastically unreasonable. Agreeing parents must still, in all cases, have the court's approval of what they agreed upon. Also, child support is always subject to court review.

Regardless of the general statement above, as a practical matter, the amount, or level, will more often than not be determined in a more mundane manner. Typically, the court will first evaluate the net monthly income of the noncustodial parent with reference to a support schedule published by the county in which the divorce proceeding is filed. As used in divorce matters, "net monthly income" generally refers to the income left over after compulsory deductions, typically federal and state withholding taxes, FICA, and SDI. Were the situation otherwise, a noncustodial parent could possibly reduce the amount of support he or she might otherwise be required to pay by causing a portion of his or her gross income to be diverted to a voluntary retirement plan, or to some other noncompulsory purpose, thereby lessening his or her net income.

These support schedules are printed guidelines that more or less arbitrarily establish a support level commensurate with a given level of net income. For instance, if you are a noncustodial parent with an established net income of, say, $1,600 per month, such a support schedule might require that you pay $175 per month for each of your children.

Because these schedules differ radically from state to state and county to county, no attempt will be made here to state categorically how much you might have to pay, except, perhaps, to suggest that at such an income level, $150 to $175 is probably the minimum you could be ordered to pay. Furthermore, some courts follow their county's guidelines unwaveringly and without serious investigation of all the circumstances, while others view their schedules only as a reference tool, and only to be consulted after a full hearing including all relevant information on both custodial and noncustodial parents.

However, today's widespread use of child support guideline schedules makes determination of the proper level of child support more or less a basic accounting function and little else. Therefore it is imperative, if you are to take skillful charge of this situation, that you consult a good divorce lawyer in the county where the divorce proceeding is initiated to determine how the issue will be resolved in your situation and how much you might expect to receive or be required to pay.

In theory, determining the proper level of child support is arrived at only after a serious consideration of the following factors:

- The financial needs of both parents and their children
- The relative income and earning capacity of each parent
- The ages of the children
- The standard of living to which the children are accustomed

Some judges will perform an exhaustive review of each of the above issues before making their orders, regardless of any support schedule's existence or common use. But don't count on the judge to do so. If your actual situation doesn't conform to the general circumstances upon which support schedules are based, you will have to bring this information to the court's attention, because you can bet that your ex-spouse won't help you out, and the judge is under no obligation to make your case for you.

For instance, if your ex-spouse is the custodial parent and earns twice as much as you do, and you can prove this to the court's satisfaction, you might be required to pay little or no support. Or if you are the custodial parent and can establish both that one or more of your children have special needs, such as constant medical attention, and that your ex-spouse can afford it, you might, and probably will, get more child support than would otherwise be ordered. In neither event, however, will you get anywhere if you don't speak up when you believe an arbitrary schedule is being unfairly applied to your unique circumstances.

As to whether or not paying the full amount of your child support order, and on time, satisfies all of your financial responsibilities to your children, the answer is no, it definitely does not. I repeat, you are jointly and individually obligated to care for all of your children's needs. These may include, in addition to the necessities of life for which your support is vital if such things are to be adequately taken care of, money for college expenses, extraordinary medical or dental care, and life and health insurance. And you can be required, if necessary, to help pay for all of these additional needs on top of what you may already be paying in child support.

Further, you can be required to maintain a security for the payment of the full amount of any such child support order, typically in the form of a beneficiary designation on your life insurance policy, which, if you do not have one, you can be required to get. And finally, the custodial parent is entitled under the law to seek your help with any of the above needs, should they arise now or in the future, and regardless of the fact that such things were not provided for in the support order as originally made.

How do I know that my ex-spouse, who is the custodial parent, will utilize the money I pay in child support for the care and maintenance of our children?

You don't. But that's not a valid legal excuse for not paying all of your support order. And paying what you're required to pay, and on time as well, will be a threshold test to any effort by you to legally alter the support order because of your expressed doubt.

If you seriously and realistically question whether your support payments are being properly used, there are three things you can do to take skillful charge of this situation:

1. Be prepared to prove that the other parent receives sufficient income to provide the necessities of life to the children and to provide for his or her own needs as well as you would want to be able to do were your situations reversed and you, instead of him or her, were the custodial parent. (Remember, the custodial parent is not required to suffer a de-

privation of his or her own interests to prove
his or her love for the children, any more than
you would be required to do so in similar circumstances.)

2. Be able to show also that, given the other
parent's now proven ability to do so, he or
she isn't providing the necessary care and
maintenance to the children. Though this
might be a difficult task, if you're successful
you may be able to get the support order
done away with entirely or perhaps even reversed, pursuant to the court's change of custody to you for having proven that the other
parent is not protecting his or her children's
best interests.

3. If your expressed doubt is really a ruse to di-
vert your own attention away from your real
feeling, which is that the other parent could
take on more income-producing work, then
you need also to be able to demonstrate that
the custodial parent has opportunities for
work that would produce such additional income, and that the custodial parent could take
on such additional work without causing any
unnecessarily adverse impact upon the children. Otherwise, the negative impact your
children might suffer would be grounds for
the court to find that the custodial parent's
increased work load would not be in your children's best interests, and therefore to deny
whatever request you might make to alter the
order.

Don't be too surprised, however, if, after you've re-
searched the above matters, you find yourself wondering
how the other parent can survive on his or her income, even
with your support payments, particularly in view of the fact
that you only have to be concerned with supporting yourself, while the custodial parent has to be concerned about
the children's needs in addition to his or her own. Unfortunately, child support schedules are too often based upon a

minimum rather than a maximum required child support at any given level of income.

I would also expect this to be the result of your efforts because, in point of fact, non-married mothers (whether divorced or single) with children are the most rapidly developing group of poor people in this country today. It is to be hoped that your research will at least satisfy your questions and persuade you to continue to pay at least what you've been ordered to pay, and maybe even to agree to increase the level as well.

What can I do to make sure that I actually do receive all of the child support to which I'm entitled under the law?

You can do four basic things that should collectively pretty well guarantee that the full amount of such support is paid. Implicit in this general comment is the importance of your realization that it is the children, and not you, to whom the child support obligation is owed. You are merely a conduit for the payment. Acknowledging this truth will help you to deal better with the paying parent's reluctance to have to pay you anything, even if it's for his or her children, by enabling you to help the noncustodial parent get properly focused upon to whom he or she owes this support obligation. In promoting your children's best interests, you need to do the following four things:

1. Make sure that all relevant financial data is brought to the court's attention before the original support order is established (this may require a lot of work on your part, and that you choose between agreeing with your spouse upon the level of support and leaving the proper level for the judge to decide).

2. Make sure, to whatever extent is possible in your state, that the original order provides for the paying of "extraordinary" expenses, such as orthodontic work or remedial reading tutors, that might arise. (This will secure the paying parent's assistance with such expenses, and without the increased cost, perhaps to

you, of a modification proceeding; and try to insert automatic child support increases into the original order as well, since this will also potentially save you the cost and aggravation of a modification.)

3. Don't do anything to frustrate the children's receipt of support by engaging in what I'll call tit-for-tat activities, such as interfering with the other parent's visitation rights or calling the other parent a bad name in front of the children, to "pay back" the other parent for his or her having been late with support checks. (Such actions by you will almost certainly decrease your children's chances of receiving the full amount of their ordered support and/or getting it on time.)

4. Use all of the available legal tools at your disposal, whenever and wherever necessary, to promote your children's best interests, including modification proceedings when circumstances warrant a change in the support, and contempt proceedings if the other parent gets more than thirty days behind in his or her support payments. If the paying parent is in another state, you can pursue the contempt proceeding in that state's courts, often with the help of the district attorney's office in whatever county that parent currently resides. You can also use other laws enacted to ensure payment of child support, chiefly the federal laws allowing the IRS to withhold income tax refunds to the extent of any outstanding child support due at a particular time, and allowing you to garnish the paying parent's wages if he or she doesn't pay his or her support for thirty or more days.

Beyond the above list, also remember always that it is in your children's best interests for you to have as positive a relationship as you can with the other parent, considering your now separated status. It is important, therefore, that you do whatever you can to see that your relationship is one in which your children's expanding needs are regularly discussed, with you and the other parent both taking responsibility to ensure that all of your children's developing needs are attended to. And work to keep the discussion focused upon what both parents can do to better provide for the children's needs, rather than allow such meetings to deteriorate into a contest to establish who's the better and more responsible parent.

Under what specific circumstances is a child support order modifiable? How much does such a legal action cost? And who pays for it?

Such orders can be modified at any time the parents agree to do so, or upon request made to the court by either parent because current financial circumstances warrant such a change. The former is by far the easier and cheaper method to modify a support order, and should be employed in preference to the latter whenever possible. However, such agreements will only work well if you take skillful charge of your situation by remembering to do all of the following:

- Have the agreement reduced to writing (preferably typed).
- Make sure that your written agreement is dated and signed by both parents, and have the signatures notarized.
- Have the specific reasons for the modification stated in the agreement. (This can be critical down the road, should one parent subsequently claim that he or she was coerced into making the agreement, and it can be extremely useful as a statement of the then-existing financial circumstances of the parents in any further modification to alter the support order.)

You can do all of the above without a lawyer's assistance, though I wouldn't recommend that you do so. In any event, however, make sure at least that each of you has any such agreement reviewed and commented upon by separate attorneys of your own choosing. As I've repeatedly stated elsewhere in this book, the relatively small fee you'll pay for such a review will be more than offset by the comfort of knowing that you are aware of all your legal rights and have legally protected your interests in the agreement. Furthermore, you'll have a better chance of not having your agreement challenged at some future date as having been entered into upon some improper ground. Once you have an agreement in the above form, it must then be filed with the court (generally at no further cost to you, if it's the same court that granted the divorce) and approved by a judge. Only then will your agreement carry the weight of a support order that has been legally modified.

In accomplishing this last and most critical task, you'd be well advised to utilize a lawyer's services to prepare the agreement in proper legal form and to ensure that all procedures for getting the agreement filed properly with the court are followed. This is necessary because courts can—and many do—have odd procedures for handling such matters, and require the filing of peculiar-looking legal documents incorporating what is perhaps a very simple agreement. I suggest using a lawyer to draft the document because it's much better for you if it's the attorney who is held responsible for any irregularities. (Besides, the fee for this limited kind of assistance is typically less than $250.)

I must impress upon you that unless you accomplish this final task properly, your efforts to get it enforced, should there be a violation of the agreement later on, will have to be by way of an *independent* lawsuit (one outside of the divorce court's power to hear), and that could cost you more than ten times the $250 just mentioned.

The other situation in which a child support order can be modified is generally whenever children's needs have substantially changed, or at any time that the parent's financial circumstances become drastically altered. Following are examples of the former.

- The passage of time. (If this is your only reason for seeking a change, at least three years is probably a minimum before such a modification would be granted.)

- The surfacing of extraordinary medical or dental expenses. (Remember, you won't incur fees and costs for getting a support order modified if you see to it that such expenses are provided for in the original order.)
- A drastic increase in the necessities of life, such as food, clothing, and/or shelter, required by the children and unavoidable by you.
- The arrival of extraordinary educational expenses either prior to or even after the age of majority. (Such expenses can be for a specialized elementary school or for college, and remember, you won't have to get your support order modified upon this ground if you ensure that such expenses are originally provided for.)

Regarding modifications owing to a change of the parents' financial circumstances, there are a number of things of which you should be aware. First, typically, though not always, the court will be primarily concerned with the paying parent's changed capacity to pay. Second, the financial circumstances of the paying parent must be significantly altered (generally at least a 30-percent change) and for a long period (normally for at least thirty days, and for sixty days to be on the safe side). Third, if you are a paying parent seeking a reduction because your income is reduced, you need to be prepared to prove that the reduction has not been voluntary by you as part of some revenge scheme of yours against the other parent (and to the ultimate detriment of your children as well), otherwise you won't be successful in your efforts. Fourth, while the paying parent's income is the primary focus of support modification proceedings, it is a change in the parents' *relative* financial circumstances that the court will be considering. This means that if you seek a child support increase because the paying parent's income has doubled, there is no relative change in the financial circumstances if your income has also doubled since the entry of the last support order, hence on this ground alone you will not be entitled to the modification.

Finally, be aware that a change in the custodial parent's

income can, on occasion, be a reason in and of itself for reducing a support order, because child support orders today are typically set with reference to child support schedules which are generally based upon the assumption that the custodial parent's income is at least 25 percent less than that of the paying parent. Therefore, if you are a paying parent whose income hasn't substantially increased since the entry of the last support order, and who can show that the other parent's income has doubled or tripled since that time, you may be able to modify your support payments downward.

As to the costs and who pays for modification proceedings, only the following general comments are really useful to you, as there are many answers to these questions. I would say the fee range for a contested modification proceeding (in which one parent files a legal request with the court and the other parent legally objects to such a request) is probably between $750 and $1,500 for moderate-income litigants, depending upon the lawyer, the state, and the intensity of the battle.

Normally, also, each parent will bear his or her own fees and costs associated with the proceeding. However, a fee award can be made at any time unless you and the other parent have otherwise agreed, if the judge feels that the present relative financial circumstances of the parents warrant such an award, and sometimes because one parent has been vindictive in the proceeding, causing an unnecessary increase in the other parent's fees and costs.

Child-Snatching: How to Cope with It, How to Prevent It

What is child-snatching?

Child-snatching is any and all conduct engaged in by either parent in contravention of a *valid, proper, existing,* and *enforceable* court order concerning the physical custody of the children of those parents. Usually, though not always, such interfamily kidnapping is an illegal attempt by a noncustodial parent to get more physical custody rights with regard to their children than that parent was originally awarded, by snatching children away from the parent presently entitled to those physical custody rights.

For a parent to be in violation of such a valid court order, that order must at least have been made by a judge, and after a hearing in which that parent was legally notified of his or her right to present evidence therein, whether or not he or she actually did so.

Even if it is a *valid* court order, it must also be a *proper* one. This means that the court making the order was the "proper" court to do so (typically, the court with the longest connection to the children, and generally the one that granted the divorce in the first place). Such an attitude is also the intent codified or made into law by the Uniform Child Custody Jurisdiction Act (UCCJA). This legislation, discussed in greater depth in the next question, has been adopted by all states in the union, with minor variations (except, as of this writing, Massachusetts, South Carolina, and Texas), and is literally the law of the land regarding all custody-related matters.

To be *existing,* the order must have been legally made before the one that you may now be trying to obtain, even if only by a few weeks or days. And finally, to be *enforceable,* (legally entitling the parent with physical custody to punish the noncustodial parent for violating the order), such an order must be one that complies with the other three criteria just discussed. Additionally, such an order is only enforceable until and unless you have obtained a subsequent valid and proper order that legally supercedes the prior existing court order.

Parental kidnapping of children is the single most tragic by-product of modern divorces. Too often, the causes for such conduct are in many ways the tragic result of parents' not fully realizing that it is their children's best interests that will suffer, and their children who will be the real and only true victims if the parents cannot find legal means of voicing their concerns for their children. There is *never* a good reason to engage in child-snatching, even though certain reasons used as justification for such conduct may seem plausible, such as the following:

- "He [or she] would have killed the kids if I hadn't taken them away from him [or her]." (If what you say is really true, it is extremely doubtful that your ex-husband would be seeing the children at all, much less be entitled to have their physical custody, assuming you have taken skillful charge of the child-related issues in your divorce.)

- "I didn't get a fair hearing. Hell, I didn't really even know what was going on." (If this is your rationale, then learn now what's going on, and find a good lawyer to properly represent your legal entitlement to access to your children.)

- "I know my spouse, and I know he [or she] will never be able to care for our children in the way I do." (If that's the case, make your attorney assert all possible methods of protecting your children's best interests while they are residing with your ex-spouse, and get a legal custody change if you can demonstrate to the court that your children are in danger.)

- "I know my children are being abused by my ex-spouse, who is the present custodial parent. [Such abuse can be psychological, emotional, spiritual, physical, or sexual.] Therefore, I must keep my ex-spouse away from our children." (If so, you probably have a whole variety of legal and very effective means to take care of any of the above situations, and ones that will not do any further damage to your children's best interests, such as the damage you would do to those interests in placing your children's lives in danger by snatching them and risking being carted off to jail for violating the terms of a prior existing, valid, and proper court order.)

- "If you'd just taken a look at the way my children are living in their mother's [or father's] home, you'd know why I just had to take them away from her." (I've either seen for myself or heard about more such incidents than you can imagine. If what you say is true, a legal modification proceeding can almost always be structured by your attorney to cause a correction of your ex-spouse's conduct, or to award you the physical custody of your children if your ex-spouse can't or won't clear up his or her act.)

Though there is no good reason for child-snatching, there are a variety of *bad* reasons to engage in such conduct, such as the following:

- Your visitation rights have been repeatedly violated by your ex-spouse. (If so, present those violations to the court that made the visitation rights order, because most such courts will take offense at having their court orders violated, perhaps to the point of finding your ex-spouse in contempt of court for his or her conduct, jailing him or her, if necessary, and maybe, in the meantime, giving you your children's physical custody.)
- You didn't win custody of your children. (The children are not your children, but rather yours *and* your ex-spouse's, and there's nothing to "win," when you are properly focused upon protecting and promoting your children's best interests.)
- You hate your ex-spouse and want to punish him or her for what you perceive as his or her transgressions. (Your children, and sadly you yourself, as well, are the only people you will punish by child-snatching conduct, as you will be a criminal felon in some states, and your children will become caught up in a web of intrigue, violence, and continual flight.)

Custodial parents are well advised not only to take precautions to prevent child-snatching (such as by specifically providing, in the child custody decree, that the children shall never be taken out of the state in which the divorce occurs, except for times and purposes to which both parents agree), but to discourage such conduct as well. You

can do this by remembering that the noncustodial parent
should never be made to feel as if he or she is a "second-class
parent." I have said this before, but it bears constant repetition when discussing what's in the best interests of your
children. Such children are entitled by law to be cared for
and nurtured by *both* of their natural parents, and parents
have a mutual and continuing responsibility, as parents, to
see to it that the other parent has all of the access to the
children that he or she wants to have, and that is reasonable
under the present circumstances. Therefore, I'd recommend that you do everything within your power to recognize and promote such access by your noncustodial
ex-husband or ex-wife, who has a right to be just as much of
a parent as you are.

*How can I deal with a child-snatching if it occurs in my
situation?*

The following situation is typical with regard to how your
question arises in divorce cases. A distraught mother comes
into my office. Tearfully, she tells me her ex-husband waited
outside of the place where their seven-year-old son goes to
school, and then whisked him away in his car. She has joint
legal custody (remember, that is custody in which both parents have a mutual say regarding important events or needs
in their child's life) but sole physical custody (in which the
child permanently resides with one, and only one, of the
two parents). Her sole physical custody rights were ordered
by the court in California, where she and her son live, and
where her divorce was granted. The boy's father was
awarded reasonable rights of visitation. Such were the
court's orders after a bitter and protracted court battle over
custody rights, in which the father had wanted sole legal
and physical custody of his son. The father had furiously told
the mother that she'd regret the court's custody order.

Now, out of the blue, he has taken their child away in
violation of the court's physical custody order. She was frantic when the child didn't arrive home on time from school,
and was ready to call the police, when her husband phoned
to tell her that he'd taken their son, Tommy, away, and that
she would never see their boy again. "Screw the court

order," he said. "You'll never find me or Tommy." The mother is now a puddle of anxiety, fear, rage, and helplessness. What can she do to get her child back?

I wish this were an exceptional case, but unfortunately more than 100,000 children each year are snatched by parents who believe they were given a raw deal in a custody battle. And Tommy's mother stands a 70-percent chance of never seeing her child again, because that's the national percentage of child-snatching cases in which that happens. The parent and child disappear into another state or country, and the parent adopts a new name.

Or, worse yet, the child-snatching parent gets a new custody order in the new state by some legal or illegal means, and then both parents spend the remaining years of their child's minority playing a game in which their child is a pawn.

The above statistic is a horrifying figure, and my heart goes out to the poor children who become victims of the tantrums of their parents. In a typical case, the snatched child doesn't want to be abducted by one of his or her parents. The child will cry out or try to escape when a parent suddenly forces the child permanently to leave the parent with whom the child has been living. And the typical parent who snatches a child is doing so not out of love of the child, but rather as a way of getting even with the ex-spouse. Divorce revenge, rather than concern for the child's best interests, is the unlovable reason for most child-snatching.

The child snatcher often is a person who is an alcoholic or child abuser, or someone with paranoid tendencies. He or she, quite likely, is trying to escape creditors, is without stable community ties, and might have job skills that could be used in other states or countries, so that when he or she abducts the child, a hideout in another area becomes possible. Like a criminal in the night, the parent may move from place to place frequently, in order to avoid being found. The child is doomed to live the life of a frightened outcast who will later become a very disturbed, antisocial adult. Realistically, I would hardly call this love for the child.

The law never paid much attention to child-snatching until it became the serious problem it is now recognized to be. Recent developments in the legal system are now trying to remedy this past neglect. In 1969 a beginning took place when the Uniform Child Custody Jurisdiction Act was passed by Congress; most states have now enacted some form of this uniform national law. Before 1969, a parent who refused to accept or abide by a custody decree awarded in one state could snatch the child away to another state and try to obtain a different custody decree in the new state in his or her favor. This often worked because each state had its own rules for determining such matters. The UCCJA prevented this undermining of valid court orders. However, it was hard to enforce because it did not provide the means to locate and punish the child snatcher. It wasn't until 1980 that Congress passed the Parental Kidnapping Prevention Act, whose purpose was to promote cooperation among the states in enforcement of custody and visitation orders, to discourage continuing interstate controversies and conflicts, and to deter interstate abduction of children. This law provides a national system for locating child-snatching parents by means of a Federal Parent Locator Service, and beefs up enforcement of state laws designed to punish such parents.

These recent legal efforts against child-snatching are better late than never, but they only scratch the surface. A truly uniform and national effort to eliminate child-snatching is still a future hope, rather than a present reality. For example, child-snatching is not currently a felony in many states. Consequently, FBI investigative services can't be used to track down child snatchers in those states that do not declare such conduct to be a felony. And bureaucratic snags and delays and complicated procedures make enforcement of the present laws frustrating to the anxious parent hoping to have a child located and returned quickly.

We can expect better laws and more simplified procedures to be enacted in the future, since child-snatching shows little signs of abating at present. Until that time comes, you can take skillful charge of situations such as these by getting your lawyer to make the most effective possible use of the existing laws in your state and in the nation regarding child-snatching. If you can afford to do so, you may need to utilize the services of a good private investigator (your lawyer will know of one) to track down a child snatcher, along with whatever such facilities your state government has for that purpose. The expense of doing so, however, may be too great for most people's pockets; $50,000 or even $100,000 is not an exceptional figure.

Should you be the parent experiencing a child-snatching, keep in mind the following suggestions:

- Don't panic. Immediately contact your lawyer and have him or her set in motion all the facilities he or she knows of—and lawyers have an enormous number of such facilities available to them—to locate and punish the child snatcher (your lawyer knows, for example, how to activate the Parent Locator Service; what warrants and contempt citations to get; how to find out whether the child's school records were transferred to a school in another state; and how to track, through banks, the post office, credit card companies, the telephone company, and motor vehicle bureaus, any changes and shifts in the child snatcher's movements).

- Don't fight fire with fire. Anything illegal that you do to rectify your ex-spouse's illegal conduct will only come back to haunt you, perhaps by jeopardizing your own physical custody rights.

- Work with your lawyer as a team; he or she may suggest you contact all the people your ex-spouse knew or worked with in order to get a lead on where your ex-spouse may have moved to. Constructive activity on your part will help enable you to overcome the feelings of helplessness that otherwise might overwhelm you.

- Don't despair if your child can't instantly be located and returned. Continue to maintain close contact with your lawyer so that he or she keeps you informed about every present and forthcoming effort to locate and return your child. And don't drop your other activities—hobbies, work, friends, or community life—while this is happening, because you need all this positive reinforcement from your daily life, and

more than ever now, if you are not to be
drowned in agony and sorrow.

By now, you've probably come to the conclusion that
the best way to deal with child-snatching is to prevent it
from ever happening at all. You're right! The child snatcher
becomes a criminal outcast, the custodial parent becomes
overwhelmed with fury and despair, and the child becomes
the traumatized victim of the game. Your divorce then
becomes a permanent nightmare, as I have seen in the faces
of many of the clients who have come to me for help.

It is with those faces in mind that I am writing these
words to urge you and your ex-spouse to reach an agreement on custody and visitation rights that both of you feel
you can live with, so that child-snatching doesn't become a
possibility that one of you might harbor in your mind. Use
your lawyers to help you reach an agreement, along with a
mediator, conciliator, or divorce counselor that your lawyers might recommend. Set aside your present dislike for
each other, as hard as that might be, and work out an agreement that is satisfying to both of you and, more important,
one that is devoted to the promotion of your child's best
interests.

If you are in agreement with what I have just said, but
your ex-spouse is an immovable brick wall of hostility, this
conduct may give you a good clue that your ex-spouse might
consider child-snatching. Your attorney, if he or she is a
good one, will also pick up on that possibility and might
want the court to sanction a custodial decree containing a
statement that removing the child to another city, state, or
country for any given length of time must require the written consent of the custodial parent (and written assurance
to the noncustodial ex-spouse that his or her visitation rights
won't be unduly frustrated by any decision you might make,
as the custodial parent, to move to another state as well).

The court might also order that the custodial parent
having physical custody of the child has the right to seek
police help if the other parent takes the child away in violation of the decree. This may warn the vengeful parent in
advance that no outrage such as child-snatching will be tolerated.

In the last analysis, however, the law is really powerless to prevent child-snatching when a parent is possessed of unremitting hostility toward an ex-spouse. All reason flies out the window when a person becomes irrationally hostile. Consequences, legal or otherwise, are seldom thought of by such parents, since vengeance is uppermost in their minds. That is all the more reason for both parents, with major assistance from their lawyers, to divest themselves of the lust for vengeance when they consider what's in their children's best interests, now that Mom and Dad are divorcing.

The Rights of Your Children
Now that You're Divorcing

What rights, if any, do our children have in the divorce?

Other than the right to express a preference in their choice of a custodial parent, your children have no legal rights in your divorce if you resolve all issues concerning them with your spouse (custody, support, and visitation), and if you do so without involving a judge or other court personnel appointed by a judge. However, this does not mean that your children don't have other rights that should be considered by both spouses when divorcing. Taking skillful charge of your divorce demands, in part, giving thoughtful consideration to the human rights of your children, so as to prevent the divorce from having any avoidable adverse impact on them. Remember, you can't divorce your children. Even after your divorce from your spouse is final, both of you will still be parents, and you will have to find some basis, however businesslike or strained, to work together if your children are to avoid being scarred for life by the divorce and its aftermath.

Although you and your spouse are divorcing because one or both of you no longer need or want to be with one another, your children still need the loving understanding and affection of *both* of you. Therefore, you should recognize that your children do have the following human rights:

- To be assured that both you and your spouse are committed to, and actually do, regularly meet with each other for the sole purpose of specifically discussing how your children are dealing with life in general, and the divorce in particular, resolving together what can be done to best correct any problems that arise.

- Not to hear their mother and father putting each other down, by saying, for instance, "Your father's a real jerk and he never pays for your support on time," or "If your mother hadn't caused the divorce, we'd be able to spend more time together."

- To have parents who want to, and do, notify each other regarding important events in the lives of their children, such as talent shows and school open houses, with both parents attending the events when possible.

- To have full and complete access to both parents, whether by telephone or letter, or in person (I've used the word *access* rather than *visitation* because the latter is a terribly inappropriate word to describe the right of a noncustodial parent to spend time with his or her children, even though *visitation rights* are what we lawyers typically refer to when discussing the issue of access to children after a divorce.

- To be told, and have continually affirmed by both parents, that both mother and father still love them, and that the children are not in any way responsible for their parents' divorce.

- Not to be "guilt-tripped" by either parent with such statements as, "If you really loved me, you'd take better care of your room," or "You must love your mother more than me, because you never call me just to say hello."

- To be free of the responsibility of performing tasks to which they are not suited, such as to be the "man of the house" now that Dad is gone, or, worse yet, to act as a go-between for parents

who can't seem to communicate with each
other.

- Not to be used by one parent as conduits of information about the latest events occurring in the
other parent's life, or, worse yet, to be used as
spies to collect damaging information on the
other parent.
- Not to be asked about their preference in regard
to whom they want to live with, unless they volunteer such information.

If you will acknowledge and honor the above human
rights, you can virtually ensure that your divorce does not
adversely affect your children, who are the only participants
in such proceedings who did not ask to be there. Furthermore, you will practically guarantee that whatever agreements you've arrived at with your ex-spouse concerning
custody, support, and access, or visitation rights, will operate smoothly, helping to promote the best interests of your
children.

If you and your spouse cannot agree on all of the issues
concerning your children, then the latter have some important legal rights and obligations in addition to the human
rights we've just discussed. First of all, they have the responsibility to answer questions posed by the judge or his appointed personnel concerning their life with both parents
and their feelings about the divorce. This can occur infor-
mally, in a family services office or judge's chambers, as well
as in open court as witnesses in your divorce proceedings.
(Please remember, calling your children as witnesses should
be avoided at all costs, as the emotional and psychological
trauma of such an event can permanently damage their
future development.)

Also, your children will typically have a legal right to
express their preference as to whom they want to be the
custodial parent, if the children are at least seven years old.
(Such expressed preferences will tend to be honored by the
judge if the children are over fourteen years of age.)

Finally, in many states your children are entitled to be
represented by a lawyer. In the great majority of cases,

however, the judge will act as the "lawyer" for your children, and protector of their best interests. I therefore urge you to consider all of the rights we've talked about here, to avoid contested custody proceedings, which can be enormously expensive as well as emotionally and psychologically damaging to your children, and, most important, to seek at all times to promote your children's best interests during and after your divorce.

9

The Quest for a New Lasting Love Relationship: Dating, Sex, Love, and Commitment Anxiety

≡

Seven divorced men sat around a living room table, facing a reporter who was questioning them for a newspaper interview about their attitudes toward women, now that they were no longer married. All of the men had been divorced for less than two years after being married anywhere from five to twenty-four years; their ages ranged from thirty to fifty.

"Would you ever want to marry again?" the reporter asked as he scanned the anxious, sad, gloomy, wounded faces around him.

Six of the men reacted as if a fire alarm button had been pushed. "No, never again!" they responded almost in unison, with an overflow of anger and hurt in their voices.

"Why not?" the reporter then asked. These were their bitter answers:

"Criticism and complaints, that's all I ever got. If my wife wasn't telling me what a lousy provider I was, she would tell me what a slob I was. Marriage is a jail sentence. Who needs it?"

"I discovered my wife had a half-dozen affairs while we were married. The last straw was finding out she was getting it on with my best friend! Deceitful bitches, that's what women are."

"Intimidation, that's what she did to me. My wife treated me like I was a bad little boy when I didn't do what she wanted. I felt like Fido the dog, begging for sex; and if I was good, like letting myself go over my head in debt to buy that damned house she wanted, then she'd spread her legs for me. You're crazy to think any other woman would be different."

"My wife was cold and unresponsive. Kissing her was like kissing a dead herring. She never could understand why I wanted to have sex more than once a month. Sex was like an obligation for her, and she would say, 'Want some tonight?' when she was ready for that one time a month she thought would keep me happy. Marriage is just another name for misery."

"Women are dull and boring. My wife was so predictable I could finish every sentence she began and guess right as to what she would say. All the yapping about new clothes and the latest hairdo. Women are so shallow."

"My wife thought more about her tennis game than she did about me. Tennis! Tennis! Tennis! I never liked the game, and it would have been nice if she had stayed home once in a while for me. I once put a padlock on the strings of her favorite tennis racket, but even that didn't stop her. All women think only about themselves, and I say the hell with them. From now on I'm only going to think of myself and use women for only one thing, to screw as many as I can."

There was one thirty-three-year-old man who did not participate in this torrent of disenchantment with women. He countered by saying, "I can't agree with any of you. I love women, and if my wife would have me back I'd return in a minute. I need a woman to make me happy, and I'd get married tomorrow if I could find a woman who would have me."

What happened to these seven men three years after that interview? All six who'd said they would never marry again indeed had married again! The seventh man, who wanted to get married again in the worst way, was still unmarried!

I was one of the six who said he would never marry again. Never is not forever. It only means that's the way you are feeling at the time you say it. All of the six, without knowing it at the time, had been in the walking-wounded stage of their development toward new love lives for themselves when they voiced their hostility. All were still too close to their past marriages, and were feeling like open wounds. They still felt that a close relationship with any member of the opposite sex was liable to lead to the same kind of painful breakup they had recently experienced. Better to protect yourself against experiencing that kind of pain again by creating a wall between yourself and all women, generalizing that every member of the opposite sex would be just like your ex-spouse. And if you got involved with women at all, you should use them for sex and nothing else, which will allow you the maximum pleasure and the avoidance of the pain of commitment. This will be your protective shield again getting hurt again.

What about the seventh man, who desperately wanted to marry again, yet three years later remained unmarried? What he was communicating to the opposite sex was his *desperation,* not his ability to be a good partner in a new relationship. His neediness, his sense of feeling unworthy, turned women off. Only a masochist would try to take on the burden of "making someone happy," if that person had no ability to make himself or herself happy.

Children expect someone to make them happy; mature adults don't expect a partner to become a twenty-four-hour-a-day entertainment industry for them. (One woman told this man that she had "baby-sat" her ex-husband throughout her ten-year marriage, and she was wasn't prepared to marry another "child"!)

If the seven persons interviewed had been women rather than men, their attitudes would have been practically the same as those of these men. Most of the women would protect themselves against the hurt of another marriage by generalizing that all men (like the man each had married) were "cold," "unfeeling," "selfish," "self-centered," "cruel," "brutal," "bullying," "critical," "complaining," "unresponsive," "dull," and "boring," and would say they would never marry again. And a few, or perhaps just one, of the women would want to marry again instantly because they felt they couldn't survive on their own.

In the early stages of divorce, the responses of these men and women are typical of the vast majority of divorced persons. On the one hand, there are those who feel so vulnerable that they vow never to become really intimate again with anyone (sex, yes; love, no!). On the other hand, there are those who believe they cannot survive physically or emotionally on their own, and need to delegate their responsibility to survive to a partner.

The attitudes expressed by the opposing statements "I'll never marry again" and "I must marry someone immediately in order to be taken care of" are mirror-images. They stem from the same source, namely, *fear:* the fear that you will make the same mistake again, and that the best thing to do to avoid that possibility is not to have anything to do with the opposite sex, other than as sexual vehicles; or the fear that you do not have the ability to live alone, and will waste away if no one is around to take care of you.

Commitment Anxiety: The Social Virus of Divorce

I have identified this fear as *commitment anxiety,* a virus that all divorced men and women are exposed to as a result of their marital breakups. Commitment anxiety is the fear that should you ever permit yourself to love someone else again, that new relationship will inevitably break up and you will again be left with the intense pain you are now feeling as a result of your divorce. After all, you allowed yourself to love, to be vulnerable to and intimate with the person you married, and what did it get you, other than the agonies you are now experiencing? Commitment anxiety arises from the unrealistic belief that any future committed relationship must inevitably repeat the experiences of your past marriage, and its disastrous ending.

Commitment anxiety flares up in its most virulent form when you see *all* persons of the opposite sex as a menace to your welfare, and equate your experiences with your ex-spouse as representative of what you can expect from every other person of the opposite sex, now that you are divorced. This is a *temporary* feeling most men and women experience in the early stages of divorce. However, should you *permanently* hold on to this notion, a lifetime of embittered isolation awaits you. In a more subtle fashion, the person who expresses an intense need to marry immediately after his or her divorce is also exhibiting commitment anxiety. That person's very neediness *prevents* his or her getting close to another person. You may have experienced uncomfortable pressure from other persons at some time in your life who came on to you too close, too fast. Your impulse is to escape that person's presence as soon as possible.

Both of these expressions of commitment anxiety are *constructive* barriers to a new intimate relationship, should you experience one or the other of them in the early stages of your divorce; they protect you from engaging in a new committed, exclusive relationship with a person of the opposite sex when you are not yet personally ready to deal with that relationship in a way that will be better than your past marriage. Should you remarry within two years after your divorce, you are more likely to repeat the ways in which you related to your partner in your past marriage. You need the time and space to become truly single, to experience your own sense of self-worth by making yourself happy, before you can be happy with one special person in a long-term committed relationship. Otherwise, you will be jumping from the frying pan into the fire. However, commitment anxiety, as we will see, becomes a self-destructive force if it outlives its initial constructive function.

Must You Remarry?

The answer to this question is "Of course not." To marry or not to marry is a matter of choice rather than of obligation. We live in a world that is far more tolerant and accepting of different life-styles than ever before. It was only yesterday that a single woman was considered an old maid at twenty-two, or a something's-wrong-with-him man at twenty-five if he was unmarried by then. The thirty-year-old single woman was viewed as "that poor woman," and the single man at thirty was considered probably gay or psychologically disturbed.

That was the time when people got married for reasons other than that they chose freely to do so: society demanded that they do so; parents pressured them with guilt to do so; friends nudged them to do so. They married because they needed a "meal ticket," or to escape from a miserable home life, or because they wanted sex. And if they were divorced, they could only wipe out this stigma by instantly remarrying in order to prove they were still acceptable members of society.

Most, if not all, of these self-defeating reasons for marrying have disappeared from our society, and society is much healthier for their disappearance. If you wish to remain single after your divorce for the rest of your life, and if you feel comfortable in doing so because it is your free choice rather than an undesired imposition, that is perfectly acceptable today.

Acting on your free choice can result in a fulfilling life. There are some divorced men and women who discover as a result of their divorces that marriage never fitted their personalities (or who found out that their true sexual orientation was homosexual rather than heterosexual) and consequently find relief and satisfaction in permanent singleness.

However, the overwhelming majority of divorced men and women are not of this type. More likely, they resemble the divorced men who were interviewed about their attitudes toward women and remarriage. Such men (and women) are only *temporarily* soured toward the opposite sex, for it is a fact that four out of five divorced men and women eventually remarry. Over one million divorced persons each year enter into new marriages with new partners—and most of them said at the beginning of their divorces that they would never become monogamously involved again. Why do they do so? Are they being dishonest with themselves? Not at all, for they were right when they said they would never remarry or love again, and they are right when they now choose to do so.

What these seemingly contradictory positions indicate is that such divorced persons were not personally ready to engage in a committed relationship, other than in a self-destructive way, when they said they would never attach themselves to one special person again. And now they have chosen to do so because they personally feel ready to engage in such a relationship out of a conviction that their past marriages will not repeat themselves.

They also discovered during the time they were single that they desired and wanted an intimate relationship, and that sharing life with another person best fitted their personalities. In the best of these remarriages, divorced men and women have progressed through the mourning process to the point of being able to choose freely to marry again because they have first renewed their lives as single persons, which has enabled them to eliminate the barrier of commitment anxiety that served as their protective shield against plunging into remarriage prematurely.

To run away from intimacy is to run away from the best part of yourself. The need to share life with another, to work toward common goals that transcend oneself, to experience being loved and to love, is deeply rooted in the human condition and is the salt that makes life worth living. The divorced person who chooses to remain single for the rest of his or her life also chooses a form of intimacy, which is often expressed as a commitment to a deeply felt cause (such as a passion to help the disadvantaged, or political activity to end the threat of nuclear war, or involvement with the concerns of a small circle of friends). And the divorced person who discovers he or she prefers a homosexual life-style will usually gravitate toward a close loving relationship with one special person, although that person now will be of his or her own sex.

Will Remarriage Lead to Another Divorce?

It probably will, if you do not learn from your past marriage about how you and your ex-spouse guaranteed a breakup through the unskillful ways in which the two of you related to each other. Unless you use the time between your divorce and your remarriage to deepen your insight into yourself and other people and become more skillful in resolving the problems that inevitably arise in *all* intimate relationships, the past will indeed repeat itself.

The old song has it that "love is better the second time around." But the old song is wrong, since one out of three first marriages end in divorce, *while almost one out of every two remarriages ends in a breakup.* Love *can* be better the second time around, but there is no guarantee. To enter into a new marriage blindly, without extracting the nuggets of wisdom that your divorce enables you to discover in the pain of your breakup, will only doom you to repeat the past in another divorce.

You do the groundwork that enables you to make a new committed relationship an improvement over your past marriage when you move through the mourning process to your self-renewal as a truly single person, which process I have discussed in previous chapters. When you have done so, you will have made twelve basic self-discoveries that enable you to become a self-renewed person. It is these self-discoveries that can start you on the road to attaining the lasting love relationships you want, and that will *not* end in another divorce:

1. The way you saw yourself after your divorce determined how you dealt with it. When you saw yourself as a guilt-ridden failure, your actions confirmed that failure over and over again. But when you subsequently saw yourself as an intelligent, well-intentioned human being, fallible like everyone else, who was capable of learning from the past rather than repeating it, positive things began to happen in your new single life.

2. The way you understood and reacted to the world outside yourself determined whether you limited your opportunities or expanded them to improve the quality of your life as a divorced person. When you felt that the entire world was condemning or rejecting you, you wallowed in self-pity and blamed others for your situation. But when you realized that this attitude was a millstone you were placing around your own neck, positive things became possible in your life again; there were

new people who offered you the emotional support that helped you extend your horizons.

3. You found you could surprise yourself. You had the capacities and resources to survive as a single person, even though you thought at first you had none. Even more important, you found out that you could relate in new and better ways to your children, to friends, to relatives, to strangers.

4. Regardless of your age, you discovered you could grow and change for the better, or could embark on new projects and gain skills you never thought possible before your divorce.

5. You learned to reexamine the values you had lived by, and discarded those you found wanting. You discovered that life was an affair of people rather than things, that what was most valuable in life was how you related to others and how they related to you. More open and empathic relations with your children, for example, proved more important than a new television set or a new car had been in your married life.

6. You learned that nothing positive would happen in your post-divorce life unless you yourself made the effort to make it happen. You had to examine the ways you might be defeating your best interests, and then act in new ways. If you were nonassertive, you became assertive; if you had no business skills, you took courses; if you were lonely, you called up people without waiting to be called by them. In the process, you found out that your greatest fear was fear itself. Doing something new was far less scary than you imagined.

7. You learned to respect the uniqueness of each person. You found out you were a person in your own right, and that your children and your ex-spouse also were separate individuals, rather than extensions of your needs. Your ex-spouse was not the monster you thought he or

she was, once you began to realize that to be different was not the same as to be bad. Differences in personality were to be acknowledged, understood, and dealt with, rather than labeled "bad" or "evil."

8. You learned not to make snap judgments about other people. Just as you found out you had a wider range of emotions, interests, and abilities than you had ever suspected, you found that your children were more perceptive than you had ever realized. (Didn't they tell you they knew your divorce was imminent long before you realized it?) Many of you discovered your parents to be more knowledgeable and caring than you had given them credit for. They had known about the irreconcilable differences between you and your ex-spouse years before your divorce; and they were more compassionate and understanding than you ever thought possible.

9. You learned there was a readiness time for coping with your problems. All problems couldn't be solved at once. Taking one day at a time and solving the problems of that day enabled you to solve other problems as they arose. The little things you did that demonstrated you could survive on your own were stepping-stones to solving larger problems. (Remember when you thought you could never handle the household repairs, now that your husband was no longer around? Remember when you felt you would starve to death or be drowned in your pile of dirty clothes, now that your wife no longer supplied household services?)

10. You learned to separate the past from the present, and began to live in the present. Instead of worrying over past mistakes or obsessing over nostalgic memories, you learned to recognize the newness in each new day. You began to deal with things as they are, rather than as they used to be or should be.

11. You learned to separate what society programmed you to believe you were from what you yourself wanted to be at this time in your life. You then acted constructively on what you wanted for yourself, not on what society had once insisted you *should* want for yourself. You can nod in recognition when you hear a divorced person say, "I don't 'should' on myself anymore."

12. You learned to be more compassionate with, and understanding of, other people. You found you were not alone, that there was a world of recently divorced people like yourself who experienced pain equal to or exceeding your own pain. And those people were willing to help you as much as you were willing to help them. You practiced kindness, cooperation, and an empathic awareness with them, and found that your life was made all the richer for your doing so.

The degree to which these twelve self-discoveries are incorporated by you in your thinking, feeling, and actions will determine the extent to which your quest for a new and better intimate relationship proves successful. Without the courage to risk the new, without taking personal responsibility for the ways in which you may be relating unskillfully to the opposite sex, without recognizing and correcting your own self-defeating behaviors, without your awareness that your feelings of being rejected, isolated, and lonely are a consequence of your self-created actions, the chances you have for a happier relationship of long duration will be slim indeed. No relationship rich in possibilities can flourish in the barren soil of fear and minimal self-esteem.

The Process at Work in Your Quest for a Lasting Love Relationship

I have previously noted that the divorced person who doesn't eventually desire to remarry (or engage in a living-together arrangement) is the exception rather than the rule. For it is not marriage as such that most divorced persons are permanently soured against, but rather the particular kind of marriage they have lived through. If the fear that such a marriage, which ended in divorce, might be repeated (what I have called commitment anxiety) remains at a very high level, there is little possibility that a new, lasting love relationship, more enriching than the relationship that ended in divorce, can materialize.

At the same time that there is a mourning process at work inside you by which you can overcome the traumas of your divorce and learn to become a truly single, self-realized person, there is a concurrent process at work by which you can learn to overcome your commitment anxiety and find a lasting love relationship that will improve upon the past rather than repeat it. This process, which is the quest for and attainment of intimacy without fear, consists of four stages of development that you will experience, once your desire to love again emerges inside yourself. At each of these four stages, your fear of intimacy decreases until you arrive at the stage where you discover that you have nothing to fear but fear itself. At the end of that process, a new, lasting love relationship not only becomes possible, but also realizable. You will not become ready to attain this goal overnight. If you are like most divorced people, it will take you at least two or more years before you are able to trust yourself to the point where you can find and attain the most appropriate and compatible partner to share your life with. The four stages of the process of overcoming your commitment anxiety so that this goal can materialize in your life are as follows:

1. The "Walking Wounded" Stage
2. The "Sex Is Everything" Stage
3. The "Come Close But Go Away" Stage
4. The "Intimacy Without Fear" Stage

If they do not recognize the existence of these stages as they experience them, many divorced people can spend fruitless years, or even decades, enmeshed in commitment anxiety, thinking they are simply spinning their wheels, and consequently ignoring the valuable learning experiences they can derive from that recognition, which would enable them to overcome their perceived inability to meet the "right" person, or their belief that meeting such a person is only a matter of luck and that they are simply unlucky, or their belief that they are doomed for the rest of their lives to be involved only in short-term relationships that lead nowhere. To avoid that possibility in your own life, an in-depth exploration of each of these four stages, which you can apply to your own experiences, is essential. Let's begin that exploration now, with a look at some legal realities of your new status.

10

Melvin Belli's Advice on How to Protect Yourself Legally in Dating and Relating

≡

Now that you are divorced or in the process of a divorce, you are free to date again. It might seem that this would be a delightful time, filled with exciting new adventures. However, these days the "field" you are playing seems to resemble a minefield more than a place of delight. Hitherto unfamiliar or unknown diseases such as chlamydia, herpes, and AIDS can turn new sexual encounters into booby-trap nightmares. . . . A breakup in a living-together arrangement can become the basis of a lawsuit even stickier than a contested divorce. . . . A demand for a prenuptial agreement before a second marriage may insult one's partner and cause him or her to break the engagement. . . .

How, then, can you deal with today's confusing, perplexing dating games? Mel Krantzler, in the previous chapter and others to follow, has provided you with a healthy psychological perspective to follow in dating and relating. In this chapter I'll be outlining the legal questions that might arise in the modern dating environment and giving you my advice on how to deal with them. There is no need for you to run scared. Knowing the legal facts is your best defense against avoidable legal entanglements.

The Legal Issues Involved in Post-Divorce Dating and Relating

Now that I'm divorced and dating again, what legal rights do I have, if any, in my new relationships?

You have the general right that all of us have to be legally protected from physical harm or from damage to your property. Whether you did so when you were married or not, you no longer have your marriage to use as a reason for tolerating abuse from anyone, particularly any kind of physical abuse. Remember, you are a single person now. And please be aware that physical harm can include infection with presently incurable diseases, such as genital herpes and AIDS. Therefore, I urge vigilant discretion in any relationships you choose to have, taking care to develop your friendships first and sexual liaisons only when you feel that it's safe for you to do so.

If you suffer a violation of any of your personal rights, you probably have a number of options. You may be able, in the proper circumstances, to sue for monetary damages if your new partner causes you mental or emotional distress, provided your state recognizes such lawsuits. All states protect your right to sue if actual physical harm is done to you, or if your property rights are violated. And recently a number of states have begun to recognize your right, in "sexual lie" cases, to do one or more of the following:

- To sue if you are impregnated and you sustain serious physical injury as a result of your lover's statement to you that "it's not possible for me to get you pregnant." (One woman, in a California case, suffered pregnancy complications resulting in her sterility while still at a childbearing age, and our highest state court upheld her right to sue for damages for her injury.)
- To sue if your new sexual partner conveniently or otherwise forgets to tell you prior to intercourse that he or she has a venereal disease such

as syphilis or gonorrhea. (In past decades, only a
few states recognized this right, but many do
today.)

- To sue if your new love infects you with a disease
such as genital herpes or, worse yet, transmits
AIDS to you. (The latter injury has not yet been
tested, so far as I'm aware, and whether wrong-
ful death suits would result remains to be seen,
but there is a clear trend in the law to hold
people responsible for any sexual lie they tell if
such lies cause serious physical injury to the sexual partner.)

I'm not trying to tell you that any of these tragic events
will necessarily happen to you, nor do I wish to scare you
away from relationships. Rather, I'm trying to suggest to you
that it is especially important at the present time to be
cautious and vigilant in regard to any of the above life-
threatening situations.

The specific rights cited above are an outgrowth of
modern sexual liability laws. The underlying basis for this
branch of the law is that the right of privacy in the sexual
relationship between consenting adults is outweighed by
society's concern for the public welfare and by the serious
and sometimes fatal injuries that can result from a sexual lie
told prior to intercourse.

Be aware of the above, and check with any good lawyer
in your city or town to find out about your rights if a sexual
lie is told to you and results in your injury. I find it sad and
tragic that lawyers and lawsuits are sometimes needed to
remind us that we have a human responsibility not to lie to
one another, and to ensure that if we must lie, we at least
not do so where there is any doubt in our minds that our
sexual activity could cause any kind of physical harm to
another person.

Be careful in your dating habits, and don't ever hesitate
to assert your rights in such situations. Your failure to do so
could cause you great physical, emotional, psychological, or
financial damage, and could perhaps cost you your life, regardless of whether you win your lawsuit or not.

*Now that I am separated and divorcing, can my spouse or
anyone else legally prevent me from dating anyone of my
choosing whenever I want to?*

No, you have complete freedom of action. However, under
certain circumstances, the dating you do now might possibly affect your right to continue to receive spousal support.
Furthermore, such dating by either former spouse can be
microscopically examined if you become involved in a court
custody battle. In this latter case, it is your children's best
interests, not your need for a new and more loving relationship, that will always be protected and promoted first, if a
court is ever asked to evaluate the issue. Here's how your
economic interests can be legally affected, and what you can
do to take skillful charge of the situation:

   If you are currently receiving financial support for
yourself from your ex-husband or ex-wife (to distinguish this
assistance from the child support you may also be receiving), you may find in whichever state you presently live that
the level of your spousal support can be reduced by order
of the court, upon your ex-spouse's request, because you
may now have a greater ability to support yourself.

   However, this can only occur legally if the monies or
property you receive from your new dating partner significantly reduce your overall living expenses. For instance,
let's assume that you're getting $1,000 a month in spousal
support, in part to cover your $560 monthly apartment
rent. If you begin seriously dating one person so much that
he or she starts living with you and paying half the rent,
your ex-spouse may be able to get a court to reduce his or
her spousal support payments by that amount. This is because your lover's financial assistance may well represent
sufficiently changed circumstance to warrant a modification
in your financial support. Continuing in that vein would
eventually result in elimination of your right to receive any
spousal support at all

   Obviously, therefore, what you must do in these situations is to keep your income and expenses clearly separated
from those of any new lover with whom you become involved. Or you might want to consider some kind of a legal

contract to protect you in the event that your ex-spouse's financial assistance to you is reduced or entirely cut off and your new relationship fizzles out afterwards. It's important to you to be individually secure in your financial circumstances now that you are single again. Learn that sometimes you are your only true friend, and avoid relying on other people to care for you financially; they may not always be with you, as your divorce has now proven.

More important than these financial concerns is the fact that your dating could affect any children of which you are either the custodial or the noncustodial parent. Your ex-spouse may be waiting for just such a relationship to seek to have child custody or visitation rights modified, and both could happen if you aren't careful. I know this to be true, because I've had the crying clients in my office to prove it.

Obviously, you can and should, first of all, avoid subjecting your children to the sexuality of your new relationships. That means you must not flaunt those experiences anywhere near your children. Your ex-spouse will consequently have difficulty getting a judge to agree that your new relationship is detrimental to the best interests of his or her children (which fact he or she must prove to cause a court to modify its previous orders regarding child custody or visitation rights).

Perhaps you don't have any children to concern yourself about, and/or don't receive spousal support. Or maybe you intend to limit yourself, at least for a while, to "casual" dating. You may, therefore, be tempted to think that the information we're discussing here doesn't apply to your situation. Well, think about that very carefully, because although you may be correct in this one regard, there are still things you may need to guard against, such as protecting your economic property interests, despite the lack of a spousal support problem. (See the discussion of premarital contracts beginning on page 338.) I'm not trying to discourage you from casual dating or from establishing new relationships. Both can be exciting and positive experiences for you, and ones that you may need to help you recover from your divorce. However, today as never before, you need to be cautious in your relationship choices, and you'd do well to consider developing friendships first, and only thereafter to think about the potential complications of a physical relationship.

My ex-husband keeps calling me and dropping by, and I really don't want to see him. Can I do anything to legally stop him?

There are a couple of legal steps you can take in such a situation. First, exhaust all reasonable measures to talk to your ex-husband about his conduct, explaining to him your feelings of wanting to live separately and apart from him. If necessary, you can get a new telephone number for your own use. The inability to talk to you whenever he wants may assist you in putting a stop to his intrusions on your privacy.

Second, if informal measures do not resolve the problem, you can request a judge who handles domestic matters to grant you a restraining order making it illegal for him to contact you except at designated times and places that the court orders.

Sadly, some of these cases can backfire on you, so be careful. If your ex-spouse has an emotional or psychological problem, the type of conduct in which he is presently engaged can be masking repressed hostility towards you. Sometimes such anger, if totally closed off by the cessation of all contact with you, can surface in the form of violence directed at you. So be cautious and thoughtful in any and all dealings with your ex-spouse. But seek legal assistance and police protection if necessary to allow you to get on with living your life and to encourage your ex-spouse to get on with living his own.

If I decide to sleep with a new lover and he spends the night at my place, do I have to be afraid of a legal action by my ex-spouse to change custody of our children, who presently reside with me?

Perhaps not, but any sexual relationship of which your children, now in your custody, are *aware* could cause you to lose them. The court's only concern with regard to your new life is for the protection and promotion of your children's best interests. It's doubtful, therefore, that this event, in and of itself, could ever be considered detrimental to those interests, unless you do something like fornicating in front of your custodial charges. How you handle it yourself in your new relationship will have more impact on the custody issue you raise than any other single factor affecting your children's best interests.

If you really want to sleep with this person, wouldn't it be more beneficial for all concerned not to make your sexual relationship an issue in some custody proceeding by keeping it private in the first place? Make that relationship public only when and if each of you is willing to commit to one another on some basis, to share the same space with each other.

Also, you will, in any event, want to be as sure as you can be that your lover doesn't have some sexual disease that is catching. Therefore, use your discretion, being mindful always of your own health and your children's best interests, and within those boundaries fully enjoy your new singleness. The courts will ask nothing more of you, and your ex-spouse will be frustrated if he or she complains.

Palimony and Related Issues

How can I legally protect my economic rights in any new relationship in which I engage after my divorce, if I decide to remarry?

If you're like an increasing number of people today, you may want to consider a prenuptial agreement, if you are contemplating consummating your new relationship in another marriage. Prior to such consideration, however, you should always seek to keep your income and expenses separated. And get proper legal advice before agreeing to put any of your hard-earned property into someone else's name as a partial owner, or selling any of your property to chase after some "pie in the sky" venture that your new lover proposes to you. There are, unfortunately, a number of people out there who can, if given the opportunity to do so, literally steal you blind and leave you a smoldering emotional wreck.

If you're a victim of such conduct, it may well be because you were also a victim of one of the five emotional divorce traps discussed in Chapter 6. The relevant trap here is the one in which a spouse has always allowed his or her partner to make the important financial decisions in their life. Be aware of such a tendency, and others like it, and take skillful charge by confronting those issues now and resolving them.

There are at least four good reasons why you might want to consider a prenuptial contract. Such agreements typically specify the rights and duties of the prospective marital partners, and property distribution in the event of death or divorce. Such agreements are made prior to marriage, hence the adjective *prenuptial.*

First of all, you may want legally to protect your individual economic interests (such as the property you have probably just fought hard to get in your last divorce). Normally there wouldn't be any reason to doubt that property you owned prior to marriage was your own, and therefore not divisible with your spouse in the event of divorce. However, if that property gets mixed up with your spouse's (commingled), or sold to acquire other property that you purchase after marriage, it can be an extremely difficult and sometimes a nearly impossible task to sort out your separate interests ten years down the road. Other examples in a similar vein are the following:

- You're contemplating putting your intended new spouse through law school. In such a case, the prenuptial contract can provide for financial compensation to you for your supporting services, and securing equivalent financial aid to you in the event of a divorce, so that you too can get some schooling.
- You've just inherited a substantial amount of property, and now find suitors beating down your door with proposals of marriage. Again, normally such property would clearly be your

own, even if acquired after marriage, but more often than I care to remember, such property gets invested in some joint enterprise in which the original inheritor ends up as the only financial loser, or it gets commingled with later acquired marital property in such a way that Houdini couldn't figure out a way to unlock the key to the property's original title.

- You have business partners who are not too keen on the prospect of potentially having to face your new spouse as an adversary, if you divorce and he or she wants a piece of the business or wants to become involved in its day-to-day operation. The agreement, here, can provide that your prospective spouse relinquishes forever any and all rights he or she might otherwise acquire in regard to the business, in the event that you divorce.

Second, you may want to consider a prenuptial agreement to establish the rights and duties of the prospective marital partners. While I fully recognize that premarital contracts can protect against legal interests being trampled upon later on, they may also tend to have a chilling effect on what is first, last, and always a relationship of trust. Contracts specifying who will walk the dog, clean the toilets or the garage, wash the diapers, or wax the cars (believe me, I've seen all these items included in prenuptial contracts) may do a great deal to undermine trust in a relationship and contribute to its destruction.

Third, if you have children from a former marriage whom you wish to inherit your property, you may want to consider a prenuptial agreement to prevent any other distribution. This situation can arise in many ways. For example, let's suppose, for the sake of simplicity, that your estate is worth $75,000 just prior to your remarriage, and your will has earmarked all of this property for your children. And let's further suppose that in spite of your efforts to increase it during marriage, your estate is still worth that amount of money when you die, five years later, and after taxes and death-related expenses are paid. If you haven't drawn up an appropriate prenuptial contract, your new spouse will probably have a right to as much as one-third or more of your estate, and in contravention of your intended distribution of your estate as provided in your will. I do not believe this would be a desirable result, and a premarital contract could be your answer.

Finally, you might want to utilize one of these agreements to protect you against losing your spousal support. Typically, a woman has struggled with great effort to get a decent level of financial assistance from her ex-spouse, and for just barely long enough to offer her a realistic amount of time to become self-sufficient. Then rises the new flame, sweeping her off her feet into a second marriage, and along the way causing her to give up her spousal support payments. Now, a year or two later, the new flame is but a flicker, and it, too, finally dies out in the smoldering ruin of another divorce. The problem now, outside of the complications of another divorce, is that this woman may not receive as much financial support this time around, or none at all, and that could place her in a real bind. The answer could well be a contract setting forth that the woman, in remarrying, is giving up her spousal support payments, and will get that same support from the new spouse if the second marriage ends in divorce.

If you decide that such a contract is for you, or if you are presently remarried, in which case it will be the prenuptial contract's after-marriage counterpart, namely the *postnuptial* agreement, there are a number of things you can do:

- Make sure that each of you is independently represented by counsel of your own choosing. This will prevent your contract from being voided later on due to proven allegations of coercion or duress which can occur in "one attorney counseling you both" situations.
- Make sure that the agreement contains language about "full disclosure" of all assets and protection against later discovered property to which you might otherwise be entitled. This

should take care of most "hidden assets" problems.
- Make sure that the agreement provides a specific remedy, agreeable to both parties, to deal
with any fraud that might be perpetrated by
either of the signing parties.

The cost of these agreements probably begins at about
$500. But you could spend $10,000 or more to draw up one
with complicated provisions, so use one suited to your particular situation and within the limitations of your pocket-
book. And always remember that your true security lies not
in any written agreement. Rather, such security comes at
the price of your honest, caring, and loving commitment to
each other, and your willingness to love each other enough
to allow for all positive things to become possible now and
in your future.

What is "palimony"?

This term gained prominence as a result of lawsuits such as
the Lee and Michelle Marvin case, and originally referred
to post-separation financial support payments related in
part to a time when the parties were living together not as
husband and wife, but rather as "pals," hence the word
palimony. The term has since become synonymous with
the enforcement of oral contacts between unmarried individuals who live together. Here is an example of a typical
palimony case:

John and Mary have been living together for six years,
and both people were working when they got together.
John didn't like the thought of his live-in lover working, and
got Mary to quit her job as a budding young architect and
keep the house instead. Mary says that she did so because
John told her that if she would stay home, do the dishes,
wash, fold, and iron the clothes, cook the meals, and otherwise care for "their" home, he'd share half of everything he
had with her. Now John has tired of Mary's company, wants
her to move out, and won't pay her a dime.

Provided that John's oral statements were made at all,
and provided also that such statements were not made by

John in return for Mary's sexual favors, but rather for the work as described by Mary, the latter may have a right to sue John for damages in this non-marriage situation. Her legal action would not be a divorce or any related proceeding, but rather a lawsuit to enforce the oral promise John is claimed by Mary to have made. Such oral contracts have always been enforceable in most states, if proven, so there is nothing new about palimony cases just because the basis for them is an oral contract.

What is new, however, is the enforcement of such contracts between consenting adults who are unmarried but living together at the time such legal agreements are claimed to have been made. Prior to the Marvin case, such lawsuits were thrown out of court on the theory that "bedroom language between lovers makes a highly questionable legal contract." The twin problems of proving that such oral statements were ever made, and, further, that they were not in any way related to sexual relations, make palimony cases very difficult to prove.

However, if the terms of the agreement are definite and specific enough and not made in return for sex, many courts will enforce the contractual terms when a lawsuit is filed and proved, complaining of a breach of an oral contract. And some courts might consider awarding Mary some financial support while the lawsuit is in progress, if part of John's oral agreement has also been to take care of Mary in the event they ever split up. This support would be palimony.

If you find yourself in a situation similar to that of John and Mary, you can take skillful charge of it by seeing a good lawyer at your earliest convenience, preferably one familiar with palimony. Get the lawyer to explain to you what rights and/or obligations you have, if any, and how best to proceed, given the law in the state and county where you live. You may want to have him or her draft a written agreement for you, similar in content to the postnuptial contract described elsewhere in this chapter.

Post-Divorce Relationships with Former In-Laws and Ex-Spouses

My child is in the hospital for an operation. My ex-husband insists upon bringing his new wife with him when he visits. This is our child and has nothing to do with her. What can I legally do about it?

The first thing you can do is to come to grips with the fact that you may be legally powerless to prevent your ex-spouse from doing exactly what he apparently intends to do. This is because nothing in what you have just described indicates, in and of itself alone, that any detriment to your son's best interests will be caused by your ex-husband's visits to see his son in the hospital, accompanied by his present spouse. Such conduct would have to be damaging to those interests in order for you to be able legally to prevent your ex-spouse from engaging in the conduct you've described. And to a court, it is your child's best interests, not your own feelings, that are at issue in any matter that concerns that child. If you want to restrain your ex-husband, you will have to find something detrimental about his conduct with regard to your son.

You can realize also that your ex-husband's new wife, by virtue of her marriage, has an interest in getting to know your son. And your ex-husband's new wife may have many experiences to share with this child that could well be in his best interests. In any event, be aware that she is under no legal obligation to prove to anyone that her contact with your son is in your son's best interests. Rather, it is you, or someone else, who would be required under present law to prove the contrary.

I say all of the above to urge you to consider whether you may harbor an emotional or psychological resistance to becoming more aware of the above legal facts and suppositional arguments. If that is the case, it's important for you to become aware that such resistance, if you do not properly work it out by yourself or in conjunction with a counselor/ therapist, can grow like cancer. It might cause you to do something that is illegal, such as frustrating your ex-hus-

band's visitation rights or stopping them entirely by snatching away your son to prevent further contact with your
ex-spouse.

*I like my ex-mother-in-law and she likes me. Can I continue
to see her, now that I'm divorced?*

There is absolutely no legal reason why you cannot. While
she may no longer be related to you by marriage, she may
be—and obviously is, in your case—still a very close friend.
And there are no laws saying that you can't see a friend, just
because you divorced the friend's son or daughter. If the
relationship is a healthy and positive one for both of you (I
wouldn't, for instance, recommend such a relationship if
you're trying to use it as a ploy either to get back together
with your ex-spouse or to do him or her emotional and/or
psychological harm), I wholeheartedly support and encourage your desire to continue such an apparently valuable
friendship, particularly at the present time, when you're
likely to need all the positive reinforcement you can get.

And if you have children, regardless of whether you
have their physical custody, the relationship with your former mother-in-law can be uniquely valuable to those children as well.

Often in the past, grandparents have had great difficulty gaining access rights to their grandchildren, even
when they had legal help from a competent lawyer. While
the situation is somewhat better today (many states now
have laws legally entitling grandparents to see their grandchildren, regardless of whether such meetings are approved
of by either of the grandchildren's parents), the fact that you
and your ex-mother-in-law continue to share a close relationship will help foster her contact with your children,
which contact is clearly in your children's best interests. So
enjoy and develop your relationship to the fullest.

*I want to see my ex-wife to try for a reconciliation. How can
I go about it?*

First, you need to find out if the other party is also willing
to consider such a move. You can answer this question with
a simple telephone call, if you are willing to acknowledge

your feeling honestly to her, and to ask that she also be honest with you. If you accomplish that task and find that your partner is willing, you can then utilize private counseling to begin to develop your reconciliation. If the cost of such assistance is presently beyond your means, look to the courts for such services. In California, such help is provided by our conciliation courts, which offer professional counseling at little or no cost to couples desirous of getting together again. Your state will probably provide similar services.

If I remarry, what are the chances of my having to go through the legal process of divorce again?

The odds will be more in your favor the longer you can put off another long-term and formalized legal commitment to another person. "Love on the rebound" seldom, if ever, produces a lasting relationship. More often than not, such experiences end up as "love on the rocks." Very broadly speaking, your next marriage will have a better-than-average chance of succeeding if it doesn't begin until at least two years after the last marriage ended. You can, however, take skillful charge by using this book as a tool to help you learn from your divorce experience, so that you can avoid repeating past mistakes.

Your understanding of the legal realities of your new status in dating and relating, as outlined in this chapter, prepares you for assimilating the in-depth exploration of the process of finding a new, lasting love relationship, which Mel Krantzler will share with you in the final four chapters of our book.

11

The Process of Finding a New Lasting Love Relationship

STAGE ONE: "WALKING WOUNDED"

This is the terror-time that is experienced at the earliest stage of your separation, when you and your soon-to-be ex-spouse have just begun to live in separate households. It may then feel as if you have just been in a car crash and are still feeling its repercussions. Dazed and disoriented, you suddenly find you're living in a foreign country, the land of the divorced, where you don't even know its language or its etiquette.

The person who said that "life is what happens to you when you're busy making other plans" must have had you in mind when he or she made that remark. One-day-at-a-time survival is of paramount importance to you at this first stage in your quest for a lasting love relationship. In fact, at this stage the desire for such a relationship may be the furthest thing from your mind. Instead, concern about your economic survival, negotiations and hassles over alimony, property division, child support and visitation rights, revised relationships with friends and relatives, and adjusting to new living quarters in an unfamiliar neighborhood are of paramount importance.

The permanent reality of your separation from your spouse has yet to be fully assimilated by your mind and feelings and behavior. Still-married habits often persist. If you are a woman, you may still be wearing your wedding ring, even after the divorce is final; or you may keep your house or apartment as a mausoleum, leaving your husband's room and mementoes and clothing untouched for months after he has permanently left. You could find yourself cooking for two when only you are at the dinner table. You may rush home to prepare dinner because your husband will soon be home, and then realize there is no reason for you to be home at that time, since he is no longer a daily part of your life.

And if you are a man, after you leave work your car may often seem to have driven itself to the house or apartment you and your wife lived together in, rather than to your new separate household. Because your new single life still feels like a scary future rather than a present reality, you might find yourself experiencing traces of wanting to hold on to the very marriage you know has ended. You do so when you involve your wife in legal hassles over minor issues, such as who gets custody of the piano or the phonograph records, thereby prolonging a connection with her. You might make excuses to visit with your soon-to-be ex-wife at your former home to argue over issues that could be more easily and appropriately handled by your lawyer, or to see how well she is looking and to find clues as to whether or not she is now dating someone. Making unnecessary phone calls is another way of perpetuating the married-habit connection, if only to criticize and complain about the way your wife is grooming the children. Arguing with each other is still a form of connection; unnecessary court appearances are a continuation of your marriage by other means.

Licking One's Wounds

As the days of your separation turn into weeks and months, the recognition that there is no turning back, that now you really must make it on your own, becomes stronger. At the same time, the fear that you cannot make it on your own also escalates as the reality that your married life is over takes hold. This is the time when self-pity is liable to overwhelm you, and you may spend endless hours bathing in the warm waters of feeling sorry for yourself.

The world looks like a menacing place, so you might entrench yourself in your home and use the crutches of alcohol or cocaine or uppers and downers to assuage your anxieties, fears, and pain, along with overdosing on endless TV programs that at least afford you the comfort of having electronic friends in your time of isolation and loneliness.

The open wound of your breakup is now throbbing with maximum intensity. The very idea of a new close, committed relationship with one special person in your life may strike you as an abomination at this time. The suggestions of well-intentioned friends who urge you to date or offer to "fix you up with someone who is just right for you" are rejected. With friends like that, who needs enemies? Don't they know you've been burned badly? You thought you had a love relationship that would last a lifetime, and received a divorce instead. Why be burned again? Forget about the opposite sex, they are all rotten.

Defiant slogans such as "A woman needs a man [or vice versa] like a fish needs a bicycle" strike a responsive chord in your soul at this time. And if a person of the opposite sex dares to look at you with even a smidgen of interest, you may glare in response as if this is a setup to victimize you, or you may avoid the glance and beat a hasty retreat. A narrow escape, thank God.

There are some men and women in this "walking wounded" stage who seem to want immediately to find someone to marry again, the sooner, the better. They are misreading their emotions, since they think that they want a lasting love relationship with a person who would radically differ from their ex-spouse, but what they really want is someone to take care of them. For, just like the men and women who proclaim they will have nothing to do with the opposite sex, these persons feel vulnerable and helpless with regard to their ability to survive on their own.

The divorced men and women who regard the possibility of any new close commitment with total distaste react in this stage with despair and isolation; those who want an instant new marriage react out of anxiety and driven neediness to have someone other than themselves take charge of their lives.

Those who wish for an instant new marriage alienate

the persons they wish to attract by their display of total neediness and sense of helplessness. They too fear and resent the opposite sex, because they imagine the opposite sex to be all-powerful, while they themselves are hostage to them because of their own weakness. Consequently, they also find themselves as isolated and despairing of their future as the men and women who vow they will never marry again.

Endings Are Also New Beginnings

The sense of helplessness and life-out-of-control that is characteristic of the walking-wounded stage is the sign of an ending *and* a new beginning. You are experiencing the irrevocable ending of your old marriage and its habits that defined your past everyday life. This ending is required as a prelude to a new beginning in which your quest for a new lasting love relationship will rest on the secure foundation of your self-renewal as a single person.

Cheer up! The walking-wounded stage will not last forever, although it seems as if it will at the time you are living through it. There is a drive toward health and self-renewal in each of us that protects us from self-destruction. Human beings cannot exist for long on a diet of hopelessness and despair, nor can self-isolation, drugs, or TV addiction cure the pain that results from the devastating loss of the intimate relationship that is the basis of the marriage bond. The search for a new intimate relationship begins when your drive toward health and self-renewal begins to tell you that enough is enough; when you become alarmed at your own drinking or drug use and stop depending on it; when you become so annoyed with TV that you turn the chatterbox off instead of automatically allowing it to ramble on through the night; when you become tired of hearing your own self-pity; when you become bored with being boring to yourself; when the house or apartment you are living in becomes more a self-isolating jail than a protective womb.

It is then that the urge to meet new people and engage in new activities arises, and it is then that the desire to have some form of personal involvement with the opposite sex emerges. Normal and natural though that desire is, you may very well have mixed feelings about its emergence: on the one hand, you may be excited over the new possibilities; on the other, you are so helpless, vulnerable, and naïve that you may very well be victimized and hurt once again should you fall in love or even be attracted to another person. When you notice these occurrences within yourself, you will be ready to start out on your quest for a lasting love relationship.

The decks are cleared for that adventure, which will lead you into Stage 2 ("Sex Is Everything") of your journey. When will you leave the walking-wounded stage? When you recognize the healthy self-renewal elements I noted above emerging within. Each person has his or her own personal time to move out of the walking-wounded stage.

In general, this stage is lived through in the first three to six months after separation. Should it go on longer than that, and you find none of the healthy self-renewal elements burgeoning within you, I recommend seeing a good divorce counselor to help you overcome your sense of disarray and despair. It is unfortunately the case that all too many divorced men and women remain trapped in this stage for many years after their divorces; the high suicide and drug addiction rates among the divorced testify to that fact. Avoid that possibility.

The Learning Experiences of the Walking-Wounded Stage

Each stage of the quest for a lasting love relationship presents you with a series of learning experiences that advance you nearer toward your desired goal. The walking-wounded stage is the first stage in that quest, and it helps you in the following ways:

1. It reinforces the irrevocability of your breakup with your spouse.
2. It is a purging process that enables you to

disengage from the habits of your old married
way of life.

3. Your self-isolation forces you to center your
attention on your own thoughts and feelings,
and to sort out the meanings of what they are
telling you about yourself.

4. It is the start of your self-healing, rather than
a time to give up on life's possibilities.

5. It is the beginning stage of a process over
time, a stage designed for you to leave when
you are ready, rather than becoming trapped
in it.

6. It serves as a protective device that guards you
against making any hasty decision to remarry
or become involved in what you may imagine
to be a committed relationship before you are
ready to make a truly insightful and mature
decision in those directions.

7. It propels you once again to reach out for an
association with the opposite sex, since the alternative of self-isolation and drugs leads to
self-destruction rather than self-renewal.

Once you have absorbed these learning experiences,
you will be ready for the second stage in your quest for a
lasting love relationship. For now you are free to engage in
relationships of your choice, without being accountable to
a spouse.

12

The Process of Finding a New Lasting Love Relationship

STAGE TWO: "SEX IS EVERYTHING"

═

This is the stage when you begin to test the waters of a lasting love relationship. It may not seem so at the time, for you are still at the level where your fear of a new commitment of any kind with the opposite sex has intensified.

The solution becomes the seeking of new sexual experiences without commitment. Having sex for its own sake—sex as entertainment, sex as fun, sex as recreation, sex as validation that you are a person who is attractive and worthy of attention. Seeing and using the other person as an object of entertainment and desire, rather than as an individual. Having sex rather than making love, for love implies commitment. This is the stage when you subscribe to Woody Allen's definition of the difference between sex and love: "Sex relieves tension, while love causes tension." And you opt for the relief of tension.

Sex has been called "the poor man's opera." In other words, sexual enjoyment is available to everyone and need cost you nothing. One can create that enjoyment with oneself when one masturbates, as well as with others.

It affords you a sense of personal power, since you are free to make that enjoyment happen by your own actions. However, in a marriage that has turned sour and has ended in divorce, sexual intercourse was neither regularly available nor the liberatingly enjoyable activity it is designed by nature to be. A grim marriage usually results in grim sex or no sex at all.

In the year or two before the final breakup of such a marriage, it is typical for a couple to have had no sexual intercourse whatsoever, or only an occasional involvement arising out of physical need rather than love. In such a case, sex has turned into an obligation, and the withholding of it has become a form of resentful punishment against a no-longer-loved spouse. Or a mutual loss of love has transformed sexual desire into sexual apathy. A vital part of your sense of self, the belief in your own sexual competency and capacity for sexual enjoyment, seems to have disappeared forever from your life.

Now that you are single, sexual feelings you long thought dead begin to blossom inside yourself. Are you really the lousy lover, the incompetent clod, the bad performer, the sexual turkey your former spouse led you to believe you were?

You are now free to test that belief as you begin to explore the world of single men and women. Will others find you attractive? Or is there truth in your ex-spouse's evaluation of your sexuality? This is the time to find out; this is the time to try to live out the fantasies you might have harbored in your now-dead marriage that you really have a great capacity to give and receive sexual pleasure, provided it is with someone other than the spouse you lived with. You had been living in the sexual desert of your marriage, but now you are free to explore the oases in single life. The thirst for enjoyable sexual activity can now be assuaged.

In this stage of your quest for a lasting love relationship, sexual interest takes center stage because it is a vital part of yourself that has long been inhibited or demeaned. Consequently, the new emergence of sexual feelings pressing for action is a sign that you are trying to recapture a part of yourself that is vitally necessary to your self-esteem. Everyone wants to be a sexual object worthy of the attention of others, but no one wants to be *only* a sexual object.

Your concentration on your sexual needs in this stage buffers you against your commitment anxiety. It's like eating your cake and having it: sexual pleasure with no relationship strings attached. Sex as the *only* thing that matters distances you from a close, loving relationship, which at this stage you would not as yet be mature enough to handle skillfully. At the same time it advances you in the direction of that goal.

Where can you find other single men and women also engaged in exploring new sexual possibilities for themselves? They are available when you are ready to send out signals that you too are available. There are presentable neighborhood bars where singles meet; there are singles dances, lectures, and workshops for you to go to; there are friends and associates at your office who know of other single people who might be interested in dating; there are singles you can meet in a restaurant and engage them in conversation; there are parties to which you might be invited where other singles are present to whom you can introduce yourself.

How you act, the aura you present to others, will determine whether or not you will meet the people you want to meet. Act sad, shy, inhibited, resentful, or defiant; isolate yourself at a party or a lecture or a dance and then complain that you can't find anyone: these are sure guarantees that you won't meet anyone.

The Changed Nature of Today's Dating Scene

What is the dating scene like today? It's certainly *not* like the time when you were dating prior to your marriage. As Ted, a recently divorced thirty-eight-year-old man new to the dating scene after being married fourteen years, told me, "It's like I've come out of the middle ages when it comes to dating again. I feel like a teenage kid who doesn't know the rules of the game. It's all so confusing. Why, the other night I automatically started to pay for the dinner check and the woman I was with called me a male chauvinist pig and insisted on splitting the bill.

"Another date I had objected to my opening doors for her; she said she was not a cripple, she could do that for herself. A woman I met casually at a party called me up and asked me for a date. I was pleased, of course, but it surprised the hell out of me that women take the initiative these days. That's always been the man's job, or at least that's what I learned when I was in my teens and early twenties."

George, forty-four, who married twenty years ago, is even more confused. "I'm damned if I do and damned if I don't when I go out on a date. One woman is put out of joint when I don't pick her up when we go out, while another *doesn't* want me to do that. Then there's the woman who was pissed off because I didn't call her up, and told me so to my face, but I thought I had never said I would. And if I pay the restaurant check, I'm an arrogant male prick, but if I don't pay it I'm considered just another guy who exploits women. If I make a pass at the end of an evening, I'm a brute who's only out for one thing. But if I don't make a pass, I'm considered a wimp or a homosexual in disguise. I really can't figure out how to deal with women these days. One woman told me she likes sensitive, tender men. Yet when I told her how I miss my kids and feel so rotten about it, and tears came to my eyes, she looked very uncomfortable and changed the subject. I never saw her again; it was like she told me to get lost because I was just a weak and helpless guy. Some women are as foulmouthed as men, and that surprises me. What are they trying to be, 'one of the boys'? And I get puzzled over some words I've never heard before. Yesterday a woman told me 'You're nice, it's too bad you're G.U.' It sounded like some kind of social disease. I later learned it meant 'geographically undesirable,' a term a lot of divorced people use. That woman brushed me off because I lived too far away from where she was living!

"I'm beginning to think there's a language called 'singlespeak,' what with terms like 'LTA,' 'unstructured relationship,' and 'POSSLQ.' I found out all three mean the same thing—living together without being married. One person told me that POSSLQ is a term used by the Census Bureau, would you believe it? It means 'persons of the opposite sex sharing living quarters,' and LTA stands for 'living-together arrangement.' Of the three terms, I like 'unstructured relationship' best. It sounds more elegant and mysterious. My divorce is forcing me to major in singlespeak!"

Every complaint and confusion expressed by divorced men about the modern dating scene can be matched by the complaints and confusions of divorced women. Barbara, a thirty-seven-year-old divorced woman with an eight-year-old daughter and an eleven-year-old son, tells me at my counseling center, "I want to be treated as an equal instead of the service industry that women like myself were trained to grow up to be. My sexual needs are just as great as any man's, and I now have the freedom to satisfy them. Yet it's not as simple as all that. It's like I'm two Barbaras. There's the 'me' who grew up to believe that men's needs came first and that I was to wait for the last piece of cake. And there's the 'me' who knows women are not second-class people and rightfully deserve to be considered the equal of men. There's the 'mo' who likes men and enjoys them sexually. But there's also the 'me' who resents men because of their economic power. I just read that women who are college graduates earn forty percent less than men who are high school graduates. I know that's true, because I'm a college graduate stuck in a low-paying job.

"So, when I go out on a date, I'd like to pay half of the restaurant bill but can't do so, which makes me feel angry. And in bed I want to be free and wild, but I'm always afraid I may hurt the man's fragile ego if I tell him what I like and want him to do to satisfy me sexually. With too many guys its 'wham, bam, thank you, ma'am.' I feel I have to settle for this because good girls are supposed to pleasure men, while women are only entitled to crumbs.

"I know in my head that this is old-fashioned thinking, but that little voice inside me that sounds just like my mother keeps telling me, 'Don't make waves, Barbara, a man's needs come first.' Sometimes I feel guilty for just being alive. Always the guilt. Guilty for wanting sexual fulfillment, guilty for wanting to be equal to men, guilty even when I take the initiative to call up a man I have met casually to suggest we go out on a date, because 'nice girls simply don't do that.'

"I always feel I'm walking on a tightrope with men, always worried that I'm being too pushy or overbearing, always worried about what the man is thinking about me. The little voice inside me keeps saying men only want one thing from a woman, so that whenever I'm on a date where the man pays, I keep thinking he wants me to pay him back by sleeping with him, even though I don't want to. So I get resentful of the poor guy right from the start of the evening, as if he were guilty of a crime that maybe he had no intention to commit. In my down moods, I say to myself, 'Why bother, maybe a nunnery is better.' And then I laugh at myself."

There are tens of thousands of Barbaras, Teds, and Georges in the singles world today. What they are saying is that the dating and sexual scene today differs dramatically from the one in which they grew up, and that the conditioning of their past is clashing with the new realities of present-day ways of relating.

It has been said that etiquette consists of tested ways to make life work more smoothly. The etiquette of dating and sexual relationships was clearly defined and generally accepted when you were involved in those activities prior to the time of your marriage. You knew what was proper and improper then, and life did work more smoothly, since the etiquette was a common language everyone spoke.

Today, however, the sexual revolution and the impact of the women's movement in the past two decades have eliminated the common assumptions you once lived by, and commonly accepted new assumptions are still in the process of being created. Hence the confusion, the misreading of intentions, the awkwardness of not knowing how to behave.

If you recognize that we are living today in a time of transition, where old etiquette patterns of dating and sexual behavior are in the process of changing into new patterns, you can begin to fit more comfortably into this new world. What's right and what's wrong in this transition time depends on your sensitivity and alertness to your partner's feelings and expectations, as well as your being up front regarding your own feelings and expectations whenever you meet, date, and go to bed with someone. Assume nothing in advance, or if you do, check out those assumptions with the person you are with to find out whether they match reality. As one woman told me, "I no longer assume anything. I've learned that 'assume' is really three words rather than one: 'ass,' 'you,' and 'me.' I'm liable to make an *ass* out

of *me* when I assume anything about *you*!" You will smooth
your way in the dating and sexual scene when you check
things out with your partner for the evening.

- *Who pays for dinner?* Discuss this in advance. A
  man usually earns more than a woman; if this is
  the case in your individual situation, tell her you
  know her income is less than yours and that you
  wish to pay for dinner, if that is what you want
  to do. If you are a woman who can afford it, then
  suggest you split the check. If you can't afford it,
  suggest that next time you would like to make
  dinner for him, or perhaps a picnic lunch.

- *Should a woman take the initiative and call a
  man whom she's recently met?* Today it is common practice to exchange business or social
  cards at a party or a lecture. Calling up later by
  either the man or woman is equally appropriate.
  A man ordinarily is pleasantly surprised and de-
  lighted when a woman makes that call, and does
  not believe that she is "loose" if she does so. If
  you tell him you have an extra ticket for a show,
  and he accepts, it's not a sign that he expects you
  to go to bed with him afterwards.

- *What is a man entitled to if he pays for your
  dinner?* Nothing except the pleasure of your
  company. If he is thinking otherwise and hints
  that he expects a sexual payoff, you don't have to
  act like a teenage virgin and say, "How dare
  you!" You can be gracious and polite in your
  refusal, telling him thanks for the compliment,
  you enjoyed the evening, but you're not ready
  yet to go to bed with him. If you find him attractive, say you'd like some time for both of you to
  get to know each other better, so let's see how
  things progress. If he feels rejected or ripped off,
  that's his problem, not yours. A man as boorish
  and insensitive as that is someone you wouldn't
  want to be involved with anyway.

- *Does a man want only "one thing"?* Only if you
  also want that "one thing." The woman sets the

limits on her behavior. This is something that every man knows and of which women are often unaware. Set the man straight by telling him of your needs and desires without giving him double signals. Don't act seductive in a low-cut dress, edge closer to him with starry eyes, and then act like an outraged Victorian maiden if he makes a serious pass or suggests the bedroom. If you don't want to go to bed, say so politely; if you do, show him the way. With very rare exceptions, men respect the limits a woman sets on her behavior; if this one doesn't, he's not worth bothering with. However, be clear in your own mind what your limits are.

- *What do women want?* If they are in the sex-is-everything stage, they want the same things a man does: sexual experiences without commitment; sexual enjoyment for its own sake, out of fear that to desire anything more will place them right back in the dependency trap of their former marriage. Women today increasingly delight in their own sexuality and are permitting themselves to fully enjoy foreplay and intercourse variations without the pretense that these are unladylike. A man should allow a woman to express *her* needs in bedroom activity. It's not a criticism of your abilities when a woman suggests ways in which she would like you to pleasure her. You will find greater pleasure together when you ask her what she would like you to do, rather than assume you have satisfied her when all you have done is to satisfy yourself.

- *What if I call up a man and he refuses my suggestion to go on a date?* You will then be joining the ranks of every man in this world, for they have had this happen to them ever since they started to date in their teens. That's the price for taking the initiative, which was presumed to be only the man's prerogative in past decades.

   Of course, such a refusal hurts. Men have

assuaged their own hurt when refused by adopting the principle "nothing ventured, nothing gained." As one man told me, "When I call up three women and two refuse to go out with me, I don't moon over the refusals. I feel I had a victory, because the third one said yes!" Refusals are part of the dating game, and in this instance the way men handle this reality is a good way for you to do so also.

• *Are men expected to make a pass at the end of a date?* This depends on the woman and how she has acted toward you all evening long. Her body signals and speech will indicate whether or not she will be responsive to a heavy or a light pass, or none at all. If you have been turned off by her, a good-night handshake and thanks for the evening are all that are required. If more seems to be in order, then it's time to play it by ear. The more alert and sensitive you are to her needs and elicit that information from her, the more appropriately you will act, whether that means coming on strong or taking it easy.

Men have generally been brought up to believe that it is obligatory on a date to make a pass as a way of proving their sexiness and maleness, whether or not the woman wants that pass, and whether or not the man actually likes the woman enough to make a pass. Eliminate that sense of obligation; freely choose to do what the situation indicates, rather than what old-fashioned ideas dictate.

• *What turns women off?* The women in my divorce adjustment seminars repeatedly say they are turned off by men who are self-centered, lacking in sensitivity, and overly possessive in public, or who are pompous, judgmental, rigid, unfeeling, dishonest (the man who says I'll call you next week but doesn't), uncommunicative, or sexually demanding. They don't like men who are unable to listen, who put down other women, who treat them like property, or who are wishy-washy or arrogant.

- *What turns men off?* Men in my seminars repeatedly object to women who are manipulative, controlling, intimidating ("What do you intend to do about our relationship?"), or coy; who overreact to a suggestion to sleep together ("forty-year-old virgins with children"); who display false modesty or do not listen; who are argumentative injustice-collectors; or who are boisterous, self-centered, insensitive, unstylish in appearance, humorless, or unable to empathize.
- *What turns men and women on?* Men and women are not very different in what turns them off, or in what turns them on. Just being yourself and demonstrating an honest, authentic interest in the person you are dating is your best guarantee for a successful evening.

Rediscovering Your Sexual Self

In the sex-is-everything stage, the dating scene enables you to rediscover your own sexuality. For most divorced men and women, the final years of a deteriorated marriage are years of physical as well as emotional alienation. In such a dead marriage, two hurt people who are not getting their emotional needs met play out their disenchantment with each other in the sexual arena. Sex becomes the battleground: sexual apathy (why bother?), sexual withholding (men, too, use the excuse that they have a headache or are "too tired"), and sexual ineffectiveness (anger toward your spouse expressed in the form of premature ejaculation, a clenched vagina or vaginismus, an inability to experience orgasm, or failure to sustain an erection) are the ways a husband and wife tell each other that their marriage is no longer livable.

The bedroom has become the bored-room. The longer

this kind of sexual warfare persists, the more your self-esteem diminishes. Belief in your own competence as a sexual being is an important component of your own self-regard as a person of value and worth. It is most often the case that both the husband and wife who have lived for many months or even years—in such a sexual no-man's-land begin to believe that they may very well be the unattractive person, the incompetent lover, the pitiful sexual performer, or the impotent wimp that their spouses give them the impression they are.

Your sexual self-esteem may therefore be at a very low level at the beginning of the sex-is-everything stage. Are you really physically attractive to persons of the opposite sex, or was your spouse right? Are you capable of orgasms or sustained erections? Do you even have the capacity to enjoy sex, since so much of your recent married life has been a time of sexual deprivation or unfulfillment? The saying is "Use it or lose it"; have you lost it?

These are the questions that might obsess you at this time, and make you hesitate to seek sexual fulfillment. Yet this is the time when the powerful drive to engage in new sexual experiences, as an affirmation that you are now no longer a married person and can exercise free choice in your life, propels you to overcome those fears and hesitations. So you take the risk.

In the very beginning of the sex-is-everything stage, surprising things might happen:

- If you are still married *in your feelings* to your ex-spouse at that time, you might surprise yourself by having sex with your ex-spouse! An encounter with your ex-spouse involving your picking up your half of the record collection may end up a half hour later in the bedroom. Mutual surprise and embarrassment are likely to be the consequence, for both of you are experiencing a release of sexual tension rather than an affirmation that all's well between the two of you.
- If you are a woman and go to bed with a person

you recently met, you may find penetration too painful and reject your partner—just as you did in your marriage!—and feel you are indeed sexually inhibited.

- If you are a man who goes to bed with a woman you met that night, you may find yourself unable to have an erection, just as you did in your marriage!

- Whether you are a man or a woman, you may find yourself unable to attain orgasmic satisfaction with a new partner, just as you did in your marriage!

- If you have always had sex in your marriage in traditional ways, believing that the missionary position was the only "respectable" one, you may repulse a new partner when oral sex or a nontraditional position is suggested. Your righteous indignation becomes a substitute for the sexual act.

Don't be overwhelmed or discouraged by incidents like these, should they occur. They are part of the divorce process, for letting go of the past also involves experiencing traces of the past that might still be present in your divorced state. The degree to which those traces of the past dominate your present behavior is an indication of the degree to which you are still married in your feelings, even though the signed piece of paper that is your divorce decree is in your files.

As John, a thirty-six-year-old man who was married for thirteen years, told me, "Whenever I go to bed with a new person, it's as if I'm still being unfaithful to my wife. Yet here I am, actually into my ninth month of divorce! It's as if there's a threesome in bed, with my ex scolding me, saying, 'No! No! No! You bad boy!' But her voice in my head is getting weaker and weaker the more I go out. Why, last week I was able to maintain my erection and was actually able to permit myself to have a climax inside my partner for the very first time since my divorce. It's taking me a while to realize I'm not married anymore."

The Freedom to Experiment

When you recognize that you are now free to experiment, and that it is necessary to move through your own inhibitory fears of possibly being rejected and found physically and sexually unworthy, with the understanding that nothing ventured is nothing gained, positive things begin to happen.

This is the time when, if you are like most divorced persons in this stage, you will begin to sprout a new wardrobe, a fresh new look for fresh opportunities. A new physical self starts to emerge: hair-coloring and hairstyle changes; the drab dresses, suits, and shirts in somber blues, browns, and blacks are discarded, and brighter, more vivid colors take their place; stylish dresses and suits and casual clothes displace the lock-step styles you once wore.

You begin to pay more attention to your physical condition and lose the excess weight you carried around with you in your marriage as if it were the heavy burden of the marriage translated into physical terms. The changes in your physical condition and your clothes, styles, and grooming make the statement that a new beginning is in the process of becoming a reality.

As more of your energies are directed toward the dating scene, you will be in for a pleasant surprise. More than a few persons of the opposite sex will find you physically attractive; you are *not* the turkey you thought you might be when you were in your marriage! Such attraction leads to the bedroom sooner or later, for we live in a society that is far more sexually permissive than the one you lived in at the time you married. Even a decade ago, living together without a marriage license was thought to be off-color; today it is taken for granted.

Safe recreational sex, as distinct from sex as an expression of love, caring, or commitment is also another activity taken for granted today, and is a consequence of the elimination of the fear of pregnancy that has resulted from the invention of the Pill and the more prevalent use of condoms and other effective contraceptive devices.

Today, Mrs. Patrick Campbell's statement about what two consenting adults should be allowed to do privately has become a reality: "Nobody should care what you do, as long as you don't do it in the street and frighten the horses." The sexual activities in the past that were once thought to be perverse or bestial (cunnilingus and fellatio, sexual positions other than the missionary position, and mutual or self-masturbation) are now regarded as normal variations to engage in or to decline as one pleases.

This kind of freedom generates excitement and anticipation if you had fantasies in your marriage of prohibited opportunities. (As one divorced man told me, "My wife always insisted on the missionary position, but I always knew I was never cut out to be a missionary.") However, mixed up with excitement and anticipation is fear and performance anxiety. (Will you like any of the variations you never had in your marriage? Will you be a "good performer" in these variations, or chicken out and disappoint your partner? And since women are more forward today in asserting their sexual needs, how will you react when a woman approaches you and says, "My place or yours?")

When you move into the try-it-you-might-like-it state of mind, these self-created barriers to discovering the wider range of your sexual nature begin to disappear. You begin to discover that you indeed have the capacity to experience orgasms, including multiple ones if you are a woman; that your penis has more staying power than your former wife ever suspected, if you are a man.

If you never had oral sex, it might become exciting rather than repulsive. If you only had sex at ten at night in a dark room, with your shouts of delight muffled so as not to disturb your neighbors, then sex in broad daylight in a bright room (where you can allow your cries of delight full force of expression) can be a liberating experience.

If you have been starved for foreplay in your marriage, you can now assert your need for it and receive it. If you often thought in your marriage how nice it would be to reverse the missionary position or to have sex on the floor or seated on a chair or in a sideways position, or to have anal sex, or oral intercourse in a "69" position, you have the freedom to realize these desires and discover whether or not they are the turn-ons you imagined them to be.

Of course, the dating and sex scene today is also fraught with some difficulties unanticipated in previous decades. The loosening of sexual restraints has brought with it a host of diseases and infections. The appearance of AIDS, in addition to the standard venereal diseases in the dating and sex scene, is a primary concern. As one man told me, "I feel every time I sleep with a new woman that I'm walking through a minefield!" I have heard similar comments from women. One man informed me that he requests a medical note that says the woman he wants to sleep with has a clean bill of health before he goes to bed with her. (This hardly makes him the most popular man-about-town.) However, discreet inquiries of a new acquaintance are in order if you are concerned about the possibility of infection, although it appears that most men and women are not sexually inhibited by this, just more careful in selecting bedmates.

Experiencing the wider range of your own sexuality, which validates your own sense of personal power to create excitement and enjoyment in your life and affirms the reality that you are indeed a physically attractive person, is the major contribution to your self-renewal as a single person in the sex-is-everything stage. However, after a time, the law of diminishing returns takes over. As you near the end of the sex-is-everything stage, a winding-down begins to happen.

The Transition to the Come-Close-But-Stay-Away Stage

Instead of looking forward to tonight's opportunity to "make it" once again, you hesitate. Dating is time-consuming, even wearying, and besides, every new person you meet is becoming a blur. It's like meeting the same person over and over again under different names. Putting on a happy face to the new person you will date, while you are worn out and drained of any sparkling conversation ideas after your last date, doesn't appeal to you. Besides, it takes so much effort and costs a bundle just for a night on the town.

Why not pass on going out tonight, just stay home, take

a nice warm bath, and listen to records or simply relax and be quiet with yourself? A notion that was once furthest from your mind, staying home when you have the opportunity to go out on a date, now sounds delightful. The boundless energy and anticipatory excitement you possessed earlier in the sex-is-everything stage seems to be disappearing. What was once so enlivening now is becoming boring. Who would have thought you would ever feel this way about sex with new persons? Wasn't that what you wanted and dreamed about in your marriage? Is it a case of "Don't ask for something; you're liable to get it"? You might even feel there must be something wrong with you because you are no longer the dating machine you once were.

On the contrary, there is nothing wrong with you when you begin to feel this way. What is happening is that you are in the process of leaving the sex-is-everything stage and are about to enter the next stage of your quest for a lasting love relationship, the come-close-but-go-away stage.

Your experience in the sex-is-everything stage has brought you a step closer toward achieving that goal. You still experience a high degree of commitment anxiety, but you have begun to experience relationships with the opposite sex, casual and short-lived though they are. You have reestablished your sense of physical self-worth and have rediscovered your sexual capabilities and widened your sexual behavior. You still see members of the opposite sex as threats, so you distance yourself from them by regarding them primarily or solely as objects for your sexual gratification.

However, the salt of sexual conquest now is losing its savor because you are beginning to discover that sex *isn't* everything. It's important, yes, but not as gratifying as you thought it would be when no other quality in the relationship was involved. Sex just for its own sake has become—surprise!—boring and disturbingly unsatisfying. The need for something more than a one-night stand has emerged and thrusts you forward toward the lasting love relationship you want but still fear.

Sometimes the realization that you are at the end of the sex-is-everything stage can come to you in a situation that starts out as just another round of sex with someone new, but turns into a jolt of new self-awareness instead.

This recently happened to Larry, a thirty-five-year-old man divorced two years previously, who told me, "I met this lovely-looking woman at a party. Turns out Linda was an airline stewardess in town for the next two days. The chemistry between us was there, and she suggested we spend the evening at her hotel. The sex was great. We balled until both of us were on the edge of exhaustion. Then, while we were quiet in bed, I began to have tender, warm thoughts about her. I wanted to know more about her as a person—something that doesn't usually occur to me. Ordinarily, when I have good sex with someone, I pick up and leave around 3:00 A.M., and go back to my place. I never liked staying all night with someone, but this time I not only wanted to stay the night, I also wanted to talk with her about other things, not just the TV shows and movies we might like, or the places we prefer traveling to. I wanted to know more about her as a person. Like where she was born, the kind of family she grew up in, what did she want to do with the rest of her life. But when I started asking her things like that, she turned on me. Boy, did she get angry. 'Don't try to play detective with me,' she said. 'I'm not here to answer any of your goddamned questions that aren't any of your goddamned business. You're here to fuck me because I want to be fucked and that's all. And I'm feeling horny again, so let's get it on.'

"I felt stunned, as if she had socked me on the jaw. Okay, I could cut the talk and get on with the action, because action was all I had wanted, wasn't it? But a funny thing happened to me. My tool became limp and I didn't even want to have any more sex with her. Instead, without saying another word to her, I got out of bed—this at two in the morning—got dressed, and left. My buddies would have thought I was nuts to do that—and I would have, too, because it wasn't like me to stop balling when a luscious lady wanted some more. After all, she was right, she was acting like I always acted before—you know, no questions asked. But it doesn't feel right anymore. Maybe I'm ready for something more than just a warm body that bounces in bed with me."

Most often, however, the realization that your sex-is-everything stage has ended sneaks up silently and subtly. It shows itself when you force yourself to date, where previously you looked forward to the chase, with energy to spare; when you feel you are spinning your wheels after a night out; when you are tired of eating out at another disappointing restaurant with someone who might look physically attractive but is boring as hell; when you become jaded with going out just for the sake of going out; when anxiety and unease displace the pleasure you used to take in the dating and sex scene. Unless you recognize these new tendencies that have surfaced within you for what they are, namely symptoms of your readiness to enter the next stage in your quest for a lasting love relationship, you may indeed keep on spinning your wheels out of sheer force of habit, and create much unnecessary unhappiness for yourself.

I have known men and women who have remained stuck in the sex-is-everything stage for years after they were ready to leave it. They are the people you can see at the "meat rack" singles bars who were there a year after their divorce and who are still there six or eight years later. They pay a high cost when they do not recognize and act on those feelings inside themselves that long ago told them they were ready for something new and better.

The Learning Experiences of the Sex-Is-Everything Stage

The sex-is-everything stage is the time when you learn the following important truths about yourself, which are essential if your quest for a lasting love relationship is to be successful:

1. You have learned you are indeed physically and sexually attractive to more members of the opposite sex than you might have thought possible when you were married. This adds an important measure of self-esteem that was lacking in your past, for you cannot attract

others if you regard yourself as unattractive.

2. You have learned to become assertive, to risk the possibility of sometimes being rejected, when you meet new people of the opposite sex. You have discovered that the pleasures of being adventurous far outweigh the losses, and that remaining shy and withdrawn guarantees you only loneliness.

3. You have met a wide range of new persons of the opposite sex, which gives you clues as to the types of people and qualities that you find most attractive. Some of those people will possess such qualities as humor, innovativeness, enthusiasm, and risk-taking; others may have stability, a sense of personal ease with themselves, warmth, tenderness, and empathy; and still others possess an ability to listen and are intelligent, knowledgeable about the world, and able to communicate openly and honestly. A sorting-out process is taking place within you, which will eventually evolve into a desire for a special person in your life who possesses a combination of most or all of those qualities you like the most.

4. You have given yourself the opportunity to live out your fantasies about the opposite sex and test them in reality. So now you can let go of any unrealistic ideas and possible regrets, which would not have been possible if you had not lived out your fantasies. You would have carried around those fantasies and regrets as a permanent millstone on your life, always plagued with feelings of what might have been.

5. You have learned to get in touch with your sexual nature, and have freed yourself from old inhibitions that diminished your capacity for sexual pleasure. Sex as play, sex as fun, sex as experimentation have replaced sex as a dirty little secret, as obligation, as manipulation, as habit.

6. You have learned, if you are a man, that you are no longer totally responsible for the sexual satisfaction of your partner. Mutual cooperation in what pleasures you and your partner takes the place of the heavy burden you once carried in your marriage of assuming that you had to give pleasure to your partner, who was the passive recipient of your actions, and that you were the culprit if such satisfaction did not occur.

7. You have learned, if you are a woman, that you have a right to sexual pleasure and to acknowledge to yourself that your own sexual desires and fantasies are not something to be ashamed of, but are human qualities that you can feel good about. Taking personal responsibility to achieve your sexual pleasure then becomes a consequence of your comfortable acceptance of your sexual nature. This means engaging your partner in open communication as to what pleasures *you* the most, as well as what pleasures him. You are no longer the passive recipient of the man's largesse, but rather an equal partner and an active participant in the activities that result in mutual sexual satisfaction.

8. You have learned, as the sex-is-everything stage ends, that sex *isn't* everything, but only seemed so because you lived in the sexual desert of your marriage. When you lack an important element in your life, such as sexual satisfaction, you tend to overestimate its significance. What you yearn for becomes the *only* thing that matters. Now that your sexual needs have been gratified, good sex is now recognized as a component of what makes for happier living, rather than the answer to all your interpersonal needs.

13

The Process of Finding a New Lasting Love Relationship

STAGE THREE: "COME CLOSE BUT GO AWAY"

Now that you've learned that sex isn't everything, the need for "something more" enters your life. Your sex drive empowered you to validate that aspect of yourself which cried out for approval—your physical attractiveness. You now know that there are people out there who consider you worth dating, worth going to bed with. A far cry from the rejection you felt in your marriage. Then why don't you just want to continue with the dating and bedding that you are doing? After all, it's out there for the taking.

It's not that your sex drive has diminished. Indeed, it is alive and well, but it's no longer the tunnel-vision, all-encompassing compulsion that drove you out of your apartment or house night after night in order to "score" or "make out." You have now discovered that you no longer want to pop into bed with just anybody, because you also want to find a *person* in the body you sleep with on any given night, and you want your own person to emerge from your body. When this happens you are in Stage 3, the come-close-but-go-away segment of your quest for a lasting love relationship.

Your commitment anxiety, your fear of a close, monogamous relationship with one special person, has diminished to the point where you can see you have *choices* rather than compulsions or obsessions with regard to the opposite sex, for you have proved that all members of the opposite sex are not "bitches" or "bastards" such as you may have thought your spouse was at the time of your divorce. You have proved that you need not be victimized by them, as you might have felt in your marriage.

And you have proved that you can attract people when you make the effort to and reach out to them, rather than waiting for them to take the first step in your direction. This emerging sense of your own personal power enables you to become less fearful and more comfortable with the person you *are*, rather than the sex-machine body you *were* in the sex-is-everything stage. You are now ready to *choose* to stay home or go out on any given night, to date or not to date, rather than always feeling compelled to do so.

Your previous compulsion to flee from your lonely residence when you came home from work arose from fear. For how could you face yourself when you were alone, with your life in disarray, feeling worthless, helpless, victimized, with no light at the end of the dark tunnel that represented your sense of self at that time. Better to run away from it all, to go out into the streets, searching and seeking. But you were running away from yourself, from your fear of making it alone. Wherever you went, you brought yourself with you. Alas, you couldn't escape yourself. However, by the time you have reached the come-close-but-go-away stage, much of this fear of meeting yourself in the privacy of your own home has diminished, for you have already proven in many aspects of your life that you indeed *can* make it on your own, as I have demonstrated in the previous chapter.

In this new stage, self-discovery begins to replace fear. You begin to make friends with yourself. Now that you see you have a free choice to date or remain alone at home (and that if you don't date tonight, someone out there will still be available to you when you have the urge to do so again), home life alone is no longer the menace to you that it once was.

Being alone out of free choice enables you to relax, pamper yourself in a warm bath, rearrange the furnishings and add new ones to your liking, write letters, call friends on the phone, read a good book, play the stereo, or selectively watch a special TV show you want to see. Most important of all, it affords you the opportunity to spend quiet time with yourself, with no activity whatsoever except meditation and self-reflection. The need now is to validate yourself, not to have others validate you. It is the time you can seize to *understand* the dating experiences you have had, and *improve* your new relationships in the future.

New Knowledge About Dating and Relating

What you and most other divorced men and women can learn about dating and relating at this time has been best expressed by a dear friend of mine, Frances Capper, who lives in San Rafael, California, the city where I live. Frances is a warm, compassionate, delightfully alive woman in her sixties who has been happily married for more than forty years to Sol Capper, a successful businessman. As she told me, "I have always had a compassion for the lonely divorced person who comes out of a marriage mold and becomes isolated with no place to go. They've been thrust away from their married friends because they were single, and I want to cultivate some new friendships for them. I generally invite them over to my home once a week with other singles, and we put on a potluck dinner together. In fact, I always say I've cooked so many chickens for those potlucks that if you counted them they would go around the world twice!

"The people I invite," she continued, "are of all ages. In my weekly get-togethers, their ages range from the late twenties to the early seventies. They have a lot in common, regardless of their ages. They joke and converse with one another once they stop labeling one another with this age thing and start to treat each other like human beings and friends for that evening. There is a slight barrier between the different ages, but I think it breaks down if it's drawn to their attention a couple of times. For instance, the last time we had a meeting I stood up and said I believed that younger people should give older people a chance, that they were going to be older themselves someday, and I said to the older ones that they should pay attention to what the younger ones had to say, too, because they might learn something, and they just naturally started talking to one another. But I think they have to be reminded once in a while in a light, humorous way.

"One young woman, Linda, who was thirty, told me that she had gotten into a conversation with an older man and didn't think she wanted to come back to the meeting; she said she felt it was like being with her uncle. But when I talked about breaking down age barriers, I noticed that she started talking to a seventy-year-old man and she had a wonderful time, and all of a sudden it didn't matter whether he was seventy or twenty. People seem to mix. Some of the mothers, although they didn't have their daughters with them, suggested to the young men that they get acquainted with their daughters. The older and the younger did mix, and they had a lot to say to one another. So Linda came back the second time and she relaxed and wound up talking to people in their forties and fifties and she had a good time, even though there were plenty of younger people there.

"There are differences in attitude between the people who are in their twenties and thirties and those who are in their mid-forties and older, when it comes to sex and dating. I think the younger people are a lot more at ease with their sexuality and their dating, and the older people are more inhibited. I think that the younger people can learn discipline from the older people about their behavior in their sexuality, and I think the older people can learn to let go a little more from seeing how the younger people handle themselves.

"The younger people are more concerned with who they are individually; they are so attracted by the physical and the sexual, but they're also attracted by the person. The sexual is beside the point; it's there if they want it or if they don't want it, and they don't make such a tremendous thing of it, it's no big deal. If it works out, fine; if it doesn't work out, that's fine too.

"The younger ones feel there is no obligation to 'put out' on a first date, while the older people have a tremendous sense of obligation: the man pays for the dinner and the woman is supposed to give sex in exchange for the meal. And the older men still have some of that attitude that they're entitled to sex because they paid for the night out.

Younger women are out there making a living, and they say
to their dates, 'It's my turn to pay,' or they will buy dinner
the next time around or invite him for a home-cooked meal
if he pays the entire bill.

"The younger women feel no obligation to go to bed on
the first date. It's a matter of free choice with them, and
they don't become defensive about it. The older women
have terrible problems with this; they find it hard to realize
that times have changed. Some of them feel that every time
they have sex with a man, it means they are in love with
him, and that means they have to marry him. Of course, that
comes from their early schooling. Some of these older
women say they don't want to go to bed with a man unless
they love him and marriage might be in the offing; friendship is not enough reason for them to go to bed. The
younger ones take it a lot lighter.

"I think the younger people want sex, but friendship,
interests in common, sports, social activities, and education
are also important. Many of the ones who have come to my
home have lots of interests, and if a woman can share that
with a man, the friendship falls into place very easily. They
can go to lectures, bike riding, a picnic, the theater, go to
a symphony, and all this comes naturally along with the sex.

"The older people go out and right away the woman
becomes defensive about whether a man wants to get in bed
with her. For example, I introduced a fifty-seven-year-old
divorcee to a gentleman who took her out to dinner and
then home. He had put his hand on her arm, the woman
later told me. She said, 'I know what he wanted, he wanted
to go to bed.' But that wasn't what he wanted; he wanted
to be warm and friendly. It was a touching thing that was
misinterpreted. So she had her defenses up high.

"I introduced another couple. The woman met this
gentleman and went to dinner and a movie with him. He
put his arm around her shoulder during the course of the
movie, and she took the arm off and then he held her hand.
She then pushed the hand away, and when they went to her
car to say good night, she said, 'I do not wish to be intimate.'
When she told me the story, I said, 'I understand what you
mean by "intimate." But this isn't what he meant or wanted.
He was just being friendly and warm, and you assume other

things.' And this is where the misinterpretation comes in, I think. Communication is very difficult between older people; they assume an awful lot because they've built up their own defense mechanisms. This woman was forty-eight and the man was about fifty.

"Regardless of their ages, women assume that men want them sexually right off the bat, but some of the time the men don't. The men might try, but they can be handled in a very polite manner. It's the handling that's important, and women who have come out of long-time marriages, and are not at home with themselves sexually, are not too comfortable at handling themselves around men.

"Many women have not been comfortable in their relationships with their husbands, so they can't relate when they get out in the single world. They don't keep themselves physically fit, and so they don't want to take their clothes off because they're afraid that men will reject them for looking bad. Somewhere along the way they've let themselves go, and they won't acknowledge it. They appear dumpy, but even a dumpy woman can be feminine and can come on in an alluring way, and a man will feel comfortable. But these women appear matronly, their hairstyles are from the forties, and their clothes look like they came out of a kitchen. They either wear too much make up or not enough. Jewelry is often overdone. A woman who is over forty-five will forget that she can ride a bike, she can take a hike, but what does she do? She sits there and makes no effort whatsoever to make herself interesting. The younger women keep themselves trim, they dress smartly, they're usually independent, and they're struggling, but they're active physically and mentally.

"Women who are forty-five and over, who have been working nine or ten years, don't fall into the 'dowdy' category. They generally dress a little sharper, they're not as threatened by men because they've been out in the professional world, and they're a lot more comfortable with me. Many women who have been subdued in a marriage for a number of years find it extremely hard to relate to men in general, because they've always had that one husband around as a support system, and it didn't matter how they

looked or how they dressed, he was always going to be there
for them.

"As for the younger men, many of them have been
workaholics in their marriages and have neglected their
emotional life when it comes to women and socializing.
I've often heard from the younger women who date these
men that they don't know what goes on with them; these
men seem to be at a distance, they're not relaxed with
themselves. That's one category. The other young men I
know have economic concerns. Nowadays it costs a lot of
money to get married, to have a baby, to raise a family.
Also, because relationships in general are so lightly handled, to carry the responsibility of a permanent relationship becomes frightening, and because there are a lot of
women around, they're not as likely to settle down as
quickly or as easily as perhaps a man from the old-fashioned world.

"People have the most difficult time learning how to
relax and socialize, to talk to one another, just to get acquainted. Their minds are jumping to these other big things
that they've got to cope with. They'll jump to the first thing
they think they're lacking in, and sure enough, they're not
going to make the first hurdle, because they didn't learn
about talking to whoever they were married to, and developing a friendship to begin with. People deal too much in
personalities. They should deal by conversing about experiences, backgrounds. How many people read, but never discuss the books they read? How many go to plays, how many
go to the park? What did they see? Did they actually see
something?

"They don't pick up on the important things about just
living that they need to talk about. They're always thinking,
'What can I get out of this? What's in it for me? Am I going
to walk out the door with a date, and is he going to walk me
to my car?' And there's this tape recording going on in their
heads and they forget what they did when they were children, relax and play a little bit. Look in their eyes, be really
interested, and listen to what they're saying. There are so
many strings in every person's lives that you can pull on. I
don't care if you were an introvert in high school, there are

so many questions you can ask a person, and one of them
leads to another.

"For example, you can start on the simplest thing that
the person has about them. You can talk about their dog.
You don't have to ask, 'What do you do?' You can say, 'You
know, I was walking along the street the other day and I saw
someone who looked just like you,' or 'You look like somebody I know,' and pull on anything. Don't make it con-
trived, be natural. I noticed this man at a wedding and he
had blue eyes, and I went over to him and I said, 'You have
the bluest eyes of anybody I've ever seen.' Give a compliment, it doesn't mean you are flirting. Everybody's got
something nice about them. My father used to say, 'You
can't get a person with vinegar, you gotta get them with a
little sugar.' Be a little nice.

"I think the questions you ask are unimportant, compared to your attitude. It's *how* you say it. If you look into
a person's eyes and you're sincere about what you're saying
. . . I don't know how many times I've done it, and it doesn't
have anything to do with being married or single. Many
divorced men and women don't practice this at all. Instead
they become tense, they look off in another direction instead of directly at a person.

"They're looking around the room to see if there is
somebody else there as an evasive kind of defense mecha-
nism. They're stiff, and they also lack a sense of humor. They
don't know how in the world to laugh at themselves. They
don't know how to look at life in a light vein. They're there
at that moment, it's not a tragedy, there's no commitment,
there's nothing other than treating the situation lightly. It's
an attitude they have to develop.

"For example, years ago, when I first learned to water
ski, I took it so seriously. I fell down all the time, so I finally
started laughing, and I laughed so hard, the next thing I
knew I was up on the skis. Socializing is the same way. Those
people who do the best are people who are just themselves.
And when you're yourself and you're natural and you don't
have all these other things going on, people *like* you; it
happens automatically because you're at home with yourself, and then they're at home with themselves in relating
to you. Learn to listen to the other person first. So many

divorced persons are so into themselves that they forget or
don't know how to listen to someone they meet. Listen first,
then talk. I know that every person I've met in my life has
some wonderful qualities. Each person is made differently,
there are no duplicates, so you can make life interesting for
yourself by just being curious and natural, and you'll discover those wonderful qualities in others, just as they will
discover them in you. Listen to them by getting outside of
yourself.

"There's one final point I'd like to share with your readers, Mel, about dating. Nowadays, dating is damned expensive. A dinner and a movie can cost a hundred dollars. And
a man who is divorced and paying alimony or child support
has a hard time making ends meet. But that shouldn't prevent him from dating.

"Look, pick up the Sunday paper, there are so many
nice things you can do with someone. Or if the weather's
good, you can go on a picnic or a walking tour. You don't
have to impress your date by spending a bundle. What your
date wants is the pleasure of your company, friendship and
conversation, a chance to learn to like you as a person, to get
to know you. That's what you want, too. And if your date
doesn't want that, but only wants an expensive evening out,
that's the kind of person to say good-bye to."

A New Look at Rejection

When you are at the start of the come-close-but-go-
away stage, you may feel isolated. Since you don't want to
date for its own sake anymore, but to be selective, to seek
out the person inside the body you date, this means reaching out for new people to meet who will be receptive to
sharing more of themselves than the kind of people you
were involved with in the sex-is-everything stage were willing to do. Can you find such people?

The fear of rejection may then return, inhibiting you
from reaching out to new people. It feels as if you're starting
from scratch again. But are you really? You have already
demonstrated your ability to reach out to new people in the

sex-is-everything stage; you've been accepted by others, despite your fear that nobody would ever find you attractive again.

But the fear will remain with you every time you embark on a new stage of your quest for a lasting love relationship, since you now want different types of people to respond to you than those who responded to you in the past. Will they do so? They will, if you don't inhibit yourself and send out signals to the people you want to meet that you are afraid of being rejected by them, which will distance you from them. I have seen it happen time and again that a man at a party will be attracted to a woman across a crowded room. She looks more attractive than the other available women present, and might even smile at him in return for his look. He then panics and avoids her eyes and makes a dash toward a far less attractive woman, ignoring his first choice.

Why? He is afraid he will be rejected by her, since she is so attractive, for what could she see in him that would make her want to talk to him, let alone go out with him? He fears rejection in advance. Sometimes the most attractive women become wallflowers at parties or in nightclubs precisely because men who might become pleasant company refuse to take the initiative of walking over to them, out of fear of rejection.

Women these days have to cope with a *new* type of rejection fear. They are now taking the initiative in meeting men much more often than they did in the past. Before, they would experience rejection passively, "all alone by the telephone." Will he or won't he call? Or they would sit primly in a chair, waiting for some man to ask for a dance.

Rejection took the form of a phone that didn't ring, or of no one asking her to dance. Now, however, when a woman takes the initiative, calling a man rather than waiting for a phone call, or walking over to a man and asking him to dance with her, she is faced with the consequences that every man has traditionally had to face, the possibility of her initiative being rejected. Since this kind of rejection is quite a new and scary experience for women, it becomes a great inhibiting factor in their reaching out for fresh relationships.

There is a different way of seeing rejection that I have

long shared with the people in my divorce adjustment groups, and that might prove helpful to you in overcoming this fear of rejection. First, don't take it for granted that you know what "being rejected" means. I've discovered that if you substitute the word *nonresponsiveness* for *rejection,* the experience no longer seems so devastating.

Rejection implies a condemnation of one's personal integrity and sense of self, and that can be very hard to cope with. I often ask the men and women who attend my seminars: "Do you really like or are you attracted to everyone you meet? When you're at a party with new people, don't you reject some by not even talking to them, while you approach and smile at others? But are you really rejecting some guests, judging them as bad people? Of course not; you're simply being nonresponsive to the kinds of signals they are sending out at the moment."

Not fitting another person's ideal does not mean that we are bad or worthless. A typical and healthy comment I have often heard is, "If somebody rejects me, it probably has something to do with that person, not with me. After all, how could he or she know what I'm like after a five-minute conversation or a few dates?"

In other words, that person is nonresponsive to you, for reasons other than the fact that you are an unworthy person. You may, for example, resemble a parent he or she disliked, or have the same name as the former spouse that person now detests, or don't have similar interests. You are *not* being rejected for the person you are. The fact that you are not being responded to has nothing to do with you as a person, but everything to do with the other person's perceptions. Put the shoe on the other foot: How many times have *you* been nonresponsive toward other people because they were, for whatever reasons, not in your style? Did that mean you considered them bad or unworthy, any more than you considered yourself to be when they were nonresponsive to you? Of course not.

Nonresponsiveness from others (as well as responsiveness) is a fact of grown-up life, for, after you leave your parents' nest, no one will ever love or care for you as much as your parents did. To expect otherwise is to invite disillusionment, bitterness, and self-isolation.

You can't be loved by everyone, and to expect that your desires will automatically be accepted and gratified by someone with whom you would like to have that happen is to invite disaster into your life. Intimacy is a two-way involvement that has to be earned.

You must be willing to take risks and to face the chance of being rejected (in the "nonresponsive" sense of the term) from time to time, otherwise you will never have the opportunity to meet people who might really mean something to you. There is always the possibility of disappointment in any contact; the mature person tries to reach out not just once but many times, knowing that with each new encounter one takes a chance.

But the risk usually has a positive payoff. As one woman said, "If I see a man I find attractive at a party and he's looking at me, I will go over and introduce myself, even though I'm a little scared. It's normal to be anxious, but I don't let it stop me. I figure that if he doesn't respond or if I find him disappointing, the world isn't going to end. On the other hand, it might well be the beginning of something pleasant, and more often than not it is."

Ninety-Day Wonders, Standbys, the Married-Man Convenience, and LTAs

In the sex-is-everything stage, you put your toes in the pool of intimacy and found the water not so icy after all. Your commitment anxiety diminished as a result, so that you are now ready to edge deeper. Not without trepidation, however. For in the come-close-but-go-away stage, the fear remains that taking the total plunge in the intimacy pool will drown you, that it will cause you the same kind of pain you experienced in your past marriage.

You now want intimacy, without the fear that the past will be repeated. However, you still cannot trust yourself to make a total commitment to one special person. The feeling that you are doomed to make the same "mistake" if you do so still pervades your soul.

You therefore make an unconscious compromise with yourself in the come-close-but-go-away stage. You hedge your bets by selectively reaching out for more interesting people (instead of bodies) than you did in the previous stage, but you *also* make certain that such new relationships are relatively short-lived or are doomed from the start to go nowhere.

In the sex-is-everything stage, relationships were uncomplicated and rarely lasted for more than two or three dates, if that. As one man in that stage told me, "I'm falling in lust every night, rather than in love." However, in the come-close-but-go-away stage, many variations in relationships are played out, and you give more of yourself in them, over a longer time.

All of these variations have one thing in common: they provide you with more intimacy than you previously thought you were capable of handling, at the same time that they allow you an escape hatch from totally committing yourself to one special person. The main forms these escape-hatch intimacies take are as follows:

Ninety-Day Wonders

A very frequent variation of escape-hatch intimacy is the ninety-day whirlwind affair, in which you are attracted to a "dynamite" person and suddenly all others temporarily vanish from your dating book. A courtship dance then occurs. There is excitement in the chase, and then a feeling of triumph in the conquest. Passionate love and full-time absorption in each other then occurs. However, there is no talk of a permanent commitment, for that topic is still too scary to broach—and if the other person should raise it, you would run for your life!

Soon the passion begins to ebb, and disenchantment starts seeping into the relationship. Flaws that went unnoticed before become evident. If you are a man, the love of your life may begin to seem too bossy, critical, and demanding for your taste. And if you are a woman, he might be insensitive and unfeeling all too often. Disillusionment sets in, and the diamond you thought you won turns out to be a rhinestone. Then the letdown occurs as you go your separate ways. However, you soon set your sights again, and there's another person you see across a crowded room. Of course he or she is the new "dynamite" attraction. . . .

Typically, this play lasts ninety days, as so many of my divorced clients tell me out of their own experience. Jack, a thirty-eight-year-old man who has been divorced for two years, told me: "My affairs all seem to have a beginning, a middle, and an end, they wind up in just about three months. So help me, each time its a speeded-up quickie marriage and divorce. There's the courtship, the romance, the knowing more about each other, then my becoming antsy and bored until there's the split-up. All in three months! I wish that had been the case in my real marriage, which lasted eleven years instead."

Jack has experienced four of these mini-marriages that end in divorce, all escape hatches from his push-pull feelings about making a total commitment to one special person, a commitment he wants, yet fears. I have called people like Jack, who can be women as well as men, "ninety-day wonders." There are so many of them in this stage that they warrant identification as a distinct group.

Standbys

Another frequent variation is the "standby." The standby is the person who cares more about you in the relationship than you care about that person. You may like him or her very much, but always feel there is something missing. You might feel friendship or even sexual passion for the person, yet somehow the chemistry for a lasting love relationship isn't there for you.

You may make that fact clear to the person, and say you like but do not love him or her. You might also say you want to date him or her, but also feel free to date others. The standby, on the other hand, will profess love for you, or far more affectionate caring than you can give in return, but will patiently acknowledge your differing feelings and profess that he or she will always be there for you despite that fact, and will remain monogamous with you, even though you continue to date others. (The standby lives in the hope that the longer the relationship lasts, in whatever form, the more you will "come to your senses" and know that he or she is the "right" person for you, and that you will eventually change your mind.)

In the beginning of the standby relationship, everything appears to your liking: you are always searching for someone "better," yet at the same time there is always someone there for you to assuage your loneliness. The standby will give you good sex, intelligent conversation, companionship, and nurturing to fall back on as you continue searching.

However, the longer the standby relationship lasts, the more uncomfortable it becomes. George, a thirty-one year-old man in such a relationship, tells why: "Gayle is such a sweet person. I've known her now for two years and she's so accepting of me, I feel like I'm an absolute heel. She's told me dozens of times she loves me, but I can't reciprocate. I have a lot of affection for her, but love, no way. I date a lot of other women, but she doesn't date anyone else, doesn't want to, she says.

"When I think of what I'm going to do on a Saturday night, I never think of her first, I'm looking for someone new. And if I can't connect, I'll call Gayle up at the last minute and she's always there for me. She's so sweet and I know she's suffering. I don't know why she puts up with me, but she does. I feel rotten, taking advantage of her. It's becoming too painful for me, and I want to break it off. The relationship is going nowhere, yet Gayle wants more of me than I can give her. How can I tell her its ended? God, I don't want to hurt her."

The standby relationship inevitably turns into a guilt-manufacturing relationship, as George is experiencing. In the beginning it seems like a good deal, but then it degenerates into an uncomfortable burden. The guilt-producer is the silent—or not-so-silent suffering standby who lets you know by words or behavior how much he or she is sacrificing for you.

And you, in turn, are made to feel guilty because you are taking advantage of the situation. Eventually the unequal relationship becomes too uncomfortable to continue, and, painful as it might be, you take action to break it off, since the pain of the breakup is far less than the pain of continuing the relationship on these terms. And that was what George later did with Gayle.

Standby relationships are not gender-limited. Many women also have standbys, and these women have had experiences similar to George's. The standby relationship gives you the advantages of a closer intimate connection than you had in the sex-is-everything stage, but still protects you from the intimacy of total commitment, which you are not as yet prepared to undertake.

Of course, you yourself might be a standby in this stage, and remain in a relationship that is stalled for precisely the same reasons that the person who seeks out a standby enters into it. The standby and the person who opts for a standby are mirror images of each other, and reflect their commitment anxiety in that mirror.

The Married-Man Convenience

At first glance, it might appear that the divorced woman who gets involved with a married man is simply in a standby situation. However, something new has been added today to this kind of escape hatch from total commitment that warrants placing it in a separate category.

Divorced women today do get involved with married men, but often not on the basis of being the silent sufferer, the woman waiting in the wings for the man to divorce his wife and then marry her. On the contrary, these women harbor no illusions that the men they relate to will leave their wives and marry them. These women, indeed, see their relationship more as a convenience than as something that victimizes them.

They receive from such a relationship a degree of affection, companionship, and caring that they were not ready for in the sex-is-everything stage; at the same time, they buffer themselves from a committed relationship in which two people share completely who they are. These are women who feel free to date others while being involved with married men. As Doris, a thirty-four-year-old woman involved in such a relationship, told me: "Harvey is a man I enjoy. He's in a terrible marriage, but told me he'll never divorce. That's fine with me, because I can't think of marriage again after my own divorce. We get together when it's convenient for both of us. He knows I date others. But men are so funny, because he almost had a fit when I told him our relationship was not an exclusive one. How do you like that for a double standard! It took time to convince him that his relationship with me wasn't exclusive. After all, he has a wife. I don't see myself as 'the other woman.'

"His marriage was rotten before I met him. You can't take another man from a woman, because he's ready for someone else by the time you meet him. Harvey is charming and intelligent and is a great sex partner, so why not have him fill up my time when no one else has anything better to offer me? But that doesn't mean I'm not looking."

The married-man convenience seems attractive to women like Doris, but there is a darker side to this picture that usually appears if the relationship lasts more than just a few months, for a relationship can't be programmed like a computer, with predictable results.

A relationship is based on feelings, which are unprogrammable. They change, develop, or deteriorate. What was once a convenience may develop into a deep sense of caring with overtones of love on the woman's part, while at the same time the man she is involved with may be trying to disengage himself from the relationship. When that happens, what was once an arrangement of convenience now becomes an excursion into loss and pain. This is precisely what eventually happened to Doris, who is now dating only single men.

There is another type of convenience relationship that some divorced women in this stage engage in: they have some homosexual male friends. June, a thirty-seven-year-old woman, tells why: "I'm pretty choosy these days, so I don't date much. The kind of men I'm interested in are not that easy to find. But I like male company and have made good friends with Bob and Todd, who are both homosexuals. I've never been biased against people just because of their sexual preference. People are people, period, and Bob and Todd are warm, sensitive, caring persons who have a lot of the same interests I have. So I go out with one or the other to dinner, to shows, to art museums, and Todd and I love tennis, so we play together. Of course there's no sex between us, but there is a lot of the kind of attentiveness and sensitivity and politeness I like in a man. These are the qualities I want in any new heterosexual relationship I feel I'm now ready for. It will be with a man who knows what he's about, and also has the kind of tenderness, compassion, and sensitivity I want."

For women like June, these homosexual friendships have revealed to her many of the qualities she would prefer in a man whom she can love, a man she has yet to meet. Her homosexual friends have given her an opportunity she would otherwise have missed.

The Living-Together Arrangement (LTA)

In recent years, living together without a marriage license has become an acceptable option for two people who wish to enter into a relationship. Even ten years ago this was considered forbidden fruit by society, something to be whispered about or apologized for. But today I hear many conservative mothers express concern when their sons or daughters say they want to marry someone. "Why marry so soon? You hardly know the person," the alarmed mothers say to their children. "Why not live together first to find out if you really should marry?" Times indeed have changed.

The living-together arrangement ordinarily occurs in the come-close-but-go-away stage for many divorced people. Where once LTAs were the province of young adults of college age, they are now an option that adults in their late twenties and older are choosing with increasing frequency.

There are those divorced persons in this stage whose thirst for intimacy has overcome their fear of living together with one special person, to the extent that they are willing to share living quarters with each other on an ongoing basis. Yet their commitment anxiety is very much present, for they live together with their fingers crossed. On the one hand, they express commitment to each other by living in the same space; on the other hand, they have the escape hatch of being able to say to themselves, "We're really not *that* committed to each other, since we're not married and are therefore free to leave the relationship anytime we want to go. It would be a breakup without pain or complications, since we were never legally tied together."

These ideas usually prevail at the start of a living-together arrangement. It all seems like the ideal solution to dampen any commitment anxiety. But more often than not, the act of living together with one special person, as the days lengthen into weeks or months, bring to the foreground all the unresolved problems and fears that still exist in each person. The high hopes that began the LTA dry up like a raisin, and the LTA then breaks up. I hear the laments in my counseling office every week.

June, twenty-eight, says, "I never knew Jerry was such a pig. When we lived together, he would drop his clothes wherever he was and expect me to pick them up. Do you think he'd ever clean the bathtub after he took a bath? Never. And when I would ask his cooperation, he'd sulk and leave the room. Who needed that!"

Marian, thirty-three, says, "Gordon was all big talk about mutual sharing and equal relationships before he moved in with me. But after he moved in, it was like he was another person. We both worked forty hours a week, yet I had to do all the shopping, the laundry, the dishes, the meals and the cleaning. He never lifted a finger. He should have hired a maid. I said, 'I quit, get someone else to be your slave!' "

Dick, thirty-eight, says, "Lois and I decided to have a joint checking account and joint credit cards once we lived together. Was that a mistake! She started to spend money like it was her last day on earth. A compulsive spender, that's what she was, what with new dresses, handbags, and shoes piled up as if our place was a warehouse. We spent more time arguing over money that we did making love. I left her before she broke me."

Tony, forty-seven, says, "Denise betrayed me when we lived together. She would say she was going out with the girls when all the time she was screwing around with other guys. I thought we were going to have a monogamous relationship, but maybe we should have talked about that before we moved in with each other."

Louise, forty-one, says, "Marty made a lot more money than I did, but I never for one moment thought he would use that to boss me. He did, though, when we lived together. He would tell me who my friends should be, when I could go out, what restaurants or movies I should go to. I had no say on any decisions. And when I'd complain, he'd say, 'Who's paying for this place!' Unbelievable."

Tom, forty-two, says, "Fran would never tell me what was bothering her. I'd never know if I'd done something that pissed her off. Like the time she felt I didn't pay enough attention to her at the parties we went to. She would simmer or remain blank-faced. But, boy, would I get it later on. She'd turn me off when I wanted sex, or would explode out of nowhere at me two weeks later. I never saw that side of her before we lived together. If I had, I wouldn't have gone near her with a ten-foot pole."

The list of disillusionments after a living-together arrangement is entered into could fill a book. But should this happen to you, it can become an important learning experience that can thrust you forward toward a lasting love relationship, rather than drag you back into a greater fear of attaining one.

If you still hold traces of the belief that a committed relationship is based on power, that you are number one and your partner is number two because you earn more money than he (or she) does, now is the time to eliminate that belief. If you have failed to communicate with a partner, begin to do so now, with the new persons you meet. If you were insensitive to the needs of your partner, then become aware of that fact and become sensitive to others. If you thought you could get the goodies of a monogamous relationship and at the same time engage in other affairs, disabuse yourself of that illusion, for it is an invitation to another breakup if you do not.

Perhaps the most important thing you can learn from the breakup of a living-together arrangement is that *any* relationship in which a degree of caring and commitment is involved will cause you pain when it ends. This is true even though you and your partner have agreed at the beginning of your LTA that should you break up, you'll still remain friends and be free of any pain, because you never had a marriage license. A license is only a piece of paper, but you and your partner are flesh-and-blood human beings whose feelings are tied up in the relationship.

I am reminded of Molly, a thirty-three-year-old woman who recently came to me for counseling. She said tearfully, "I feel so foolish, because I shouldn't be crying. I just broke up with Justin after living with him a year, and it hurts in spite of the fact that we both told each other at the time we moved in together that should we ever break up, there would be no hard feelings between us. Yet I feel angry with him, and so empty and alone. I try to explain to my friends that I feel bad and messed up, but they can't understand me. They tell me I should be happy instead, because we wanted to avoid the agony of what happened to us in our previous divorces, should we ever break up. But I never expected it to turn out this way. Maybe I am being foolish, maybe my friends are right in saying I should be happy instead of sad."

No, her friends were wrong. Molly was right to feel she had lost something of importance, a relationship that did have some qualities of caring and attachment, during the time she and Justin spent together. The loss needed to be mourned; she was entitled to her anger and sadness. Once you enter into a relationship, it has a logic of its own, no matter how much you might wish to shape it in advance. In a living-together arrangement, you might become more attached to your partner, while your partner might become less enchanted with you. Or both of you might become disillusioned with each other.

And pain is the consequence of these changes in the relationship. To say cavalierly in advance that you and your partner can split up without any pain because you don't have a marriage license is to deny the reality of what it means to be human. Remember that rocks split up, but people bleed.

What you can learn from a living-together arrangement that turns sour is that exposure to the possibility of pain is inherent in any relationship, if that relationship is worth anything. Rather than run away from the pain, acknowledge it and understand its meaning; there is necessary pain and unnecessary pain in whatever relationship you might enter into. Much of the pain involved in an ended living-together relationship is *unnecessary*, because it is self-created out of unawareness and unskillfulness in dealing with the issues in the relationship. Once that is understood, you can correct your behavior and move forward toward intimacy without fear, the final stage in your quest for a lasting love relationship.

The Learning Experiences of the Come-Close-But-Go-Away Stage

Whether you have been involved in ninety-day wonder, standby, married-man convenience, or LTA relationships (or a combination), you will have derived many positive learning experiences from them in this stage. Those learning experiences in their totality diminish your commitment anxiety to a minimal level at which you realize that your goal of a new, lasting love relationship based on intimacy without fear is now within your grasp:

1. You have learned to make friends with yourself, so that you no longer equate living alone with living lonely.
2. You have learned to trust yourself, becoming more selective and insightful in the people you choose to date.
3. You have been able to cope with rejection and prevail over it.
4. You now know that sex *and* friendship, shared interests, mutual support, mutual respect, intelligence, and caring are the necessary elements that make for a stimulating, long-lasting relationship, and you are now prepared to settle for nothing less than involving yourself with a person who agrees with you on these basics.
5. You have learned that allowing yourself to be-

come vulnerable again, which is the price of greater intimacy, has not destroyed or victimized you, as you once thought would happen if you shared more of yourself than just your body with another person. You have not only survived new hurts, but have become a more self-aware, compassionate human being in the process.

6. You have stopped your generalizing that all persons of the opposite sex are enemies you would like to get even with, and are now seeing each of those persons as an individual in his or her own right.

7. You now see each new person you are dating as a promise rather than as a threat, a person who offers you the possibility of nurturing a good relationship if the seeds of such a relationship seem to be present.

8. You no longer think in terms of using the people you date, but rather of sharing more of both of your lives together for mutual benefit.

9. You have taken risks and found the risks worth taking, and have become a more knowledgeable, compassionate, confident person as a result.

10. You now know you are stronger than you ever thought you could be, for you have demonstrated repeatedly that you can make positive things happen in your relationship.

11. You have learned that all of your relationships in the come-close-but-go-away stage were learning experiences rather than failures. They protected you against a too-hasty decision to remarry, because you were not ready to do so as yet, and they forced you to take a look at what you were doing (as well as what your partner was doing) in each of these relationships that made them end, so that you can now handle yourself more skillfully in any new relationship.

12. You have learned that you still have a bit of commitment anxiety left within you, but now you are willing and able to seek and find a lasting love relationship in which intimacy without fear will at last triumph over the remains of your commitment anxiety.

The Process of Finding a New Lasting Love Relationship

STAGE FOUR: INTIMACY WITHOUT FEAR

Your readiness to arrive at the intimacy-without-fear stage in your quest for a lasting love relationship begins with an ending: the relationships you may have experienced in the come-close-but-go-away stage no longer serve the purpose of satisfying your emotional needs, as they did when you began them. At the start of the come-close-but-go-away stage, you were still guarding yourself against becoming too emotionally involved with any one person, because your commitment anxiety level was still too high to enable you to risk that possibility. At that time your emotional security still depended on your ability to escape from any of the relationships you involved yourself in, should you feel yourself becoming too close to any of your partners. Your self-esteem, your belief in your ability to trust yourself not to become victimized in a relationship, had not yet developed to the point where you could risk a *total* commitment to any one person. Fear of such intimacy still outweighed your desire for a life that would be monogamously shared with one special person on a permanent basis. If you toyed with such a vision, it was always darkened by the distinct feeling that you would be helplessly dominated, stifled, held in thrall, and diminished by such a commitment, as you felt you had been in your past marriage. Consequently, the relationships you entered into in the come-close-but-go-away stage effectively satisfied your needs for closeness *and* distance with persons of the opposite sex when you began them.

However, by the time you are ready to disengage yourself from the come-close-but-go-away stage, the very relationships you once entered into with such clarity now seem unsatisfying: the living-together arrangement, which once seemed like such an ideal solution, is now tarnished with disillusionment, since you may have been through a series of them with different partners only to find they ended painfully. The ninety-day-wonder affairs have become tedious in their repetitiveness, so why put out any more effort to engage yourself in a new one? It's as if now that you've seen one, you've seen them all. The married-man convenience has become an inconvenience; you begin to feel shallow and second-best in that kind of relationship, even though you may have started it on what you thought were equal terms. The standbys you had always sought out are now persons you wish to escape from, since they seem to manufacture more guilt in you than pleasure. And should you yourself have been a standby, always becoming involved in a no-win, self-victimizing position now becomes unbearable.

The Need for a "Something More" Relationship

Instead of being signs of your personal helplessness and failure, these developments are really signs that you have begun the final stage of your quest for a lasting love relationship. They are signs that what satisfied you previously is no longer satisfying enough; you now want an in-depth emotional involvement with one special person. The people you were previously involved with did not afford you the opportunity to have that kind of in-depth relationship; the chemistry, the emotional bonding were not present in sufficient amounts. Of course, you wanted to become involved with people like that, which is why those relationships happened in the first place. But now you want something more.

However, you can't attain "something more" without disengaging yourself from "something less," which is what you had been having with the kinds of people who colluded

with you in those relationships. This means you may now
find yourself in your dating activities with feelings of loneliness and isolation similar to those you felt at the time your
sex-is-everything stage ended. For these feelings are telling
you that you no longer wish to pursue relationships that you
once eagerly wished to be involved in. When this happens,
you may think you have been spinning your wheels rather
than progressing, since you have disengaged from your past
relationships because they now appear in retrospect as shallow and unfulfilling, but you have yet to find any new relationship that will satisfy your recently emerged need for an
in-depth commitment. It's as if you have your feet solidly
planted in midair, a scary feeling indeed. Consequently,
your behavior at this time might appear confusing and disturbing to you. You might, for instance, try to run away from
these feelings of loneliness and isolation by retrogressing to
the sex-is-everything stage, hopping into bed with sex objects rather than persons once again, or reverting to the
walking-wounded stage, in which you once again take a
bath in the warm water of self-pity. However, these are very
short-term reactions, since they no longer assuage your
needs as they once did. You've already learned too much,
progressed too far to feel comfortable again in these stages.
You can't go home again, but only forward. So you stop
wallowing in self-pity, stop the sexual affairs you use as tran-
quilizers, and begin to experience a period of solitude
rather than loneliness, which could include an interval of
constructive celibacy. This is the time for reflection, a time
to measure how far you've come, rather than how far you
have yet to go to attain a lasting love relationship. Focusing
on how far you've come can give you the courage to go
farther in this direction, for by now you've traveled light-
years toward your goal without, perhaps, even being aware
of that fact. The future is near, rather than farther away
than ever, as you might have been thinking. When I ask the
men and women in my divorce adjustment groups who are
ready to commence the intimacy-without-fear stage in their
lives how far they've moved toward this goal since their
divorces, here are some of their typical responses:

Harlan, thirty-nine, says, "I once said I'd never date
again because no one would ever want to go out with a man

whose wife had left him. I must have had marbles in my head, because in the past three years I can't even count the number of women I've dated. My ex was just one person, not every woman in the world. I discovered I'm likable and fairly attractive, and that when I make the effort, dating is no big deal."

Donna, thirty-three, says, "I felt just like Harlan when my divorce happened. That was four years ago. I've had no trouble finding men. They're out there when you're ready to find them. But I do have trouble staying in a relationship. I've been in three living-together arrangements that ended with me walking out. But that's because I picked some really shallow guys to live with. I'm not dating at the moment, because I'm being more selective from now on; I want a man who's interested in a long-term commitment, not a short-term affair. He may be hard to find, but he's out there."

Perry, forty-seven, says, "My former wife, Edna, accused me of being a thinking machine instead of a human being. Much as I hate to admit it, she was right. She would get very angry when she would ask me what I was feeling about something, like a problem with our kid, and I would always reply, 'Well, I *think* that . . .' She would scream at me, 'No, no, no! *Not* what you think, it's what you *feel* about it that I want to know.' I never could understand what she meant by that, because feelings to me were always something to be ignored because they were irrelevant. Well, I've learned the hard way since my divorce how wrong I was. I fell apart during the first year after we separated, crying and being scared of my own shadow. I never even knew I had such feelings. And I've met a lot of women who think me the better man for being sensitive and aware of their feelings as well as my own, as I do now. I don't wear my heart on my sleeve, but I do know damn well the difference between thinking and feeling now."

Ellen, twenty-nine, says, "I thought that a marriage meant the end of having problems. Instead, my marriage with Jack was just one problem after another. So I left him, thinking I had married the wrong guy. But in the last two years I've discovered there are problems in *any* relationship, whether you're married or not, what with all the men

I've dated. It's dawned on me that if I want no problems, I shouldn't have a relationship at all. But I like men, I don't want to be a nun. So, the next time I get involved, I'm going to try to be a partner in solving problems rather than being scared of them."

Barry, thirty-six, says, "I left my marriage because my wife couldn't talk to me about anything except her clothes, the baby, and the house; she bored the hell out of me. I'm sorry to say I had contempt for women, based on my experience with my wife, and thought all of them were muddle-headed and ignorant. Since I've been dating I've found there are a lot of savvy, bright ladies in this world who can give me a run for my money in the brains department, and if I ever marry again, it's going to be one of them."

Muriel, forty-four, says, "I had a hatred for all men after John left me. We had been married twenty years, and my entire life revolved around him and our house and two children. I had slaved in our house to help him in his career by making everything comfortable for him. He didn't do a stitch at home, not even volunteer to clean off the table after he had eaten. I hated all men when he left. I can remember what I put in my diary then: 'All men want is a maid rather than a partner. Who wouldn't want a maid? I certainly would. I'm not the least bit interested in cooking, cleaning, or caring for a man anymore. They are all bastards who use women and throw them away'. After John left, four years ago, I had to find a job, since the only job I ever had was my marriage. I'm now an insurance salesperson and get to meet a lot of men, and find them a lot different from John. Men have a tough time too. Working for someone can be a terrible strain. It's a cutthroat world in business, which I never knew before. I thought John had all the glamour, being outside the home, while I had all the dullness, but the outside world can be pretty heavy-duty. Plenty of men are insecure and running scared, always worried about what the boss will say or do to them. I'm no longer angry at men as I was, and I suppose I show it, because I have more dates than I can handle now."

Bill, fifty-one, says, "With my ex-wife, I always felt that having sex with her was a performance trip. I would ask her, 'Did you have an orgasm?' If she said no, I felt like a failure.

And if I couldn't sustain my erection or couldn't even get it up when I was too tired, I would consider myself a failure. Since my divorce, I've learned from the women I've dated that that's a lot of baloney. Sex isn't a report card. A lot of women want hugs and snuggling even more than sex. In fact, Lorraine, the current lady I'm dating, said that tenderness is more important than the hardness and size of my penis inside her. I'm much more relaxed about sex now; I don't grade myself every time I sleep with someone any longer. Lorraine gave me a book about how women feel about sex. It's an eye-opener, and I brought it along today because there's a passage in it I'd like to read to the group. I know other guys have had hang-ups, just like I did, about their penises. The book is called *Ladies Own Erotica,* and a group of women in their forties wrote it. The section I want to read is called 'Address to a Penis Owner.'

We are not anti-penis. In the feminine experience the penis can add the finishing touch to satisfaction, but is not sine qua non. No, indeed. We have been brainwashed into paying more homage than is due to this particular attachment of the male anatomy, and far too much has been made of its rise and fall. The fact that we admire a Greek statue no less when the penis has crumbled off should be sufficient proof that male beauty does not depend on this unique feature. Freud, of course, was wrong when he claimed that women suffer from penis envy; it is the men who do. Sadly, a man without a penis is no man at all in our culture, and in male mythology the penis distinguishes a valiant man from a timid one.

We do appreciate a lusty penis when it knows its place. Penis owners should keep in mind that a well-trained penis is a joy to hold and cuddle. If it knows a trick or two, so much the better. A well-behaved penis is indeed woman's best friend, but we object to those mindless penises that indiscriminately push their way in and out of our folds like sewing machines.

We suspect that the penis culture was tantamount to the survival of the race. Understandably, then, the penis is still an important showpiece, and while it also adds much gratification to its owner, it offers comparatively less to the fulfillment of female desires.

If this comes as a shock to you, penis owner, please look at yourself from the female point of view. What is natural to you, who handle your penis many times a day, is quite unnatural to us. To us, the penis is a foreign object. I think no man knows how alien his rod is to the girl who is confronted with it for the first time, when she is told to stroke it, to lick it, to like it. We know neither the power that comes with owning this tool nor the fear of losing it. Since we don't have anything as obvious and as embarrassingly untrustworthy in our love-making paraphernalia, we share your concern for its ups and downs, so much so that we have obliterated your own needs for gratification. We are not trying to diminish your appendage, but we want to enlarge upon those parts of you that have been unjustly ignored. These are the parts that are essential to our pleasure: your hair, your eyes, your lips, your tongue, your chest, your thighs, your voice, and most importantly your hands.

It is these kinds of experiences and the self-knowledge you derive from them that build up your trust and confidence in yourself to make right decisions rather than new mistakes when you search for a new relationship. You've come light-years away from those early days of your separation from your former spouse when you were the walking wounded and feared your own shadow, let alone a person of the opposite sex. The commitment anxiety that has dogged your steps throughout the three previous stages of your quest no longer has the power to inhibit your desire to meet the one special person you want to share a lifetime with. Now intimacy without fear becomes probable as well as possible for you.

Where is that One Special Person?

There is no special time or place in which you will find that one special person. That depends on your own personal readiness to meet him or her, which may be a few years after your divorce, or many years later. The intimacy-without-fear stage can arrive at *any* time in your life after your divorce; it depends on how well you have learned the lessons of the previous stages in the quest for a lasting love relationship, and whether or not you have been stuck in one stage or another for a longer period than necessary. When you are ready to search for a new relationship out of the conviction that a totally committed relationship can be a promise of a better life resulting from two equal people sharing a lifetime together in which they grow individually as much as they grow as a couple, you set the stage for your search to become successful. This is the time when you are relatively happy with your life as a single person, hard-earned as it was, but wish to become happier through the sharing of your life with another person. You desire a lasting love relationship out of strength rather than weakness, for you've learned that no one but you yourself can make you happy; another person can only reinforce and enhance the happiness you already possess.

When you feel this way about yourself, you will create the circumstances in which you will find that one special person. Your search for that person will become a non-search, for you will not be desperately seeking someone to "make you happy" because you are feeling so miserable about yourself, owing to your fear that you cannot make it alone in the world. You've already proved you can survive emotionally, socially, and physically. You won't come on too close, too strong, too fast, and make people sidestep you. You won't be shy and isolate yourself at social affairs or parties and then complain that nobody cares for you. You will simply be yourself, a person who sends out signals that you like people, reach out to them, get involved in activities where many different kinds of people meet, and like to listen to them and find out who they are as individuals. You will be sending out signals from your personality and behavior that you are ready to meet that one special person simply by being who you are. A deliberate, conscious effort to search for that special person then becomes unnecessary; in fact, it would be self-defeating. For when you feel driven to find such a person, you guarantee that you will *not* find that person, for such a compulsion originates out of fear rather than free choice.

By simply being who are, you no longer send out the kinds of signals to others that you did in the previous three stages, for you do not wish to attract those types of people now. In the walking-wounded stage, you sent out signals that told everyone of the opposite sex you didn't want to involve yourself with anyone. In the sex-is-everything stage, you sent out signals that attracted people like yourself who were not ready for anything except a self-centered, sex-based relationship. In the come-close-but-go-away stage, you sent out signals to a more selective number of persons who were then ready, like you, to know more about the *person* they popped into bed with, but were fearful of becoming too close to that person. Now you are ready for a total commitment, and the signals you send out by your personality and behavior will attract people who are also ready for that kind of relationship. Consequently, you will no longer attract the sex-object person or the don't-come-too-close person who is still too emotionally needy and insecure to be a good partner. In fact, people such as these will intuitively steer clear of you, since they will feel you're not the type of person who can satisfy their needs, and they will be right.

In your present state of readiness you could meet the person you want to meet in the most unexpected places. I can remember the time, fourteen years ago, when I met my wife, Pat, at a party I didn't want to go to. I was invited to a Christmas tree-trimming party, which I went to for lack of anything better to do. I had asked who would be there, and felt that most of them would be dull. Well, the food and liquor ought to be good, I thought. But Pat was present that night, and we spent the entire evening being turned on by each other's presence, as we still are. The stories I hear from many others abound with similar situations, meeting that special person when it seemed least likely. A beginning happens with an elevator chat, a comment at the water cooler in your workplace, a blind date, a hello at a fitness center, a friend arranging a meeting with someone you might find interesting, a workshop you attend, a restaurant where you're eating alone but you engage in conversation with someone sitting a seat away, a new person you see on your jogging course. It can happen anywhere, at any time.

Who Is that One Special Person?

Now that your commitment-anxiety wall has been torn down, the person you become attracted to and who is also right for you may be a surprise. He or she might, and frequently does, turn out to be very different from your previous notions about who that special person might be. Frances Capper, who has so much experience in matching up singles (she herself has been the catalyst for more than fifty marriages of previously divorced persons), has this to say on the subject:

"One of the things I tell my divorced friends who wish to remarry is to tear up the laundry list they have in their heads about the kind of person they want. They can miss out on a person that's right for them when they say to me that they will only go out with a person who must measure up to what they think they want. One woman will tell me she won't go out with anyone shorter than she is, and another will say, 'If he's bald, forget it.' And a man will say the woman he wants has to have a college degree and no children, and must not be over thirty-five. Things like that are all nonsense, like what happened to Marvin. One rainy Sunday afternoon this six-foot-tall divorced man came to me. He sat down, had a cup of tea, and got to talking, and he said he wanted a woman who was five feet two, quiet, very gentle. So I went to the phone and called a woman who was five feet nine, and I invited her over and they never stopped talking. She came that afternoon and had rain boots on that made her look six feet tall. He became totally fascinated with her. He dated her a year, lived with her for two years, and now they're married and living in Sonoma. She was the absolute opposite of everything he said he wanted. And how many times I see that; people get these labels in their minds, and don't leave themselves open. Most of the people I introduce and who eventually marry aren't anything like the lists they make of who they thought they wanted."

You may already have found that one special person you want to find. There may have been occasions when you met a person you thought attractive, but then became disenchanted after a first date. You may then have been in the come-close-but-go-away stage, while that other person had just emerged from the walking-wounded stage, for example. He or she may have bored you to tears by talking only about how rotten his or her ex-spouse was, and how terrible life is. You had been through that stage a long time ago, and wanted to get on with what was happening in the present rather than talking about the past, and therefore dropped that person. However, when you understand that divorce is a process over time, and that the person who wallows in the past at the beginning of a divorce will not be the same person a year or two later (just as you are not the same person), you can still continue to be in touch with that person. You need not regularly date him or her, but can check in from time to time with a phone call or a luncheon date to catch up on his or her progress. The chemistry can grow between the two of you to the point where *both* of you are at the intimacy-without-fear stage. When you are alert to the fact that the people you meet might not be in the same stage you are in, but can catch up to that stage, the possibility of one of those persons becoming that special person in your life might be greater than you think.

That one special person in your life might also be the person you are involved with in a living-together arrangement. While LTAs are typically prevalent in the come-close-but-go-away stage, the two of you might progress to the intimacy-without-fear stage together. This doesn't happen nearly as frequently as breakups occur, for most LTAs are conceived of as escape hatches from a total commitment rather than as affirmations of such a commitment. However, if you have entered into an LTA with a clear understanding that this is to be a monogamous relationship in which the both of you will try to resolve problems rather than run away from them, and will practice truly open communication, this could lead to a total commitment truly based on intimacy without fear. Such an LTA has to be conceived of as an experiment in changing old, self-defeating habits and relating in new ways to your partner, rather than the ways in which you related in your old marriage, if it is to progress to the intimacy-without-fear stage. It has to be conceived of as an experiment, without any initial belief that it must develop into marriage at a certain time. Every alternative, including the possibility of a breakup, must be allowed for, with the understanding that even if the LTA breaks up, *both* parties win, because it could be a constructive learning experience. The LTA must be allowed to develop on the basis of how skillfully the two people relate to each other every day, if it is to become anything more than a temporary affair. When you establish an LTA on this basis, the possibility of its becoming an intimacy-without-fear relationship is very real.

Sometimes the person you are ready to meet is one you may have met many years ago and lost contact with during your marriage. There is an urge among divorced men and women to come to terms with what might have been unfinished business in the past. Not infrequently, a divorced man may try to contact a woman he dated in college, who later married someone else. Now that he is divorced, he calls her to find out what has happened in the intervening fifteen or twenty years. She, too, may be divorced or widowed, and the relationship is renewed. Or a divorced woman may meet an old flame at a high school reunion two decades later and start to date again, since that old flame is also divorced. More often than not, these renewed associations lead nowhere; the two people have changed far too much in different directions, and the chemistry simply isn't there. However, there are exceptions to every rule, and sometimes the relationship is not only renewed but develops into an intimacy-without-fear marriage.

Commitment Anxiety and Remarriage

When you have found that one special person and both of you decide to remarry, you can expect commitment shock to enter both of your lives. The closer you get to the wedding date, the more fearful you might become. The initial euphoria of making the commitment starts to give way to waves of commitment anxiety, which you thought had disappeared. Commitment anxiety reaches its highest level in the weeks prior to remarriage, and may even end the marriage before it begins, as it did with Len, forty-two, a client of mine:

"I've tried to remarry three times to three different women," he told me. "The first time, I chickened out three months before the marriage date. The second time I told my fiancée I couldn't go through with it six weeks before, after we had printed the wedding announcements. The last time I thought I would make it. But I got the shakes, terrible shakes, a week before we would be going down the aisle and I cancelled the ceremony. I wanted to marry, but I kept remembering the eighteen-year marriage I had, which was terrible most of the time. I've been divorced six years and I like my freedom, and the thought of giving it up was too much for me. I kept thinking, 'My God, what am I doing? Do I want another horrible eighteen years?' The three women I wanted to marry were all nice people, but my wife was too, before we were married. So I felt it was bound to happen the same way again, and had nightmares and the sweats the closer I got to the wedding dates, until I couldn't stand it any longer and broke off the relationships."

Intense commitment anxiety can exhibit itself in many ways after a marriage date has been set: the slightest problem can trigger off monumental shouting matches; an innocuous mention of an old flame can cause an outburst of fury from a wary groom; a future wife may lash out at her fiancé because he ignored her at last night's party; and, not infrequently, the soon-to-be husband or wife might engage in an affair only weeks before the marriage is to occur, and leave clues, such as the phone number of the third party, in an easily discovered place. Pandemonium, rage, and a breakup might then ensue.

In my own case, everything progressed smoothly after Pat and I decided on the marriage date. Then, the night before our marriage was to take place, my commitment anxiety, which I thought had ended, pounced on me like a Frankenstein monster. It took the form of a second-degree burn on my right foot. I had been pouring hot water into a funnel to make some coffee (something I had done countless times without ever having an accident), but made the absentminded "mistake" of pouring the boiling water on my right foot instead. I had flimsy slippers on, so the boiling water seeped through. I remained transfixed and continued to pour the water on my foot as if I had no control over the pot, and stopped doing so only when the pain became intolerable. I had to be rushed immediately to the hospital to be treated for a second-degree burn. Rather than be "burned" again in marriage, I chose a more direct form of self-punishment! However, commitment anxiety didn't triumph in this instance. Pat and I married on time, and I sported a bandaged right foot at the ceremony.

Why Commitment Anxiety Escalates

Why does commitment anxiety become so overpowering just after you think everything is settled? The date has been agreed upon, and you've chosen to remarry of your own free will, so why fear another walk down the aisle? The main clue resides in the word *another* in the last sentence. Since all a divorced person knows at a gut level about marriage is what he or she personally experienced in a marriage that turned sour and ended in divorce, to talk about "another" marriage conjures up in your feelings more of the same punishment. This is a vision too intolerable to contemplate. When Jonathan Winters remarks that "the difference between a first and a second marriage is the difference between West Point and Annapolis—only the costumes have changed," he is saying the same thing, that marriage is marriage; when you've seen one, you've seen them all, and all of them are the same kind of servitude. It matters not that intellectually this simply isn't true, that it is an absurd and false generalization. (I certainly knew intellectually the falseness of this equation when Pat and I set our marriage date.) What matters is that your head and your heart are not connecting. Your head (your intellect) is telling you to take the risk, to *improve* upon your past marriage, while your heart (your emotional makeup) is telling you that you will be burned again. And since your emotions, not your intellect, form the soil in which commitment anxiety lives and grows, it can erupt with surprising, nonintellectual force when your preservation of self is threatened.

However, in this instance, it only *appears* that your sense of self, your freedom to be who you are without fear of someone destroying that freedom, will be wiped out by a new marriage. For it is precisely because you have *already* earned the right to be your own person that you chose to remarry; your decision to remarry comes from your strength within yourself, not your weakness. Yet the resurgence of your commitment anxiety is telling you that you will be marrying out of weakness.

Paradoxically, it is precisely because commitment anxiety no longer has the power to determine the fate of your relationship, as it did in the previous three stages, that it gives the *illusion* that it is all-powerful in determining whether or not you remarry. Your commitment anxiety at the time you are about to remarry is making one last, dying effort to continue to determine the way you relate to the opposite sex. If you are aware of this, you will not let it control your life, the way it controlled people like Len, when you decide to remarry. Should some traces, or even great amounts, of commitment anxiety exist when you make that decision (and some amount of it probably will appear!), you can notice it rather than become terrified; you can then make your head and heart connect with the knowledge that you've grown too much as a person since your divorce to allow your new marriage to repeat your past marriage. Commitment anxiety then vanishes, and you can begin an intimacy-without-fear marriage.

The Way to Prevent Another Divorce: The Intimacy-Without-Fear Marriage

I have noted previously that love is not automatically better the second time around, since a larger percentage of remarriages than first marriages end in divorce. This happens because too many divorced persons simply repeat the way they related in the old marriage, so that the new marriage becomes a repetition of the past relationship rather than an improvement over it, with a new divorce at the end of the tunnel. These are people who still persist in believing that finding a good partner is a matter of luck, and that should their marriage turn sour, why, it's all the other person's fault, of course. Persistence in maintaining this point of view can only guarantee a lifetime of serial divorces.

If you want your new relationship to be more than just a way station on the road to another divorce, creating an intimacy-without-fear marriage is your best insurance against that possibility. I use the word *creating* because that is indeed what a married couple must do to make their marriage a lifelong journey in which happiness outweighs stress and discontent with the relationship. To create, the dictionary tells us, means to make something new. In an intimacy-without-fear marriage, you and your spouse are joint partners in making something new of your relationship, rather than falling back on the ways you related in your past marriages.

How to Make Your Remarriage a Success

To make your remarriage work may require a total revision of what you and your partner thought a workable marriage consisted of when you married the first time. Our society has changed dramatically since the time you previously married, and in the process of very rapid social change, concepts of what marriage is and what it should be have also changed. If you were married the first time at least fifteen years ago, you probably regarded marriage as an inevitability rather than a free choice. Society then demanded that you marry at a certain age (in your early twenties) as proof of your "normal" adulthood. The wife stayed home and proved her normality by immediately having three or four children, while the husband worked (a two-career family was a sign that "the poor woman" had an incompetent husband who couldn't adequately provide for her support). The man made all the major decisions and the wife was his support system, a second-best person who was supposed to be proud of that position. Divorce was a sign of personal failure, to be avoided at all costs. And if the marriage was agonizing (an alcoholic husband, a promiscuous wife, a total mismatch of personalities), your inner voice, along with relatives and friends, told you to hang in there and take the bitter with the sweet (or without the sweet, if that's all there was). Marriage was for life, even though the marriage might be lifeless. Society placed its stamp of approval on your marriage by telling you that your career success, your credit, and your social life depended on it. Think back to seven years ago, if you were married then (the average divorce occurs after seven years of marriage). Many changes had taken place. Divorce was on the rise, but still rather hesitantly acknowledged; two-career families were increasing rapidly, so that the old stereotype that a man should be the sole support of his family was losing its validity; the women's movement was demanding that women be given full legal equality with men, and that marriage be an equal partnership; living-together arrangements were increasing in number. Yet, along with those changes, many traces of old-style marriage still remained seven years ago. Many men still felt terribly uncomfortable when their wives worked; married women still deferred to the king-of-the-castle male; having children was still seen as a sign of a "normal" marriage.

How times have changed, even in the past seven years! Marriage today is what you make it. There are no norms anymore. Women today have the *choice* of remaining housewives or working at careers if their husbands have an adequate income. Men welcome the additional paycheck a wife brings home, and may brag about a wife's career—although they still may feel threatened if their wives earn more than they do! To have children is a personal choice, not the obligation that society once imposed on you. The LTA is an acceptable option now, a part of casual cocktail conversation. Men acknowledge today that women are equal to them in ability and intelligence (many women would say more than equal!), and accept the concept of an equal partnership in a marriage, even if their deeds do not always match their words. *Single* is no longer a dirty word if you are divorced or have never married, whether you are in your twenties or older. Career success and credit no longer depend on your being married, nor do your social possibilities. Divorce has become a normal life crisis, rather than an exotic option that only movie stars and the very rich could afford or talk about.

Despite these changes, you may still have many of the cobwebs of what marriage is "supposed" to be like still in your mind and in your behavior when you remarry. These cobwebs I call the "movie marriage in your mind." It consists of the accumulated experiences of the ideas you held when you married the first time: the cultural inheritance of old ideas about marriage you derived from seeing how your parents related when you were growing up; the media assault on your mind from the movies, books, and TV shows you were exposed to earlier in your life. And if you are unaware of the persistence of unusable and unworkable ideas about how your marriage can work, they can sabotage your remarriage so that it becomes an intimacy-*with*-fear relationship instead of one devoid of fear.

I often counsel remarried couples who, out of their own unawareness, brought to their new marriage the cobwebs of many "movie marriages in the mind," creating situations that brought them to the edge of divorce. Jill and Paul, for example, two very bright, career-oriented thirty-two-year-olds, verbally agreed before their marriage that both would take an equal part in household chores. This worked well for the first two years. But when Jill had their baby, suddenly Paul reverted to the traditional king-of-the-castle male, refusing to help with caring for any of the child's needs and ignoring his wife's pleas for help while she prepared dinner and minded the baby as Paul kept watching the six o'clock news. Jill's frustration with this state of affairs was inevitable. What Paul had done was to revert unconsciously to the traditional role he had witnessed in his own family as he was growing up, where his father had acted the same way Paul was acting now. "Raising a kid is woman's work," was the message he received from his father, and that message was controlling him now. When this was brought to Paul's attention, he began to become much more cooperative than he had been in the past.

Marjorie, a thirty-eight-year-old remarried woman, complained to me that her new husband always seemed to be calling the shots as to where to go, what movies to see, what friends she could invite home. Her needs were never considered. But when I asked her if she asserted her needs and her differences with her husband at the time these situations arose, she said she did not. She would bite her lip, store up her resentment, and then explode over some trivial point weeks later, leaving her husband irritated and confused. Marjorie fully believed in women's right to equality in marriage, yet she was fearful of making waves with her husband in situations where she felt her needs should be considered as well as her husband's. She had promised herself that when she remarried she would never again be the mousy creature she was in her first marriage. Yet great traces of that unassertiveness persisted in her new marriage. What was happening? It turned out she still subconsciously believed that nice girls never made waves, and that the man of the house always came first. She had always seen her mother act that way toward her dad, and she, as a grown woman of thirty-eight, was acting just like her mother, something she had vowed never to do! The persistence of past emotional baggage such as this can erupt in surprising ways in a new relationship, sabotaging what you truly want from that relationship. The only way to deal with this phenomenon when it occurs in your remarriage is to notice it when it happens, identify it as a trace of who you were in the past rather than who you are in the present, and then correct its tendency to control your behavior before it turns into actual behavior. Marjorie learned to overcome her tendency toward unassertiveness by doing precisely that. When her husband said, "This is the restaurant we're going to tonight," even though she would like to go to another one, she would notice herself biting her tongue and going along with his decision. However, she would then take the next step of breaking with her old behavior pattern. Marjorie told me this was scary for her to do at first, for she thought she would invite anger from her husband if she disagreed, just as she had witnessed the anger of her father when he was crossed. "Imagine my surprise," she later told me. "Tom didn't get angry at all. In fact, he told me he would welcome my suggestions, that he was tired of always making the decisions for both of us. How do you like that! It's so much easier now. We compromise. Sometimes I get my way

about things, sometimes he does. It's the kind of equal relationship I had wanted in the first pace."

When things go wrong in an intimacy-without-fear relationship, problems are solved rather than swept under the
rug. Divorced men and women who enter such a marriage
are not controlled by the fear that openly discussing problems, and seeking solutions for them as they happen, will
destroy the marriage. They know that problems *don't* go
away when you don't talk about them; they remain to haunt
the marriage, and can eventually destroy the relationship.
Jill and Marjorie knew this, and had the strength of their
divorce experiences behind them to cope successfully with
the threats to their new married lives.

Eliminating the Eight Major Misconceptions About Marriage

You lay the groundwork for intimacy without fear that
your new marriage will turn out to be a repetition of your
past marriage when you come to terms with any and all of
the remnants of the "movie marriage in your mind" that
may still be present at the time you remarry. Awareness of
their presence is the key to eliminating them. The eight
major misconceptions that I have observed when remarried
couples have come to me for counseling are listed below.
Ask yourself how many of them may still pervade your
thinking and behavior.

1. *Your spouse is simply the extension of your
   own emotional and physical needs.* That may
   have been the way Mom and Dad related,
   where a wife was brainwashed to believe she
   was the public service industry of her husband. Recognize that today this attitude is an
   invitation to another divorce. No one person
   can satisfy all of your needs, and to require
   that of your spouse is to ask the impossible.
2. *Marriage means togetherness.* If traces remain
   of the old-fashioned belief that your spouse
   must think, act, and feel the way you do all the

time, or else he or she doesn't love you, eliminate that notion from your consciousness and behavior. Today a marriage can only work successfully if two people grow as individuals in their relationship. "Two-getherness" must replace "togetherness."

3. *A good marriage is a problem-free marriage.* Life consists of problems, whether you are married or single or divorced. Problems are challenges to you and your partner's ability to resolve them skillfully rather than ignore or run away from them.

4. *Love is a possession; you "win" the love of your partner by marrying, which means there is also the possibility of "losing" that love after marriage.* If you consider love a "thing" to win and hold on to, you will guarantee its loss, for you will always fear that you might be deprived of such a precious possession, and try to protect it jealously. Love is an *activity,* not a possession, which is renewed each day in the ways you and your wife act toward each other. Your only guarantee of maintaining love is to show empathy, compassion, friendship, flexibility, compromise, kindness, and respect toward each other in your *daily* lives.

5. *Good sex depends on your capacity always to have orgasms and sustained erections.* These cobwebs can lower your self-esteem and result in a false belief that your partner doesn't love you. Sex is not a performance, a test in which you must always get an A, or else you are a failure. Good sex in today's marriage means mutual gratification, which can and does occur simply through a demonstration of tenderness—hugging and snuggling should times arise when physical ability is not equal to orgasmic intercourse. Good sex is a celebration of the fact that your marriage is working well, rather than a requirement that you become an orgasm-manufacturing machine.

6. *You marry because your partner will make you happy.* When you expect your partner to become your permanent entertainment industry, you probably are asking for something that only you can give yourself: a sense of feeling personally happy. To enter into a marriage because you need someone else to assuage your boredom, discontent, and low self-esteem is to place an impossible burden on your partner. Happiness is a two-way street; you and your spouse become happier together when both of you are already happy with yourselves.

7. *Your marriage can be improved by having sexual affairs with others when your spouse gets boring.* Nothing will erode the basic trust that you have built with your marriage partner more than "getting a little bit on the side." Those who practice having outside affairs (once known as an "open marriage") invite a divorce or chronic mistrust, should the marriage continue. In today's marriage, monogamy freely chosen (not with fingers crossed) is essential for making that relationship work successfully. Recognize that there must be trade-offs in everything you do in life. In exchange for choosing to be monogamous, you give up the opportunity to relate sexually to others. But in doing so you gain a loving relationship based on trust, one of life's most valuable elements. And should you become bored with your partner, it's a sign that you are ready to relate in new and better ways toward each other, rather than a sign that the grass is greener outside the marriage.

8. *Change in a marriage is something to be feared and guarded against.* In your past marriage you may have complained that your spouse changed and was no longer the person you married, and you felt ripped off and betrayed. Recognize that change is inevitable in

a marriage, and should be welcomed rather than feared. Both of you will become older, and the longer the marriage lasts, the more your priorities will change. The glow of romantic love in the beginning may diminish, but the glow of caring and companionship may increase, and interesting new facets of your own and your partner's personalities may later emerge. Change then becomes a challenge to know yourself and your spouse better, rather than an excuse for ending that marriage.

The Qualities of an Intimacy-Without-Fear Marriage

An intimacy-without-fear marriage is a normal consequence of your divorce, when you have successfully incorporated the learning experiences of the four stages of your quest for a lasting love relationship, which have been reinforced by your proving to yourself that you are a person of value, competency, and worth in all phases of your divorce experience. Your readiness to take the marriage step is an affirmation of your competent individuality rather than a sign of your inability to make a happy life for yourself alone. You trade some of the advantages of singleness (such as your ability to please yourself and choose your activities without being accountable to anyone else) for the more valuable experience of sharing a life together with someone who is your best friend and lover. The self-centeredness of the single life gives way to reciprocal enhancement of two lives in partnership. This requires changes in the way you related to your spouse in your past marriage. Throughout your divorce, you have already proved you can change for the better. You've responded with competence and skill to the many new challenges your divorced life thrust upon you, and have successfully survived experiences you once thought would crush you. (Remember those early times in your divorce when you thought you couldn't survive another day?)

In an intimacy-without-fear marriage, you and your

partner are kind teachers and receptive students to each other as well as lovers, equal partners, and authoritative parents. You do not flinch from the difficulties that inevitably arise when two persons live in the same household, but discuss and resolve them instead. You know that you probably ran away from sticky problems in your last marriage, and that this only compounded your alienation from your partner. When some of the cobwebs of the "movie marriage in your mind" that destroyed your past marriage begin to manifest themselves in your new marriage, your partner, as a kindly teacher, can draw attention to your inappropriate behavior, and you, as a receptive student, can correct it without feeling that your spouse is attacking or demeaning you. You in turn will do the same for your spouse. You want the best *for* each other and *from* each other, and this way of relating will elicit the best from each of you.

In an intimacy-without-fear marriage, you marry because you each want to be the number-one person in the other's eyes. Today there is no other adequate reason to marry, for old-style marriage has proved unworkable. Marrying out of fear of being single, marrying to have sex, marrying to escape a bad family situation, marrying because society demanded you marry to prove you were a "normal" adult, marrying because of parental pressure to do so—all of these now-outmoded pressures that once drove a person into marriage (perhaps they drove you into your previous marriage) no longer obtain if a marriage is to become a lasting love relationship rather than just another excursion into unhappiness. Today, you remarry out of free choice, which means you must take personal responsibility for the way you relate to your partner, rather than allowing the relationship to drift into disaster by ascribing all of the difficulties you will encounter to the other person. You've already taken personal responsibility as you moved through the mourning process of your divorce and learned how to become single. Your next challenge is to learn to become married in a way that will ensure that your new marriage will be the lasting love relationship you always wanted but never had. Now you can measure up to that challenge.

The Learning Experiences of the Intimacy-Without-Fear Stage

In this stage, you have learned that your readiness time to experience each of the four stages of your quest for a lasting love relationship has been determined by you yourself, once you became aware of these stages and what they signified, as well as the clues in each stage that indicated when you were ready to progress to the next stage. You will have sought out a good divorce counselor when you felt stuck in any one stage, in order to free yourself to move your life constructively ahead.

In addition, you have learned that your own personal growth did not end when you felt comfortable and relatively happy with yourself as a single person. Rather, that was the time when you were ready to take the next step in your journey beyond divorce, the time to engage in a lasting love relationship.

Perhaps the best summation of what you learned about how to make a love relationship last is expressed in a poem written by Eve Merriam, a woman who has experienced divorce and remarriage:

The Eskimos Have No Word for Divorce

but a boat is called a *kayak*.

The first time out in one
seems clumsy
when you have been accustomed to
an American canoe
that glides so easily
(and can just as easily
overturn
if you do not hold your bow and stern
firmly in mind and
separate.
You must know where your place is
and keep it wholly

do not try to shift
and remember to hold your paddle clearly to one side—
left or right   don't dabble.)

In a *kayak*
you sit anywhere you like
and always dip with
a double paddle
neither side is the head
either side is the head
since both pull with equal weight
and you grasp in the center:
kayak, a most peculiar word
that you can spell
from either end
and come out
even.

Selected Bibliography

Survey of Single Life:

Simenauer, J. and D. Carroll. *Singles: The New Americans.* New York: Simon and Schuster, 1982.

Sex and Sexuality:

Advanced Study of Human Sexuality. *Safe Sex in the Age of AIDS.* New York: Citadel, 1986.

Boston's Women's Health Collective. *Our Bodies, Ourselves.* New York: Simon and Schuster, 1984.

Zilbergeld, Bernard. *Male Sexuality.* Boston: Little Brown and Co., 1978.

Social Trends:

Cherlin, Andrew J. *Marriage, Divorce and Remarriage.* Cambridge: Harvard University Press, 1981.

Children of Divorce:

Gardner, Richard A. *The Boys' and Girls' Book About Divorce.* New York: Bantam, 1970.

Group for the Advancement of Psychiatry. *The Joys and Sorrows of Parenthood.* New York: Charles Scribner's Sons, 1983.

Le Shan, Eda. *What's Going to Happen to Me?* New York: Aladdin Books, 1986.

Child Custody:

Wolley, Persia. *The Custody Handbook.* New York: Summit Books, 1979.

Men and Divorce:

Cassidy, Robert. *What Every Man Should Know About Divorce.* Washington: New Republic, 1977.

Gardner, Richard A. *The Parent's Book About Divorce.* New York: Doubleday, 1977.

The Nature of Love:

May, Rollo. *Love and Will.* New York: Dell Publishing Co., 1973.

Remarriage and Step-Parenting:

Krantzler, Mel. *Learning to Love Again.* New York: Harper and Row, 1987.

Maddox, Brenda. *The Half-Parent.* New York: Signet, 1976.

Religion and Divorce:

Young, James J., C.S.P. *Divorcing, Believing, Belonging.* Ramsey, New Jersey: Paulist Press, 1984.

Rambo, Lewis R. *The Divorcing Christian.* Nashville: Abingdon Press, 1983.

Interpersonal Relationships:

Blumstein, P., and P. Schwartz. *American Couples.* New York: William Morrow & Co., 1983.

Zimbardo, Phillip G. *Shyness.* Menlo Park: Addison-Wesley, 1977.

Personal Safety:

Castleman, Michael. *Crime Free.* New York: Simon and Schuster, 1984.

Career Horizons:

Bolles, Richard A. *What Color Is your Parachute?* Berkeley: Ten Speed Press, 1987.

What Men Are Like:

Astrachan, Anthony. *How Men Feel.* New York: Anchor Press/Doubleday, 1986.

Farrell, Warren. *Why Men Are the Way They Are.* New York: McGraw-Hill, 1986.

What Women Are Like:

Dowling, Colette. *The Cinderella Complex.* New York: Pocket Books, 1981.

Friedan, Betty. *The Second Stage.* New York: Summit Books, 1981.

Shaevitz, Marjorie Hansen. *The Superwoman Syndrome.* New York: Warner, 1984.

Spiritual Growth and Change:

Fromm, Erich. *To Have or to Be?* New York: Harper & Row, 1976.

Jampolsky, Gerald G. *Love Is Letting Go of Fear.* Berkeley: Celestial Arts, 1979.

Le Shan, Lawrence. *How to Meditate.* New York: Bantam, 1974.

Peck, M. Scott, M.D. *The Road Less Traveled.* New York: Simon and Schuster, 1978.

A New Look at Marriage:

Krantzler, Mel. *Creative Marriage.* New York: McGraw-Hill, 1981.

Dating and Single-Person Etiquette:

Martin, Judith. *Miss Manners' Guide to Excruciatingly Correct Behavior.* New York: Warner, 1983.

Merser, Cheryl. *Honorable Intentions.* New York: Holt, Rinehart and Winston, 1984.

The Legal, Economic, and Social Consequences of Divorce:

Weitzman, Lenore J. *The Divorce Revolution*. New York: Free Press, 1985.

Remarriage and Living-Together Contracts:

Weitzman, Lenore J. *The Marriage Contract*. New York: Free Press, 1981.

Taking Care of Yourself Financially:

Porter, Sylvia. *Sylvia Porter's New Money Book for the Eighties*. New York: Avon, 1986.

Taking Care of Yourself Legally:

Belli, Melvin and Allen Wilkinson. *Everybody's Guide to the Law*. New York: Harcourt Brace Jovanovich, 1986.

Drug Addictions and How to Break Them:

Beattie, Melody. *Codependent No More*. New York: Harper/Hazelden, 1987.

Woititz, Janet Geringer. *Adult Children of Alcoholics*. Pompano Beach, Florida: Health Communications, Inc., 1983.

Index

About the Authors

MELVIN M. BELLI, SR., is one of the world's foremost trial attorneys. A graduate of the University of California's Boalt School of Law, Mr. Belli has made his international reputation with many famous cases and has earned the title "King of Torts." He has also worked on many divorce cases, including divorces of Rita Hayworth, Barbara Hutton, Martha and John Mitchell, Nick Nolte, and others. He is the author of sixty-two other books on the law, including, most recently, *The Belli Files: Reflections on the Wayward Law; Everybody's Guide to the Law;* and the five-volume revised edition of *Modern Trials.* Mr. Belli continues to make his home and practice law in San Francisco.

Psychologist MEL KRANTZLER, Ph.D., who is a clinical member of the American Association for Marriage and Family Therapy (AAMFT), is internationally recognized as the outstanding authority on the psychology of divorce. He is the author of the best-selling *Creative Divorce,* which has sold more than two million copies since its first publication, as well as two other bestselling books: *Creative Marriage* and *Learning to Love Again.* Dr. Krantzler has been an innovator in teaching courses on divorce in colleges throughout the country, and in originating divorce group counseling; he is currently the director of the Creative Divorce, Love and Marriage Counseling Center, located in San Rafael, California.

CHRISTOPHER S. TAYLOR, an attorney with extensive experience in divorce and related areas of the law, lives in Oakland, California.

BESTSELLING BOOKS FROM ST. MARTIN'S PAPERBACKS— TO READ AND READ AGAIN!

———————————— ⌑ ————————————